The Language Organ

Linguistics as Cognitive Physiology

Challenging and original, *The Language Organ* treats human language as the manifestation of a faculty of the mind, a mental organ whose nature is determined by human biology. Its functional properties should be explored just as physiology explores the functional properties of physical organs. The authors argue that linguistics investigates cognition, taking as its object mental representations and processes rather than externally observed grammatical patterns (which constitute evidence, but are not themselves the object of study). Such a view has untraditional consequences for the kinds of argument and analysis that can be offered in understanding the nature of language. The book surveys the nature of the language faculty in its various aspects: the systems of sounds, words, and syntax; the development of language in the child and historically; and what is known about its relation to the brain. It discusses the kinds of work that can be carried out in these areas that will contribute to an understanding of the human language organ. The book will appeal to students and researchers in linguistics, and is written to be accessible to colleagues in other disciplines dealing with language as well as to readers with an interest in general science and the nature of the human mind.

STEPHEN R. ANDERSON is Professor of Linguistics and Cognitive Science at Yale University. He is the author of *The Organization of Phonology* (1974), *Phonology in the Twentieth Century* (1985), and *A-Morphous Morphology* (1992).

DAVID W. LIGHTFOOT is Dean of the Graduate School, Georgetown University. He is the author of eight books, most recently *The Development of Language* (1999).

The Language Organ

Linguistics as Cognitive Physiology

Stephen R. Anderson

Yale University

David W. Lightfoot

Georgetown University

CAMBRIDGE
UNIVERSITY PRESS

PUBLISHED BY THE PRESS SYNDICATE OF THE UNIVERSITY OF CAMBRIDGE
The Pitt Building, Trumpington Street, Cambridge, United Kingdom

CAMBRIDGE UNIVERSITY PRESS
The Edinburgh Building, Cambridge CB2 2RU, UK
40 West 20th Street, New York, NY 10011–4211, USA
477 Williamstown Road, Port Melbourne, VIC 3207, Australia
Ruiz de Alarcón 13, 28014 Madrid, Spain
Dock House, The Waterfront, Cape Town 8001, South Africa

http://www.cambridge.org

First published 2002

Printed in the United Kingdom at the University Press, Cambridge

Typeface Times 10/12 pt.   *System* LaTeX 2$_\varepsilon$ [TB]

A catalogue record for this book is available from the British Library

ISBN 0 521 80994 0 hardback
ISBN 0 521 00783 6 paperback

Dedicated to the memory of
Victoria Fromkin,
who was way ahead of us in
the investigation of language
as an aspect of the mind/brain

[H]uman cognitive systems, when seriously investigated, prove to be no less marvelous and intricate than the physical structures that develop in the life of the organism. Why, then, should we not study the acquisition of a cognitive structure such as language more or less as we study some complex bodily organ?

Noam Chomsky 1975, p. 10

Contents

Preface   *page* ix

1   Studying the human language faculty   1
    1.1 Linguistics and the mind/brain   3
    1.2 Linguistics as history   5
    1.3 Linguistics as the study of *E*-language   12
    1.4 Linguistics as the study of *I*-language   14

2   Language as a mental organ   18
    2.1 We know more than we learn   18
    2.2 The nature of grammars   23
    2.3 Back to the puzzles   25
    2.4 The acquisition problem   34
    2.5 Conclusion   40

3   Syntax   41
    3.1 The emergence of syntax within linguistics   41
    3.2 Successive merger and deletion   43
    3.3 Case   61
    3.4 Conclusion   66

4   Sound patterns in language   67
    4.1 Phonetics as theory   68
    4.2 Phonology: language-particular structure   73
    4.3 Morphophonemics and *I*-language   83

5   Describing linguistic knowledge   92
    5.1 Phonological knowledge as it appears in borrowing   93
    5.2 Can rules express phonological knowledge?   96
    5.3 Constraint-based theories of phonological knowledge   99
    5.4 The extension of constraint-based description   109

6   Phonetics and the *I*-linguistics of speech   111
    6.1 Representations and the study of sound structure   111
    6.2 A linguistic basis for phonetic representation   114
    6.3 Speech microprosody: a research program   127
    6.4 Conclusion   129

7   Morphology   131
    7.1   The lexicon   132
    7.2   Words and "morphemes"   134
    7.3   Productivity   152
    7.4   Conclusions about lexical organization   155

8   Language change   157
    8.1   Long-term directionality in the twentieth century   157
    8.2   Grammars and time   161
    8.3   English auxiliary verbs   162
    8.4   Syntactic effects of the loss of case   175
    8.5   Chaos   183

9   "Growing" a language   186
    9.1   Principles of Universal Grammar: active early   186
    9.2   New phenomena   191
    9.3   Experimental technique   194
    9.4   Nature of the trigger   198
    9.5   Acquiring sound patterns   206
    9.6   Conclusion   214

10 The organic basis of language   216
    10.1 Only humans have language organs   219
    10.2 Language is a function of the brain   221
    10.3 Language is a particular faculty   236
    10.4 Conclusions   238

References   244
Index   257

Preface

One of the great success stories of post-Second-World-War intellectual inquiry has been the extent to which linguists have been able to make the syntactic and phonological structure of natural language into a serious object of explicit formal study. This work has uncovered principles of surprising subtlety, abstractness, and deductive richness; it has also raised fundamental questions concerning the ontogenetic and phylogenetic developments by which knowledge of this kind could develop in the organism. Much of this progress results fairly directly from the adoption of an explicitly **biological** perspective on the subject: instead of seeing language as an external phenomenon, as a collection of sounds, words, texts, etc. that exists apart from any particular individual, contemporary linguistics increasingly concerns itself with the internal organization and ontogeny of a special kind of knowledge. The specific form that this aspect of human cognition takes appears, we will argue, to be a species-specific property of human beings, and thus rooted in our biological nature.

As our subtitle promises, we will describe linguistics, the scientific study of (human natural) language, as cognitive **physiology**. An individual's use of language involves that person's brain: the way this brain works depends at least in part on childhood influences and whether the person was raised in New Haven, New Delhi, or New Guinea. The relevant aspect of the brain's structure that responds to these differences in experience is the person's language organ, but to characterize it we need to take seriously the notion of physiology as the study of **functions**.

Webster's *Second International Dictionary* tells us that physiology is

[t]he branch of biology dealing with the processes, activities, and phenomena incidental to and characteristic of life or of living organisms; the study of the functions of the organs, tissues, cells, etc. during life, as distinct from *anatomy*, which deals with their structure. The final analysis of these processes and phenomena is mainly physical and chemical. The phenomena of mental life are usually regarded as outside the ordinary scope of physiology (see PSYCHOLOGY).

Like many dictionary definitions, this one combines the central conceptual content of the word with other characteristics that are as much the product of historical accident as of basic meaning. The core notion seems to be that of the study of functions and processes as opposed to static structure, but that by itself does not tell us much about just what sorts of object might properly fall within the scope of this science.

A central aim of this book is to explore the notion that physiology should extend, if it is to be productive, beyond the study of isolable physical structures and organs. As we see it, the range of "phenomena . . . characteristic of life" whose functional organization can be usefully attributed to the biology of the organism exhibiting them, and substantively studied, goes well beyond those for which we have a "final analysis" which is "mainly physical and chemical." Excluding "the phenomena of mental life" from physiology surely reflects, at least in part, the ancient Cartesian dualism of mind and body in rejecting the study of cognition from the biological domain. However, this dualism was soon undermined, largely because of what we came to learn about the "body" not long after Descartes. Newton reintroduced "occult" causes and qualities, to his own dismay, and the Cartesian theory of body was shown to be untenable. Hence, there is no absolute distinction between body and mind, because our notions of the body need to be enriched beyond the simple mechanisms envisioned by Descartes.

Accepting the notion that "the mind is what the brain does," as much modern cognitive science does, entails that cognitive phenomena essential to the life of an organism are good candidates for biological study: as with other organs, we can study them at an appropriate functional level and not just in the narrow terms of a physical or chemical analysis of living tissue. There is no longer any motivation for a sharp delineation between functional organization that is associated with discrete anatomy and that whose relation to physical implementation is less obvious and discrete. In all cases, we need to identify an appropriate level of abstraction at which significant generalizations about biologically determined function can be stated. We shall illustrate such a level of abstraction: the study of "*I*-language."

Does it make sense to take linguistics as a paradigm for this sort of analysis, though? In modern academic life, linguistics as a discipline suffers from a lack of clear general perception. All too commonly, the notion that there is anything very complex or technical about the study of language seems contrary to common sense: after all, just about everyone (even little kids) can speak a language perfectly well, so what could be that intricate about it? Of course, when you learn a new language you have to learn a lot of words, and little details like where the verb goes in a German sentence, but surely that's not **science**. If there is something to study there, this attitude continues, it must be things about the histories of languages (Which ones are related to which others? Where did the word *boondocks* come from?), or else about the way we use language in society (Does bilingual education make sense? How do men and women do different things with the same words?).

As a result, linguistics departments sometimes have a bit of a hard time making ends meet. Often enough, when universities feel the need to save some money, linguistics is one of the first departments to feel the impact, since surely what people do there is either trivial or else could be perfectly well done elsewhere (in the language departments, or in Anthropology, Sociology, Psychology, etc. – "real" disciplines).

Even the location of the linguistics department is often problematic. Some places have linguistics in the humanities, some in the social sciences; but the things linguists do on a day-to-day basis seem ill suited, at least in many cases, to either of these labels. Our own personal inclination is to locate the core focus of linguistics in the biological (or at least natural) sciences, along with the rest of cognitive science, as is indeed the case in a few enlightened institutions. Of course, linguistics is construed in different ways by different scholars; the particular view we take in this book would surely not be shared by all faculty in all linguistics departments.

We will argue (in chapter 1 below) that this disciplinary ambiguity actually reflects the historical development of our understanding of what is essential in the study of language. The first (non-speculative) studies of language in the nineteenth century really were focused, at least originally, on the detailed study of words and texts, their histories, and their importance for an understanding of the history of individual languages and language families. This kind of activity falls squarely within the domain of the humanities, and much historical work on language today continues to fit that characterization.

Around the turn of the twentieth century, however, the ideas of Ferdinand de Saussure caused students of language to pay much more attention to the **synchronic** realities of language, and less to its history. An initial attempt to understand the nature of this object took language to be fundamentally a set of social conventions for conveying meaning, and its reality comparable to other aspects of society and culture and thus transcending any individual to reside in the entire community of language users. The modern discipline of sociolinguistics continues to study the relation between language and society, in ways including the correlation of social and linguistic differences, the relation between discourse structure and social goals, the formulation of rational national language policies, and many other things.

In the middle years of the twentieth century the externalization of language through its construal as a social object, entailed by Saussure's views, was reinforced by behaviorist ideas that treated all study of strictly internal, mental phenomena as unscientific at best, even nonsensical. Surely some of that attitude lingers on in the definition provided by *Webster's Second* above, along with simple Cartesian dualism. At any rate, the activity of linguists at this time was largely devoted to the development of techniques for reducing the data of unfamiliar or "exotic" languages to manageable form, an effort that continues to be of great interest to anthropologists among others.

With the work of Noam Chomsky, and his colleagues and students, however, a completely new focus arose. Chomsky stressed from an early point that if we want to understand the essential nature of language, a study of its external manifestations in speech, texts, communicative behavior, etc. may provide relevant evidence, but that should not be the fundamental object of inquiry in the field. What we want to understand, that is, is not a text or a spoken utterance, but the system of knowledge within a speaker that underlies (significant and well-defined aspects of) it. Linguistics is thus in its most essential aspect a component of the study of the mind, the study of a system of human knowledge (the language organ) that forms a part of our larger cognitive organization. It has developed a level of abstraction that appears to be appropriate for the formulation of significant generalizations about language: what we will call "*I*-language" below, an individual, internal system. We know something of the properties of *I*-language, though certainly not all, and an appropriate level of abstraction seems to be emerging which permits productive research. Efforts toward detailing the properties of *I*-language in a variety of areas constitute the subject matter of this book.

As modern cognitive science has come increasingly to reject the dualism of mind and body, and to see our mental life as the product of physical processes and events, it has become possible at least to consider the possibility that aspects of cognition have a structure in themselves that is determined as much in its form by our biological nature as is the structure and functioning of physical organs like the liver or the skin. And when we look into the matter with care, we find that there are indeed many strong reasons to consider that the cognitive organization underlying our ability to acquire and use a language is as much a part of our genetically determined biology as the structure of our eyes or skeleton.

This might lead us to expect that the right way to study language might be to identify and characterize discrete, separable regions of the brain that are responsible for it, and then to explore the operation of this tissue in precise detail. It would surely be at least premature to take this approach, however. We are far from being able to associate specific neural tissue, except at the very grossest levels, with specific cognitive functions. We can observe that injuries to certain brain regions result in particular cognitive deficits, and that shows that the tissue involved must indeed be serving some purpose that is essential to the cognitive function in question, but that is not at all the same thing as saying that this is the specific region which "computes" the relevant cognitive property. Even when rapidly developing imaging techniques allow us to identify metabolic activity in specific regions of the (normal) brain that is associated with language-related activities, we are still far from being able to relate those activities in any direct way to molecular or cellular events and processes.

In truth, our understanding of the overall architecture of cognition is still very sketchy, imprecise, and surely inaccurate. Before we can even pose serious questions about the specific physical underpinnings of cognitive activity, we need to know much more about just what that activity consists in. We can provide inferential, limiting arguments that show beyond a doubt that there is a large biologically determined component to cognitive abilities such as language, but that is a long way from showing exactly how neurophysiological activity in specific regions of the brain (and elsewhere) corresponds to the production and understanding of language.

While this conclusion may well imply that it will be some time before linguistics is moved definitively out of humanities and social sciences and into the biology building, we are encouraged to pursue the prerequisites to such an understanding. In particular, we need to understand the "processes, activities, and phenomena" characteristic of our mental life, the organization, development, and interaction of cognition. Of course, to do that, we have to look at the right things; and in the case of language, that means studying language as a highly structured kind of knowledge rather than as a collection of external events. And we submit that this study of the organization and functioning of the human language capacity is every bit as "physiological" as the study of the processes that take place in the kidney, even though the "organ" involved is defined (for the present, at least) in functional rather than anatomical terms.

The study of language over the past half century or so has provided cognitive scientists with models for how one might go about studying cognition more generally. In this, linguists have been distinctly lucky in comparison with other students of the mind, precisely because our knowledge of language has so many evident and observable consequences, and is so much more open to study than other domains. Historically, linguistics has provided a model for other fields on more than one occasion: witness the basic importance of linguistic notions in the development of "structuralist" analysis quite broadly in the social and human sciences. More recently, linguistics has also provided a prototype for the study of cognitive systems in general (even if the ultimate application of this analogy should prove to be an understanding of just how different cognitive systems, including language, can be from one another), as well as a focus for the application of valuable techniques such as the cognitive neuropsychological exploration of (normal) cognitive architecture on the basis of functional deficits consequent to brain damage.

Linguists in fact have quite a bit to contribute to the general study of cognition. In the study of action and motor control, for example, the results of phoneticians are potentially an incredibly rich source of evidence. There is probably no single area in which we have a finer grained understanding of the details of muscular activity and movement in time and in space than in the case of speech articulation; or in which such low-level detail can be put into correspondence with so specific an understanding of higher-level abstract representations of the intentionality underlying the movements in question. Yet it is only quite recently that work in phonetics and in the general study of action has begun to converge and "cross-pollinate."

A central problem in understanding any cognitive system is that of seeing how its structure can develop within the individual organism. In this study, the language organ offers quite unparalleled advantages. We can detail with great precision the evidence available in the course of language acquisition; we have a reasonably clear notion of the character of the system which is eventually attained, and we can formulate precise hypotheses about the intermediate stages through which the organism passes on the way to this knowledge. As such, we can study the interplay between considerations particular to a single cognitive system (generally, the content of "Universal Grammar") and those that generalize across cognition in general. The study of the development of linguistic competence in the child is an enormously important exemplar for more general studies of cognitive development.

Linguists have not always gone to enough trouble to inform a broader scientific public about the implications of our work. Surely the huge expansion of the field within academia during the 1960s and 1970s was largely due to a perception that this discipline did potentially offer a privileged kind of "window on the mind," but in actual practice linguists have tended to neglect the obligation to make good on the promissory notes thus issued. The technical details of the field are indeed fascinating to pursue, as well as specialized, complex, and fairly opaque to outsiders. When linguists pursue these technicalities (in the same way that physicists pursue the details of physics without feeling a need continually to inform the outside world about the importance of their discipline), the result is a continuing lack of understanding on the part of the general public of just what the science of language is all about, and why it matters.

This book has several aims, then. One is to establish for the non-specialist the biological nature of the human language faculty, and to give an account of the organization of that faculty to the extent we can discern it. Another is to give these same non-specialist readers a sense of the complex interplay between the empirical phenomena of language and the basic questions of cognitive organization we would like to be able to ask.

We have writen primarily for our colleagues in anthropology, history, German, biology, physiology, and a variety of other fields in which they approach language from their own disciplinary perspective and on the basis of their own expertise. They sometimes ask us in the Faculty Club about how linguists view things: this book is an extended answer to those questions, among others. Scholars with different backgrounds – physiologists and historians, for example – will disagree on which parts of the book are easy and which are harder reading. Like restaurateurs, we aim to cater to a range of different tastes within an overall framework.

In the process, we introduce a good deal of the specialized apparatus of modern linguistics, which displays an intricacy that may surprise some. Indeed, one of our fondest memories is of the time when one of us, at a rather boring meeting, was sitting next to Dr. Rita Colwell, the distinguished biologist who would later become director of the National Science Foundation. Dr. Colwell idly picked up a book on morphosyntactic theory from her neighbor, leafing slowly through it with apparently mounting interest. "Well !" she eventually remarked, handing the book back. "You really do have to be a rocket scientist to be a linguist !" Certainly no more so than to be a microbiologist, but perhaps more than is generally appreciated.

For our linguist colleagues, we also have some important goals. Apart from encouraging them to make the more general implications of their work known beyond our own small community, we want to stress the significance of seeing language as an internal fact about speakers, a form of knowledge, or "*I*-language" as Chomsky has called it, as opposed to its external manifestation as utterances, texts, sets of sentences, or social conventions – "*E*-language" in Chomsky's terms. While a growing part of the rhetoric of the field adopts a position similar to ours, actual practice often devotes more significance to these external phenomena than might be scientifically justified. Beginning graduate students need to understand this, and some of our tables are set for them.

We try, in parts of this book, to explore some of the intellectual history of the discipline which might be responsible for wrong emphases. This historical orientation serves at least two goals. On the one hand, it allows us to contrast a contemporary understanding of important issues with earlier alternatives, plausible in themselves but positions on which the views presented can (we hope) be seen as improvements. And on the other hand, it is important not to neglect the role of inertia in science. In fact, many attitudes of scientists (linguists included) turn out on closer analysis to be simply the unexamined residue of earlier stages of their science, positions that have survived major changes of outlook simply because they did not directly engage the central issues at play in periods of substantial scientific change. Understanding this fact, together with the true nature of the basic scientific questions that need to be asked about language, will perhaps help us to arrive at a more coherent account of this fascinating part of our nature as humans.

There is a fair amount of technical material in this book: details about exotic languages, formal apparatus for describing parts of linguistic knowledge, etc. This is partly in service of introducing serious readers to the real nature of the field, and partly because it is unavoidable if the fundamental points are to be made in a serious way. Despite advice from many that the inclusion of many references in the text will put off non-specialist readers, we have tried to document our discussion from the standard literature. These references are of two general sorts: some are intended to make it possible for skeptics, or for those who simply want to know more about a particular point, to see where our position is grounded. The reader may in general presume that such additional exploration is not crucial to understanding the point at issue, and regard these citations as so much baroque ornamentation. Other references are provided specifically to point readers to fuller discussions of areas which we cannot go into here in adequate detail; these are generally signalled as such, and should again be considered as supplementary rather than required reading assignments.

We have tried, overall, to make this book as self-contained as possible, defining our terms at least to an extent that should make our usage comprehensible to a non-specialist who is willing to make the effort to understand us. The reader who has read carefully Steven Pinker's very useful book *The Language Instinct* should have all of the tools that are necessary to make it through this one. Some parts will be slower going than others, however. The reader may perhaps take comfort in the fact that most chapters can be appreciated in the absence of a complete understanding of some of the others.

Linguistics is a field with many subareas, and the basic concepts and methods of each are to some extent distinct. We have not by any means attempted to cover the entire field (lexical semantics, for example, is not treated at all, nor is parsing, or computational analysis, etc.), but we have tried to provide a representative piece from several of the major areas of grammatical theory, and from some other areas that are of special importance for the kind of questions we wish to address. In all cases, we see that we need to get beyond the everyday notions of "languages," "words," "sounds," and the like – external, extensional notions from *E*-language – and to work at a higher level of abstraction in order to capture significant generalizations.

Chapter 1 summarizes the way ideas have changed over time concerning the basic object of inquiry in linguistics. Philologists thought of texts as the essential reality; in the nineteenth century, the neogrammarians looked at individual sounds and words; structuralists assumed that language should be studied in itself, but thought of structure as somehow immanent in an external, social reality. American structuralists thought they could characterize linguistic behavior from a purely external point of view, until Chomsky's review of Skinner and the subsequent triumph of mentalism over behaviorism in the study of cognition showed us that the real object we ought to be studying is the nature, development, and organization of linguistic knowledge – the language organ.

Against the background of this understanding of what linguistics is centrally concerned with, chapter 2 sets the stage for more detailed consideration of the various subparts of the study of the language organ. We argue that the properties of language cannot be understood if we take it to develop by the inductive application of general learning strategies to the data available to the child, and present evidence that the language faculty is a species-specific, biologically determined capacity.

Chapter 3 deals in more detail with the domain where the cognitive nature of the subject was clearest from the start, syntax. Prior to the late 1950s, linguistics focused almost entirely on the smallest units of language, sounds, words, and minimal meaningful elements ("morphemes"), where the model of the Saussurian sign has most plausibility. "Syntax" was largely a promissory note to the effect that such sign-based analysis would eventually encompass the larger units of phrases, sentences, etc. When the productive mechanisms of syntactic formation came under scrutiny with the rise of transformational generative grammar, however, the challenge to the notion that language is essentially an inventory of signs became apparent. The resulting insights had profound effects in all areas of the field.

Chapter 4 deals with phonology, the study of what Edward Sapir meant by the title of his paper "Sound Patterns in Language" (Sapir 1925). The study of the linguistic organization of sound led, in structuralist linguistics, to the notion of the "phoneme" as a minimal unit of contrast. This idea, in turn, was seen as fundamental by students of several other disciplines, and for many constitutes the main claim of linguistics to scientific status. A focus on the definition of this unit, however, resulted in a resolutely surface-oriented view of language, which was only with great difficulty replaced by a more internalist picture. In fact, generative phonology more or less accidentally discovered the right alternative to the externalism of phonemics. In what is generally seen to be the foundational moment in the development of a generative approach to phonology, Morris Halle offered an argument against classical phonemics that had profound effects on the field. What is of interest here is the fact that the true force of Halle's argument against phonemes only becomes apparent when the object of inquiry in the study of language is taken to be a form of knowledge (*I*-language), not the properties of sounds, words, sentences, etc.

The concern of chapter 4 is with the nature of **representations** in phonology, the description of the way languages use sound properties to distinguish linguistic elements from one another and the changes that have taken place in our conception of the relation between phonological form and surface phonetic form. Chapter 5 continues the discussion of phonology by asking how the regularities of linguistic knowledge in this domain are to be characterized. We discuss reasons to believe that the kind of configuration-specific rules in terms of which early generative phonology operated can profitably be replaced with systems of more general constraints. We view the rise of theories of this sort (such as "Optimality Theory") as being of a piece with the more general abandonment in syntax and elsewhere of construction-specific rules in favor of general principles.

Chapter 6 deals with phonetics, often thought of not as a theoretical aspect of the study of language, but rather as just a set of tools for objectively observing and recording external facts. We argue, in contrast, that phonetics as it forms part of linguistics is necessarily based on the development and articulation of a highly abstract theory of the organization of speech production and perception – a theory that identifies and characterizes the linguistic aspects of speech events to the exclusion of their other physical and physiological correlates. There is no external, language-independent basis for this abstraction; and indeed some of the "phonetic" aspects of speech may not be overtly realized in any measurable way, but must be inferred from linguistic organization. Again, the coherent nature of this aspect of language only makes sense in terms of the cognitive construal of language as a form of knowledge, rather than as E-language.

Chapter 7 introduces the field of morphology. A language's stock of words is usually seen as merely an inventory of signs – some of which may be internally complex, and to which additions may be made in regular ways, but fundamentally a collection. We argue that the nature of word structure necessitates a conception of the lexicon instead as a form of knowledge, of a kind not reducible to syntax and/or phonology.

Chapters 8 and 9 concern the related subjects of linguistic change and the acquisition of grammatical knowledge by the child. Language change is argued not to be driven by the imperatives of external forces acting on linguistic objects, as the founders of modern historical linguistics (the neogrammarians) saw it, but rather as a working out of the possibilities made available by the human language faculty in the presence of limited and often ambiguous data. Similarly, the acquisition of a first language by the child is better seen as the growth of a cognitive capacity in a way sensitive to (but not simply determined by) the partial and degenerate data available in the environment. In both of these (tightly interconnected) respects, a coherent view of the regularities involved necessitates a cognitive, rather than an E-language perspective.

In the concluding chapter, we return to the problem of the organic basis of language as it develops in humans. Abundant evidence shows that this is an aspect of the organization of the mind/brain, which naturally raises the question of where in the brain this faculty is to be found. While some partial answers in the form of apparently concrete loci for certain aspects of the language capacity have been proposed, it is reasonably clear that the brain's organization is subtler and more complex than this. If language is indeed an "organ," it is one in a functional sense, not localized in the manner of the kidney. In this respect, however, language is simply typical of the functional organs that, collectively, make up the mind.

The original idea for this book arose when Dr. Joseph Hoffmann, editor of the *Annual Review of Physiology*, asked us to prepare an article for that journal that would suggest to physiologists what linguists were talking about when they referred to a language "organ." The result was Anderson and Lightfoot 1999, which serves as the basis for chapter 2 and much of chapter 10 of the present book. We are grateful to Dr. Hoffmann not only for giving us an opportunity to discuss this issue for a discerning and sophisticated audience of non-linguists, but also for making us think about the importance of the basic issues raised by that question and the need to present them to a broader audience.

We have received useful comments on various drafts of parts of this book from Dana Boatman, Norbert Hornstein, Ray Jackendoff, and Charles Yang, as well as from referees for Cambridge University Press. Some of the research on which chapters below are based was supported by awards (SBR 9514682 and BCS 9876456) from the National Science Foundation to Yale University.

Figure 6.1, is reprinted from J.-M. Hombert, 'Consonant types, vowel height and tone in Yoruba,' *UCLA Working Papers in Phonetics* 33 (1976), 40–54.

Figure 10.1, is reprinted from Richard L. Gregory (ed.) *The Oxford Companion to the Mind* (Oxford, Oxford University Press: 1987), 620.

Figure 10.2, is reprinted from D. Purves et al. (eds.), *Neuroscience* (Sunderland, MA: Sinauer), 159.

1   Studying the human language faculty

If you meet someone at a cocktail party and tell them you are a carpenter, or a veterinarian, or an astronomer, they are likely to be quite satisfied with that, and the subsequent evolution of the conversation will depend, at least in part, on the depth of their interest in woodworking, animals, or the universe. But if you tell them you are a linguist, this is unlikely to satisfy whatever curiosity they may have about you: "Oh, so how many languages can you speak?" is the most common reply at this point. But in fact, many – probably even most – linguists actually speak few if any languages in addition to their native tongue, in any practical sense. A "linguist," at least in academic disciplinary terms, is not a person who speaks many languages, but rather someone concerned with the scientific study of language more generally.

That still doesn't settle matters, though. As we will discuss below, different generations of scholars have had rather different notions of what was important enough about language to warrant study. Languages have histories, and relationships with one another that at least superficially parallel genetic connections, and one can study those things. Most often, languages are spoken, and it is possible to study the anatomical, acoustic, and perceptual aspects of speech. Different spoken forms can mean different things, and we might study the kinds of things we can "mean" and the ways differences in the forms of words are related to differences in their meanings. Literature, rhetoric, and the texture of ordinary verbal interchange show us that we can do many different things with words, and we might take an understanding of these various potential uses as the goal of a scientific study of language.

All of these approaches to language, however, assume that language is an essentially ubiquitous activity of human beings. As an infant, every human being normally acquires a knowledge of (at least one) language, knowledge that is acquired while exposed to a limited amount of speech in the child's surroundings and that allows him or her to participate in the verbal life of the community within a relatively short time. Surely the most basic questions to ask if one wants to understand the phenomenon of language concern the nature and form of that knowledge, the way it arises and the way it relates to other aspects of human cognition.

The study of language and cognition during the past several decades has given increasing credibility to the view that human knowledge of natural language results from – and is made possible by – a biologically determined capacity specific both to this domain and to our species. An exploration of the functional properties of this capacity is the basic program of the present book. These develop along a regular maturational path, such that it seems appropriate to speak of our knowledge of our language as "growing" rather than as "being learned." As with the visual system, much of the detailed structure that we find seems to be "wired in," though interaction with relevant experience is necessary to set the system in operation and to determine some of its specific properties. We can refer to experience that plays such a role as **triggering** the organization of the system, exploiting a term taken from ethology.

The path of development which we observe suggests that the growth of language results from a specific innate capacity rather than emerging on a purely inductive basis from observation of the language around us. The mature system incorporates properties that could not have been learned from observation or any plausibly available teaching. The deep similarity among the world's languages also provides support for the notion that they are the product of a common human faculty.

These fundamental, apparently native properties are shared by the gestural languages which develop spontaneously in Deaf communities, quite independently of one another or of the language of the surrounding hearing community. We must conclude that they are neither the result of simple shared history nor necessary consequences of the articulatory/acoustic/auditory modality of language in its most familiar form, spoken language. The development of structurally deficient pidgins into the essentially normal linguistic systems found in creoles, as a result of transmission through the natural language learning process in new generations of children, provides additional evidence for the richness of that process.

The domain-specificity of the language faculty is supported by the many dissociations that can be observed between control of language structure and other cognitive functions. Focal brain lesions can result in quite specific language impairments in the presence of otherwise normal cognitive abilities; and *vice versa*. Natural as well as acquired disorders of language also support the proposal that the human language faculty is a product of our genetically determined biological nature: there is evidence that certain language deficits show a clear distribution within families, patterns that epidemiological and other studies show to be just what would be predicted of relatively simple heritable traits (Gopnik and Crago 1991, Tomblin 1997).

Finally, the species-specificity of the human language faculty is supported by the very fact that (absent severe pathology) every human child exposed in even limited ways to the triggering experience of linguistic data develops a full, rich capacity which is usually more or less homogeneous with that of the surrounding community. Meanwhile, efforts to teach human languages to individuals of other species, even those closest to us, have uniformly failed. While a certain capacity for arbitrary symbolic reference can be elicited in some higher apes (and perhaps even in other animals, such as parrots), syntactic systems even remotely comparable to those of human languages seem to be quite outside the capacity of non-humans, despite intensive and highly directed training.

These considerations make it plausible that human language arises in biologically based ways that are quite comparable to those directing other aspects of the structure of the organism. The language organ, though, is not to be interpreted as having an anatomical localization comparable to that of, say, the kidney. Our understanding of the localization of cognitive function in brain tissue is much too fragmentary and rudimentary. Certain cortical and subcortical areas can be shown to subserve functions essential to language, in the sense that lesions in these regions disrupt language functioning (sometimes in remarkably specific ways), but an inference from this evidence to a claim that "language is located in Broca's (and/or Wernicke's) area" is quite unwarranted. The linguistic capacity which develops naturally in every normal human being appears to be best understood in functional and not anatomical terms, at least for the time being. We will return to these issues of the physical basis of linguistic knowledge in chapter 10; until then, let us take it as given that **some** such physical basis must exist, and concentrate on the nature of linguistic capacities.

1.1   Linguistics and the mind/brain

The major puzzles in linguistics concern the fact that our biological nature makes it possible to acquire a richly structured kind of knowledge, much of which is only indirectly evidenced (if at all) in the data available to the learner. This is the "poverty-of-stimulus" problem, which will occupy us in chapters below. It follows that any sensible student of language would want to take as his or her basic agenda the investigation of the details of this knowledge, and the foundation for its growth in the individual. This understanding of what linguistics is all about, however, with the focus on language organs, is actually a relatively recent one.

In the Introduction, we noted the problem of where linguistics departments fall in the geography of modern academia. As the central concerns of the field have moved away from historical issues and the study of languages for their own sake, and toward a more general understanding of the phenomenon of language, the reaction has often been to move linguistics out of the humanities and into the social sciences. This has not been particularly comfortable, however, since the most important questions about the nature of language do not really respond to the assumptions and methods of the disciplines concerned with group phenomena that arise fundamentally as a part of social reality (anthropology, economics, sociology, political science, etc.). The problem of relating group behavior to the properties of the individual, and its appropriate resolution, was already prefigured some time ago in an even broader form by Edward Sapir, a notable visionary in his approach to language and to culture more generally.

In his classic article in the first number of the journal *Psychiatry* (Sapir 1938) and in many other writings, Sapir urged that a true understanding of the nature and effects of culture must necessarily be founded on an understanding of the individuals who participate in culture and society: "In the psychological sense, culture is not the thing that is given us. The culture of a group as a whole is not a true reality. What is given – what we do start with – is the individual and his behavior."[1] And the central term in this understanding is the nature of the mind and personality of the individual, not an external characterization of his actions and responses or some system that somehow exists outside of any particular person.

Trained by Franz Boas as a cultural anthropologist, Sapir devoted most of his professional life to the study of language and the development of the nascent discipline of linguistics (see Anderson 1985, chap. 9 and Darnell 1990 for sketches of his personal and professional life). For Boas, as for Sapir, language was a key to all other understanding of cultural realities, since it is only through an appreciation of the particularities of an individual's language that we can hope to gain access to his thoughts and conception of the world, both natural and social. Sapir, indeed, is widely associated with the notion of "linguistic relativity," according to which the structure of an individual's language not only reflects but even contributes to determining the ways in which he construes his world.[2] Language thus occupies a central place among the phenomena that can lead us to an understanding of culture; and it must follow that the way to study language is in terms of the knowledge developed in individual speakers, not in terms of such externalities as collections of recorded linguistic acts. In the history of linguistics, Sapir is remembered especially as one who emphasized the need to study what speakers know and believe (perhaps unconsciously) about their language, not simply what they do when they speak.

In addition to his primary focus on linguistics, Sapir also wrote widely of more general issues in the nature of society, culture, and personality. His *Psychiatry* piece was far from isolated in the sympathy it showed with the project of psychiatry and psychoanalysis. This interest in psychiatric issues and approaches

---

[1] Sapir 1994, p. 139. The quotation is from a recent reconstruction of Sapir's lectures on these topics.

[2] This is the so-called "Sapir–Whorf Hypothesis."

was certainly not isolated from his work as a linguist and anthropologist. On the contrary, as reflected in the title of his article ("Why cultural anthropology needs the psychiatrist"), he felt that the mode of understanding essayed by the psychiatrist was really the only path to a true appreciation of cultural phenomena, given the claim above that the individual is the basic reality in this study.

Why the psychiatrist, in particular? One must remember that the 1930s, when Sapir was active in general studies of personality and culture, was the time when ideas from the positivist and behaviorist traditions predominated in scientific investigations of psychological questions, and of course these were precisely antagonistic to a sympathetic investigation of the nature and contents of the mind and personality. Psychiatry, in contrast, was centrally occupied with exactly this, and so the fundamental place of the individual in language and culture entailed a need for the kind of light that could only be shed on core issues by psychiatric investigation and understanding.

While no one denied Sapir's stunning brilliance as a linguist, both as a theoretician and as an analyst, many of his colleagues at the time considered this "mentalist" aspect of his thought to be an eccentricity – even an aberration – something to be excused rather than imitated. After all, linguistics was on its way to attaining genuine status as a science precisely through adopting the behaviorism of the day, focusing on purely mechanical methods for collecting and arranging linguistic data so as to arrive at a purely external analysis of linguistic behavior, eschewing all metaphysical talk about "minds" and such-like unobservables (cf. Bloomfield 1933). Over time, however, the field of linguistics has arrived at essentially the same conclusion Sapir did, by its own path and making only a little use of the insight he had to offer.

1.2   Linguistics as history

While the study of language up through about the 1870s was as much a branch of philosophy as an empirical science, scholars began to adopt genuinely scientific methods around that time. Linguistics grew, in part, out of the study of philology: how do we establish the correct form of an ancient text, given that we have perhaps only several corrupted manuscripts to go on? A method developed for comparing manuscripts to establish the most likely ancestral form from which they all derived.[3]

When nineteenth-century scholars came to the conclusion that whole languages, not just individual texts, could be regarded as related in this way, the COMPARATIVE METHOD came to be applied to the problem of how to

---

[3] The connection between philological methods in dealing with ancient manuscripts and the *Stammbaum* or "tree" model of inter-linguistic relationships is discussed by Hoenigswald 1963, who suggests that the method of reconstructing the geneology of manuscripts developed by F. Ritschl may have influenced the conceptions of his student A. Schleicher.

reconstruct an ancestral language (e.g., Proto-Indo-European) from which a number of attested modern languages could be derived. In the case of texts, it is clear how an original form comes to be corrupted: scribes make mistakes. But what is the analog in the case of whole languages? Nineteenth-century linguists came up with the conception of "sound change": systematically over time within part of a speech community, certain sounds change into others. Thus, voiced stops like *b*, *d*, *g* may be uniformly replaced by the corresponding voiceless stops *p*, *t*, *k*, for example (see (1.2) below). When we reconstruct an earlier form of language, what we are trying to do is to undo the sequence of sound changes by which the modern language came about.

Where this became scientific was when people suggested that there was a general lawfulness to these changes, and proposed the principle of REGULARITY OF SOUND CHANGE. That is, unlike the random pattern of scribal errors, sound changes operate in a uniform way, and do not affect individual words idiosyncratically. Furthermore, scholars hoped that it would be possible to derive the range of possible sound changes from a study of the physics and physiology of speech, assuming that sound changes reflected regularities that could ultimately be deduced from natural laws of these domains, and not purely arbitrary, random events.

The point of these observations is that at this stage, the object of scientific inquiry about language was pretty much defined by the scope of the available genuinely explanatory principles, and this meant that linguistics was "about" the histories of languages (and of individual words within those languages). The basic question of the field could be put as: how do languages come to be as they are through (DIACHRONIC) change over time? As a result, historical linguistics was the only kind of linguistics there was at the time. Towards the end of the nineteenth century, Hermann Paul (1880, p. 20) was able to pontificate that "Es ist eingewendet, dass es noch eine ander wissenschaftliche Betrachtung der Sprache gäbe, als die geschichtliche. Ich muss das in Abrede stellen" (It has been objected that there is another scientific view of language possible besides the historical. I must contradict this).

Linguistics was thus resolutely about change, and for nineteenth-century linguistics, what changed was a "language": essentially, an inventory of words. The systematicity of linguistic change arose from the nature of its basic mechanism: change of sounds, which thereby affected all words in which the relevant sounds (or sound combinations) occurred. There was more to language than just words, of course, but everything else was attributable either to a universal "logic" or to individually variable "habits," and these matters did not greatly interest the linguists of the time. The job of the linguist, then, was to write the history of words, their pronunciations, and their meanings. This understanding of what linguistics is about still characterizes some parts of the field, though classical historical linguistics is a relatively small subdiscipline today.

Words are transmitted from one generation to the next, and they may change their form in the course of that transmission. Latin *pater* "father" became *padre*, *père*, *patre*, *pai*, etc. in the modern Romance languages. One could characterize such changes by writing "sound laws" such as the principle that a dental stop came to be pronounced with vocal fold vibration (that is, [t] came to be pronounced as [d]) between a vowel and a vocalic *r* at some point in the transition from Latin to Italian and Spanish. The important observation which made it possible to envision a science of this sort of thing was the fact that while such changes affected particular words, they were in principle formulable in terms of phonetic environments alone, without direct reference to the words themselves. Changes in the set of words, then, were the consequence of the working of sound laws, and linguistics could potentially develop a science of these that could hope to explain the development of languages over time.

In this view, languages are the basic objects of reality, entities existing in their own right "out there," waiting to be acquired by speakers. Linguists sought to determine and quantify the degree of historical relatedness among sets of languages, and this relatedness was expressed through tree diagrams or cladograms such as that in (1.1), introduced by August Schleicher (1861–62).

(1.1)

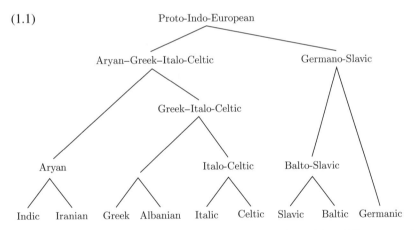

(After Schleicher 1861–62; note that many of the details in this model would be contested by scholars today.)

As has often been pointed out, the Schleicher-style cladograms, familiar from all textbooks on historical linguistics, capture only what biologists call "homologies," similarities which result from common historical origins, and not "analogies," similarities which arise from common developments. This was recognized very early, and nineteenth-century linguists supplemented the "tree-theory" picture with "wave-theory" models representing common innovations shared by geographically contiguous languages.

These cladograms assume that languages are like species, as articulated by Schleicher 1863, and that they derive from one another in some coherent historical or evolutionary development. But we should realize some of the idealizations that are involved. Trees of this kind idealize away from the fact that languages do not split sharply at some specific point and suddenly emerge in their full individuality. The splitting process is more gradual and is initiated by minor divergences. We might say that the first change which affected, say, Latin and not any of the other languages, is the bifurcation point, the point at which Latin suddenly splits away. That is not enough, though: saying that French and Italian are both (separately) descended from Latin glosses over the fact that they are descended from different forms of Latin, and that "Latin" is a cover term for many different forms of speech. In fact, the analogy between languages and species is not ultimately a very useful one, and the conventional tree models of historical linguists would require vast elaboration to be equivalent to modern biological cladograms based on the molecular genetics of organisms.

Schleicher-style family tree models also do not provide a very insightful way of talking about relatedness, since they deal only with historically derived similarities. These models were developed to capture relatedness among lexicons, which were taken to be pretty much unstructured inventories of words (see chapter 7 below). If one goes beyond the mere word-stock, however, and envisions relatedness more broadly than just in terms of similarities resulting from a common history, very different relations would emerge.

If one thinks of grammars, individual systems of knowledge, language organs, developed on the basis of exposure to some relevant linguistic experience and emerging according to the requirements of the linguistic genotype (UNIVERSAL GRAMMAR) as children set predefined parameters in appropriate ways, one can then compare the grammars of English speakers with those of German speakers, and ask whether those grammars are more or less similar to each other than either are to the grammars of Italian speakers. After all, the child acquiring a language has no access to the historical sources of the linguistic forms in the input, and accordingly no bias toward having linguistic ontogeny recapitulate phylogeny, in Ernst Hackel's famous phrase.

German grammars are quite different from English grammars: they have the object preceding rather than following the verb (*Ich glaube dass Hans Maria liebt* "I believe that Hans loves Maria"); they require the finite verb to appear in second position in main clauses (*Im Dorf gibt es nicht zu viele Hunde* "In the town there are not many dogs"); they have very different word order possibilities within the verb phrase. In fact it is quite possible – even likely – that English grammars might be more similar to grammars with which there is less historical connection. From this perspective, looking at the parameters in the current linguistic literature, English grammars may be more similar to

Italian than to German, and French grammars may be more similar to German than to Spanish.[4] There is no reason to believe that structural similarity should be even an approximate function of historical relatedness – assuming that there is in fact a non-circular notion of historical relatedness to be discovered.

Nonetheless, nineteenth-century linguists focused on languages, seen as inventories of words composed from basic inventories of sounds, which could change over time. Languages so conceived appeared to change in systematic ways which could be formulated as regular correspondences, each the product of some combination of sound changes that could be expressed as sound laws independent of the identities of the individual words affected. By the end of the nineteenth century, linguists knew that this was not the entire story: there were other regularities of language change which could not be stated in purely phonetic terms, suggesting that at least in these cases it was not the language (construed as an inventory) or its sounds that were changing, but rather some kind of more abstract system. This was dealt with in a terminological move: there were regularities of "sound change," but there could be other sorts of change that worked differently. These were called "analogical change," and were assumed to be governed by quite a different, more mysterious, kind of regularity.

Nineteenth-century linguists focused on the surface forms of words, which are the products of human behavior, rather than on internal processes that underlie and shape that behavior. They thus dealt with *E*-language rather than *I*-language in the terminology of Chomsky 1986. Not all aspects of language have satisfying accounts in these terms, though, and it is often necessary to invoke underlying processes and abstract systems that are not manifest parts of the observable facts of *E*-language. This is true for such famous instances of regular sound change as Grimm's Law, which affected many types of consonants in a related way in a sort of cycle (cf. (1.2a)); or the Great Vowel Shift in English (cf. (1.2b)), which changed all of the long vowels in another sort of cycle, raising all vowels one step and making diphthongs of the highest vowels. Thus, [swe:t] "sweet" (pronounced with a vowel similar to that of modern *skate*) became modern English [swi:t]; [ti:m] "time" (pronounced rather like modern *team*) became [taim]; [hu:s] "house" (with a vowel similar to that of modern *loose*) became [haus], etc.). Grimm's Law and the Great Vowel Shift affect many sounds at the same time, and represent changes in systems, not simply in inventories.

---

[4] Linguists idealize and speak of French grammars, but a "French grammar" has much the same status as a "French liver," a convenient fiction. Individuals have livers and individuals have grammars. Grammars may be similar to one another, and we may seek similarities between the grammars of "English speakers," whoever they may be exactly. In doing so, we must be prepared to find differences between the grammars of a man in Houston and a woman in Leeds.

(1.2) a. Grimm's Law

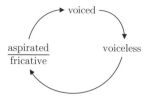

b. The Great English Vowel Shift

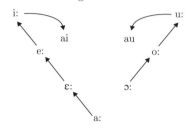

Because the historical linguists of this period were working with the external forms of language, rather than with internal, underlying processes and abstract systems, it makes sense that their attention was confined to phonological and morphological aspects of language, and they paid little attention to change in syntactic systems. It makes no sense to think of (sets of) sentences, products of behavior, as being transmitted from one generation to another, because language acquisition is clearly not a matter of learning sets of sentences. This limitation was not seen as a matter of concern: they simply worked on what they felt they had useful tools to elucidate. The debates of the time were primarily about the nature and causes of sound change.

A part of what made the study of sound change appealingly scientific was the fact that its systematicities could be related to those of another domain: the physics and physiology of speech. When we describe Proto-Indo-European /p,t,k/ as becoming /f,θ,χ/ in the Germanic languages (e.g., prehistoric *patr* becoming modern English *father*, *tres* becoming *three*, etc.), we can unify these by saying that one kind of formational occlusion (complete blockage of the oral cavity followed by a rapid release, accompanied by a brief burst of noisy airflow) is replaced by another (incomplete blockage of airflow, allowing for noisy, turbulent flow during the period of occlusion). With this unitary formulation in hand, we can hope to find reasons why one sort of occlusion should be replaced by another, a rather more hopeful task than that of finding reasons why one arbitrary set of symbols should be replaced by another equally arbitrary one.

It is natural that the development of rigorous methods in historical linguistics more or less coincided with the beginnings of serious investigation of the phonetics of speech using instrumental techniques that were precise and quantifiable (if quite primitive by today's standards). It was widely assumed that the terms of an explanatory theory of speech production and perception would serve as the underpinnings of an equally explanatory theory of sound change, and it is no accident that among the important figures in the late-nineteenth-century development of comparative Indo-European studies was Eduard Sievers, author of the basic text of the period on the science of phonetics, Sievers 1881.

But in spite of the promising start provided by increasingly precise accounts of speech, sound laws were clearly not reducible to measurable aspects of the physical world. Grimm's, Grassmann's, and Verner's Laws (three changes whose discovery and formulation played particularly important roles in the development of the doctrine of the regularity of sound change) were not general laws like Boyle's Law: they were rather particular contingent events that had taken place at a given point in history, but were not universally valid. As such, they required a deeper explanation. Changes were taken to be **directional**, as in biology. Rask (1818) held that languages became simpler. Schleicher (1848) identified a progression from isolating to agglutinating to inflectional types, although this was said to hold for preliterate societies, whereas Rask's drive to simplicity was relevant for literate societies. Darwin (1874, pp. 88–92) thought that languages changed in the direction of having shorter, "easier" forms.

There was widespread agreement that language change followed fixed developmental laws, and that there was a direction to change, but there was active disagreement about what that direction was. By the end of the nineteenth century there was an enormous body of work on sound correspondences among historically related languages, and vast compendia of changes that had taken place, especially in the Indo-European languages. There were, however, few ideas about why those changes had taken place.

First, the notion that languages became simpler, more natural, easier to pronounce, etc. was quite circular: "simpler," etc. was what languages change to, and there was no independent definition in a framework dealing entirely with historical change. Second, the idea that languages change toward greater simplicity (or whatever) gives no account of why a given change takes place when it does – as opposed to the laws of gravity, which apply to all objects at all times. To that extent, invoking notions of directionality was no more law-like than the laws of Grimm, Grassmann, and Verner, which directionality was intended to explain.

There were attempts to break out of this circularity, by invoking psychological causes, but the psychology itself was implausible and unexplanatory. Grimm (1848) attributed his consonant changes to the courage and pride associated with the German race's advance over all parts of Europe. Jespersen (1909) ascribed the shift in the meanings of verbs like *like, repent* etc. (whereby Middle English sentences like *pears like me* became modern *I like pears*) to the greater interest taken in persons than in things at one stage in the history of English. For other examples, see Lightfoot 1999. Hardly anyone was satisfied that the result of such speculations provided a genuine science of (the history of) language.

1.3   Linguistics as the study of *E*-language

In the early years of the twentieth century, then, the data of linguistics consisted of an inventory of sound changes occurring for no good reason and tending in no particular direction. The historical approach had not brought a scientific, Newtonian-style analysis of language, of the kind that had been hoped for, and there was no predictability to the changes. One of the greatest figures in historical linguistics at the time was Ferdinand de Saussure, whose revolutionary work on the vowel system of Indo-European (de Saussure 1879) established much of the research agenda in historical linguistics for the twentieth century; and it is something of an irony that he was the first to argue forcefully that these historical issues were only a very small part of the story, and that the science of language would have to provide an account of the nature of the linguistic systems that we find today in their own terms, not just their histories.

Saussure (de Saussure 1974) argued that when we look at language, we must distinguish the **system** of a language (called "*langue*") from concrete acts of speaking or language use ("*parole*"). What is systematic about language is to be sought in an analysis of *langue*, but for Saussure, the locus of linguistic change is not there, but rather in usage, or *parole*. It follows that linguistic change itself cannot be the object of a fundamental science of language.

Following Saussure's lead, the historicist paradigm – the notion that there are principles of history to be discovered, which would account for a language's development – was largely abandoned by the 1920s (see Lass 1980 for thorough discussion). Indeed, there was a virulent anti-historicism in the writing of several major figures of this period, including not only Saussure but also Franz Boas, Edward Sapir, and Leonard Bloomfield. They worked to some extent on language change, but abandoned historicism, and with it the earlier program of seeking to explain how it was that languages come to be as they are.

Perceived problems included the circularity of the historical principles invoked, and the kinds of psychological claims that had been made. Sapir (1929, p. 208) wrote that the psychological interpretation of language change was "desirable and even necessary," but that the existing psychological explanations were unhelpful and "do not immediately tie up with what we actually know about the historical behavior of language." Bloomfield (1933, p. 17) complained about the circularity of psychologizing, saying that there was no independent evidence for the mental processes other than the linguistic processes they were supposed to explain. The historicist paradigm was not really refuted or shown to be wrong: rather, it was abandoned as yielding diminishing returns and not asking the truly fundamental questions about the nature of language. Work on language change continued to flourish, but subsequent generations did not, by and large, appeal to historicist explanations.

In chapter 8 below, we will ask what accounts of language history we can give if we take a different, more contingent approach. We shall shift away from a study of the results of behavior and toward a study of the states and properties of the mind/brain that give rise to those products, and we will see that a rather deeper (if quite different) understanding of change results. But at this point, let us continue to trace the evolution of thought about what linguistics ought to concern itself with.

Saussure's concern to re-orient linguistics from the study of *parole* to that of *langue* gave rise to structural linguistics, or the study of linguistic systems: the sounds and grammatical structures of, e.g., French, as opposed to the history of how Latin originals became the individual words of Modern French. Saussure himself argued that the right basis for such an understanding was to construe the linguistic system as something with a reality that was primarily social: a set of conventions among speakers of a given language to do things in a certain way. For him, *langue* was a system existing outside of any individual, located rather in the speech community that employs a particular code.

The nature of that code was that of a structured inventory of SIGNS, where each sign consists of the unity of some expression with the semantic content which it signifies (thus, "[kæt] means 'Felis catus' "). The structural value of any unit in the system derives from the principle that each sign is distinct from every other sign: thus, the value of *cat* is provided by the facts that in terms of expression, [kæt] is different from [ræt], [kɔt], [kæn], etc.; while in terms of content, a *cat* is distinct from a *lion, tiger, dog*, etc. The system of signs (*langue*) is what makes communication possible within a speech community; it constitutes the common knowledge of that community, and is therefore independent of the particular properties of any individual member of the community, or of any individual utterance that may be produced on a particular occasion by a speaker of the language (an act of *parole*).

While Saussure's conception of *langue* as a primarily social entity was not widely adopted, his replacement of diachronic change by synchronic system as the object of study in the field was. Structural linguistics evolved in various ways through the first half of the century, and a consideration of those developments is well beyond the scope of the present book (see Anderson 1985, among many other sources, for further discussion).

With the rise of strongly empiricist, verificationist views in the philosophy of science during this period, the study of language eventually became mired down in the assumptions of behaviorist (or as Leonard Bloomfield, a major influence in this development, preferred to put it, "mechanist") psychology. On

that view, scientific investigation can only concern itself with external observables. Properties of mind (if indeed there are such) are intrinsically beyond the
reach of science. Bloomfield in particular (contrary to his subsequent reputa-
tion in some circles) did not deny the existence of the mind, but maintained that
its properties were so far beyond the reach of (current) science as to make its
investigation pointless.

What was consistently true through this period was that the primary object
of inquiry in the field was not something historical, but something present to
contemporary speakers of a given language. This was always something external, and the basic question of the field had become: what are the properties
of the sets of sounds, words, sentences, etc. recorded in attested acts of speaking? Whether thought of as deriving from social conventions or as the external
responses corresponding to particular stimuli, linguistic objects were consistently seen in this external mode. The commitment to an *E*-language view of
what linguistics studies was thus axiomatic and complete.

1.4   Linguistics as the study of *I*-language

The study of *E*-language entails the study of languages as sets of externally
observable elements – sounds, morphological units, words, phrases, sentences,
texts, etc. But there is no reason to believe that such sets are actually coherent
or well-defined objects of inquiry. That is, there is no precisely definable notion
of a "language," such that one can show in some non-circular way that a given
sentence is "a sentence of English" (see Chomsky 1986, Lightfoot 1999, and
others). A given sentence might be used by a particular speaker in Arkansas, but
not by another speaker in Yorkshire. Does that make it a sentence of English?
Apparently the answer is "yes" for at least some Arkansas speakers, but "no"
for at least some Yorkshire speakers.

There is no general algorithm for characterizing the sentences of English,
and there is no reason to expect to find one. If different speakers of the "same"
language speak differently, there can be no general algorithm. Languages in
this extensional sense are conglomerations of the outputs of various grammars,
where each grammar is represented in the mind/brain of (at least) one individual
speaker. It is not, of course, **necessary** that people who consider themselves to
speak the "same" language should have different grammars, different language
organs, but it is certainly not necessary that their grammars be the same, either,
and empirical evidence suggests considerable variation within particular speech
communities. Some of this variation, as it is reflected in differences in output of
the grammars concerned, may be identified by speakers as reflecting different
"languages," but this is a sociological notion, not a linguistic one. For example,
speakers across a large part of the former Yugoslavia used to consider that they
spoke "Serbo-Croatian," but as a result of changes in political identity, some of

these came to be speakers of "Serbian," others of "Croatian," "Bosnian," etc. – all of this in the absence of any significant change in the grammars of the speakers involved.

The *E*-language set of sentences in use in a speech community, then, is not a coherent object of study because it corresponds to the outputs of a diverse range of (possibly very different) grammars. Indeed, even the *E*-language notion of the set of sentences produced by a given speaker cannot serve this purpose. Ignoring the fact that an individual speaker will typically control a number of (possibly very different) styles, corresponding to different grammars, the actual set of sentences produced and/or understood by a speaker is a completely accidental consequence of the range of things s/he has had occasion to say or hear. Insofar as there are systematic properties of this collection, they are systematicities either of non-linguistic experience or of the underlying grammar, but not of the set of sentences itself. "Languages" in the *E*-language sense are not well-defined entities. They do not "exist" independent of contingent, concrete acts of speaking; they do not "descend" from one another; and there is no reason to believe that their study will reveal any interesting properties. They are convenient fictions, like the rising and the setting of the sun. It follows that if we want to develop a genuine science of language, this must be concerned instead with the *I*-language notion of grammars, the properties of a person's language organ.

In the 1950s, the intellectual coherence and scientific status of American structuralist theories of (*E*-)language were not seriously in doubt. When an alternative to the distribution-based theories of linguistic structure then in vogue[5] developed around the work of Noam Chomsky, this did not initially challenge the notion that the goal of linguistics was to provide rigorous and principled descriptions of the set of possible utterances that constitute a particular language. As Chomsky worked out his ideas, however, it became clear that the conceptual underpinnings of the field were in principle incapable of providing a substantive account of language.

The central difficulty for existing theories was the problem of how language could be acquired. Chomsky (1959) presented a devastating critique of Skinnerian behaviorism that centered on this issue, an assessment that eventually had far-reaching effects in psychology, but whose immediate consequence was a shift of seismic proportions in the expectations scholars had for linguistic theory. He observed that when we consider language use ("verbal behavior" in Skinner's terms), we must recognize that

[t]he child who learns a language has in some sense constructed the grammar for himself on the basis of his observation of sentences and non-sentences (i.e. corrections by the verbal community). Study of the actual observed ability of a speaker to distinguish

---

[5] Harris 1951 was perhaps the epitome of this approach.

sentences from non-sentences, detect ambiguities, etc., apparently forces us to the conclusion that this grammar is of an extremely complex and abstract character, and that the young child has succeeded in carrying out what from the formal point of view, at least, seems to be a remarkable type of theory construction. Furthermore, this task is accomplished in an astonishingly short time, to a large extent independently of intelligence, and in a comparable way by all children. Any theory of learning must cope with these facts. (Chomsky 1959, p. 57)

These remarks had a number of profound consequences. For one, they made it clear that the generalized mechanisms of behaviorist learning theory, based on attributing as little structure as possible to the organism in particular domains, was quite incapable of dealing with the acquisition of human language. For another, they brought the problem of learning to the forefront in the study of language: where previously linguists had generally been content to characterize the language itself, Chomsky made it clear that an understanding of language cannot proceed without asking how a speaker's ability to use it arises in development.

But for linguists, the most profound effect of these arguments was a shift in our conception of the object of study in the field. Chomsky stressed that the basic problem is not one of characterizing what people **do**: it is rather one of characterizing what they **know**. The central reality of language is the fact that we call someone a speaker of, say, Japanese, because of a certain kind of knowledge that he or she has. If that is the case, linguists need to find a way to study the structure of this knowledge, and while the things people say and do can constitute important evidence, that is not all there is, or even the most important thing. This knowledge is what we are calling a person's language organ.

In this focus on the nature of language as a form of knowledge, an aspect of the structure of the mind, linguists have thus returned to a conception much like Sapir's of the centrality of the individual to an understanding of linguistic and cultural phenomena. The decline of behaviorist assumptions in the last several decades of the twentieth century necessarily led to a much broader consensus about the need to understand the mind in its own terms: if Bloomfield was indeed right that the mind was beyond the reach of current science, the thing to do was to develop the relevant science, not study something else.

Much of academic psychology still finds itself preoccupied with externalist issues, and for one reason or another rejects the validity or utility of conceiving its object in terms of the minds of individuals described at some appropriate level of abstraction. The result has been the rise of cognitive science as a discipline whose goal is precisely a science of the mind. Combining ideas from linguistics, computer science, philosophy, anthropology, and cognitive psychology, this emerging field focuses squarely on the nature of mental and cognitive life.

Linguists and linguistics have been important in these developments, in view of the fact that it is in this sphere that the central role of the individual can be studied particularly concretely and productively. Cognitive science thus plays for the contemporary linguist the kind of role Sapir foresaw for psychiatry: one that makes it possible to study phenomena that emerge from the individual by providing methods for investigating the content of the individual's mind and the structure of mental life. If the insight of Sapir's 1938 paper now appears in somewhat different form, its validity has only been reinforced by subsequent developments in the study of language.

The result of the developments surveyed above has been the rise of a consensus that linguistics really is (a branch of) cognitive science: the object of study, *I*-language, is an aspect of the structure of the mind/brain, the language organ, defined at some level of abstraction, which must be studied as such and whose study can lead to further insights about the architecture of cognition. This view is certainly not a universal one: some linguists, for a variety of reasons, continue to focus on external objects and events rather than on the form of linguistic knowledge. It is also important to note that many linguists who would assent in principle to the view we have presented nonetheless continue to pursue in practice the study of particular linguistic phenomena in ways that remain unchanged from their origins within an *E*-language conception of the discipline. In what follows, we will attempt to draw out the differences in approach that follow from this shift of attention, and the relation between such abstract, general considerations and the everyday practice of linguistics.

Here we have sketched some aspects of the path by which the field of linguistics has arrived in its own way at what were essentially Sapir's conclusions. In subsequent chapters, we will outline some of the basic properties and substructures of language organs, considering as we proceed **how** we have been able to discover them.

2   Language as a mental organ

In this chapter, we pursue an important source of evidence for the claim that human language has a specialized basis in human biology: the relation between what a speaker of a language can be said to "know" and the evidence that is available to serve as the basis of this knowledge. The apparently common-sense notion that an adult speaker's knowledge of his/her language arises by simple "learning," that is, as a direct generalization of experience, turns out to pose a logical paradox. We begin with two brief examples that illustrate this point, and then explore the consequences of this for the mechanisms that must in fact underlie the development of language organs in normal human speakers.

2.1   We know more than we learn

A striking property of language acquisition is that children attain knowledge which, quite literally, **infinitely** surpasses their actual experience. On the basis of very limited experience, a productive system, a grammar, arises in each speaker which not only encompasses the actual facts to which they have been exposed, but also permits the production and comprehension of an unlimited range of novel utterances in the language. There must, therefore, be much more to language acquisition than mimicking what is heard in childhood; and there is more to it than the simple transmission of a set of words and sentences from one generation of speakers to the next.

2.1.1   Two grammatical puzzles

Consider some subtleties that people are usually not consciously aware of. The verb *is* may be used in its full form or its reduced form: English speakers can say either *Kim is the professor here* or *Kim's the professor here*, *He is happy* or *He's happy*. However, certain instances of *is* never reduce: for example, the underlined items in *Kim is happier than Tim is* or *I wonder who the professor is here*. Most speakers are not aware of this, but we all know, subconsciously as it were, that we can not use the reduced form in such cases. How did we come to know this? As children, we were not instructed to avoid the reduced form in certain places. Yet, all children typically attain the ability to use the forms in the adult fashion, and this ability is quite independent of intelligence level or educational background. Children attain it early in their linguistic development. More significantly, children do not try out the non-occurring forms as if testing a hypothesis, in the way that they "experiment" by using forms like *goed* and *taked*. The ability emerges perfectly and as if by magic.

Another example. Pronouns like *she, her, he, him, his* sometimes may refer back to a noun previously mentioned in a sentence (2.1a–c). However, one can only understand (2.1d) as referring to two men, Jay and somebody else; here the pronoun may not refer to Jay, unlike (2.1a–c).

(2.1) a. Jay hurt his nose.
b. Jay's brother hurt him.
c. Jay said he hurt Ray.
d. Jay hurt him.

To extend this point, consider some more complex examples, as in (2.2):

(2.2) a. When Jay entered the room, he was wearing a yellow shirt.
b. Jay was wearing a yellow shirt when he entered the room.
c. When he entered the room, Jay was wearing a yellow shirt.
d. He was wearing a yellow shirt when Jay entered the room.
e. His brother was wearing a yellow shirt when Jay entered the room.

In all of the sentences in (2.2) the pronoun (*he* or *his*) may refer to some other individual, not mentioned. It may also refer to Jay – in all cases, that is, except (2.2d), where the wearer of the yellow shirt can only be understood to be someone other than Jay. Again, all speakers understand these sentences in the same way, but we may legitimately be puzzled at the source of this commonality. It is quite unlikely to have come from any explicit instruction: as far as we know, these points about the interpretation of pronouns had not been systematically noted, even by grammarians, prior to the late 1960s (Ross 1967, Langacker 1969, Reinhart 1976, McCawley 1999).

As adults we generalize that a pronoun may refer to another noun within the same sentence except under very precise conditions (as in (2.1d) or (2.2d)). But then, how did we all acquire the right generalization, particularly knowledge of the exceptions? In the case of (2.2d), we might be tempted to say that it is only natural that a pronoun should not be able to refer to an individual mentioned only later in the sentence, but the evidence of (2.2c,e) shows that such "backwards anaphora" is in fact possible under some circumstances. Furthermore, we will see in chapter 9 that even very young children know when backwards anaphora is possible and when it is not.

2.1.2   *Where does this knowledge come from?*

In approaching both of these problems, recall the nature of our childhood experience: we were exposed to a haphazard set of linguistic expressions. We heard various sentences containing both the full verb *is* (*am*, *are*) and the reduced form *'s* (*'m*, *'re*). We also heard sentences containing pronouns, in some of which the pronoun referred to another noun in the same sentence, and in others to a person not mentioned there. The problem is that, because we were not informed about what **cannot** occur, our childhood experience provided no evidence for the "except" clause(s), the cases in which the reduced form is impossible or where a pronoun and a noun in the same sentence may not corefer. That is, we had evidence for generalizations like "*is* may be pronounced [z]"[1] and "pronouns may refer to an individual named by a noun in the same sentence," but no evidence for where these generalizations break down.

As children, we came to know the generalizations and their exceptions, and we came to this knowledge quickly and uniformly. Yet our linguistic experience was not rich enough to determine the limits to the generalizations. We call this the problem of the POVERTY OF THE STIMULUS. Children have no data which show them that *is* may not be reduced in some contexts and they have no data showing that *him* may not refer to Jay in (2.1d). These two small illustrations are examples of the form that the poverty-of-stimulus problem takes in language. It may look as if children are behaving magically, but there is no magician and magic is no answer.

There are two "easy" solutions to the poverty-of-stimulus problem, but neither is adequate. One is to say that children do not overgeneralize, because they are reliable imitators. That is, children do not produce the reduced *'s* in the wrong place or use a pronoun in (2.1d) or (2.2d) wrongly to refer to Jay, because they never hear language being used in this way. In other words, children acquire their native language simply by imitating the speech of their elders. We know this cannot be literally true, because everybody constantly says things that they have never heard. We express thoughts with no conscious or subconscious consideration of whether we are imitating somebody else's use of language. This is true of the most trivial speech: in saying *I want to catch the 3:25 pm bus, which leaves from outside Borders bookstore*, one is using a sentence that one has almost certainly not heard.

The alternative of saying that we form new sentences "by analogy" with specific sentences we have heard before simply conceals the problem, because it does not account for the fact that some possible "analogies" are good and others are not. Why does the existence of the contracted *'s* in *Tim's happy* not provide an analogical foundation for a similar reduced form in *Kim's happier*

---

[1] We follow the convention in linguistics of enclosing phonetic representations in square brackets.

than Tim is? Why do the sentences (2.2a–c,e) not provide an analogical basis for coreference between *Jay* and *he* in (2.2d)? The point is that language learners arrive at certain very specific generalizations, and fail to arrive at certain other logically possible ones, in ways that cannot be founded on any independent general notion of induction or analogy.

A variant on this "solution" is to claim that children learn not to say the deviant forms because they are corrected by their elders. Alas, this view offers no better insight for several reasons. First, it would take an acute observer to detect and correct the error. Second, where linguistic correction is offered, young children are highly resistant and often ignore or explicitly reject the correction. Third, in the examples discussed, children do not overgeneralize and therefore parents have nothing to correct; this will become clearer when we discuss experimental work on young children later in this chapter and in chapter 9.

So the first "easy" solution to the poverty-of-stimulus problem is to deny that it exists, to hold that the environment is rich enough to provide evidence for where the generalizations break down. But the problem is real, and this "solution" does not address it.

The second "easy" answer would be to deny that there is a problem on the grounds that a person's language is fully determined by genetic properties. In that case, there would be nothing to be learned. Yet this answer also cannot be right, because people speak differently, and many of the differences are environmentally induced. There is nothing about a person's genetic inheritance that makes her a speaker of English; if she had been raised in a Dutch home, she would have become a speaker of Dutch.

The two "easy" answers either attribute everything to the environment or everything to the genetic inheritance, and we can see that neither position is tenable. Instead, language emerges through an interaction between our genetic inheritance and the linguistic environment to which we happen to be exposed. English-speaking children learn from their environment that the verb *is* may be pronounced [ɪz] or [z], and native principles prevent the reduced form from occurring in the wrong places. Likewise, children learn from their environment that *he*, *his*, etc are pronouns, while native principles entail that pronouns may not refer to a preceding noun under specific circumstances. The interaction of the environmental information and the native principles accounts for how the relevant properties emerge in an English-speaking child.

We will sketch some relevant principles below. It is worth pointing out that we are doing a kind of Mendelian genetics here, in the most literal sense. In the mid-nineteenth century, Mendel postulated genetic "factors" to explain the variable characteristics of his pea plants, without the slightest idea of how these factors might be biologically instantiated. Similarly, linguists seek to identify information which must be available independently of experience, in order for a grammar to emerge in a child. We have no idea whether this information is encoded directly in the genome or whether it results from epigenetic, developmental properties of the organism; it is, in any case, native. As a shorthand device for these native properties, we shall write of the linguistic genotype, that part of our genetic endowment which is relevant for our linguistic development. Each individual's genotype determines the potential range of functional adaptations to the environment (Dobzhansky 1970, p. 36), and we assume that the linguistic genotype (what linguists call Universal Grammar or UG) is uniform across the species (apart from fairly severe and specific pathology). That is, linguistically we all have the same potential for functional adaptations and any of us may grow up to be a speaker of Catalan or Hungarian, depending entirely on our circumstances and not at all on variation in our genetic make-up.

It is important to understand that UG in this sense is not to be confused with the grammar of any particular language: to say that would be close to the second fallacious approach to the problem of the poverty of the stimulus which we discussed above. Rather, UG can be seen as the set of principles by which the child can infer, on the basis of the limited data available in the environment, the full grammatical capacity which constitutes a mature speaker's (unconscious)[2] knowledge of a language.

Since children are capable of acquiring any language to which they happen to be exposed between infancy and puberty, the same set of genetic principles which account for the emergence of English (using **genetic** now in the extended sense we have indicated) must also account for the emergence of Dutch, Vietnamese, Hopi, or any other of the thousands of languages spoken by human beings. This plasticity imposes a strong empirical demand on hypotheses about the linguistic genotype; the principles postulated must be open enough to account for the variation among the world's languages. The fact that people develop different linguistic capacities depending on whether they are brought up in Togo, Tokyo, or Toronto provides a delicate tool to refine claims about the nature of the native component.

We conclude that there is a biological entity, a finite mental organ, which develops in children along one of a number of paths. The range of possible paths of language growth is determined in advance of any childhood experience. The language organ that emerges, the grammar, is represented in the brain and plays a central role in the person's use of language. We have gained some insight into the nature of people's language organs by considering a wide range of phenomena: the developmental stages that young children go through, the way language breaks down in the event of brain damage, the manner in which people

---

[2] Needless to say, not everything we want to say a person "knows" is accessible to direct reflection and articulation. This is a point which has been made at great length in the literature of philosophy, psychology, and diverse other fields, and which we will not attempt to justify here.

analyze incoming speech signals, and more. At the center is the biological notion
of a language organ, a grammar.

2.2   The nature of grammars

Children acquire a productive system, a grammar, in accordance with the requirements of the genotype. If asked to say quite generally what is now known
about the linguistic genotype, we would say that it yields finite grammars, because they are represented in the finite space of the brain, but that they range
over an infinity of possible sentences. Finite grammars consist of a set of operations which allow for infinite variation in the expressions which are generated.
The genotype is plastic, consistent with speaking Japanese or Quechua. It is
modular, and uniquely computational.

By **modular** we mean that the genotype consists of separate subcomponents
each of which has its own distinctive properties, which interact to yield the
properties of the whole. These modules are, in many cases, specific to language. The grammar is one such module. Another may be a distinct "parser"
which interacts with the grammar to assign structures and meanings to incoming speech signals, and thereby captures our capacity to understand spoken
language in real time. Within the grammar, one module of innate linguistic
capacity contains abstract structures which are compositional (consisting of
units made up of smaller units) and which fit a narrow range of possibilities.
These structures reflect computational operations which encompass the ability
to relate one position to another by movement (or what we treat as copying and
deletion below, p. 24). Another module is the mental lexicon, a list of word-
forms and their crucial properties. Research has undermined the notion that the
mind possesses only general principles of "intelligence" which hold of all kinds
of mental activity.

These modules may or may not be separately represented in neural tissue:
for example, Grodzinsky (2000) has recently argued that movement relations –
and not other aspects of syntactic form – are computed by specific tissue within
the classical Broca's area. We return to these matters in chapter 10: the claim of
modularity does not in any sense rest on such physical separation, however. It
refers, rather, to the fact that various aspects of linguistic knowledge are logically
and functionally independent of one another, yielding the full complexity of
human language through the interaction of individually rather simple systems.

To see the kind of compositionality involved, consider how words combine.
Words are members of categories like noun (N), verb (V), preposition (P),
adjective/adverb (A). If two words combine, then the grammatical properties of
the resulting phrase are determined by one of the two words, which we call the
head: we say that the head **projects** the phrase. If we combine the verb *visit* with
the noun *Chicago*, the resulting phrase *visit Chicago* has verbal and not nominal

properties. It occurs where verbs occur and not where nouns occur: *I want to visit Chicago*, but not **the visit Chicago*[3] nor **we discussed visit Chicago*. So the expression *visit Chicago* is a verb phrase (VP), where the V *visit* is the head projecting the VP. This can be represented as a labeled bracketing (2.3a) or as a tree diagram (2.3b). The verb is the head of the VP and the noun is the complement.

(2.3) a. [_{VP} _Vvisit _NChicago]

      b.

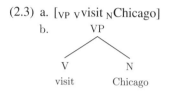

In general, two categories "merge" to form a new category. So an "inflectional" (I) element like *will* might combine with the VP *visit Chicago*, to yield the more complex expression *will visit Chicago*, with a structure [_{IP} _Iwill [_{VP} visit Chicago]]. The auxiliary, inflectional *will*, heads the new phrase and projects to a phrasal category IP. This means that *visit Chicago* is a unit (VP), which acts as the complement of *will* (it completes the meaning of *will* and is structurally the sister of *will*), but *will visit* is not a unit; that is, there is no single node which dominates *will visit* (and nothing else) in this example. The unit consisting of *will* and its complement can, in turn, be the basis of yet more structure in merging with a subject phrase (e.g., [_{DP} _Dthe _Nstudent]) to form a full IP: *The student will visit Chicago*.

The units defined by these trees are the items which the computational operations manipulate; they are the items which are copied and deleted, and to which reference (including coreference) can be assigned. Non-units are not available to these operations.

One of the computational operations involved is that of copying an element already present and merging it with the tree. This accounts for the fact that in the surface forms of many sentences, elements occur in positions other than those with which their syntactic function is naturally assigned, i.e., displaced. For example, an expression like *What city will the student visit?* (where *what city* is understood as the complement of *visit*) can be described by a structure along the lines of (2.4). *Will* is copied in a position labeled C (for "complementizer"), which in such question constructions precedes the rest of the IP, and *what city* is copied as a specifier to that head. The copies are deleted, which we indicate with "e" (for empty) and an index. We take phrases like *what city* and *the student* to be determiner phrases (DP), where *what* and *the* are determiners projecting as DPs; more on this in chapter 3 (see note 1 there).

---

[3] Following a standard convention in linguistics, we indicate phrases or sentences which are not well-formed in English with a preceding *.

(2.4)

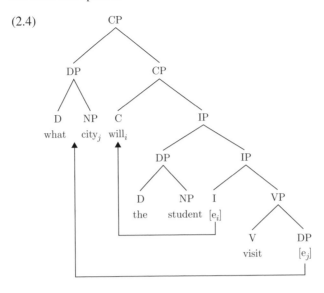

The syntactic component of a speaker's language organ, then, can be represented by a system of rules that describes (or "generates") the set of structures (similar to that in (2.4)) occurring in sentences of the language; it characterizes the range of possible structural relations between displaced elements and their functional positions, etc. Other aspects of a full grammar provide explicit accounts of the relation between this kind of syntactic organization and the way the words of sentences are constructed and pronounced. We will have more to say about these various areas of grammar in later chapters. The set of possible grammars of this type is narrowly limited by the principles of UG, which require that systems within this range (and no others) are in principle attainable by the specific principles available to the child, with differences among them corresponding to differences in the child's experience.

2.3   Back to the puzzles

Let us return now to the poverty-of-stimulus problems raised above in section 2.1, beginning with that of 's, the reduced form of *is*. Recall that this reduced form is not available in some cases, though it is possible in other, superficially quite similar, examples.

(2.5) a. I wonder who the professor is/*'s here.
       b. I wonder who the professor is/'s talking about now.

Poets make linguistic jokes from these phenomena. The Gershwins were famous for contraction jokes: in *Girl Crazy* (1930) a chorus begins *I'm bidin' my time / 'Cause that's the kind of guy I'm*, which is not normal English.

What differentiates the two cases in (2.5), such that the reduced form *'s* is possible in the one instance but not in the other? One potential difference emerges if we consider the structures of the sentences in (2.5) in more detail. In particular, if we take into account the notion that the element *who* has been displaced from its natural position in the sentence, we see that the position from which this movement takes place differs in the two cases:[4]

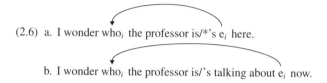

(2.6) a. I wonder who$_i$ the professor is/*'s e$_i$ here.

     b. I wonder who$_i$ the professor is/'s talking about e$_i$ now.

We can notice that in example (2.6a) the verb *is*/*'s* immediately precedes the trace of the displaced element *who*, while in (2.6b) it does not. The correct generalization seems to be that reduced forms of auxiliary elements cannot immediately precede empty elements, such as the trace of displacement in these cases.

This does indeed describe many of the relevant circumstances under which reduced auxiliaries are impossible, but it is too narrow to be satisfying. There is no direct evidence for the situation in which reduced forms are excluded, so some native principle must be involved, but it seems unlikely that such a principle as "reduced auxiliary verbs cannot appear before an empty element such as a trace" forms a distinct part of the human genetic endowment for language; or rather, to the extent that it does, it must surely be as a by-product of something more general and principled.

We might attempt to improve on this hypothesis as follows. Note that, in a sentence like *Kim's happy*, the auxiliary element *'s* is grammatically the head of the IP, taking the adjective phrase (AdjP) *happy* as its complement. In pronunciation, however, it forms part of a single unbroken unit with the preceding word *Kim*, as the apostrophe in the conventional spelling *'s* suggests, despite the fact that the sequence *Kim+'s* does not constitute a phrase syntactically.

In the case that interests us, reduced forms of auxiliaries such as *'s* (as well as *'ve*, *'re*, and the reduced forms of *am*, *will*, *would*, *shall*, and *should*) do not have enough phonological "substance" to be words on their own, and thus necessarily combine with a word on their left to make up a single phonological word in the pronunciation of sentences in which they occur. In terms of pronunciation, that is, *Kim's* in *Kim's happy* is just as indissoluble a unit as *birds* in *Birds fly*.

---

[4] As above, we indicate the source of a copied element with an empty symbol "*e*," generally referred to in the syntactic literature as a TRACE. The identical subscripts attached to the copied element and its trace indicate that both have the same reference.

Not every element that functions as a unit from the point of view of the syntax corresponds to a whole word in pronunciation. Syntactic units that do not contain enough phonetic material to make up a whole word by themselves, such as the reduced auxiliaries in English, are referred to as (simple) CLITICS. Clitics are little words which occur in many, perhaps all languages, and have the property of not being able to stand alone.

In some languages, these elements attach systematically to the word to their left; in others, to the right, and in others the direction of attachment depends on details of the syntactic and/or phonological structure. This is a property of particular languages that is plausibly learned from overt data: the child need only determine that some element is a clitic (in the sense above), and then see whether it is pronounced indissolubly with the word on its left or on its right. What is consistently the case, however, is that syntactic elements that do not constitute words in their own right must attach to some other word as clitics in order to be pronounced at all. This much plausibly reflects properties of UG.

The phonological evidence clearly supports the claim that in English, clitics attach to their **left**, not their right. This direction of association is supported by the fact that the pronunciation of the clitic varies from [s] to [z] to [əz] as a function of the final sound of the **preceding** word (2.7a); and is completely insensitive to the shape of the word on its right. This variation in shape is exactly the same as that which we can observe in the shape of the regular plural ending (spelled *(e)s* but pronounced in the same three ways as *'s*), again as a function of the final sound of the preceding word (2.7b). Similarly, while the third person singular present ending of verbs is always spelled *-s*, it shows the same variation in pronunciation (2.7c), as does the ending of possessive forms (2.7d).

(2.7) a. Pat's ([s]) leaving, Kim's ([z]) coming in, and Chris's ([əz]) replacing Jan.
b. packs ([s]), pals ([z]), passes ([əz])
c. infects ([s]), cleans ([z]), induces ([əz])
d. Pat's ([s]), Kim's ([z]) (or) Chris's ([əz]) corkscrew

In *Kim's happy*, the element *'s* is a clitic in terms of its pronunciation. This does not alter the fact that in syntactic terms, it is a verb which serves as the head of the phrase [$_{IP}$ *'s happy*], a simple structure which involves no displacement or deletion. Compare this with the case of the underlined *is* in *Kim's happier than Tim is*, though. This latter element is also a verb that serves as the head of a phrase, though what it is followed by within that phrase is something which is understood but not pronounced. Syntactically, the phrase has the structure [$_{IP}$ *is* e], where the unpronounced element *e* is understood as *happy*.

Now recall that our problem is to account for the fact that not only are sentences like (2.8a) impossible in English, but language learners know this without ever having been explicitly told not to use reduced auxiliary forms in such positions.

(2.8) a. *Tim's happier than Kim's.
      b. Tim's happier than Kim is.

What differentiates the bad sentence (2.8a) from its well-formed near-twin (2.8b)? The only difference is between the final phrase [IP 's e], in (2.8a), *vs.* the phrase [IP*is* e], in (2.8b). While reflecting no distinction of syntactic structure or meaning, this difference does have one consequence: in each of the sentences in (2.8) the final phrase contains only a single element, but in (2.8a) that element is a clitic (*'s*), while in (2.8b) it is the word *is*.

We already know that a clitic cannot (by definition) constitute a word by itself. A rather natural part of the theory of sound structure is the PROSODIC HIERARCHY (see Nespor and Vogel 1986 for basic discussion of this notion), according to which **utterances** are composed of **phrases**, phrases of **words**, words of smaller units called **feet**, which are themselves composed of **syllables**.[5] It stands to reason that since a clitic by itself cannot constitute a word, **a phrase** consisting only of a clitic would contain no word, and would thus be ill-formed. We might, then, attribute the ill-formedness of (2.8a) in English to the fact that it contains the ill-formed phrase [IP *'s* e].

It may appear that we have played a sort of shell game here, trading on the fact that the word "phrase" has more than one sense: on the one hand, it refers to a unit of pronunciation, associated with particular intonational contours, possibilities for pause, etc. and composed of smaller units of pronunciation, (phonological) words. On the other hand, however, a "phrase" can be interpreted as a unit of syntactic organization, composed of units of grammar and meaning whose actual pronunciation is, for syntactic purposes, quite irrelevant. Thus the final syntactic phrase in both sentences in (2.8) consists of two elements: a verb (*'s* or *is*) and an adjective (*e*, interpreted as "happy"). The explanation we are proposing requires us to say that because [IP *'s* e] is syntactically a phrase, its pronunciation as a **phonological** phrase would be ill-formed because it would not contain enough phonological material to make up even a single word. But what justifies us in the apparent equation of syntactic and phonological notions of "phrase"?

We must note that syntactic phrasing is not always faithfully reflected in phonological phrasing. In a sentence like *This is the cat, that chased the rat, that ate the cheese, . . .* the boundaries of phonological phrases coincide roughly with the commas. As a result, *that chased the rat* is a phonological phrase here, but not a syntactic phrase: syntactically the phrasing is something like [DP the cat [IP that chased [DP the rat [IP that ate the cheese . . .]]]].

---

[5] Various authors have proposed slightly different inventories of prosodic constituent types, but without affecting the overall point here in any material way.

While the correspondence between syntactic and phonological phrase structure is not a simple isomorphism, neither is it arbitrary and unconstrained. As we will see below in chapter 9, children are sensitive at a very early age (around eight to ten months) to the phonological organization of utterances into phrases, and there is no doubt that they use this structure as a crucial key to discovering the syntactic organization of sentences and phrases. In order to do this, however, they must assume that in general a syntactic phrase will correspond to a phonological phrase. If this is the case, things that are true of phonological phrases will tend also to be true of syntactic ones; and we have seen that a phonological phrase consisting of some phonetic material, but not enough to make up even a single well-formed word, is itself ill-formed. From this property of the Prosodic Hierarchy, together with an assumption that syntactic and phonological phrases will in general correspond, we can arrive at the following principle:

> (2.9) Every syntactic phrase which corresponds to any pronounced material must contain enough material to make up at least one phonological word.

The principle in (2.9) is not by itself an independent part of UG, but it is plausible to suggest that it follows as a theorem from things that are: the Prosodic Hierarchy and the assumption of a correspondence between syntactic and phonological constituency.

Armed with (2.9), we can now see the basis for our earlier observation that reduced forms of the auxiliaries cannot immediately precede empty elements, as in the ill-formed sentence (2.8a). The problem is not with the empty element itself, but rather with the fact that where a phrase consists of an auxiliary verb together with a following element such as an adjective, and that following element is unpronounced, the use of a full (rather than clitic) form of the auxiliary is necessary to provide the phrase with enough phonetic substance to satisfy (2.9).

Sentence-internal understood elements can have similar effects, as in *I wonder where$_x$ the concert* [$_{IP}$ [$_{IP}$*is* e$_x$] *on Wednesday*]. Here *where$_x$* has moved from the position indicated as e$_x$, but is still understood there. The verb *is* (whether reduced to its clitic form *'s* or not) has to be combined with a word that stands in a certain kind of structural relationship to it: it forms a phrase together with its complement. This phrase is subject to (2.9), and so if the complement does not provide a word (because it has been deleted), the auxiliary must: *'s* itself would not suffice to supply a well-formed phonological correspondent to a syntactic phrase, and so does not tolerate a deletion site to its immediate right that would exhaust the phrase of which *'s* is the head.

On Wednesday is not the complement of *is* in this example: rather, it is the deleted *where$_x$*. In chapter 3, we argue that this kind of deletion results from incorporation of a copied word into an adjacent word. The non-occurrence of *I *wonder who the professor's here, *I wonder where the concert's on Wednesday,* **Kim's happier than Tim's,* etc., suggest that clitics like *'s* cannot host a deleted (understood) item in this way.

How do these facts interact with the observation we made above that clitic elements are in fact attached to material on their left, forming part of a phrase with that material in actual pronunciation? Such "migration" of clitic material from one phrase to another does not actually alter the force of (2.9). In (2.10a), for example, *happy* is the complement of *is* and therefore reduced *'s* may attach to the preceding word without leaving the phrase it heads phonologically deficient. The same is true for the first *is* of (2.10b). However, *Tim* is not the complement of the underlined *is* in (2.10b); in this case, the subject *Tim* and the copula verb *is* have permuted. As a result, the underlined *is* is the only overt representative of its phrase, and cannot be reduced.

> (2.10) a. Kim's happy.
> b. Kim is (/'s) happier than is(/*'s) Tim.

But while the principle in (2.9) is plausibly derivable from general requirements that are part of UG, and a consequence of (2.9) is that a reduced *is* may not be the only phonological material representing the syntactic phrase of which it is the head, this is not the whole story. Consider the following examples:

> (2.11) a. John, my dear's, a bastard.
> b. *John's, my dear, a bastard.
> c. He is/*'s TOO going to fix it.
> d. Fred is tired of Spinoza, just as Mary is/*'s of Schopenhauer.
> e. She's a better scientist than he is/*'s an engineer.

In all of these cases, the reduced auxiliary is impossible in circumstances where the **syntactic** phrase it heads contains other material that ought to satisfy (2.9). There is, however, a property that characterizes the sentences in (2.11): the fact that each involves a construction with special intonation. In each of the bad cases, the material immediately following the auxiliary *is/'s* is set off as (part of) a separate (phonological) phrase in pronunciation.

At this point, we know enough to provide an account of the circumstances under which reduced auxiliaries are impossible. Suppose that we start with the syntactic structure of the sentence, and then identify the corresponding pronunciation, in terms of phonological phrases. Simplifying somewhat, we can say that the most natural phrasing is one that mirrors the syntax: syntactic phrases correspond to phonological phrases. Some constructions, however, are exceptions to this in that they enforce a phonological phrase boundary in a place where one might not be motivated syntactically. These include the various parenthetical insertions, emphases, and ellipses illustrated in (2.11). Once phonological phrases have been delimited, we can say that any such phrase that contains some phonological material, but not enough to constitute at least one phonological word, is *ipso facto* ill-formed. Since clitics do not qualify as full phonological words, any phrase consisting of a clitic alone will suffer such a fate. In actual pronunciation, finally, prosodically deficient elements (simple clitics) are attached phonologically to the word on their left.

Though fairly intricate, this account provides an answer to the problem sketched at the outset: how to account for the fact that the child comes to know when the reduced forms of the auxiliary elements are or are not possible, in the absence of direct evidence. In order to achieve this, the child needs to learn that in English (a) the elements *am*, *is*, *has*, etc. have simple clitic alternants *'m*, *'s*, etc.; (b) clitics attach to their left; and (c) certain constructions (parenthetical insertions, emphasis, ellipses) get phrased in a special way phonologically. All of these facts are directly attested in the linguistic data available to the child, and can thus be learned without difficulty.

But these observable phenomena interact with principles of UG, which are part of the child's initial linguistic endowment, and thus do not have to be learned, principles which are not language-particular but rather apply to all languages: (a) notions of the phonological word and phrase, together with the requirement that phonological phrases must be made up of at least one phonological word; and (b) the preference for parallel structure in syntax and in prosodic organization. Jointly these will entail that a syntactic phrase with a clitic element such as *'s* as its only phonological content will be excluded, without requiring the child to have overt evidence for the badness of such examples, as we have seen above.

Part of what a child growing a grammar needs to do is to determine the clitics in his or her linguistic environment, knowing in advance of any experience that "clitics" are small, unstressed items attached phonologically to an adjacent word in ways that may be contrary to the syntactic relations they bear to surrounding material. This predetermined knowledge – the nature of clitics and the fact that they cannot by themselves satisfy the requirement that phrases be represented by at least one phonological word – is contributed by the linguistic genotype and is part of what the child brings to language acquisition. The environment provides examples such as *Pat's happy, Bob's happy, and Alice's happy too*. The child can observe that the three instances of *'s* in these cases vary in their pronunciation ([s] after *Pat*, [z] after *Bob*, and [əz] after *Alice*). This variation is quite systematic, and, as noted, follows the same principles as those that determine the form of the plural ending in *cats*, *knobs*, *palaces* among other endings in English. These facts confirm that *'s* must be a clitic, and must attach phonologically to its left.

Under this approach, the child is faced with a chaotic environment and in scanning it, identifies clitics . . . among many other things, of course (Lightfoot 1999). This is the answer that we provide to our initial problem, and it is an answer of the right shape. It makes a general claim at the genetic level ("clitic" is a predefined category) and postulates that the child arrives at a plausible analysis on exposure to a few simple expressions. The analysis that the child arrives at predicts no reduction for the underlined *is* in *Kim is happier than Tim is, I wonder who the professor is here*, and countless other cases, and the child needs no correction in arriving at this system. The very fact that *'s* is a clitic, a notion defined in advance of any experience, dictates that it may not occur in certain contexts. It is for this reason that the generalization that *is* may be pronounced as *'s* breaks down at certain points and does not hold across the board.

Consider now the second problem, the reference of pronouns. An initial definition might propose that pronouns refer to a preceding noun, but the data of (2.1) and (2.2) showed that this is both too strong and too weak. It is too strong because, as we saw, in (2.1d) *him* may not refer to Jay; in (2.1b) *him* may refer to Jay but not to Jay's brother. The best account of this complex phenomenon seems to be to invoke a native principle which says, approximately (2.12).

> (2.12) Pronouns may not refer back to a higher nominal element contained in the same clause or in the same DP.

In (2.13) we give the relevant structure for the corresponding sentences of (2.1). In (2.13b) the DP *Jay's brother* is contained in the same clause as *him* and so *him* may not refer back to that DP: we express this by indexing them differently. On the other hand, *Jay* is contained inside the DP and is not "higher" than *him*, so those two nouns do not need to be indexed differently – they may refer to the same person and they may thus be coindexed. Again we see the constituent structure illustrated earlier playing a central role in the way in which the indexing computations are carried out. In (2.13d) *Jay* is in the same clause as *him* and so the two elements may not be coindexed; they may not refer to the same person. In (2.13c) *Jay* is not contained in the same clause as *he*: *Jay* and *he* may thus refer either to the same person or to different people. In (2.13a) *his* is contained inside a DP and may not be coindexed with anything else within that DP; what happens outside the DP is not systematic; so *his* and *Jay* may corefer and do not need to be indexed differently.

> (2.13) a. [$_{IP}$ Jay$_i$ hurt [$_{DP}$ his$_{i/j}$ nose]]
> b. [$_{IP}$ [$_{DP}$ Jay$_i$'s brother]$_k$ hurt him$_{i/j/*k}$]
> c. [$_{IP}$ Jay$_i$ said [$_{IP}$ he$_{i/j}$ hurt Ray]]
> d. [$_{IP}$ Jay$_i$ hurt him$_{j/*i}$]

The idea that pronouns refer to a preceding noun is shown to be too weak because sometimes, as in (2.2c,e), the pronoun refers to a **following** noun. In this case, the relevant principle seems to be that such "backwards anaphora" is not possible if the pronoun not only precedes the noun, but is also "higher" (in a precise sense whose details are not relevant to our present concerns) in the syntactic structure than the noun which is to serve as its antecedent.[6] In (2.2c), the pronoun precedes *Jay*, but this is acceptable because the pronoun appears within a subordinate clause, and thus is not relevantly "higher." In (2.2e), the pronoun is subordinated by virtue of appearing as a possessor within a larger DP. In (2.2d), however, the pronoun appears as subject of the main clause, and is thus (in the relevant structural sense) syntactically higher than the following noun, which therefore cannot serve as its antecedent.

We could have illustrated these points equally well with data from French or from Dutch, or from many other languages, because the principles apply quite generally, to pronouns in all languages. If we assume a native principle, available to the child independently of any actual experience, language acquisition is greatly simplified. Now the child does not need to "learn" why the pronoun may refer to Jay in (2.13a) or (2.13b,c) but not in (2.13d); in (2.2a–c,e) but not in (2.2d), etc. Rather, the child raised in an English-speaking setting has only to learn that *he, his, him* are pronouns, i.e. elements subject to Principle B (see note 6). This can be learned by exposure to a simple sentence like (2.1c) (structurally (2.13c)), uttered in a context where *he* refers to Jay; that suffices to show that *he* is neither an anaphor nor a name – the other possible noun types, according to most current views – and hence must be a pronoun.[7]

One way of thinking of the contribution of the linguistic genotype is to view it as providing invariant principles and option-points or PARAMETERS. There are invariant principles, such as that clitics attach phonologically to adjacent words by virtue of their prosodically "weak" character; that phonological phrases are based on words, which are based on smaller prosodic units; that phonological and syntactic phrases are generally related in a particular way; that pronouns cannot be locally coindexed and that names may not be coindexed with a higher DP, etc. Taken together, these have consequences, such as the principle in (2.9) which requires phrases that are pronounced at all to contain at least one full phonological word. Meanwhile, there are also options: direct objects may precede the verb in some grammars (German, Japanese) and may follow it in others (English, French); some constructions may have special intonation associated with them; clitics in some grammars attach to the right and in others to the left, etc. These are parameters of variation and the child sets these parameters one way or another on exposure to particular linguistic experience. As a result a grammar emerges in the child – a language organ, part of the linguistic

---

[6] The principle alluded to in the last paragraph, that pronouns may not be locally coindexed, is Principle B of the binding theory; (2.12) is only an informal (and partly inaccurate) rendering of Principle B. Here we allude to Principle C, that names may not be coindexed with a higher DP anywhere. In chapter 9 we discuss the acquisition of Principle C.

[7] Anaphors are elements that are locally coindexed, according to Principle A of the binding theory, while names, by Principle C, are never coindexed with a higher DP.

phenotype. The child has learned that *'s* is a clitic and that *he* is a pronoun; the genotype ensures that *'s* cannot be the only phonological material within a syntactic phrase and that *he* is never used in a structurally inappropriate context.

2.4   The acquisition problem

In the preceding sections we have looked at some specific acquisition problems and considered what ingredients are needed for their solution. Now let us stand back and think about these matters more abstractly.

The child acquires a finite system, a grammar, which generates structures which correspond more or less to utterances of various kinds. Some structural principle prevents forms like **Kim's happier than Tim's* from occurring in the speech of English speakers, as we have seen. Children are not exposed to pseudo-sentences like this or informed systematically that they are not to be produced. Speakers come to know subconsciously that they cannot be said and this knowledge emerges somehow, even though it is not part of the environmental input to the child's development. It is not enough to say that people do not utter such forms because they never hear them: people say many things that they have not heard, as we have noted. Language is not learned simply by imitating or repeating what has been heard.

2.4.1   The poverty of the stimulus

This poverty-of-stimulus problem defines our approach to language acquisition. Since the late 1950s, much of the linguistic literature has focused on areas where the best description cannot be derived directly from the data to which the child has access, or is underdetermined by those data, as in the examples with the clitic *'s* and the pronouns discussed above. If the child's linguistic experience does not provide the basis for establishing a particular aspect of linguistic knowledge, another source must exist for that knowledge.

This is not to say that imitation plays no role, but only that it does not provide a sufficient explanation. This is worth emphasizing, because antagonists sometimes caricature this approach to language acquisition as "denying the existence of learning," when in fact we merely deny that learning is the whole story, a very different matter. The quoted phrase comes directly from a remarkable article in *Science* (Bates and Elman 1996), in which the authors assert that "Noam Chomsky, the founder of generative linguistics, has argued for 40 years that language is unlearnable" and that they, on the other hand, have "rediscovered" learning!

Caricatures of this type show up in the writing of people who claim that all information is derived from the environment and that there is no domain-specific genetic component to language acquisition. These people deny the poverty-of-stimulus problems, claiming that children may derive all relevant information from their linguistic environment. Bates and Elman provide a recent and particularly striking instance of this line, claiming that artificial neural networks can learn linguistic regularities from imperfect but "huge computerized corpora of written and spoken language."

Nobody denies that the child must extract information from the environment; it is no revelation that there is "learning" in that technical sense. After all, children learn to speak one way when surrounded by speakers of French and another when surrounded by speakers of Italian. Our point is that there is more to language acquisition than this. Children react to experience in accordance with specific principles.

The problem demanding explanation is compounded by other factors. Despite variation in background and intelligence, people's mature linguistic capacity emerges in fairly uniform fashion, in just a few years, without much apparent effort, conscious thought, or difficulty; and it develops with only a narrow range of the logically possible "errors." Children do not test random hypotheses, gradually discarding those leading to "incorrect" results and provoking parental correction. In each language community the non-adult sentences formed by very young children seem to be few in number and quite uniform from one child to another, which falls well short of random (see chapter 9). Normal children attain a fairly rich system of linguistic knowledge by five or six years of age and a mature system by puberty. In this regard, language is no different from, say, vision, except that vision is taken for granted and ordinary people give more conscious thought to language.

These, then, are the salient facts about language acquisition, or more properly, language growth. The child masters a rich system of knowledge without significant instruction and despite an impoverished stimulus; the process involves only a narrow range of "errors" and takes place rapidly, even explosively between two and three years of age. The main question is how children acquire so much more than they experience and how the growth takes place.

A grammar, the language organ, represents what a speaker comes to know, subconsciously for the most part, about his or her native language. It represents the fully developed linguistic capacity, and is therefore part of an individual's phenotype. It is one expression of the potential defined by the genotype. Speakers know what an infinite number of sentences mean and the various ways in which they can be pronounced and rephrased. Most of this largely subconscious knowledge is represented in a person's grammar. The grammar may be used for various purposes, from everyday events like expressing ideas, communicating, or listening to other people, to more contrived functions like writing elegant prose or lyric poetry, or compiling and solving crossword puzzles, or writing a book about the language organ.

We do not want to give the impression that all linguists adopt this view of things. In fact, people have studied language with quite different goals in mind, ranging from the highly specific (to describe Dutch in such a way that it can be learned easily by speakers of Indonesian), to more general goals, such as showing how a language may differ from one historical stage to another (comparing, for example, Chaucerian and present-day English). However, the research paradigm we sketch, which construes a grammar as a biological object, the language organ, has been the focus of much activity since the late 1950s and it seems to us to provide the most satisfying approach to the attempt to understand the fundamental nature of language.

2.4.2   The analytical triplet

A grammar, for us, is a psychological entity, part of the psychological state of somebody who knows a language. For any aspect of linguistic knowledge, three intimately related items are included in a full account of this state. First, there is a formal and explicit characterization of what a mature speaker knows; this is the grammar, which is part of that speaker's phenotype. Since the grammar is represented in the mind/brain, it must be a finite system, which can relate sound and meaning for an infinite number of sentences.

Second, also specified are the relevant principles and parameters common to the species and part of the initial state of the organism; these principles and parameters make up part of the theory of grammar or UG, and they belong to the genotype.

The third item is the trigger experience, which varies from person to person and consists of an unorganized and fairly haphazard set of utterances, of the kind that any child hears.[8] The universal theory of grammar and the variable trigger together form the basis for attaining a grammar.

In (2.14) we give the explanatory schema, using general biological terminology in (2.14a) and the corresponding linguistic terms in (2.14b). The triggering experience causes the genotype to develop into a phenotype; exposure to a range of utterances from, say, English allows the UG capacity to develop into a particular mature grammar. One may think of the theory of grammar as making available a set of choices; the choices are taken in the light of the trigger experience or the primary linguistic data (PLD), and a grammar emerges when the relevant options are resolved. A child develops a grammar by setting the open parameters of UG in the light of her particular experience.

> (2.14) a. linguistic triggering experience (genotype $\longrightarrow$ phenotype)
>   b. primary linguistic data (Universal Grammar $\longrightarrow$ grammar)

Each of the items in the triplet – trigger, UG, and grammar – must meet various demands. The trigger or PLD must consist only of the kinds of things that children routinely experience and includes only simple structures (see chapter 9

---

[8] The notion of a trigger is from ethologists' work on the emergence of behavioral patterns in young animals.

for discussion). The theory of grammar or UG is the one constant and must hold universally such that any person's grammar can be attained on the basis of naturally available trigger experiences. The mature grammar must define an infinite number of expressions as well-formed, and for each of these it must specify at least the sound and the meaning. A description always involves these three items and they are closely related; changing a claim about one of the items usually involves changing claims about the other two.

The grammar is one subcomponent of the mind, a mental organ which interacts with other cognitive capacities or organs. Like the grammar, each of the other organs is likely to develop in time and to have distinct initial and mature states. So the visual system recognizes triangles, circles, and squares through the structure of the circuits that filter and recompose the retinal image (Hubel and Wiesel 1962). Certain nerve cells respond only to a straight line sloping downward from left to right within a specific, narrow range of orientations; other nerve cells to lines sloped in different directions. The range of angles that an individual neuron can register is set by the genetic program, but experience is needed to fix the precise orientation specificity (Sperry 1968).

In the mid-1960s David Hubel, Torsten Wiesel, and their colleagues devised an ingenious technique to identify how individual neurons in an animal's visual system react to specific patterns in the visual field (including horizontal and vertical lines, moving spots, and sharp angles). They found that particular nerve cells were set within a few hours of birth to react only to certain visual stimuli, and, furthermore, that if a nerve cell is not stimulated within a few hours, it becomes totally inert in later life. In several experiments on newborn kittens, it was shown that if a kitten spent its first few days in a deprived optical environment (a tall cylinder painted only with vertical stripes), only the neurons stimulated by that environment remained active; all other optical neurons became inactive because the relevant synapses degenerated, and the kitten never learned to see horizontal lines or moving spots in the normal way.

We see learning as a similarly selective process: parameters are provided by the genetic equipment, and relevant experience fixes those parameters (Piattelli-Palmarini 1986, 1989). A certain mature cognitive structure emerges at the expense of other possible structures which are lost irretrievably as the inactive synapses degenerate. The view that there is a narrowing down of possible connections out of an overabundance of initially possible ones is now receiving more attention in the light of Hubel and Wiesel's Nobel Prize winning success. On the evidence available, this seems to be a more likely means of fine tuning the nervous system as "learning" takes place than the earlier view that there is an increase in the connections among nerve cells.

So human cognitive capacity is made up of identifiable properties that are genetically prescribed, each developing along one of various preestablished routes, depending on the particular experience encountered during the individual's early life. These genetic prescriptions may be extremely specialized, as

Hubel and Wiesel showed for the visual system. They assign some order to our experience. Experience elicits or triggers certain kinds of specific responses but it does not determine the basic form of the response.

This kind of modularity is very different from the view that the cognitive faculties are homogeneous and undifferentiated, that the faculties develop through general problem-solving techniques. In physical domains, nobody would suggest that the visual system and the system governing the circulation of the blood are determined by the same genetic regulatory mechanisms. Of course, the possibility should not be excluded that the linguistic principles postulated here may eventually turn out to be special instances of principles holding over domains other than language, but before that can be established, much more must be known about what kinds of principles are needed for language acquisition to take place under normal conditions and about how other cognitive capacities work. The same is of course true for other aspects of cognitive development. Only on such a basis can meaningful analogies be detected. Meanwhile,

we are led to expect that each region of the central nervous system has its own special problems that require different solutions. In vision we are concerned with contours and directions and depth. With the auditory system, on the other hand, we can anticipate a galaxy of problems relating to temporal interactions of sounds of different frequencies, and it is difficult to imagine that the same neural apparatus deals with all of these phenomena . . . for the major aspects of the brain's operation no master solution is likely. (Hubel 1978, p. 28)

2.4.3   Real-time acquisition of grammars

In the domain of language, there is good evidence that the sophisticated distinctions that we discussed at the beginning of this chapter do not result from learning and that the hypothesized genetic (or epigenetic: recall our earlier extension of this term) constraints seem to be at work from the outset. Experimenters have constructed situations in which the over-riding temptation for children would be to violate the relevant constraints. The fact that children conform to the hypothesized constraints, resisting preferences they show in other contexts, shows that the constraints under investigation are active for them, and that this is true at the earliest stage at which they might be manifested (Crain 1991).

Stephen Crain and Rosalind Thornton (1998) developed an elicitation task that encouraged children to ask questions like *Do you know what that's up there*, if these were compatible with their grammars. They hypothesized that children would generally show a preference for the reduced 's form whenever this was consistent with their grammars. This preference would be revealed in a frequency count of legitimate forms, like *Do you know what that's doing up there?* Comparing the frequency of the reduced forms in the contexts where adults find reduced forms unacceptable with that of non-adult reduced forms more generally would indicate whether or not children's grammars contained the hypothetical genetic constraint. If the genetic constraint is at work, there should be a significant difference in frequency; otherwise, not.

The target productions were evoked by the following protocols, in which Thornton and Crain provided children with a context designed to elicit questions.

(2.15) Protocols for cliticization:

a. Experimenter: Ask Ratty if he knows what that is doing up there.
Child: Do you know what that's doing up there?
Rat: It seems to be sleeping.

b. Experimenter: Ask Ratty if he knows what that is up there.
Child: Do you know what that is up there?
Rat: A monkey.

In (2.15a), the child is invited to produce a sentence where *what* is understood as the object of doing: *Do you know what$_x$ that is doing e$_x$ up there?* Since the resulting phrase of which *is* is head, [$_{IP}$ is [$_{VP}$ doing e$_x$]], contains at least one phonological word in addition to *is* itself, *is* can be replaced with the clitic form *'s* without resulting in an ill-formed correspondence between syntactic and phonological structure. However, in (2.15b), the child produces a sentence where *what* is understood as the complement of *is*, but is not pronounced in that position: *Do you know what$_x$ that is e$_x$ up there?* (cf. *That is a bottle up there*). Here a deletion site is the only other component of the phrase headed by *is*. As a result, that phrase ([$_{IP}$ is e$_x$]) only corresponds to a phonological word to the extent that *is* itself is a word – and not merely a clitic. This fact prevents the *is* from cliticizing in adult speech; no adult would use the reduced form to produce **Do you know what that's up there?* (cf. *That's a bottle up there*).

Crain and Thornton found that young children behaved just like adults, manifesting the hypothetical genetic constraint. The children tested ranged in age from 2 years, 11 months, to 4 years, 5 months, with an average age of 3 years, 8 months. In the elicited questions there was not a single instance of the reduced form where it is impossible in adult speech. Children produced elaborate forms like those of (2.16), but never with *'s*, the reduced form of *is*.

(2.16) a. Do you know what that black thing on the flower is? (4 years, 3 months)
b. Squeaky, what do think that is? (3 years, 11 months)
c. Do you know what that is on the flower? (4 years, 5 months)
d. Do you know what that is, Squeaky? (3 years, 2 months)

There is, of course, much more to be said about grammars and their acquisition, and we will return to this topic in chapter 9 below. There is also an enormous technical literature, but here we have briefly illustrated the kind of issue that work on real-time acquisition can address under our *I*-language approach.

2.5   Conclusion

Recent theoretical developments have brought an explosive growth in what we know about human languages. Linguists can now formulate interesting hypotheses and account for broad ranges of facts in many languages with elegant abstract principles, as we shall see. They understand certain aspects of language acquisition in young children and can model some aspects of speech comprehension.

Work on human grammars has paralleled work on the visual system and has reached similar conclusions, particularly with regard to the existence of highly specific computational mechanisms. In fact, language and vision are the areas of cognition that we know most about. Much remains to be done, but we can show how children attain certain elements of their language organs by exposure to only an unorganized and haphazard set of simple utterances; for these elements we have a theory which meets basic requirements. Eventually, the growth of language in a child will be viewed as similar to the growth of hair: just as hair emerges at a particular point in development with a certain level of light, air, and protein, so, too, a biologically regulated language organ necessarily emerges under exposure to a random speech community.

From the perspective sketched here, our focus is on grammars, not on the properties of a particular language or even of general properties of many or all languages. A language (in the sense of a collection of things people within a given speech community can say and understand) is on this view an epiphenomenon, a derivative concept, the output of certain people's grammars (perhaps modified by other mental processes). A grammar is of clearer status: the finite system that characterizes an individual's linguistic capacity and that is represented in the individual's mind/brain, the language organ. No doubt the grammars of two individuals whom we regard as speakers of the same language will have much in common, but there is no reason to worry about defining "much in common," or about specifying precise conditions under which the outputs of two grammars could be said to constitute one language. Just as it is unimportant for most work in molecular biology whether two creatures are members of the same species (as emphasized, for example, by Dawkins 1976), so too the notion of a language is not likely to have much importance if our biological perspective is taken and if we explore individual language organs, as in the research program we have sketched here and which we elaborate in later chapters.

3 Syntax

3.1 The emergence of syntax within linguistics

Before the development of generative grammar in the late 1950s, linguists focused almost entirely on the smallest units of language: sounds, minimal meaningful elements ("morphemes" like *ed*, *ful*, *con* – see chapter 7 below for more on this notion), and words, where the model of the Saussurian sign has most plausibility. "Syntax" was largely a promissory note to the effect that such sign-based analysis would eventually encompass the larger units of phrases, sentences, etc. Meanwhile, what went by that name was largely a kind of applied morphology: some instructions for what to do with the various kinds of words (inflected and otherwise).

For example, drawing from our bookshelves more or less at random, we find that Morris Jones' (1913) comprehensive grammar of Welsh is divided into two sections, phonology and accidence (inflectional properties), and has nothing under the rubric of syntax. Arthur MacDonnell's (1916) grammar of Vedic Sanskrit has two chapters on sounds, four chapters on inflections, and a final chapter entitled "Syntax". There he has some observations about word order and agreement phenomena, and then a discussion of the uses of cases, tenses, and moods. He notes that the subjunctive mood has a fundamental sense of "will" and lists the uses of the subjunctive mood in main clauses, relative clauses, and with "relative conjunctions." Joseph Wright's grammar of the Gothic language (1910) also has one final chapter on syntax, in which he illustrates the use of the various cases, the agreement properties of adjectives, some uses of the pronouns, verb voices, tenses, and moods. These works are entirely typical.

One could think of languages as made up from a small inventory of sounds, a larger inventory of morphemes, and a lexicon containing the words. Those inventories might be transmitted from one generation of speakers to another and language acquisition could be seen as a process of children acquiring the relevant inventories. That is not implausible for these small units, although the view turns out to be inadequate for reasons that we shall discuss in the next few chapters; and there was no productive way to think of syntax or of larger units in that fashion. Certainly children do not just acquire a set of sentences as they become mature speakers. Perhaps they acquire some set of basic structures and construction-types, which may then be elaborated into some open-ended set, and there were efforts to build models along those lines. But that involved positing some kind of system, an open-ended, recursive system, and the available models did not have that capacity. Certain "typological" approaches, inspired by Greenberg (1963), adopted *E*-language formulations in identifying harmonic properties of languages which have "predominant subject–object–verb" word order, for example, asking to what extent such languages would show, say, noun–adjective order.

When the productive mechanisms of syntactic structure came under serious scrutiny, with the development of generative grammar, it became apparent that even though a description of the words of a language is certainly necessary, it is not sufficient: languages cannot be viewed simply as inventories of signs. The resulting insights had profound effects in all areas of the field. There has been a tremendous amount of work over the last forty years, yielding discoveries in language after language and theories which apply productively to wide ranges of phenomena in many languages. Since pregenerative work on syntax was so scant, there is little to be learned from a comparison. Rather, in this chapter we shall take two features of current models – deletion and Case theory – and we shall show some of the ramifications of these ideas, how they are shaped by the cognitive, *I*-language nature of our analyses, how they capture details about language structure, remembering that God is in the details, and the devil, too.

The details are fascinating in themselves; they represent distinctions which are not reported in standard language textbooks, they are not taught to second-language learners, and, indeed, for the most part they were not known until rather recently, when they were discovered by theoreticians. There is no way that these distinctions could be communicated directly to young children as they develop their language capacity. However, the distinctions we shall dis-cuss are not the object of our inquiry, but data which provide evidence about the inner mechanisms of the mind. Our problem is to pick one or two more or less self-contained illustrations of those mechanisms, parts of the internal systems represented in individual brains and acquired under normal childhood conditions.

The earliest attempts to carry out the program of generative grammar quickly revealed that even in the best studied languages, elementary properties had passed unrecognized, that the most comprehensive traditional grammars and dictionaries only skim the sur-face. The basic properties of languages are presupposed throughout, unrecognized and unexpressed. This is quite appropriate if the goal is to help people to learn a second language, to find the conventional meaning and pronunciation of words, or to have some general idea of how languages differ. But if our goal is to understand the language faculty and the states it can assume, we cannot tacitly presuppose "the intelligence of the reader." Rather, this is the object of inquiry. (Chomsky 2000, p. 6)

3.2   Successive merger and deletion

We begin by returning to the basic mechanisms for building syntactic structure
that we began to discuss in chapter 2. One way to think of this (developed in
recent "Minimalist" work) is that the mental lexicon contains words belonging
to various categories. They may be drawn from the lexicon and "merged" into
a syntactic structure, which is built bottom-up. To adjust our earlier example:
the verb *visit* might merge with a determiner phrase[1] (DP) *what city* to yield a
verb phrase (VP) containing a head, the verb *visit*, and its complement [DP what
city]: [VP V visit [DP what city]]. The inflectional element (I) *will* now may be
merged with the VP, yielding the inflection phrase (IP) in (3.1a). Subsequently
the determiner phrase *the student* may be merged with the resulting IP, to yield
another IP in which the DP *the student* is the specifier (Spec) of the IP already
formed (3.1b); this yields the sentence *The student will visit what city?* with the
structure of (3.1b–c). The structures may be represented as a labeled bracketing
(3.1b) or as an equivalent tree (3.1c); the linear brackets of (3.1b) and the
tree diagram of (3.1c) carry precisely the same information about constituent
structure. The structures define the units of expressions: *what city* is a unit but
student will is not; *will visit what city* is a unit, but not *will visit*. The units are
the items manipulated by the computational mechanisms; they are the items
which may be copied, deleted or indexed in ways that we shall explore in a
moment.

(3.1) a. [IP I will [VP V visit [DP what city]]]
       b. [IP [DP the student][IP I will [VP V visit [DP what city]]]]
       c.

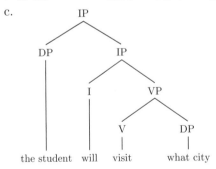

This kind of merger may continue indefinitely, building structures of arbitrary
size through simple recursive devices. All languages may draw on three kinds of
recursive devices which enable one to take any sentence and make it longer: coordination (*Reuben and Phil and Fred and . . . went fishing and caught lobsters*

---

[1] DPs are headed by a determiner like *the* or *what*, which in turn is followed by a noun phrase. This
yields structures like [DP D the [NP N student [PP P of physics]]], [DP D what [NP city]], [DP [SpecDP
Kim] [DP D 's [NP tall mother]]], or [DP D we [NP linguists]].

and . . .), complementation (*Reuben said that Phil said that Fred thought that . . .*), and relativization (*This is the cow that kicked the dog that chased the cat that caught the mouse that ate the cheese that . . .*).[2] It is always possible to construct a more complex sentence.

Instead of considering how the language capacity deals with the (literal) infinity of possible structures, let us explore the property of "displacement": words and phrases may occur in displaced positions, positions other than those corresponding to their interpretation. In an expression *What did you see in Berlin?*, *what* is understood as the direct object of *see* (cf. *We saw the Reichstag in Berlin*), but it has been displaced. It is pronounced at the front of the sentence but understood in the position of a direct object, to the right of the verb. English-speaking children hear sentences like these and consequently the displacement operation is learnable; children learn from experience that a *wh*-phrase typically occurs at the front of its clause, even though it is understood elsewhere. Chinese children have no such experiences and their grammars have no comparable displacement. They hear questions like "You saw what in Berlin?" in Chinese, where (the equivalent of) "what" is pronounced in the same position in which it is understood.

Displacement can be viewed as a special case of merger: an item already in the structure is copied and merged, with subsequent deletion of the copied element. There are other ways of viewing the displacement effect, of course, but let us pursue this account. For an example, let us continue with the structure of (3.1b). The I element *will*, which is already present in the structure, might now be copied and merged with (3.1b) to yield the more complex (3.2a), with a complementizer phrase (CP) headed by the copied *will*; the lower *will* is subsequently deleted to yield (3.2b). Now another step: the DP *what city*, the direct object of *visit*, may be copied and merged, yielding (3.2c), (where *what city* is the specifier of the CP), with subsequent deletion to yield (3.2d), the structure of the sentence *What city will the student visit?*

(3.2) a. [$_{CP}$ $_C$will [$_{IP}$ [$_{DP}$ the student] [$_{IP}$ $_I$will [$_{VP}$ visit what city]]]]
   b. [$_{CP}$ $_C$will [$_{IP}$ [$_{DP}$ the student] [$_{VP}$ visit what city]]]
   c. [$_{CP}$ [$_{Spec_{CP}}$ what city] [$_{CP}$ $_C$will [$_{IP}$ [$_{DP}$ the student][$_{VP}$ visit what city]]]]
   d. [$_{CP}$ [$_{Spec_{CP}}$ what city][$_{CP}$ $_C$will [$_{IP}$ [$_{DP}$ the student][$_{VP}$ visit]]]]

We shall focus here on a condition for deleting elements after they have been copied: the manner in which elements may be deleted limits the way that

---

[2] It has been suggested by Hale 1976 that in some (Australian aboriginal) languages, the functions of relative clauses are actually filled by a kind of "adjoined" structure which is more like a form of coordination than it is like the embedded relative clauses of, e.g., English. This does not compromise the point that in these languages, too, sentences can be arbitrarily extended by the introduction of the functional equivalents of English relative clauses.

elements may be displaced, as we shall see. We shall postulate a Universal Grammar (UG) condition on deletion, which will interact with what children learn about English to distinguish the kinds of sentences that one might hear from those which do not occur.

Let us be clear on the logic of the enterprise here. English-speaking children, unlike their Chinese-speaking counterparts, learn from their environment that "*wh*-phrases" (as we will call question phrases like *who, when, what city*, etc. – even though Chinese "*wh*-phrases" do not involve the sound *wh*) are displaced to the front of their clause. We want an analysis which entails that that is *all* they need to learn from the environment in this regard. In fact, there are many interesting distinctions involving *wh*-expressions, as we are about to see. We seek an analysis, however, in which those distinctions are not themselves learned directly from the environment, since much of what we will discuss is not explicitly present in the child's experience and thus could not be learned in this way. Rather, these aspects of the knowledge that develops – the language organ – follow from such relatively simple, directly attested facts as the clause-initial position of English *wh*-expressions in combination with what is contributed by general genotypic properties, or UG.

3.2.1   *Delete* that

First, observe a very simple instance of deletion: English complementizers or "sentence introducers" like *that* may be deleted in structures like (3.3).[3]

(3.3) a. It was apparent [$_{CP}$ that/e Kay had left].
       b. The book [$_{CP}$ that/e Kay wrote] arrived.
       c. It was obvious [$_{CP}$ that/e Kay had left].

This operation does not apply in languages like Dutch and French, where the complementizers *dat* and *que* are invariably present. Nonetheless, the English-specific operation is learnable, because children typically hear sentences in both forms, sometimes with the complementizer present, sometimes not: *It was apparent that Kay had left/It was apparent Kay had left*. Therefore an operation "Delete *that*" meets the basic requirements for inclusion in the grammars of English speakers: children have evidence for it. (3.3a) is the structure for the sentence *It was apparent (that) Kay had left*, (3.3b) for *The book (that) Kay wrote*, and (3.3c) for *It was obvious (that) Kay had left*.

However, as with virtually every grammatical operation, we find that some aspects are not determined by normal childhood experience. In particular, generalizations typically break down and the point at which they break down cannot be determined by the data available to children; we shall see many

---

[3] As in chapter 2, "e" indicates an empty element, in these structures a deleted *that*.

examples over the next few pages. This matters if grammars are elements of individual cognition, emerging in people's brains on exposure to some linguistic experience: we need to tease apart what can plausibly be learned from the environment and what cannot. Our current generalization, "Delete *that*," breaks down in that certain instances of *that* may not be deleted. Consider (3.4), where only the structure with *that* occurs in speech: **It was apparent to us yesterday Kay had left*, **The book arrived Kay wrote*, **Kay had left was obvious to all of us*, **Fay believes, but Ray doesn't, Kay had left* (a boldface "**e*" indicates an illicit empty item, a place where *that* may not be deleted).

> (3.4) a. It was apparent to us yesterday[CP that/*e Kay had left]
>   b. The book arrived [CP that/*e Kay wrote].
>   c. [CP that/*e Kay had left] was obvious to all of us.
>   d. Fay believes, but Ray doesn't, [CP that/*e Kay had left].

This is a standard poverty-of-stimulus problem. Since children are not told that a sentence like **Kay had left was obvious to all of us* does not occur (corresponding to (3.4c), with no *that*), principles of UG are implicated. The fact that *that* is deletable can be derived directly from experience, since children hear sentences in both forms with and without a sentence-introducing *that*, but the fact that *that* may **not** be deleted in the structures of (3.4) has no comparable basis in experience, since children are exposed only to utterances which actually occur and they are not supplied with lists of utterances which do not occur, as we discussed in chapter 2. Therefore knowledge of the limits to a generalization like "Delete *that*," of the exceptions where it does not apply, must come from elsewhere; this knowledge is not derivable from the external world and it must reflect internal properties.

All of this represents subconscious knowledge that every speaker of English has. To know English is to know where *that* may, may not, or must appear: to know the distribution of *that*. No one taught us these things, and the distinctions we have just noted will come as news to nearly all of our readers who have not studied syntax. Some of this knowledge is learnable in the sense that it can be derived from normal childhood experience, but much is simply not accessible in this way.

The difference between (3.3) and (3.4) is that in (3.3) *that* is the top-most element in a clause (CP) which is the complement of an adjacent, overt word. A complement is something which completes the meaning of a word, and the CP is the complement of *apparent* in (3.3a), *book* in (3.3b), and *obvious* in (3.3c), and in these contexts *that* may be deleted. In (3.4) the embedded clause [CP *that Kay had left/wrote*] is the complement of *apparent* in (3.4a), *book* in (3.4b), nothing in (3.4c), and *believes* in (3.4d). In no case is the CP the complement of the **adjacent** word in (3.4) and therefore *that* may not be deleted. Evidently, *that* may be deleted only if its clause is the complement of an adjacent, overt word.

Somehow this limitation must be derived from intrinsic, native properties; it cannot be a direct consequence of environmental information, because children are not informed about what does not occur. This is crucial. "Delete *that*" is a very simple generalization, easily learnable by children on the basis of normal experience, but we see that a UG principle is implicated; we need some sort of internal principle to prevent the system from over-generating, yielding structures like those of (3.4) with *that* deleted, which do not occur in normal speech. Let us formulate the principle in question as (3.5).

> (3.5) UG CONDITION: an element may be deleted if it is the top-most item in a complement of an overt, adjacent word.

3.2.2   *Deleting copies*

Returning to the deletion of copied elements in the structure-building operations, we now see that the identical condition holds for deleted copies, marked henceforth as an indexed "e." In (3.6a), *who* is deleted in the position marked as e_i, where it is the complement of *see*. In (3.6b), *who* is copied first at the top of its local CP and then at the top of the higher CP;[4] in each case, the lower element may be deleted, because it is the complement of an adjacent, overt word *saw* or the top-most item in the complement of *say*. These are the structures for the well-formed sentences *Who did Jay see?* and *Who did Jay say that Fay saw?*

> (3.6) a. Who$_i$ did Jay see e$_i$?
>   b. Who$_i$ did Jay say [$_{CP}$ e$_i$ that Fay saw e$_i$]?

Our UG condition on deletion (3.5) makes lots of nice distinctions, which we shall illustrate, but let us again be clear on the logic. The idea is that there are simple generalizations that children can learn from their environment, for example, "Delete *that*" or "Delete a copied *wh*-phrase." However, these generalizations break down, and the points at which they break down cannot be a function of external, environmental information, because there is none. Therefore we need to formulate an appropriate internal condition which interacts with the learned generalizations so that the system does not over-generate to produce the non-occurring (3.4), but yields only the kinds of sentences which actually occur. Condition (3.5) suffices for (3.4), and more.

---

[4] It is crucial that movement is local: a *wh*-phrase moves first to the front of its own clause. From there it may move on to the front of the next clause up.

Consider (3.7a), which illustrates a common-or-garden conjoined sentence. Here the second verb may be unpronounced, as we see from (3.7b). In (3.7b), we say that there is a "gapped" verb, which is understood to be present in the position indicated but not pronounced.

(3.7) a. Jay introduced Kay to Ray and Jim introduced Kim to Tim.
b. Jay introduced Kay to Ray and Jim GAP Kim to Tim.
c. *Which man$_i$ did Jay introduce e$_i$ to Ray and which woman$_j$ (did) Jim GAP *e$_i$ to Tim?
d. *Jay wondered what$_i$ Kay gave e$_i$ to Ray and what$_j$ Jim (did) GAP *e$_j$ to Tim.
e. *Jay admired e$_i$ greatly [$_{DP}$ his uncle from Paramus]$_i$ but Jim (did) GAP *e$_j$ only moderately [$_{DP}$ his uncle from New York]$_j$.
f. Jay gave his favorite racket to Ray and Jim GAP his favorite plant to Tim.
g. *Jay gave e$_i$ to Ray [$_{DP}$ his favorite racket]$_i$ and Jim (did) GAP *e$_j$ to Tim [$_{DP}$ his favorite plant]$_j$.

The fact that verbs may be gapped in this way in all (as far as we know) forms of English is readily learnable: children hear sentences like *Jay went to Rome and Fay to Paris, Jay introduced Kay to Ray and Jim Kim to Tim*, and so on, and they can infer from their experience that verbs may be omitted in conjoined sentences. This is not a universal fact and we are told that such gapping does not occur in Chinese; children in Beijing do not have the requisite experiences.

The system as we have it now predicts (as a result of (3.5)) that, where gapping occurs, a *wh*-phrase cannot be deleted to the right of the gap (see 3.7c,d) if the *wh*-phrase is the complement of the gapped verb but the verb is not overt. Sentences corresponding to these structures fail to occur: **Which man did Jay introduce to Ray and which woman (did) Jim to Tim?* (3.7c), **Jay wondered what Kay gave to Ray and what Jim to Tim* (3.7d). Similarly with the non-*wh*-words displaced in (3.7e,g); (3.7e,g) illustrate a generalization that we shall return to below, to the effect that a "large" DP may be displaced to the far right of its clause. This principle is learnable on exposure to sentences like *Jay admired greatly his uncle from Paramus, Jay introduced to Fay all the students from Los Angeles*. Our condition on deletion prevents this learned generalization from over-generating to yield (3.7e,g), and we seem to have the right kind of interaction between intrinsic and acquired properties.[5]

---

[5] There are various kinds of conjoined structures, and there is more to be said – in fact, much more – about ellipsis operations. For example, while the sentence corresponding to (3.7c) is ill-formed, one encounters sentences like *Which man did Jay introduce to Ray and Jim to Kim?* and *Which man did Jay introduce to Ray and which woman to Tim?* We have no intention of providing a comprehensive account of ellipsis operations here. Our goal is rather to illustrate

The same point holds for a deleted *that* to the right of a gapped verb (3.8b) and a deletion at the front of an embedded clause (3.8c). (3.8a) is a well-formed structure yielding the normal, everyday sentence *Jay thought Kay hit Ray and Jim that Kim hit Tim.* However, (3.8b,c) are ill-formed; the deleted *that* in (3.8b) and the deletion at the front of the indicated CP in (3.8c) fail to meet our condition, not being in a complement of an adjacent, overt word; so the structures do not occur, nor do the corresponding sentences **Jay thought Kay hit Ray and Jim Kim hit Tim* (3.8b), **Who did Jay think Kay hit and who (did) Jim (that) Kim hit?* (3.8c).

(3.8) a. Jay thought Kay hit Ray and Jim GAP [$_{CP}$ that Kim hit Tim].
      b. *Jay thought Kay hit Ray and Jim GAP [$_{CP}$ *e Kim hit Tim].
      c. *Who$_i$ did Jay think Kay hit e$_i$ and who$_j$ (did) Jim GAP [$_{CP}$ *e$_j$ (that) [$_{CP}$ Kim hit e$_j$]]?

Our UG condition (3.5) captures these distinctions with a plausible bifurcation between internal properties and information which is learned from the environment. Children learn from their environment that a sentence-introducing *that* may be deleted, that a copied *wh*-phrase may be deleted, that verbs may be omitted in conjoined sentences, that large DPs may be displaced to the far right of their clause. Our internal UG condition (3.5) guarantees that these learned operations do not over-generate to yield non-occurring structures and their corresponding sentences.

There are more subtleties holding of the speech of every mature speaker of English, which follow from this particular condition of UG, making deletion possible only in certain structures. Again, these are distinctions known subconsciously to every speaker of English: to know English means having these distinctions, even though they were not taught to us and they could not be derived entirely from our direct experience.

A simple possessive phrase like *Jay's picture* is three ways ambiguous. Jay might be the owner or the painter of the picture, or the person portrayed, i.e. the object. Traditional grammarians label the last of these readings an "objective genitive." Following the traditional intuition, modern linguists say that the structure for the reading in which Jay is the object, the person portrayed, is (3.9): *Jay* is copied from the complement position, where it is understood, to the possessive position, where it is pronounced. Its copy is deleted in the usual fashion, where it is adjacent to and the complement of the noun *picture*.

(3.9) a. [$_{DP}$ Jay$_i$'s [$_{NP}$ picture e$_i$]]

But now consider *The picture of Jay's.* Here the ambiguity is different and the phrase is only two ways ambiguous. It means that Jay is the owner or the

some poverty-of-stimulus problems and the kind of reasoning that is involved in solutions to them.

painter of the picture, but not the object: the expression cannot refer to a picture in which Jay is portrayed, somewhat surprisingly. Similarly in *A picture of the Queen's*, the Queen can be the owner or the painter but not the person portrayed. This is something that most adults are not aware of: indeed, it was not observed until recently and certainly is not something we impart explicitly to children.

Again, a condition of UG must be involved and it is our condition on deletion (3.5). Possessive elements like *Jay's* only occur introducing DPs and therefore must be followed by an NP even if nothing is pronounced (see note 1). If nothing is pronounced, then the noun heading the NP must be null (e). So *The picture of Jay's*, where Jay is the owner or the painter, would have the well-formed structure of (3.10a), where the indicated NP is empty and understood as "picture." If *The picture of Jay's* were to have the impossible reading where Jay is the person portrayed, the "objective genitive," then the structure would be (3.10b) and the copied element to be deleted (e_i) is the complement of another empty element, the same empty noun understood as "picture." The deletion of the copied Jay is illicit because there is no adjacent overt word (cf. 3.9). Similarly for *The picture is Jay's* (3.10c) and *The picture which is Jay's* (3.10d), which also lack the objective genitive reading for *Jay* and whose structures involve an illicit deletion.

(3.10) a.   The picture of [$_{DP}$ Jay$_i$'s [$_{NP}$ e]]
        b.   *The picture of [$_{DP}$ Jay$_i$'s [$_{NP}$ e *e$_i$]]
        c.   *The picture is [$_{DP}$ Jay$_i$'s [$_{NP}$ e *e$_i$]]
        d.   *The picture which is [$_{DP}$ Jay$_i$'s [$_{NP}$ e *e$_i$]]

Data like these are not the input to language acquisition; rather, they emerge from the properties of the system which is triggered by simple, accessible data available in children's everyday experience and now we understand how. Children hear expressions like *Jay's picture*, understanding it to mean "picture of Jay," and thereby learn that English, unlike many other languages, has displaced objective genitives; the UG condition then blocks structures like (3.10b,c,d).

For a further illustration of the utility of our UG condition (3.5), the deviant (3.11c) has an illicit deletion right-adjacent to the gapped verb. Because the verb is a gap, deletion of he_i there (the top-most element of the complement) is illicit, as is now familiar. That is the only relevant difference from (3.11a), which is perfectly comprehensible and straightforward, involving no ill-formed deletion. (3.11b) is also well-formed: here there is no gapped verb and *known* licenses the deleted copy.

(3.11) a.   It is known that Jay left but it isn't GAP that he went to the movies.
        b.   Jay is known [e$_i$ to have left] but he$_i$ isn't known [e$_i$ to have gone to the movies].

  c. *Jay$_i$ is known [e$_i$ to have left] but he$_i$ isn't GAP [*e$_i$ to have gone to the movies].

Before we change gear, consider one last distinction. The sentence corresponding to structure (3.12a), *The crowd is too angry to organize a meeting*, is ambiguous: the understood subject of the embedded clause, written here as "e," may refer back to *the crowd* (the "anaphoric" reading, indicated by coindexing), or it may be arbitrary in reference, meaning "anybody" (indicated by the "arb" index): either the crowd is going to organize the meeting or somebody else, unspecified.

  (3.12) a. The crowd$_i$ is too angry [$_{CP}$ e$_{i/arb}$ to organize a meeting].
          b. What$_i$ is the crowd$_j$ too angry [$_{CP}$ e$_i$ [e$_j$ to organize e$_i$]]?

The ambiguity corresponds to an ambiguity of structure: the anaphoric reading occurs if the CP is the complement of *angry*; while if the CP is not a complement, but some kind of adjunct (where the CP is a sister not to *angry* but to some higher phrasal category), then the embedded subject is taken to be arbitrary in reference. Take this on faith (we cannot argue it here) and see what follows.

The interrogative sentence corresponding to (3.12b), *What is the crowd too angry to organize?*, is not ambiguous in the same way and allows only the anaphoric reading, in which the understood subject is *the crowd*; it cannot be understood to mean that some other, unspecified person is to organize something. This is because *what* originates as the complement of *organize* and moves first to the front of the embedded CP, and then to its final position. Two instances of *what* must be deleted, in the positions indicated. The fact that *what* is deleted at the front of the embedded clause indicates that the clause is the complement of *angry* and not an adjunct: if it were not the top-most item in the complement of *angry*, it would not be deletable (as a result of (3.5)). As a result the understood subject must be anaphoric, e$_j$. It is inconceivable that children learn from experience that structures like (3.12b) do not have the ambiguity of (3.12a). This can only be a function of the general properties of the language organ, as on our analysis.

Our UG condition on deletion does a lot of work; it enables us to distinguish many well-formed and deviant structures, and to do so in such a way that we can offer plausible stories about what is learned and what is not learned by children who will become speakers of some form of English. Children learn that there is deletion of sentence-introducing *that*s, displacement of *wh*-phrases, copied objective genitives, and right-moved large DPs; our UG condition on deletion (3.5) then makes the distinctions we have discussed. Notice, by the way, that we have been focusing on a property of our model, deletion, and not on phenomena from some language; in fact, the deletion cuts across many sentence types and constructions. The mathematical model we are working with defines topics of research, as is usual in scientific work, and phenomena of the kind that we have discussed constitute evidence for the properties of the model.

3.2.3   Incorporating deleted items

Let us now take things a step further. One way of thinking of deletion in the light of our discussion so far would be to take the structural position left empty by a deleted item to be incorporated, clitic-like, into an adjacent phonological host of which it is the complement. So in (3.12b) the lowest e_i incorporates into the verb *organize*; the higher e_i incorporates into *angry*; however, in (3.11c) the boldface $*\mathbf{e}_i$ cannot incorporate into an adjacent overt word, because there is not an overt word in an adjacent position. In (3.7c), e_i incorporates into *introduce*, but $*\mathbf{e}_j$ has no adjacent overt word to incorporate into. And so on. We will pursue this in a moment.

This perspective generalizes to some of the phenomena involving the reduced *'s*, *'re*, *'ve*, etc., discussed in chapter 2. If these reduced forms are cliticized to their left, as we suggested, then we can understand why the second *is* in *Tim's happier than Kim is* may not be reduced (**Tim's happier than Kim's*): at some level the structure for such a sentence contains *Tim is happier than Kim is happy* and *happy* deletes only if it has a full phonological host to its left. If reduced *is* (*'s*) is itself a clitic, then it cannot host the deleted *happy*. Similarly for *I wonder what$_i$ that is e_i up there*, where the lower *what* could not be deleted if there were no host to its left and therefore *is* must occur in its full, unreduced form (compare the non-existent **I wonder what that's up there*).

We can now unify these phenomena by saying that the reduced *is* is not an appropriate host for a deletion site: since it is itself a clitic, it is not a full phonological word, as we argued in chapter 2, and not an appropriate host for a deleted item. Similarly, one finds the simple *The concert's on Wednesday*, which is well formed because there is no deleted element requiring a host, but not **I wonder where the concert's on Wednesday*, since the structure would be . . . *where$_i$ the concert's e_i on Wednesday* and there would be no host for e_i.[6] The facts discussed in chapter 2 concerning the distribution of reduced forms of *is*, *am*, *have*, etc. thus interact with another story, reflexes of our UG condition (3.5).

Note that the total picture involving the reduced auxiliaries is not provided by either part of our account alone. Thus, at least some examples of the types

---

[6] Here is a nice distinction: *Max is dancing in London and Mary is in New York* is ambiguous: Mary might be dancing in New York or perhaps running a restaurant. However, the same sentence with a reduced *is* is unambiguous: *Max is dancing in London and Mary's in New York* means only that Mary is in New York, not necessarily dancing there. If Mary were dancing in New York, the structure would be . . . *and Mary is [e] in New York* and the empty verb would require a full phonological word as its host, for which the reduced *'s* would not suffice.

represented by (2.11) do not involve deletion, and so (3.5) would have nothing
to say about them. On the other hand, some examples involving displacements
(and thus deletion) would not fall under (2.9) either:

> (3.13) Tired$_i$ as he [$_{IP}$ is/*'s [$_{AdjP}$ e$_i$ of his job at the car-wash]], Fred
> won't go looking for something better.

In many examples involving deletion affecting the entire complement of an
auxiliary, the two conditions converge to rule out the reduction of auxiliaries,
but each has a separate role to play in other examples.

If we adopt this view, then the notion of a host for a deletion site illumi-
nates more distinctions, which have to do with the extractability of subjects of
embedded clauses. Many years ago Joan Bresnan postulated a Fixed Subject
Constraint to capture the observation that subjects of finite embedded clauses
seemed to be fixed, unmovable. Now we can dispense with a distinct Fixed
Subject Constraint and relate the cases it was intended to account for to what
we have discussed in this section, explaining them through our UG condition
on deletion.

We noted that English embedded clauses are introduced by a complementizer
which may or may not be pronounced; so, sentences corresponding to (3.14a)
occur with and without *that*. This is also true if a *wh*-item is copied from
the embedded object position (3.14b): *that* may or may not be present. The
deleted complementizer in (3.14a) incorporates into the adjacent verb *thought*,
as indicated. Similarly the deleted *wh*-word at the front of the (embedded)
clause in (3.14b) incorporates into the adjacent *think*, whether or not *that* is
present. The same goes for the deleted *wh*-word which is the complement of
saw in (3.14b). In each case, the deleted element is the top-most item of the
host's complement.

> (3.14) a. I thought [$_{CP}$ that/e [$_{IP}$ Ray saw Fay]].
>
> b. Who$_i$ did you think [$_{CP}$ e$_i$ that/e [$_{IP}$ Ray saw e$_i$]]?
>
> c. *Who$_i$ did you think [$_{CP}$ *e$_i$ that [$_{IP}$ *e$_i$ saw Fay]]?

However, a *who* in an embedded subject position may not incorporate into an
adjacent *that* (the boldface *e$_i$ in 3.14c): *Who do you think that saw Fay? That*
cannot host the deleted item: incorporation is not possible and the deletion is
illicit (hence the boldface).[7]

The same is true of indirect questions introduced by a word like *how*: a direct
object incorporates into the adjacent verb *solved* in (3.15b) (*Which problem do
you wonder how John solved?*), but a subject *wh*-word may not incorporate into

---

[7] The higher element, at the front of the clause, poses no problems, incorporating into the higher
verb, *think* in (3.14c), *wonder* in (3.15a,b), etc.

how (3.15a), the ill-formed structure for the non-occurring sentence *Who do you wonder how solved the problem?* It cannot be the case that complementizers like *that* and *how* are not appropriate hosts for deletion sites because they are not full, phonological words in some sense, because (apart from the phonologically unmotivated nature of this move) the same is also true for expressions like *what time* in indirect questions like (3.15c), **Who were you wondering what time finished the exam?*

(3.15) a. *Who$_i$ do you wonder [$_{CP}$ e$_i$ how [$_{IP}$ *e$_i$ solved the problem]]?

b. Which problem$_i$ do you wonder [$_{CP}$ e$_i$ how [$_{IP}$ John solved e$_i$]]?

c. *Who$_i$ were you wondering [$_{CP}$ e$_i$ what time [$_{IP}$ *e$_i$ finished the exam]]?

d. Which exam$_i$ were you wondering [$_{CP}$ e$_i$ what time [$_{IP}$ Kim finished e$_i$]]?

In these cases, what blocks the incorporation of the deletion site into the preceding word is the requirement in (3.5) that only the **top-most** element in the complement of a word can incorporate into that word. This suggests either that *e$_i$ in (3.15a,c) is not the top-most element in the embedded finite clause (perhaps the finite verb, the bearer of the clause's inflectional marking, is its structural head) or else that the clauses [$_{IP}$ *e$_i$ solved the problem] (3.15a) and [$_{IP}$ *e$_i$ finished the exam] (3.15c) are not properly the complements of *how* and *what time*, respectively. We leave this open here.

A *wh*-word also may not be deleted in subject position if its clause (an "indirect question" in traditional terms) is part of a relative clause. In (3.16b) the *wh*-word has been copied from an underlying object position (where the deleted *who* is the complement of and incorporated into *bought*) and the result is a more or less normal sentence: *This is the sweater which I wonder who bought.* However, (3.16a) is impossible, where *who* cannot be deleted in subject position; [$_{IP}$ e$_i$ bought e$_j$] is not the complement of the adjacent *what*. The sentence corresponding to (3.16a) would be the impossible **This is the student who I wonder what bought.*

(3.16) a. *This is the student who$_i$ I wonder [$_{CP}$ what$_j$ [$_{IP}$ *e$_i$ bought e$_j$]].

b. This is the sweater which$_i$ I wonder [$_{CP}$ who bought e$_j$].

Now consider another limitation on the deletion of subjects, but here in a simple, unembedded clause. As we mentioned in connection with (3.7), English has an operation whereby a "large" DP may occur in a displaced position at the far right of its clause. In (3.17a) the moved element, *All the students from LA*, is understood as the complement of the verb *introduced* and it may be deleted in its original position, incorporated into the adjacent verb. In (3.17b) the moved element is in a subject position, but the subject of a non-tensed or "infinitival" clause; it is the top-most item in the complement of the verb *expect* and may be incorporated. Crucially, unlike the case of finite embedded clauses (which, like other finite clauses, must have subjects), a subject associated with an embedded non-finite verbal expression is not structurally subordinate and can incorporate. However, the generalization breaks down at a certain point: the sentence corresponding to (3.17c) sounds very un-English (**Are unhappy all the students from LA*), and the problem is that the deletion site is neither a complement nor the top-most element in any complement.

(3.17) a. I introduced e_i to Mary [$_{DP}$ all the students from LA]$_i$

      b. I expect [$_{CP}$ e_i to be at the party] [$_{DP}$ all the students from LA]$_i$

      c. *[*e_i are unhappy] [$_{DP}$ all the students from LA]$_i$

So if we take deletion to involve incorporation into an appropriate host word, this move has the effect of blocking it where such incorporation is impossible, thus preventing the copying of *wh*-phrases from the subject of tensed clauses. This blocks the generation of ill-formed structures like those of (3.14c), (3.15a,c), (3.16a), and (3.17c), while permitting the well-formed structures. This enables us to understand a wide range of data, as we have sketched.

3.2.4 *Understanding some diversity*

As the next part of our story, we will see that our condition on deletion (3.5) also enables us to understand some remarkable diversity among languages.[8] The restriction on the deletion of the subjects of tensed clauses apparently conflicts with a desire/need to ask questions about subjects of tensed clauses, just as one may ask questions about entities in other structural positions. The evidence for this claim is that strategies are adopted to circumvent the effects of this UG principle in certain contexts, and these strategies are manifested quite differently in individual languages. Because they vary so much, these individual strategies obviously do not reflect genotypical principles directly, but they do exist and they take on such diverse forms because of our genotypical principles.

---

[8] As more languages have been examined with carefully worked out models, it has become clear that earlier work had underestimated not only their complexity and the extent to which they are determined by initial conditions, but also their diversity (see Chomsky 2000, p. 7).

We have argued for our UG condition (3.5) here entirely on the basis of poverty-of-stimulus facts from English, but the condition holds at the level of UG, and therefore of all grammars; and we expect to be able to argue for the condition from the perspective of any language showing displacement properties. Indeed, we can and probably should make those arguments, but to do so would exhaust the tolerance of our publisher if not our readers, so we will demonstrate some consequences for linguistic diversity more succinctly. Rather than give comparable arguments from several languages, we shall illustrate one effect as it is manifested in various languages.

Luigi Rizzi (1990) identified three kinds of strategies used in different languages to circumvent the UG ban on extracting the subject of a tensed clause, here subsumed under our condition on deletion (3.5). Each strategy employs an *ad hoc*, learned device which licenses extraction from a subject position. The particular devices are quite different from language to language, and our UG condition on deletion helps us understand that diversity.

> (3.18) Three strategies to license an extracted subject:
> a. Adjust the complementizer so as to license the extraction
> b. Use a resumptive pronoun in the extraction site
> c. Move the subject first to a non-subject position and then extract

English exploits strategy (3.18a) and permits extraction of a subject if the complementizer *that* is adjusted – in fact, not present, as in *Who do you think saw Fay?*, which has the structure (3.19). Recall that *who* originates as the subject of *saw*. Because it is a *wh*-expression, it is copied at the front of its local clause, and then at the front of the upstairs clause. So two copies need to be deleted in the positions indicated. The lowest deletion (the subject) is licensed by the higher coindexed (agreeing) position at the front of the CP (and is incorporated into the coindexed position),[9] and the higher deletion at the front of the CP is licensed by and incorporated into the verb *think* (being the topmost item in *think*'s complement). In the comparable (3.14c) and (3.15a), there was no host for the deleted item. In other words, subjects of tensed clauses in English are movable only if the CP contains only an empty, unpronounced, coindexed or "agreeing" item: that permits a subject *wh*-word to be incorporated

---

[9] Example (3.16a) illustrates the importance of indexing, a complex matter. Indexed elements are effectively overt. This can be seen in a language where verbs are displaced. French *Qui voyez-vous?* "Who do you see?" has the structure (i), where e_j is the deletion site of *voyez* and hosts e_i, the deleted *qui*.

(i) [$_{CP}$ qui$_i$ voyez$_j$ [$_{IP}$ vous e_j e_i]]

By contrast, the English "gapped" verbs in (3.7) and (3.8) do not result from displacement and, therefore, behave differently.

appropriately.[10] *That* and *how*, on the other hand, in these positions are not appropriate hosts, as we saw in connection with (3.14c) and (3.15a).

(3.19) Who$_i$ did you think [$_{CP}$ e$_i$ [$_{CP}$ e$_i$ saw Fay]]?

French also exploits strategy (3.18a), but somewhat differently. The complementizer *que* is never deleted (3.20a). Again we see that objects may be extracted freely: *Qui crois-tu que Marie a vu? Qui* originates as the direct object of *vu*, is copied at the front of its local clause, and then at the front of the upstairs clause (3.20b). The trace of the lowest *qui* is incorporated into *vu* and the higher one is incorporated into *crois*, as indicated. But a subject is not extractable in a comparable way and *que*, like English *that*, cannot host a deleted subject: **Qui crois-tu que a vu Jean?* (3.20c). However, French speakers can adjust the complementizer *que* to the "agreeing" form *qui*, if and only if it is followed by a deletion: *Qui crois-tu qui a vu Jean?* Effectively the agreeing form hosts the deleted element (3.20d).

(3.20) a. Je   crois   [$_{CP}$ que [$_{IP}$ Marie a   vu   Jean]].
           I   think   that   Marie has seen Jean
           I think that Marie has seen Jean.

       b. Qui$_i$ crois-tu   [$_{CP}$ e$_i$ que [$_{IP}$ Marie a vu e$_i$]]?
           who think you   that Marie has seen
           Who do you think Marie has seen?

       c. *Qui$_i$ crois-tu [$_{CP}$ e$_i$ que [$_{IP}$ *e$_i$ a vu Jean]]?

       d. Qui$_i$ crois-tu [$_{CP}$ e$_i$ qui [$_{IP}$ e$_i$ a vu Jean]]?

Here we see a very specific, *ad hoc* device, in this case an operation changing *que* to *qui*, whose sole motivation is to permit deletion of a subject DP. In French the agreeing complementizer is an overt *qui*, while in English the comparable form is the deleted, unpronounced complementizer.

Rizzi identified similar devices in a variety of languages, which host deleted subjects. West Flemish (a language like German and Japanese and unlike English and French, where direct objects precede their verb; hence the rightward cliticization of the direct object in (3.21a)) behaves similarly to French: the usual form of the complementizer is *da* (3.21a) but a special "agreeing" form *die* occurs where a deleted subject needs to be hosted (3.21b).

[10] In chapter 9 we discuss the course of language acquisition by children who use "medial" *wh*-items, as in *What do you think what Cookie Monster eats?* (Thornton 1995). Such children retain medial *wh*-items longest in contexts where the *wh*-word is extracted from a subject position and where it acts as a kind of "agreeing" complementizer: *Who do you think who's under there?*

(3.21) a. Den vent da$_i$ Pol peinst   [$_{CP}$ e$_i$ da Marie e$_i$ getrokken heet]
the man that Pol thinks   that Marie photographed has
The man that Pol thinks that Marie has   photographed

    b. Den vent da$_i$ Pol peinst$_i$ [$_{CP}$ e$_i$ die e$_i$ gekommen ist]
the man that Pol thinks   that come is
The man that Pol thinks has come

Norwegian is similar to West Flemish: it shows a special complementizer *som* only in embedded questions with a subject deleted (3.22a); its function seems to be to host a deleted subject which otherwise would violate our UG condition. It never occurs with a deleted object (3.22b).

(3.22) a. Vi vet   [$_{CP}$ hvem$_i$ som/*e [$_{CP}$ e$_i$ snakker med Marit]].
we know   who   that   talks   with Mary
We know who talks with Mary.

    b. Vi vet   [$_{CP}$ hvem$_i$ (*som) [$_{CP}$ Marit snakker med e$_i$]].
we know   who   that   Mary talks   with
We know who Mary talks with.

In these four languages we see copied subjects being deleted if the complementizer is adjusted in some fashion: deleted in English, amended to an agreeing form in French, or with a special form in West Flemish and Norwegian. In all cases there is a kind of agreement. Hebrew is a bit different. Hebrew also does not allow deletion of a subject DP (3.23a), although objects extract freely (3.23b), as is now familiar. Subjects are extractable under special circumstances. A special device adjusts the complementizer, in this case cliticizing the complementizer *še* onto an adjacent head (3.23c). In (3.23c) the complementizer cliticizes rightward onto *lo*, vacating the complementizer position and permitting the subject to be incorporated leftwards, as in the analysis of (3.23d) (see Shlonsky 1988). Because the complementizer position has been vacated, the subject is extractable; this is reminiscent of the English device of emptying the complementizer position not by cliticization but by deletion.

(3.23) a. *Mi$_i$ ein ex joda'at   [$_{CP}$ 'im *e$_i$ mešaret bamilu'im]?
who not you know   whether serves in reserves?
Who do you not know whether (s/he) serves in the reserves?

    b. Et mi$_i$ ein ex joda'at [$_{CP}$ 'im hamilu'im me'aifim e$_i$]?
acc+who   not you know   whether the reserves tire
Who do you not know whether the reserves tire him/her?

   c. Mi at ma'mina   [CP šelo ohev salat xacilim]?
      who you believe   that not likes salad eggplants
      Who do you believe doesn't like eggplant salad?

   d. Mi$_i$ at ma'mina [CP e[IP e$_i$ še+lo ohev salat xacilim]]?

The second general strategy is to use a "resumptive" pronoun in positions where incorporation is not possible (3.18b). Swedish exploits this strategy: (3.24a) shows that a complementizer does not host a deleted subject, as is now familiar; instead, the resumptive pronoun *det* appears and so there is no deletion, no empty element to be licensed. On the other hand, if no complementizer is present, the resumptive pronoun does not appear and the deleted item incorporates first into the empty complementizer and then into the verb of which its clause is the complement (3.24b), more or less along the lines of English and Hebrew, exploiting strategy (3.18a) in this instance (Engdahl 1985, p. 40).

(3.24) a. Vilket ord$_i$ visste ingen [CP hur det/*e$_i$ stavas]?
       which word knew no one   how it/e   is spelled
       Which word did no one know how it is spelled?

    b. Kalle$_i$ kan jag sla vad om [CP e$_i$/*han kommer att klara sig].
      Kalle can I   bet   about e/he   is going to succeed
      Kalle, I can bet (*he) is going to succeed.

The West African language Vata adopts the same strategy, but here even for local movement in a simple, unembedded clause. Again we see the familiar subject–object asymmetry: an extracted subject has a resumptive pronoun in its underlying position, never a deletion (3.25a), while the opposite is true for an extracted object (3.25b). To express English *Who ate rice?*, one says "Who did he eat rice?," with a resumptive pronoun in the subject position, and not "Who ate rice?"; to express English *What did Kofi eat?*, interrogating the direct object, one says "What Kofi ate?," with no resumptive pronoun (the lower "what" is incorporated into its verb *le*), and not "What Kofi ate it?" The resumptive pronoun is used only where a *wh*-word may not be incorporated.

(3.25) a. Áló$_i$ *(ò$_i$)   le   saká la?
       who   (he)   eat   rice WH
       Who ate rice?
    b. Yi$_i$ Kòfí   le (*mí$_i$) la?
      what   Kofi   eat (it)   WH
      What did Kofi eat?

Italian, on the other hand, manifests a third strategy: moving the subject first to a non-subject position (3.18c). Subjects may occur to the right of the

VP (3.26a): *Credo che abbia telefonato Gianni* "I think that Gianni has tele-phoned." Here *wh*-words may be incorporated leftward into an adjacent verb, and that is the position from which they are copied; so (3.26b) is the structure for a sentence like *Chi credi che abbia telefonato?* "Who do-you-think has telephoned?"

(3.26) a. Credo [$_{CP}$ che [$_{VP}$ abbia telefonato Gianni]].
 I-think that has telephoned Gianni
 I think that Gianni has telephoned.

 b. Chi$_i$ credi [$_{CP}$ che [$_{VP}$ abbia telefonato e$_i$]]?
 who do-you-think that has telephoned
 Who do you think has telephoned?

The Arabic dialect of Banni-Hassan employs a similar device. Here subjects may occur in front of the verb or after it, as in Italian. Indeed, there is a morpho-logical distinction between a post-verbal subject *miin* "who" and its preverbal counterpart *min*. If the complementizer *innu* "that" occurs (3.27a), then the post-verbal subject form is required. In other words, if the complementizer is present, it cannot host a deleted element (just like English *that*, French *que*, West Flemish *da*, Hebrew *še*, Swedish *hur*, Italian *che*, etc.) and consequently the element must move from the post-verbal position, showing the appropriate morphology; the structure is (3.27a). On the other hand, if the complemen-tizer is absent, then the subject may be incorporated leftwards, hosted by the higher verb *gaal*, as illustrated by English above (3.19), and the preverbal sub-ject is a possible extraction site; the pronoun shows the appropriate preverbal morphology (3.27b).

(3.27) a. Miin/*min$_i$ Fariid gaal [$_{CP}$ innu [$_{VP}$ kišar e$_i$ albeeda]]
 who Fariid said that broke the egg
 Who did Fariid say broke the egg?

 b. Min/*miin$_i$ Fariid gaal [e$_i$ [$_{VP}$ kisar albeeda]]?

We have discussed a bewildering range of facts, but a comprehensible pattern emerges from the data. UG blocks extraction of subjects, because unlike overt verbs, nouns, and indexed null elements, complementizers cannot host deleted items. However, for reasons of expressibility, speakers "need" to extract sub-jects; that is what the evidence from specific languages shows. Because of the UG constraint, they are forced to adopt *ad hoc* strategies which eliminate illicit deletions (Swedish, Vata), provide a post-verbal alternative to them (Italian, Banni-Hassan Arabic), or adjust the complementizer in some way so as to license them through an agreeing form (English, French, West Flemish, Hebrew, Norwegian).

The UG constraint explains the need for *ad hoc*, language-specific devices. Each of the devices we have examined is learnable, assuming children are prohibited genetically from extracting embedded subjects in the normal case. That is, children are exposed to positive, accessible data which demonstrate the language-specific operation that adults use: the deletability of *that* in English, the operation changing *que* to *qui* in French, the need for a resumptive pronoun **only** in subject positions in Swedish and Vata, etc. The conditions under which these apply follow from our UG condition (3.5). We therefore have accounts for the specific languages, which meet our basic requirements. We also see that the consequences of a condition of the linguistic genotype may be circumvented sometimes in the interest of expressivity, and we understand why there is such diversity in these cases.

Our UG principle on deletion (3.5), requiring that deleted elements are incorporated in a clitic-like fashion into an adjacent, overt head, was postulated on the basis of poverty-of-stimulus arguments. It provided a way to tease apart generalizations that a child might induce from her environment and the limits to those generalizations, preventing them from over-generating and yielding non-occurring structures. We know that the principle has similar effects in other languages, but we have not illustrated that here. Instead, we have illustrated some effects in a variety of languages relating to the extractability of subjects. That suffices to show that our principle is operative in other languages, although it certainly has many more consequences than we have illustrated here for analyses of French, West Flemish, and so on.

3.3   Case

Let us turn now to a second aspect of UG, which connects with matters central for traditional grammarians, the existence of cases. As it turns out, this notion – familiar to anyone who has studied German, Russian, Latin, Greek, etc. – is both closely similar to and subtly different from a more abstract relation on syntactic structure which plays a central role in the theory of UG.

3.3.1   *Morphological case*

It is a striking property of natural languages that a noun often shows a different form depending on its function. Modern English manifests these "case" alternations only in the pronoun system. A pronoun shows one form if it is the subject of a finite verb ("nominative," or "nom"), another if it is the complement of a verb or of a preposition ("accusative," or "acc"), and another if it acts as the specifier of a DP ("genitive," or "gen") (3.28).

(3.28)   a. *He* saw *him* in [DP *his* car].
          b. *They* saw *them* at [DP *their* house].

Other languages have much richer morphological systems. Finnish has, strictly speaking, fifteen different cases, of which nine are local, expressing location, destination, and source, each of which may appear alone or with markers for interior and exterior. Source is thus indicated by the suffix *tta*; if the phrase indicates "from inside," the noun may have the ELATIVE case marker *sta*, and if the phrase indicates "from outside," the noun may have the ABLATIVE case suffix *lta*. Other languages have a COMITATIVE case indicating accompaniment, an ABESSIVE or PRIVATIVE case to mean "not having" (Finnish *rahtatta* is [money+abessive] "without money, moneyless"); some Australian languages encode the opposite idea in a PROPRIETIVE case indicating "having" (Kalkatungu *putuyan* [stomach+proprietive], means "pregnant"). Languages may display quite an array of different inflectional endings on nouns. If one adds all combinations of orientation markers and regular case markers, one can identify forty or more markings in some Finno-Ugric and Northeast Caucasian languages. Barry Blake's (1994) book *Case* takes his readers on a wonderful trip through a spectacular range of case systems.

Old English had a morphological case system, with essentially four cases – quite simple when compared to Finnish. Figure 3.1 gives four sample paradigms, for different types of nouns. The demonstrative (*sē*, etc.) has somewhat richer inflection than the nouns.

	"that stone"	"that ship"	"that tale"	"that name"
		Singular		
Nominative	*sē stān*	*þæt scip*	*sēo talu*	*sē nama*
Accusative	*þone stān*	*þæt scip*	*þā tale*	*þone naman*
Genitive	*þæs stānes*	*þæs scipes*	*þǣre tale*	*þæs naman*
Dative	*þǣm stāne*	*þǣm scipe*	*þǣre tale*	*þǣm naman*
		Plural		
Nominative	*þā stānas*	*þā scipu*	*þā tala*	*þā naman*
Accusative	*þā stānas*	*þā scipu*	*þā tala*	*þā naman*
Genitive	*þāra stāna*	*þāra scipu*	*þāra tala*	*þāra namena*
Dative	*þǣm stānum*	*þǣm scipum*	*þǣm talum*	*þǣm namum*

Figure 3.1   Old English (nominal) case inflection

Morphological cases are not just ornamental decorations but they interact with core syntactic operations. Polish, like Russian, shows an accusative marking on direct objects (3.29a), but the marking is genitive if the verb is negated (3.29b).

(3.29) a. Janek   przyniósł   kwiaty.
           John   bought   flowers [acc]
           John bought flowers.
       b. Janek   nie   przyniósł   kwitów.
           John   not   bought   flowers[gen]
           John did not buy flowers.

3.3.2   Case theory

Surprisingly, the intertwining of case with core syntactic operations shows up
even in languages with no overt, morphological case system. This indicates
that there is more to case than meets the eye: case must represent a significant
abstraction, regardless of overt markings, and "case theory" has become part of
modern models. The idea is that all grammars have some kind of case system,
but only some have morphological case; the rest have abstract Case. From now
on we shall use **Case** to refer to that abstract notion of case, and lower case **case**
(sorry) to refer to overt, morphological markings. The distinction is crucial for
our discussion.

Any lexical head (noun, verb, adjective, preposition) may have a complement
DP. However, DPs are pronounced only in certain positions, and these are
positions where they have Case (by analogy with a traditional understanding of
the distribution of case). The abstract Case system of modern English is simple.
Verbs and prepositions generally assign (accusative) Case to their complement
DPs, as is overt in the form of pronouns: *Kay $_V$ saw him $_P$ with them*. The
subject of a finite verb receives (nominative) Case (*he, they left*) and a DP in the
specifier of a larger DP is Case-marked by the clitic *'s* and has (genitive) Case:
Kay's, his, their book. These are the positions which receive Case and these are
the positions in which a DP may be pronounced.

DPs may be understood in other positions, but unless that position is Case-
marked, the DP may not be pronounced there; it must be copied into a position
in which it is Case-marked in order to be pronounced. This, in fact, is the
motivation for certain movement: DPs move in order to be Case-marked. All
overt DPs must be Case-marked in order to be pronounced.[11] That is the essence
of Case theory.

So, if a DP originates in a position which is not Case-marked, somehow it
must acquire Case. In (3.30) DPs move to another DP position. *Kay* is understood as the complement of *arrested* and *picture*, and as the subject of *like*, but

---

[11] One position in which a DP is not Case-marked and may not be pronounced is the complement
to an adjective: **Kay is proud Ray*. Such structures are salvaged not through movement but
through the insertion of the meaningless preposition *of*, whose sole function is to assign Case
to the DP. The preposition *for* plays a similar role in salvaging the subject of an infinitival verb:
*him to learn Greek would be difficult vs. *for him to learn Greek would be difficult*.

these are not Case-marked positions. Again, the Case-marked positions are the complement of verbs and prepositions and the specifier of a DP. In (3.30) Kay does not originate in such a position; in (3.30a) Kay originates as the complement not of a verb *arrest* but of a participle *arrested*, and passive participles (unlike verbs) are not Case assigners. In (3.30b) Kay originates as the complement of a noun, not a Case assigner, and in (3.30c) the original position isn't the complement of anything nor the specifier of a DP nor the subject of a finite clause. Consequently *Kay* may not be pronounced in those positions and must move to a position where it does receive Case: one does not find anything like **Ray was arrested Kay*, **Ray's picture Kay*, **Ray seems Kay to like Jay*, or **it seems Kay to like Jay*, because, in each example, *Kay* is in a position which is not Case-marked.

> (3.30) a. Kay$_i$ was $_{participle}$arrested e$_i$.
> b. Kay$_i$'s $_N$picture e$_i$. (meaning "picture of Kay")
> c. Kay$_i$ seems [e$_i$ to like Ray].

If a DP originates in a Case-marked position, on the other hand, then it does not move. *Kay* originates as the complement of a verb in (3.31a) and may not move (3.31aii), as the complement of a preposition in (3.31b) and may not move (3.31bii), and as the subject of a tensed verb in (3.31c) and may not move (3.31cii). Compare the analogous structures of (3.30), which differ crucially in that *Kay* originates there in non-Case-marked positions and must move.

> (3.31) a. i. Somebody $_V$arrested Kay.
> ii. *Kay$_i$ $_V$arrested e$_i$. (intended to mean "Kay arrested herself")
> b. i. Picture $_P$of Kay.
> ii. *Kay$_i$'s picture $_P$of e$_i$.
> c. i. It seems Kay likes Ray.
> ii. *Kay$_i$ seems [e$_i$ likes Ray].

If we are going to distinguish the positions from which movement takes place in modern English in terms of case ((3.30) *vs.* (3.31)), we need an abstract notion of Case, defined independently of morphological endings, because morphological case does not exist in the language outside the pronoun system. Abstract Case is what is at work in the distinctions of (3.30)–(3.33).

In (3.30a), the deleted *Kay* (e$_i$) is not the complement of a verb or preposition or any other Case assigner, but of the participle *arrested*, and it has no Case. Similarly in (3.30b), e$_i$ is the complement of the noun *picture* and has no Case. And in (3.30c) e$_i$ is the subject of an infinitive verb and is Caseless. As a result, the deletion sites in (3.30) are positions from which the DP *Kay* moves to another DP position and receives Case there. In (3.31a), on the other hand, the deletion site is the complement of a transitive verb, of a preposition in (3.31b), and in (3.31c) it is the subject of a tensed verb. All these positions are Case-marked, DPs may be pronounced in these positions, and these are not positions from which they must move to other DP positions; indeed, they may not move. We draw the relevant distinctions in terms of an abstract notion of Case.

Conversely, *wh*-movement shows the mirror image: a *wh*-phrase moves to the specifier of CP, not to another DP position, and it may not move there from Caseless positions (3.32), but only from Case-marked positions (3.33). (3.32) and (3.33) correspond to (3.30) and (3.31), respectively. In (3.33a) the deletion site is the complement of the verb (as in (3.31a)), in (3.33b) the complement of the preposition *of* (as in (3.31b)), and in (3.33c) the deletion site is the subject of a tensed verb (as in 3.31c).

> (3.32) a. *Who$_i$ was Kay $_{participle}$arrested e$_i$?
>   b. *Who$_i$ did you see a $_N$picture e$_i$?
>   c. *Who$_i$ did it seem [e$_i$ to like Ray]?

> (3.33) a. Who$_i$ did Kay $_V$arrest e$_i$?
>   b. Who$_i$ did Kay see a picture $_P$of e$_i$?
>   c. Who$_i$ did it seem [e$_i$ likes Ray]?

3.3.3   *Links between morphological case and abstract Case*

This shows that Case is a fundamental item in grammars, even when it is not morphologically marked. Current work within the Minimalist Program is investigating the intertwinement of Case and syntactic operations, with intriguing results. One way of thinking of the relationship between the morphological and abstract systems is to claim that abstract Case occurs in all grammars and must be **realized** in some fashion; morphological case is then one means of realizing abstract Case. We shall return to the relationship between morphological case and abstract Case in chapter 8, when we examine some interesting syntactic effects of the loss of morphological case in the history of English.

Meanwhile we have illustrated another principle of UG, which characterizes the positions in which DPs may be pronounced. That principle forces certain DPs to move, to be copied elsewhere. In that event, the copied element has to be deleted; in section 3.2, we examined some aspects of the way in which deletion takes place. All the deletions illustrated in this section meet the requirements discussed in section 3.2.[12] That is true, for example, of the deleted items in (3.30); e$_i$ is the complement of the adjacent participle *arrested* in (3.30a), of

[12] We have assumed but not demonstrated that copied elements **must** be deleted. Therefore, if they cannot be deleted, not meeting the requirements for incorporation into an appropriate host, the resulting structure is ill-formed. We adopt the analysis of Nunes 1995: copied elements must be deleted because if they weren't, there would be two instances of, say, *what* and those two instances are non-distinct. If they are non-distinct, they cannot be linearized in the phonology. This would take us further into grammatical theory than we want to go here, but interested readers can follow the details in Nunes 1995.

the adjacent noun *picture* in (3.30b). In (3.30c), the trace e_i, it is the top-most element of the complement of *seems*, and thus these are all legitimate deletion sites. That is also true of the deletion sites in (3.31): e_i is the complement of the adjacent verb *arrested* in (3.31a), the adjacent *of* in (3.31b) and it is the top-most element of the complement of *seems* in (3.31c), all legitimate deletion sites. The problem with the structures of (3.31) is that they violate, not the condition on deletion (3.5), but Case theory: *Kay* receives Case in its original position and therefore may not move. Case theory interacts with our principle of deletion (3.5) and together they characterize the possibilities for moving DPs, i.e. copying and deleting them. We will leave it as an exercise for the reader to determine that the deletions in (3.32) and (3.33) also meet the requirements discussed in section 3.2.

3.4   Conclusion

Here we have put a searchlight on two aspects of current syntactic theory, deletion and Case, and shown how they help to capture distinctions typical of English speakers, and how they distinguish what a child learns from the environment from what she knows independently of experience. It is these detailed distinctions which make up the subconscious knowledge that people have when they are speakers of some form of some language. That knowledge is characterized by the kinds of grammars that people have, by their cognitive systems. It is too gross to say merely that structures are made up of subunits or that languages with case systems tend to have freer word order than languages without a rich morphology. Modern work takes us beyond *E*-language bromides like this.

4   Sound patterns in language

In this chapter and the two following ones, we turn from issues of syntactic organization in natural language to the systematicities of sound structure. There is a conventional division between PHONETICS, or the study of sounds in speech, and PHONOLOGY, the study of sound patterns within particular languages. As we will see, there is a reasonably clear conceptual distinction here, and we will follow it in devoting most of this chapter and the next to the more obviously linguistic domain of phonology while postponing substantive discussion of the nature of phonetics until chapter 6, after some necessary preliminaries in section 4.1. We will attempt to tease apart these notions, but that process will reveal that questions of sound structure, seemingly concrete and physical in their nature, are actually abstract matters of cognitive organization – aspects of *I*-language and not measurable external events.

Ideally, we should broaden our scope a bit: signed languages also have a "phonology" (and a "phonetics") despite the fact that this is not based on sound, although we cannot go into the implications of that within the scope of this book.[1] In recent years, the study of signed languages has revealed the fact that their systems of expression are governed by principles essentially homologous with those relevant to spoken language phonology and phonetics. This close parallelism reinforces the conclusion that we are dealing here with the structure of the mind, and not simply sound, the vocal tract, and the ears (or the hands and the eyes).

A rough way to distinguish phonetics from phonology is as follows: phonetics provides us with a framework for describing the capacities of the organism – the range of articulatory activities humans use (or can use) in speech, the properties of the sounds that result, and the way the peripheral auditory system deals with those sounds. A learner still has to determine how these capacities are deployed in the language of the environment, but the capacities themselves and their relation to physical events develop in the organism independent of particular

---

[1] A basic survey of the formational system of American Sign Language is provided in Klima and Bellugi 1979. Diane Brentari (1995) discusses the relation of this system to the phonological systems of spoken languages; some more technical papers on this topic will be found in Coulter 1993.

languages, in ways we will examine briefly in chapter 9. Phonology, in contrast, provides us with a framework for describing the knowledge of sound structure that is acquired as part of learning a specific language.

The limitation of phonetic concerns to properties that are actually employed in speech is significant. Phoneticians do not, in principle, consider non-linguistic sounds – burps, coughs, whistles, etc. There are purposes for which a representation that goes well beyond anything that might be linguistically significant can be motivated: consider the interests of the psychotherapist, for example, who might attend closely to much more than the purely linguistic content of a patient's vocalizations. Phoneticians and other linguists, however, have generally agreed that a representation of just those properties that might distinguish linguistic utterances in some language is the appropriate starting point for such a notion.

A PHONETIC REPRESENTATION, then, specifies the sound properties of an utterance that differentiate it from all other possible human linguistic utterances, in terms of all the dimensions that function in human languages. Such a representation can be interpreted as a language-independent set of instructions for pronouncing the utterance.

PHONOLOGICAL (or "phonemic") REPRESENTATIONS, in contrast, specify the sound-related properties of linguistic elements (morphological units, words, whole utterances) that distinguish these from other elements of the same "granularity" **within the same language**. This involves the way differences in sound are (and are not) used to differentiate one linguistic element from another within the systems of particular languages; the way sounds are modified (or replaced by other sounds) in particular environments, in ways particular to individual languages; and other matters. A theory of sound structure, on this picture, must specify at least the following things:

(4.1) a. What information belongs in the phonetic representation;
       b. What a phonological representation looks like, and how it may differ from a phonetic representation; and
       c. What principles relate one to the other, and how these are organized.

4.1   Phonetics as theory

Before we explore the goals and content of phonology, it is necessary to say a bit about the nature of phonetics, and the relation between the acoustic signal and our perception of it. Phonetics is the place where linguistic data seem most clearly **observable**. That is, sound seems to be a measurable physical phenomenon which you can actually get your hands on (or at least your ears). In contrast, phonological structure, syntax, semantics, and so on are all something we infer from judgments and intuitions: sentences do not come with little trees on them (representing their syntactic organization) which we could study directly, for instance. Because it deals with observables, phonetics seems to many people not to be much of a "theory" at all: just a sort of neutral observation language in which we describe utterances. On that view, a phonetic description might be more or less accurate, but there is no other sensible way to evaluate it.

In fact, in the nineteenth and early twentieth century, phoneticians proceeded along just this line: they attempted to refine their techniques for measuring as many dimensions as possible of speech with maximal precision. As equipment got better, and researchers' observations could be more and more fine-grained and accurate, there was an explosion of data – a result that had the paradoxical effect of convincing most students of language that they were on the wrong track.

Much of what was being turned up, for instance, followed from the observation that speech is continuous: what is taking place at any particular moment is at least a little bit different from what is going on just before or just after that moment. As a result, if the phonetician attempts to measure everything at every moment where there are distinct values to be recorded, there is no limit in principle to the amount of measuring to be done. It is clear that a full characterization of an utterance as a physical event requires us to recognize an unlimited number of points in time – but it is also clear that our understanding of the utterance in **linguistic** terms is not thereby improved.

In fact, we usually represent the phonetic structure of an utterance in a much simpler way: as if it were a sequence of separate units, like beads on a string, each one a "sound" representing about the same amount of phonetic material as a letter in common writing systems. A phonetic representation usually has the form of a sequence of segments, where each of these is characterized as a point in a multi-dimensional space. The dimensions of this space are the phonetically relevant properties of sounds. These include articulatory details such as the location of the highest point of the tongue body, presence (*vs.* absence) of vibration of the vocal cords, rounding of the lips, etc. This is rather like a sequence of snapshots, one per segment, where each one shows just the detail about the articulatory apparatus that we deem relevant.

This characterization may seem to be simply a direct observation statement about the utterance – after all, if the representation is really **phonetic**, there surely couldn't be anything too abstract about it, right? And isn't it the case that an utterance of the English word *pit* "really" consists of the sound *p*, followed by the sound *i*, followed by the sound *t*?

But in fact while a phonetic representation has a certain claim to "objectivity," it is not just a mechanical recording of utterances. Rather (like any serious record of an observation), it is a **theory** of what it is about the physical form of this utterance that is of linguistic significance: it deals in abstractions.

Observers who are completely in agreement on the measurable, physical facts can nonetheless disagree strongly on their interpretation, and thus on the correct phonetic transcription of a given utterance. A physicist, on the other hand, would be quite unhappy with a phonetic representation as a characterization of acoustic or biomechanical reality. We will have much more to say about the actual content of a theory of phonetic representations in chapter 6, but at this point it is still worth establishing that there is something substantial here to have a theory of.

Compare the characteristics of a tape recording of an utterance of the word *pit* with a transcription of that same utterance: [pʰɪt]. There are (at least) three important ways in which the transcription is an idealized abstraction from the actual signal:

> (4.2) SEGMENTATION pretends the flow of speech can be divided into a sequence of discrete intervals (here, three such segments);
> SEGMENTAL INDEPENDENCE pretends each of these intervals contains all and only the information about a single phonetic segment (thus ignoring co-articulation); and
> A SYSTEM OF FEATURES chooses some aspects of speech production to talk about and ignores others.

However intuitive it may seem, there is no physical warrant for representing the continuous event as a sequence of (some small number of) discrete points. Even the spaces in writing between words do not correspond to anything that is (necessarily) present in the speech signal. Our division of the speech signal into a sequence of discrete words is actually a **theory** of its structure. Sometimes, more than one theory can be consistent with the same signal, which is the source of a class of unintended distortions called *mondegreens*. The word comes from the misconstrual of a line from a seventeenth century Scottish ballad, where "they hae slain the Earl of Murray, and hae laid him on the green" was heard as " . . . and the Lady Mondegreen." Jackendoff (1994) cites the fact that the English sentences *We needed a cantor* and *We need a decanter* sound the same without context or a particularly careful pronunciation, a relation described by saying that the two sentences are *oronyms*. In such a case, a listener needs other evidence to choose between multiple theories of the same utterance, and often (particularly in the case of songs) such evidence is simply lacking.

Just as the division of utterances into words is a matter of linguistic structure, and not physics, so also is the division of words into letter-sized units. This is the abstraction involved in SEGMENTATION. Both from an articulatory and from an acoustic point of view, that is, utterances give us no justification for cutting them up as we do. For example, X-ray movies or other ways of picturing the speech apparatus at work show continuous fluid movement of the articulators: there are no (appropriate) discontinuities to tell us where to cut. This is not to say that the acoustic facts do not have discontinuities: they often do, but usually not where we want them. For instance, the acoustic structure of a stop consonant like the initial [pʰ] at the beginning of *pit* looks like three separate parts, not one – but where the last one is integrated with the properties of the following vowel in such a way as to make it impossible to separate them.

Secondly, there is the abstraction of SEGMENTAL INDEPENDENCE. The segmental picture suggests that all of the properties of a segment are located at the same point, and that segments do not overlap. But in fact, this is not at all the way speech works. Instead, there is an enormous amount of co-articulation, or overlapping of articulatory gestures. This is both anticipatory (right-to-left) and perseverative (left-to-right), and it smears the segments together so as to make it impossible to define their identity except relative to their particular context.

Another consequence of coarticulation is the fact that what counts as the "same" sound may be heavily context-dependent. For instance, the [g] sounds in *ghoul* and *geek* are quite different, as a function of differences in the vowel that follows. This kind of intersegmental interaction is quite typical of speech articulation: at any given point in time, what is going on is likely to be the product not just of one but of several of the "segments" in the utterance. Even if we could find discontinuities, then, we would not in general be able to present a snapshot that is physically real and consists exclusively of the (invariant) properties of a single segment we wanted to characterize.

So why do we do this (segmentation)? Because we have learned that this idealization is actually more appropriate and useful than the literal truth. The segmental representation is really the only basis for finding the regularities that obtain in languages with respect to the forms shown by individual words. Of course, it is only adequate once we specify the relation between such a picture and the vastly more complex reality that we could (in principle) measure, and phoneticians therefore take on (at least implicitly) the responsibility of describing the ways in which the representations they work with are implemented in all of their messy detail.

The phoneticians of the nineteenth century were concerned to say how transitions between segments fill in the intervening values of a continuous function – a function which we only specify at some small finite number of points (corresponding to the distinct segments we recognize in the utterance). Having done that, though, the segmented result is more enlightening for further linguistic study than a full reconstruction of the actual continuous nature of the facts. It is an appropriate level of abstraction from those facts because it organizes the data in a way that is more coherent: a way that allows us to see their structure, otherwise obscured by detail.

There is a third idealization involved in phonetic representations: these are also abstract in that they choose some things to characterize at the expense of others. We might describe the sound [i] (roughly the vowel of *Pete*), for instance, as a "high front unrounded oral vowel." This tells us about some things involved in the production of [i]: the position of the highest point of the tongue body, the configuration of the lips, and the position of the velum. It says nothing about what the rest of the tongue is doing (except that it is "lower" than the point we described), or what the epiglottis is doing, or how wide the nose itself is opened, what the facial muscles are doing, how loudly the speaker is talking, what his (or her) precise vocal range is, etc. These omissions are not because the values of these other properties cannot be determined: rather, they represent an implicit claim that these and other aspects of the physical event are not linguistically significant (or else that they can be predicted from the other things that we **have** described).

No language, for example, ever seems to contrast utterances on the basis of degree of spreading of the nostrils, or of loudness of the voice. Nor do languages differ systematically in this respect (such that, e.g., language A is spoken louder than language B, and to speak language A softly gives you a foreign accent). Linguistically relevant transcriptions, then (as opposed to what might be of interest to a psychiatrist or other specialist in non-verbal behavior) do not need to record the width of the nasal opening, or the loudness of the voice. In fact, we can go further, and say that *a fortiori*, such a transcription **should not** record these properties – at least not if "phonetics" refers to the linguistically relevant dimensions of speech. The choice of a set of parameters (or DISTINCTIVE FEATURES) is (part of) a phonetic **theory**: the data alone do not establish their own meaning, or impose a particular choice of a set of features as a matter of physical necessity.

What is required is a representation that will describe all and only those aspects of sound production that can play a part in the system of **language**. This is **linguistic** phonetics, after all, and not physics, or physiology. Any degree of freedom in the representation should correspond to something that at least potentially could be under linguistic control. The segmented phonetic representation actually stands at a level of abstraction some distance away from the physical reality, and there must be an explicit statement of the relation between the two, a matter which will occupy us further in chapter 6. Theory kicks in, even at the level of representing the sounds of language.

Phonetics connects with claims about innateness and Universal Grammar (UG), etc.: linguistic phonetics is an attempt to delineate exactly the aspects of sound structure that are available for use in natural languages – the things that one has to be able to control (potentially) as part of learning a particular language, matters which fall within the domain of the language organ. There are indeed a number of independent dimensions with this property, but certainly not an infinite number – and more to the point, not everything that one could measure is a candidate. And if a discrete, segmented representation is close to what is linguistically significant, the dimensions of control in speech are rather abstract and removed from the continuous, concrete physical reality.

What is part of UG, then, and thus innate, is not the actual sound of any words, but rather a set of abstractly organized possibilities. The child approaching the task of learning a language knows in advance what to pay attention to, and what range of possibilities might be important. In fact, as we will discuss in chapter 9, children attend to these matters in astonishingly structured detail from the very beginning: according to some research, indeed, even before birth. If the terms of analysis are given in advance, then we can begin to understand how humans cope with the infinite variability of experience in a common fashion, in such a way that we arrive at shared representations and analyses of speech events.

4.2   Phonology: language-particular structure

In contrast to the "general purpose" nature of phonetics, phonology studies the ways in which sounds are organized and related **internal to individual languages**. While phonetics is concerned to provide a universal framework for the linguistic sound properties of human speech, phonology is concerned with questions such as those of (4.3).

> (4.3) INVENTORY: Which of the possible sound types made available by phonetic theory actually occur in utterances in language X?
> CONTRAST: Which of the phonetic differences that occur in language X can serve to distinguish utterances (words, sentences) from one another in this language?
> CONTEXTUAL LIMITATION: Even though some property P occurs in language X, are there environments (characterized in terms of other properties) from which P is excluded, or where the value of P is fixed? Where P is a property of some element, and might be expected to occur in a position from which it is excluded, what – if anything – appears in its place?
> ALTERNATION: When the "same" linguistic element (morpheme, word, sentence) appears in different forms in different environments, what systematic differences occur in its pronunciation? What conditions govern the range of phonetically different elements that count as the "same" morpheme, word, etc.?

Of course phonological **theory** is concerned to specify the range of answers to these questions that are possible in general. As such, it is another universal property of the human language faculty, since we presume that the range of answers (and indeed the set of appropriate questions) is independent of any particular language. Just as the child brings a set of phonetic categories to the task of language learning, there is also a limited range of properties that characterize the systems of individual languages in comparison with one another. Phonological theory attempts to describe the dimensions of this aspect of *I*-language.

4.2.1   Phonological representations

In this section, we discuss the basic nature of phonological representations, showing the kinds of abstraction that are involved. We shall see that there are actually a wide range of quite different approaches that all correspond in one way or another to the fundamental insight underlying the concept of "phonological representation," implying distinct notions of the phonology–phonetics relation. Within the linguistics of the mid-twentieth century, certain *a priori* notions about the nature of this relation implied that some significant facts about linguistic sound structure had to be relegated to some other aspect of the grammar, for which yet a third kind of representation was proposed: MORPHOPHONEMICS.

Phonetic representations are an idealization from the complex facts of speech to a sequence of discrete, internally homogeneous segments. Each segment is characterized with respect to a set of features on a limited, universal list. The point of such a theory is to provide a principled account of what we include and what we leave out in giving a **language-independent** characterization of particular utterances: importantly, we leave out the irrelevant and the predictable. But if phonetic theory provided our only account of the sound properties of languages, we would leave unexpressed the fact that many things which are not predictable in general are nonetheless quite predictable by principles specific to a given language. When we know the language of a given utterance, many of its properties that are significant from the perspective of general phonetics can be seen to be determined by the system of that language, rather than being distinguishing properties of just that utterance.

For instance, the aspirated character of the stop in English *pat* (phonetically [pʰæt]) must be indicated phonetically, since the languages of the world contain many instances of unaspirated voiceless stops in essentially the same position (e.g., French [pat] *patte* "paw"), and in some cases the two possibilities even contrast (e.g. Punjabi [pət] "honor" vs. [pʰət] "split"). And yet somehow this aspiration seems less relevant from the point of view of English: indeed, most English speakers are quite unaware of it.

This is not to say that a phonetic representation of utterances is wrong, but only that there are facts of another order to be described as well, another (distinct) level of analysis that must be available for the sound structure of utterances. We want not only a characterization in the language-independent terms of phonetic theory, but also one that takes into account the sound pattern of a particular language, in terms of which we can identify the ways in which sound properties function in that language.

Following a line originally stressed by Ferdinand de Saussure (1974, an edition drawn from notes on his courses first published in 1916), we want this phonological representation to be systematically constrained so that differences between the representations of two utterances correspond to differences in their linguistic content, not simply their physical properties. For reasons that will become apparent, we will often refer to the phonological representation as the "underlying form" of an utterance. And to further confuse matters, the history of this kind of representation results in a tendency to call its elements "phonemes" and thus to speak of a "phonemic" representation. There are subtle distinctions to be made here, but by and large "phonological," "underlying" and "phonemic" representations are all ways of talking about the same thing.

The essence of what this representation is all about is expressed by the following principle:

(4.4) Two phonological representations should differ only insofar as they correspond to different messages within the language in question.

Thus, in English, phonetic representations contain both [pʰ] (as in *pit*, phonetically [pʰɪt]) and [p] (as in *spit*, phonetically [spɪt]); but we do not want to allow two **phonological** representations to differ only in that one has a [pʰ] where the other has a [p], since it is never the case that this difference alone serves to distinguish meanings in English. Simplifying slightly, aspirated [pʰ] appears always and only at the very beginning of stressed syllables, while unaspirated [p] appears elsewhere (after a syllable-initial *s* or under conditions of reduced stress). A similar generalization applies to other voiceless stops (*t, k*) in English.

The point is that a speaker's knowledge of English, her language organ, includes some characterization of a set of principles defining the notion of "phonological representation in English" that exclude two such representations from both being possible, even though the definition of "phonological representation in Punjabi" (for instance), which consitutes a part of a Punjabi speaker's language organ, **does** allow two representations that differ only in this way. Just as the notion of "phonetic representation" provides us with an implicit definition of "possible human linguistic utterance" or the like, a phonological representation is the basis of an account of what the possible linguistically distinct utterances are in a given language. The phonological principles that are thus inherently particular to a specific language form a part of *I*-language, and it is part of the task of learning a language to determine the appropriate set of such principles from among those made available by phonological theory.

We have formulated the principle in (4.4) in extremely general terms, in order to try to accommodate the many different ways in which linguists have thought of phonological representations. We can distinguish at least three variant conceptions of how to satisfy the requirement of the phonemic principle (4.4).

One approach, which we can call a theory of INCOMPLETELY SPECIFIED REPRESENTATIONS, proposes that where some property is predictable within a given language, we omit it altogether from phonological representations within that language. It is then a function of the rules mapping phonological onto phonetic form to fill in the unspecified features. On this picture, phonological representations in a given language are arrived at by quite literally abstracting away from the predictable properties of utterances in the language in question.

Many people assume that the incompletely specified view is the only possible (or coherent) way to think of phonological representations, but this is not the case. Some scholars, such as Edward Sapir, have maintained a FULLY SPECIFIED BASIC VARIANT view of phonological form. This notion also focuses on the idea that only a limited number of the sound types that are phonetically possible can be the basis of contrasts in a given language, but instead of effectively omitting all of the non-contrastive properties, it treats a group of (phonetically distinct) sounds that do not contrast with one another as a sort of equivalence class, represented by a kind of "prototype" sound.

On this picture, we say that English has only one kind of voiceless stop in phonological representations, but this is nonetheless a fully specified phonetic segment. Suppose (for concreteness' sake) that we choose to have underlying unaspirated voiceless stops like [p]. Then the phonological representations of *pit* and *spit* are /pɪt/ and /spɪt/, respectively,[2] and one of the things that must be specified about the relation of phonological form to phonetic form is that some /p/s are realized phonetically as [pʰ]s.

These two views are different, but they both satisfy the phonemic principle. On the fully specified basic variant view, no two English phonological representations could differ only in that one has a p^h where the other has a p because English phonological representations only have /p/s, and not /pʰ/s. On the incompletely specified view, such a difference could not arise because the property of aspiration is not present at all in phonological representations (in English).

There is a third way to satisfy principle (4.4) which has been maintained by some other phonologists, including on one reading (Anderson 1985), Saussure himself. We can call this a FULLY SPECIFIED SURFACE VARIANT view. On this picture, we let phonological representations look just like phonetic ones: *pit* = /pʰɪt/, *spit* = /spɪt/. But we also say that a phonological representation in English is only well-formed if it conforms to a set of defining regularities. For instance, a representation in which an aspirated stop follows an /s/ within a syllable is ill-formed, and on the other hand a representation in which an unaspirated stop appears at the beginning of a stressed syllable is also ill-formed.

Now if we get the restrictions right (and tight enough), we have satisfied the phonemic principle even though our representations do not look any different from phonetic ones! That is because if we take two representations that differ

---

[2] Note that the usual convention is to put phonological representations within /s and phonetic representations within square brackets.

only in that one has a p^h where the other has a p, one or the other of these is going to be ill-formed because it violates some constraint, and is thus ruled out as a phonological representation in English.

If all of these approaches to phonological representation can satisfy the basic desiderata for such a notion, as expressed in (4.4), does it make any difference which one we choose? In fact here, as elsewhere, the issue of an appropriate level of abstraction arises, and the determination of the properties of that level is ultimately an empirical question. If all three of the varieties of phonological representation just considered can be made to fare equally with respect to the basic principle in (4.4), there may still be other ways in which they are distinct in their ability to facilitate an insightful account of the complete reality constituted by sound structure in *I*-language. When we consider not simply the nature of phonological form itself, but also the systematic formulation of its relation to other aspects of language (including phonetic form, word structure, and other matters), differences will emerge.

4.2.2   *Relating phonological and phonetic form*

The differences among possible conceptions of phonological representation considered in the previous section are connected with different conceptions of how phonological form is to be related to phonetic form. On the incompletely specified view, what has to be done to get from phonological to phonetic form is to "fill in the blanks": i.e., to specify the values of redundant parameters. On the fully specified basic variant view, on the other hand, the relation consists not in filling in the blanks, but rather in **changing** a "prototypical" value of a given parameter in a context-dependent fashion. Finally, on the fully specified surface variant view, there is no alteration of the representations at all, but rather a system of constraints serves to define directly the range of potentially contrasting forms within a given language. In choosing among these possibilities, the phonological theorist asks which leads to a more enlightening and comprehensive view of the nature of *I*-language.

Independent to some extent of the mechanics of the phonology–phonetics relation, another issue is just how "abstract" that relation can be. In particular, during the 1940s and 1950s, many linguists came to agree on a condition that should be imposed on the relation between the two representations, radically limiting the permissible degree of abstraction in phonological form by requiring that phonological form be directly and unambiguously derivable from phonetic representation. This is often called the BIUNIQUENESS CONDITION:[3]

>   (4.5) The phonetic and the phonological representation can each be uniquely recovered from the other.

[3] See Anderson 1985, pp. 312ff. for some discussion of these matters.

With regard to the path from phonological to phonetic representation, everyone would accept this (at least up to the point of free variation): it just means that the principles of the phonology have to operate so as to assure a determinate result.

In the other direction, though, the requirement that a phonological representation can be uniquely determined on the basis of phonetic form alone is not so obvious. In particular, (4.5) means that two phonological representations cannot be "neutralized" in the sense that both map onto the same phonetic form, for if they were, there would be no way to resolve the ambiguity without appealing to something outside of phonetic representation. But many cases in many languages seem to have that character, *prima facie*.

For instance, obstruents in German are always [–Voice] in final position. This has the consequence that both *Bund* "association" and *bunt* "varicolored" are pronounced [bʊnt], although the difference reappears when the stops cease to be final (cf. *Bunde* [bʊndə] "associations," *bunte* [bʊntə] "varicolored (fem nom sg)"). To maintain biuniqueness, we would have to say that both *Bund* and *bunt* have the same phonological representation (e.g., /bʊnt/), because there is no way to tell for a given instance of phonetic [bʊnt] which word it represents. But this conclusion is quite counter-intuitive.

Why did scholars believe in the necessity of a condition like biuniqueness? In fact, the notion that phonological form should be biuniquely related to phonetic substance grows fairly directly out of the notion that both are characterizations of utterances as they exist apart from speakers themselves: that is, of the *E*-language conception of what is being described in linguistics, with phonological representations hugging the (supposedly objective) phonetic ground and minimizing their abstractness. As we will see, the abandonment of condition (4.5) is intimately tied up with the replacement of that conception of the field by one that takes *I*-language, the speaker's knowledge of the language, as the proper object of linguistic inquiry.

There are at least three sorts of reason that seem to characterize the motivations for earlier scholars' assumption of the condition in (4.5), all deriving from the *E*-language orientation of linguists at the time. First, speech perception was assumed to work in a purely passive, bottom-up mode, starting from the acoustic input (alone) and yielding a linguistic percept. If phonological representations correspond to this perceptual reality, they would then have to be recoverable on the basis of data in the signal alone.

Secondly, a bias toward procedural accounts of linguistic structure dominates the linguistic literature (at least in North America) from the 1930s through the early 1950s. Linguists were not supposed to have any biases or preconceived notions of what languages were like, since it was assumed they could differ without limit (i.e., that there are no universals). Further, since meaningful elements are constructed out of sound units, it seemed logical to linguists of the time that one had to have a complete account of the latter before trying to identify the former. But in that case, the phonetic data are all the analyst has to go on when constructing an analysis, so the analysis has to be the sort of thing that can be attained on that basis. The conceptual mistake that follows is to identify what the language "must be" with a particular path by which the linguist can discover its structure. This has the (presumably unintended) consequence that linguistic theory winds up describing the behavior and knowledge of linguists, rather than that of speakers.

Finally, many felt that what the phonemic principle "really" required was that phonological representations encode linguistic contrast. If we take contrast to be something that can be operationally determined by asking speakers "do the utterances U_1 and U_2 contrast or not?" (or any one of a thousand variants of this), the principle again follows, since all and only those differences that can be unambiguously recovered from phonetic presentation alone will correspond to contrasts in this sense.

As this view became more explicit, however, it became clear that it failed to do justice to the facts of language. First, students of the nature of perception came to entertain the possibility that rather than simply registering its input, the mind actively constructs hypotheses about the world, and compares them with the incoming data to validate a particular interpretation. Perhaps the purest form of this picture is the notion of "analysis by synthesis," according to which percepts are quite generally constructed by the perceptual system itself (the "synthesis") and then confirmed (as the "analysis") to the extent that the available data do not contradict them.[4] The kind of "motor theory" of speech perception which we will presume in chapter 6 below generally makes somewhat similar assumptions. These and other active views of perception made it clear that the perceptual system might well involve (at least in part) "top-down" generation and testing of hypotheses, and not only simple, bottom-up identification of the acoustic signal. If that is the case, though, more than one such hypothesis might be consistent with the same surface facts, and thus more than one phonological representation might represent a speaker's interpretation of the same phonetic form.

Secondly, when we recognize that there are in fact substantive universals of language, it becomes clear that linguists are not limited in their grammar-writing to simple induction over collections of surface data, and also that the analysis of different parts of the grammar (e.g., sound structure and word structure) can proceed hand-in-hand. Thus, there is no reason to believe that the surface facts alone directly constrain the range of possible grammars.

Finally, it turns out that "contrast" is a lot harder to define operationally than it initially appears. True, we do need to be able to define this notion (insofar

---

[4] See Stevens and Halle 1967 for the specific application of this view to the problem of speech perception.

as it is a coherent one), but it does not follow that contrast ought to be the only thing determining what a phonological representation should be like. A coherent view of this relation, in fact, along with the other matters discussed just above, emerges only when we realize that the basic object of inquiry in the study of sound structure (as with the rest of language) is the language organ, a form of knowledge, rather than a direct characterization of external events.

4.2.3   *Morphophonemic representations*

Let us explore the consequences of accepting the biuniqueness condition (4.5) for our ability to provide an adequate description of the content of *I*-language knowledge of sound structure. We will see that adherence to this condition actually prevents us from articulating some regularities that clearly constitute part of what speakers know about their language.

Consider an example that is similar to that of the final devoicing we saw above in German, but with a bit more structure. In Korean we find the following set of obstruent consonants in initial position and between vowels:

$$(4.6) \quad \begin{array}{cccc} p^h & t^h & \check{c}^h & k^h \\ p' & t' & \check{c}' & k' \\ p/b^5 & t/d & \check{c}/\check{j} & k/g \\ & s & & \\ & s' & & \end{array}$$

In final and preconsonantal position, on the other hand, we find only $[p^\urcorner, t^\urcorner, k^\urcorner]$, sounds in which the consonantal closure is not immediately released into a following vowel or brief aspiration. In different forms of the same basic word, final or preconsonantal $[p^\urcorner]$ will correspond to any one of the labials, $[t^\urcorner]$ to any of the coronals (the second and third columns in (4.6)), and $[k^\urcorner]$ to any of the velars.

In medial position, any of the segments in the chart in (4.6) can occur. What is obviously the same stem, however, changes shape when a medial consonant comes to be in final or preconsonantal position. For example, an object case suffix /-ɨl/ appears in Korean in (object case) forms like those in (4.7).

$$(4.7) \quad \begin{array}{l} \text{a. nadɨl "grain"} \\ \text{b. nat}^h\text{ɨl "piece"} \\ \text{c. nasɨl "sickle"} \\ \text{d. na\check{c}}^h\text{ɨl "face"} \\ \text{e. na\check{j}ɨl "day"} \end{array}$$

---

[5] For the sounds in this row, the first (p, t, č, k) occurs initially and the second (b, d, ǰ, g) occurs between vowels. Since the members of these pairs are in complementary distribution, we treat them as units.

In isolation, though (as for instance in the citation forms of the same words), all of these stems are pronounced in the same way: as [natˑ].

The matter of how to analyze the object case forms in (4.7) phonologically is straightforward, since all of the segments in the chart are in contrast, and we can set up phonological representations essentially equivalent to the phonetic ones (though we still need to abstract away from the environmentally conditioned variation in voicing in p/b, t/d, etc.). But what about the phonological analysis of [natˑ]? We seem to have two choices.

On the one hand, we might say that [natˑ] always has the same phonological representation (e.g., /nat/), one which satisfies biuniqueness (4.5), because it can always be uniquely, if uninformatively, recovered from the phonetic form. The alternative is to say that there are at least five (and potentially eight) different phonological forms that all correspond to the surface form [natˑ], such that it is not possible to tell in isolation which phonological representation should be associated with any given phonetic one (hence violating biuniqueness).

Most linguists are tempted to posit phonological representations /nat/, /natʰ/, /nas/, /načʰ/, /nač/, etc., and to say that there is a principle by which any final or preconsonantal coronal obstruent (in phonological representation) is replaced by (phonetic) [tˑ] (with corresponding rules for labials and for velars). This violates biuniqueness, but it seems to express something real about the language. What is the basis of this feeling?

In essence, the situation is the following. For any given lexical element of the language, the prevocalic variant in which it occurs is idiosyncratic, but constant: e.g., the word for "day" appears with the same consonant in [najei] "in the daytime" as in [najɨl] "day (obj)," as well as in any other form where the stem-final consonant is followed by a vowel. In contrast, forms of, e.g., "sickle" in which the stem is immediately followed by a vowel always show a stem-final [s]. Given the form that occurs before a vowel, the final or preconsonantal form is predictable, but not *vice versa*. That is, we can establish **as a general principle of the language** that any segment which is [+Obstruent,+Coronal] in medial position (i.e. [t, tʰ, s, č] etc.) will correspond to [tˑ] in final position. From the non-medial form, however, we cannot predict the medial one in a unique way.

Given a biunique notion of the relation between phonological representations and phonetic form, /nas/, /nač/, etc. cannot be the phonological representations of words all pronounced [natˑ], since there would be no way to recover one of these (as opposed to any of the others) from a given instance of [natˑ]. Any phonological representation is a representation of the **sound properties** of a message, but biuniquess further limits the sound properties that can potentially differentiate one message from another to ones that are overtly realized in the phonetic form of utterances expressing that message – an *E*-language notion.

But what else could "sound properties" possibly mean? In fact, what differentiates e.g. /nas/ from /nač/ as the phonological representation for [natˑ] is something a native speaker of Korean knows about the form the item in question takes **in general** and not just in this utterance. As a part of speakers' knowledge of the language, these relations clearly belong in a full account of the *I*-language Korean, part of a Korean speaker's language organ. Any theory of phonological form which prevents their expression is thereby seen to be inadequate as a general account of the structure of the language faculty.

Note that the proposal to distinguish /nas/, /nat, /nač/, etc. (all realized phonetically as [natˀ]) is still a matter of the "sound properties differentiating one (potential) message from another," however. We have not, for instance, proposed a way to give different representations for, e.g., *pair* and *pear* in English, since these words never differ in their sound properties. While the differences among Korean /nas/, /nat/, /nač/, etc. are manifested in some (though not all) phonological environments, there are no such differences among English *pare*, *pear*, *pair*.

When American structuralists in the 1940s and 1950s came up against this sort of example, they could not incorporate it into a (biunique) phonemic representation. Since their focus was on an *E*-language conception of the object of their study, and for other reasons sketched above, they considered biuniqueness a valuable requirement *a priori* on phonological form, and were not particularly troubled by this conclusion. On the other hand, examples such as the Korean one here (and the widely discussed case of final de-voicing in German, Russian, and a variety of other languages) made it clear that even if these facts did not belong in the "phonology," there was still more to be said to include them in an overall description.

To allow for this, they constructed a new kind of object: a "morphophonemic" representation. This was assumed to represent a more abstract characterization of linguistic elements, related in a non-biunique way to phonemic representations as in (4.8).

(4.8) Morphophonemic form   Phonemic form   Phonetic form

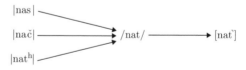

These morphophonemic representations were not taken too seriously as realities of language by most phonologists at the time, precisely because they were not recoverable in a biunique fashion from the phonetic data: they were regarded simply as linguists' conveniences for representing a lot of data in a compact fashion. This makes perfect (ideological) sense: the need for a phonological representation of the "morphophonemic" variety does not spring from *E*-language considerations, which were the focus of attention at the time, but rather from the need to express the content of speakers' knowledge of the language. From our perspective, however, it can readily be seen that these representations actually articulate something important that a speaker **knows**, hence properties of that individual's language organ: they (and not the biunique phonemic forms) uniquely determine the full range of shapes a given linguistic element will display across environments, which is surely part of the characterization of the "sound properties" that oppose that element to other elements). An account of sound structure as *I*-language must thus include these matters; while the necessity of the biunique phonemic representation, in contrast, remains to be established.

4.3   Morphophonemics and *I*-language

Biuniqueness has been abandoned as a requirement by most phonologists for many years, and in practice the phonological representations of the 1960s and later have looked much more like the "morphophonemic" representations of the 1950s than like the phonemic representations of that era. Given the intellectual investment of the field in a biunique, surface oriented, *E*-language interpretation of the phonemic principle at the time, how did this change in outlook come about?

There is a standard version of the history of phonology – a kind of creation myth that has as its background the picture of structuralists in America (and also in Europe) concentrating on the discovery of (biunique) phonemes as minimal units of surface contrast through the 1930s, 1940s, and 1950s. Then at the end of the 1950s (according to this interpretation), Morris Halle presented some data from Russian, facts concerning voicing assimilation in that language, from which it was immediately clear that the whole notion of phonemes as they were conceived at the time was indefensible and led inevitably to loss of generality. As a result (with allowances for entrenched prejudices and the time necessary to retool), phonologists reoriented their attention toward the previously marginalized domain of morphophonemics, and phonemics was replaced by generative phonology.

To what extent does that picture correspond to reality? Let us look at the facts, historical and linguistic, which can teach us something about shifts in scientific paradigms, among other things. Halle's argument was first presented at a 1957 meeting (Halle 1957), and appears in print two years later in *The Sound Pattern of Russian*:

In Russian, voicing is distinctive for all obstruents except /c/, /č/, and /x/, which do not possess voiced cognates. These three obstruents are voiceless unless followed by a voiced obstruent, in which case they are voiced. At the end of a word, however, this is true of all Russian obstruents: they are voiceless, unless the following word begins with a voiced obstruent, in which case they are voiced. E.g., [m'ok l,i] "was (he) getting wet?," but [m'og bɨ] "were (he) getting wet"; [žeč l,i] "should one burn?," but [žeǯ bɨ] "were one to burn."

In a phonological representation which satisfies both condition (3) [phonemic→ phonetic determinacy] and (3a) [phonetic→phonemic determinacy], the quoted utterances would be symbolized as follows: /m'ok 1,i/, /m'og bi/, /žeč 1,i/, /žeč bi/. Moreover, a rule would be required stating that obstruents lacking voiced cognates – i.e., /c/, /č/, and /x/ – are voiced in position before voiced obstruents. Since this, however, is true of all obstruents, the net effect of the attempt to meet both condition (3) and (3a) would be a splitting up of the obstruents into two classes and the addition of a special rule. If condition (3a) is dropped, the four utterances would be symbolized as follows: {m'ok 1,i}, {m'ok bi}, {žeč 1,i}, {žeč bi}, and the above rule could be generalized to cover all obstruents, instead of only {č}, {c} and {x}. It is evident that condition (3a) involves a significant increase in the complexity of the representation.[6] (Halle 1959, 22f.)

Halle's argument is standardly adduced as having persuaded phonologists to abandon the phonemics of the time, and take up the rather different pursuits and abstractions of generative phonology. The logic of the argument is that a description interposing a level of representation meeting the biuniqueness condition (4.5 above) between the morphophonemic and phonetic representations, as in (4.8), leads necessarily to a situation in which a regularity of the language (here, the assimilation of voicing in clusters of obstruents) cannot be stated in a unitary way.

As we will argue below, the force of this argument rests in its focus on the need for a grammar not only to assign the correct representations to linguistic forms but also to give an account of the **rules** of the language, rules which correspond directly to components of a speaker's linguistic knowledge. By "rules" here, we do not of course refer to the pronouncements of prescriptive grammarians, but rather to the collection of regularities that can be shown to characterize an important component of the way individuals produce and understand sentences of their language – the language organ, as represented by a "grammar." As we shall see in chapter 5, these regularities can be formulated in a variety of ways. What matters is that the replacement of biunique phonemic representations by "morphophonemic" ones must have followed from the replacement of *E*-language conceptions of language by those of *I*-language. While quite plausible in retrospect, however, the extent to which that logic was actually apparent to the linguists of the time who heard Halle's argument is not obvious.

It is reasonably clear that the force of Halle's argument cannot have come from its novelty, since similar arguments had been offered before. Halle, indeed, cites one (though curiously, not one of the better known cases noted below):

Analogous examples can be cited from many languages. An especially interesting example is discussed by G. H. Matthews, "A Phonemic Analysis of a Dakota Dialect" [*IJAL* 21. 56–59 (1955)], who shows that the labial and dental nasal consonants are automatic alternants of the cognate stops as well as of /m/ and /n/, while the velar nasal is an alternant of the velar stop exclusively. (*Ibid.* p. 22, note 12)

---

[6] Halle uses braces – {} – to indicate a morphophonemic representation, as opposed to biunique phonemic representations in /s and phonetic representations in square brackets.

In fact, the example Halle refers to is *not* analogous in the relevant details to the Russian case. Matthews shows that /b,t,k/ are replaced by [m,n,ŋ] in syllable-final position after a nasal vowel in this form of Dakota. But he also makes it clear (Matthews 1955, p. 57, note 3) that "[m, n] do not otherwise occur in this position." This is thus a case of "partial overlapping," rather than neutralization, and the example does not necessitate the loss of a generalization in order to maintain a biunique analysis. Since the nasalization rule for stops following a nasal vowel does not involve a mixture of neutralization and allophonic effects, but can be formulated entirely as a relation between phonemic and phonetic forms, its unitary nature is not compromised by the principle requiring phonemic forms to be uniquely recoverable from the surface phonetics. Other examples that **do** have this character, however, were known at the time, as we will note.

There were actually several examples that had been discussed in the literature before Halle's paper that involve facts whose logic is entirely parallel to that of Russian voicing assimilation. It is instructive to look at the treatment they received, because it shows us something about the extent to which linguists of the period held to the principles of their theory.

One way of dealing with such facts is illustrated by Bloomfield's discussion of Menomini. Here, as in Russian, we have an apparent generalization which (when applied to morphophonemic forms) involves a mixture of phonemic and subphonemic effects. But instead of concluding that this showed the inadvisability of phonemic representations, Bloomfield interprets the facts as showing that the allophonic variation is probably phonemic too, after all. "If it looks like a phoneme, walks like a phoneme, quacks like a phoneme, it must **be** a phoneme" (with apologies to Walter Reuther).

If postconsonantal y, w, or any one of the high vowels, i, ī, u, ū, follows anywhere in the word, the vowels ē and ō are raised to ī and ū, and the vowel o in the first syllable of a glottal word is raised to u: mayīčekwaʔ *that which they eat*, cf. mayēček *that which he eats*; ātɛʔnūhkuwɛw *he tells him a sacred story*, cf. ātɛʔhnōkɛw . . . Since ū occurs only in this alternation, it is not a full phoneme. (Bloomfield 1939, §35)

"Not a full phoneme." What does that mean? In the inventory of "the actual Menomini phonemes," the element ū appears in parentheses, and is identified as a "semi-phoneme" (Bloomfield 1939, §5). Bloomfield must have been somewhat uncomfortable with this analytic result, because in a later treatment, his posthumously published grammar of Menomini (edited by Charles Hockett), he gives some rather marginal arguments that ū̲ is a ("full") phoneme after all.

Since the occurrence of u̲ʼ is normally confined to the forms in which it replaces o̲ʼ under the regular alternation of 1.8 [referring to the rule above], it might be viewed as a mere positional variant of o̲ʼ. In this alternation, however, the difference of o̲ʼ and u̲ʼ is parallel with that of e̲ʼ and i̲ʼ, two sounds which unmistakably figure as separate phonemes. Moreover, the difference of o̲ʼ and u̲ʼ is maintained by persons in whose speech this alternation has lost its regularity. Also, the sound of u̲ʼ (and never of o̲ʼ) is

used in a few interjections: <u>capuʼq</u> "splash!," <u>kuʼh</u> "stop it!" A contrast of <u>oʼ</u> and <u>uʼ</u>
appears in the foreign words <u>coʼh</u> "Joe," <u>cuʼh</u> "Jew." (Bloomfield 1962, §1.16)

Fairly clearly, the invocation of such marginal evidence (the speech of individuals who do not really control the phonology of the language and the
pronunciation of a synchronically non-Menomini word) stretches the intuitive
notion of what phonology is about in order to maintain consistency.

A somewhat different response, and a real triumph of honesty in dealing
with such facts, is illustrated by Bernard Bloch. Discussing (in Bloch 1941) an
example from English that is logically just like Halle's, he notices exactly the
same point Halle makes: an apparently unitary rule must be broken in two as a
result of the requirements for a phonemic representation. But does he conclude
that (biunique) phonemes should be discarded? Not at all. Instead, he concludes
that science has saved us from a seductive but ultimately false generalization.
In essence, he denies the intuitively obvious analysis of the facts on the basis
of *a priori* theoretical considerations.

These reactions are among the more principled. In fact, when we look at the
examples that began to accumulate by the 1950s which suggested that phonemic representations had properties that led to incorrect or otherwise deficient
analyses, we see that linguists of the time found various ways to preserve their
principles in the face of the apparent facts. On an issue other than biuniqueness,
this can be illustrated from reactions to the famous example of *writer/rider*,
where the surface contrast is in the "wrong" place as illustrated in (4.9). For
many speakers, the pronunciations differ in terms of the length of the first vowel
and not in terms of the the medial stop, which is pronounced in the same way
(typically as a sort of "flap") in both words.

(4.9) [rajDɚ] "writer" *vs.* [raˑjDɚ] "rider" $\overset{?}{=}$ /rajtr/ *vs.* /rāˑjtr/ *or* /rajtr/
       vs. /rajdr/

One possible way to deal with such a situation is to force the theory to provide
the correct result. When the principles lead to absurdity, adapt the principles
so that they will yield what you know intuitively to be correct. An example of
this approach is provided by Harris' (1951) procedures of "rephonemicization,"
which allow the linguist to massage the analysis in a variety of ways so as to
arrive at a satisfying analysis even though the basic premises of the theory do
not naturally provide one.

An alternative is to follow the principles consistently, and if they lead to
absurdity, then deny the facts. With respect to the specific facts in (4.9), this is
illustrated by Householder's (1965, p. 29) conviction that "I can tell you from
experience that you will, if the words are in fact consistently distinguished,
invariably find one or more of several other differences [between the flaps of
writer and *rider*]." That is, even though all of the apparent evidence suggests

that the difference between w*riter* and *rider* (in the relevant dialect) is a matter of the quantity or quality of the stressed vowel, a sufficiently assiduous search for phonetic detail will uncover some basis for assigning the difference to the medial consonant (where it intuitively "belongs") and treating the patent vowel difference as allophonic.

The difficulties that emerged for the phonemic theory of this period follow directly from the fact that it was a theory of *E*-language. The biuniqueness condition (4.5) and the approach to language that motivated it forced the terms of the theory to limit themselves to descriptions of the external observables supposedly provided by phonetics. As a result, facts indicating that speakers' knowledge of a language is not limited in this way had to be dealt with in uncomfortable ways or not at all.

A phonological representation is, by its very nature, a characterization of the sound properties that distinguish linguistic objects for a speaker of a given language. In order to translate this notion into a description of external reality, however, phonemicists found it necessary to rebuild it on the basis of observable properties and operational tests, ideas that turn out to be quite problematic in practice and to lead to a host of difficulties that in fact have nothing important to do with phonology itself. As we will see in chapter 6, even the notion of a purely *E*-language approach to phonetic description turns out to be inadequate.

When we ask why Halle's argument should have been so earth-shaking, it is hard to say. Not only did it not involve a completely novel complex of facts, it is not even the case that it shows biunique phonemic analyses in general to lead to loss of generalization. This is a point that several authors have made, with respect to earlier theories such as that of Trubetzkoy (1939), one of the founders of the European variety of phonological theory to which generative phonology often traces its roots.[7]

Principled discussion in the 1940s and 1950s of facts that were embarrassing for phonemic theory did not in general consider, as Halle did, the possibility that the appropriate conclusion to be drawn was that the basic premises of structuralist phonology were misconceived. On the other hand, Halle's argument when it was presented in 1957/1959 was of a sort that had been offered in substance before; and in any event, it did not really suffice to prove its point in a fully general form. So why, then, did it have such major consequences, while other similar cases had little or no effect? It appears that the special force of Halle's argument came from the fact that it was embedded in a theory that was not limited to representations and the alphabets of elements that compose them:

---

[7] For discussion of alternatives to Halle's analysis within Trubetzkoy's framework – involving the notion of the "Archi-phoneme" – and also within current generative phonology, see Anderson 2000, from which the present section is derived.

[T]he effectiveness of Halle's argument . . . lay in the emphasis it put on the centrality of rules in a phonological description. Note that the entire argument rests on the observation that, in certain situations, a level meeting the conditions of bi-uniqueness requires some unitary regularity of the language (here, voicing assimilation) to be split up into two effectively unrelated rules. Now in a theory (such as American structuralist phonemics) in which only the representations of forms have "real" status, such an argument is nonsensical or at best irrelevant: the principles relating one representation to another (the rules) are simply parts of the definitions of individual elements of representations, and have no independent status whatsoever in the grammar. If they can be formulated in a simple and concise way, so much the better: but the notion that the elements of representations themselves should be chosen for the convenience of the rules was inconceivable.

The immediate consequence of Halle's discussion was a change in phonology in the direction of much more abstract representations than those permitted within a theory which concentrated on biunique phonemics. But it must be emphasized that this move was, in an important sense, an ancillary consequence of a more fundamental reorientation in phonological research: a shift from a concentration on the properties of phonological representations and their elements to a much greater stress on the rules of a grammar. Naturally, concern with questions of representations and their nature did not disappear overnight. Nonetheless, the recognition was dawning that rules as well had to be taken seriously as part of a grammar if language was to be examined as a complex cognitive system rather than an inventory of phonemes, morphemes, words, and constructions. Since the study of rules, their properties, and their organization into linguistic systems was virtually unexplored territory, this reorientation had a much more important effect on the nature of phonological research than the mere fact that generative underlying representations are more abstract than biunique phonemic ones. (Anderson 1985, pp. 321f.)

Halle's innovation, on this view, was the focus he put on the need to get the **rules** right in the statement of a language's phonology, and not simply to provide the right representations. These rules, as part of the content of a speaker's language organ, are intrinsically an aspect of *I*-language. So long as linguistic theory remained focused on the (*E*-language) issue of how to represent utterances in a principled alphabet, though, an argument based on the need to do justice to the rules could have no real force, since the content of the statements that relate phonology to phonetics had no independent external (*E*-language) status of the sort the utterances themselves have.

Ultimately, the shift of attention from ALPHABETS (inventories of basic representational elements) and representations based on them to RULES is significant because it reflects a more profound shift in the object of inquiry, from the study of the properties of observable linguistic events, the forms, to the study of the knowledge speakers have of their language that underlies their production and perception of such events. Rules are preeminently a characterization of speakers' knowledge, while the representations are in some sense primarily a characterization of the forms. The change is thus a shift from the study of language as an external, physical or social reality to the study of the structure and organization of an aspect of human cognition: from *E*-language to *I*-language.

Now during the heyday of American structuralism, it was pretty much out of bounds to study internalized knowledge: all there was to study was the observable external form. But by the 1950s the world was gradually coming to be more receptive to talk about minds, and so such a shift was at least logically possible. The link between rules and individual cognition is quite explicit, at least by the time of Chomsky and Halle's fundamental statement in *The Sound Pattern of English* (Chomsky and Halle 1968, pp. 3f):

The person who has acquired knowledge of a language has internalized a system of rules that determines sound–meaning connections for indefinitely many sentences . . . [W]e use the term "grammar" to refer both to the system of rules represented in the mind of the speaker-hearer . . . and to the theory that the linguist constructs as a hypothesis concerning the actual internalized grammar of the speakerhearer.

As late as 1965, when Fred Householder provided Chomsky and Halle with a debating platform for use in going through the bases of alternative approaches to phonology, it is clear that at least a significant fraction of the field did not (and perhaps could not) understand the notion that linguistics might have speakers' knowledge, rather than the properties of linguistic forms, as its proper object. Householder was certainly a very intelligent man, and an experienced linguist, but the very idea of linguistics as the study of an aspect of the mind was quite incomprehensible to him. In discussing the claim of Chomsky (1964) that "A grammar that aims for descriptive adequacy is concerned to give a correct account of the linguistic intuition of the native speaker," Householder (1965, p. 14) finds that "[o]nly . . . 'observational adequacy' is intelligible (at least to me) . . . it is sheer braggadocio to talk about descriptive adequacy, even if one knew how to discover what a 'correct account of the linguistic intuition of the native speaker' is."

By the mid to late 1960s, as new generations of students appeared whose training originated in the work of Chomsky, Halle, and their colleagues at Massachusetts Institute of Technology, the basic point about the central importance of rules – the need to get those right because they are really what the study of language is all about – came to be more generally appreciated. But recall that the persuasiveness of Halle's original argument rests crucially on one's willingness to take seriously this need to get the rules right. And in fact it took ten years or so after Halle's original presentation for this to become a generally accepted notion,[8] so it is clear that whatever was responsible for the rise of generative phonology, it probably was not simply the logic of Halle's conclusion about the obstructive role of phonemes in a descriptively adequate account of Russian voicing assimilation.

So what in fact **did** happen to change the direction of phonologizing in the early 1960s? A part of the responsibility undoubtedly should be laid to a

---

[8] See Anderson 2000 for a more detailed account of the relevant history.

principle that *"plus c'est la même chose, plus ça change."* That is, by the end of the 1950s, phonemic theory had increasingly become a settled discipline within which only quite minor adjustments seemed necessary (or possible). With little left to do, new generations of students inevitably looked for new challenges – and new approaches that would provide them. While the fundamentally distinct scientific premises of the new theory of generative grammar may have been apparent to its originators, students did not have to appreciate these differences to see that something quite new and different was going on, and that they could make real contributions to it.

It is important to understand the content of our creation myths, since they tell us something about the structure we actually give to our world. On the other hand, it is also important not to confuse them with explanations of how the world actually came to be the way we find it. In the end, Halle's argument about Russian voicing assimilation probably did not in itself persuade the linguists of the time to drop their externalist presumptions, their phonemes and their exclusive focus on representations, so as to become mentalists focusing on rules as the expression of internalized knowledge. But on the other hand, it is exactly in the context of that development that we still have to see the logical force of the original argument. We really only come to appreciate the sense of this important argument after the shift in point of view that it supposedly produced has been achieved.

It is not particularly satisfying to discover that a field can change its character fairly rapidly for reasons that are primarily pragmatic, and not purely principled. But on the other hand, this case is instructive, not just in its own right, but because it suggests that the same kind of influence may have been responsible, on a smaller scale, for a number of the changes we have seen since then (and probably many times before).

For example, phonological theory in the period immediately before and after the publication of Chomsky and Halle 1968 was intensely occupied with highly formal concerns, issues such as rule ordering and the role of formally defined notational conventions in producing an explanatorily adequate theory of grammar.[9] Within a rather short period in the late 1970s, these were almost completely abandoned in favor of the study of "auto-segmental representations" – a notion of the organization of phonological (and phonetic) representations in terms of the synchronization of properties with respect to the time-course of speaking. This considerable shift of attention did not come about because auto-segmentalists solved the earlier problems, however, or even showed that they were misconceived. Rather, it happened because auto-segmental work

---

[9] That is, a theory which has enough internal deductive structure to ensure that for any given set of empirical facts, exactly one grammar will be provided – and that grammar will be the "descriptively adequate" one, in the sense introduced by Chomsky above of providing a "correct account of the linguistic intuition of the native speaker."

developed an impressive array of fascinating results within a rather short time, especially in an area that had previously been rather intractable (the study of tone). Only much later was it shown that some classical chestnuts of earlier work, like the analysis of length, could really be **solved** in auto-segmental terms, in ways that had just not been available within the framework of standard segmental phonology (see for instance the discussion in Kenstowicz 1994, pp. 410ff. and references there).

In this chapter, we have considered the way in which the shift from a focus on *E*-language to speaker's knowledge or *I*-language went along with changes in linguists' views of the nature of phonological representation, and of the scope a description must have if it is to be adequate to its object. We have said little, as yet, about the form such a description should take. In the next chapter, we turn to those matters, where we will see that linguists' views of the nature of the field have changed again, as consequences of the need to focus on *I*-language have gradually been absorbed.

5   Describing linguistic knowledge

In the previous chapter, we traced the path of linguists' interests in sound structure as these evolved from an *E*-language-based focus on representations alone to an *I*-language approach. Over time, it has come to be appreciated that knowledge of language includes not only (representational) questions of what speakers of a language know about the sound properties of its words, etc., but also the characterization of what they know about overall regularities that transcend particular items (see Anderson 1985). In the domain of sound structure, the description of these regularities originated in important respects from the study of what had been previously thought of as "morphophonemics" (see section 4.2.3 above). It inherited from that work a descriptive framework going back to one of the oldest grammatical traditions about which we have evidence, that of ancient Indian grammarians such as Pāṇini (*c.* 500 BC). In those terms, regularities are formulated as a system of rules, each of which performs some limited, local modification of a representation. Collectively, and in the context of a theory of the way they interact with one another, these rules describe a mapping between phonological representation and overt phonetic form.

Until relatively recently, linguists assumed that the description of a speaker's knowledge of overall regularities, of the general principles that are not part of any individual word or other linguistic form, was essentially equivalent to such a system of rules. Around the early 1990s, however, a challenge arose to this position, in the form of proposals (associated with the framework of OPTIMALITY THEORY (OT)) claiming that the rule system could and should be replaced with a hierarchy of ranked, violable constraints on surface form. Descriptions in terms of rules and in terms of constraints are, on the face of it, rather different, but both have as their goal a description of the linguistic knowledge of a speaker – that is, of the language organ. We attempt below to give some of the flavor of the issues involved, and of the similarities and differences between the two approaches.

The discussion here is limited to phonological matters, but the consequences of these considerations are potentially much broader. In the concluding section, we return briefly to this matter.

5.1   Phonological knowledge as it appears in borrowing

In asking what a speaker of a language knows about its sound structure, most of the relevant evidence comes from a close study of the regularities that seem to characterize forms, their pronunciation and systematic relations among them within the language, under normal circumstances of use. Sometimes, however, this knowledge is put to use in other ways, whose study provides another source of evidence about what speakers know. In phonology, one example is the way words of one language are adapted when borrowed by another language. We consider here some of the conclusions we can draw from one such case, the way French words are adapted when borrowed into the West Atlantic language Fula.[1]

French and Fula have rather different inventories of sounds, as well as different structures within which those sounds appear. The sounds of standard French are given in figure 5.1.

Consonants

	labial	coronal		dorsal
		+anterior	−anterior	
stops	p/b	t/d		k/g
fricatives	f/v	s/z	ʃ/ʒ	
nasals	m	n	ɲ	
glides			ɥ/j	w
liquids		r/l		

Vowels [i, y, u, e, ø, o, ɛ, ə, œ, ɔ, a; ã, ɔ̃, œ̃, ɛ̃]

Figure 5.1   The sounds of French

These segmental units appear within syllables that may have zero, one or two consonants in their onset, possibly followed by a glide, preceding an oral or nasal vowel, followed optionally by one or two additional consonants as a coda. Monosyllabic words illustrating some of these various possibilities are in (5.1), where "V" represents the vowel of the syllable and "C" and "G" represent a consonant and a glide (or semi-vowel) respectively.

(5.1) V   *eau*   [o] "water"
       GV   *oui*   [wi] "yes"
       CV   *peaux*   [po] "skin"
       CGV   *moi*   [mwa] "me"

---

[1] Fula is a language spoken in various forms by some 12–15 million people across West Africa. In much of this region, the colonial language was French, and use of French in a variety of circumstances continues in many countries. The discussion here is based on the work of Carole Paradis and her colleagues (e.g., Paradis and LaCharité 1997); where dialect differences are relevant, the forms are those of a Futa Toro speaker.

CCṼ	*plein*	[plɛ̃] "full"
CCGV	*croix*	[krwa] "cross"
CCGVC	*truite*	[trɥit] "trout"
CVC	*lac*	[lak] "lake"
VCC	*ours*	[urs] "bear"
CVCC	*parc*	[park] "park"
CCGVCC	*croîotre*	[krwatr] "to grow"

These can be reduced to a formula for the structure of the French syllable, given as (5.2).

(5.2) FRENCH SYLLABLE STRUCTURES: (C(C))(G)V(C(C))

The sounds of Fula are rather different from those of French. These are given in figure 5.2.

Consonants

	labial	coronal		dorsal	laryngeal
		+anterior	−anterior		
stops	p/b	t/d	č/ǰ	k/g	
prenasal stops	ᵐb	ⁿd	ⁿǰ	ᵑg	
implosives	ɓ	ɗ	ʄ		
fricatives	f	s			h
nasals	m	n	ɲ	ŋ	
glides	w	j		(w)[2]	
liquids	r/l				

Vowels i, u, ɛ, ɔ, a (long and short); ɛ and ɔ have closed variants [e] and [o] in the vicinity of a high vowel or another raised mid vowel.

Figure 5.2   The sounds of Fula

The structure of syllables in Fula also differs from French. As summarized in (5.3), Fula allows at most a single consonant as a syllable onset, followed by either a short or a long vowel (but not a sequence of glide plus vowel or other diphthong), followed by at most a single consonant as an offset.

(5.3) FULA SYLLABLE STRUCTURES: (C)V(:)(C)

When French words are borrowed into Fula, their forms are generally changed so as to adapt to the possibilities offered by the language. For instance, Fula

[2] The segment [w] appears in both the labial and the dorsal columns, because it involves both lip and tongue body in its articulation. The duality has consequences for the way the segment behaves with respect to regularities of the language, as shown in Anderson 1976.

does not have the sound [ʒ] (similar to the consonant at the end of the English word *garage*), and when French words containing this sound are borrowed, it is replaced by [s] as in the examples in (5.4).

(5.4)

French		Fula	gloss
barrage	[baraʒ]	baras	dam
collège	[kɔlɛʒ]	kɔlɛ:s	school
journal	[ʒurnal]	su:rnal	newspaper

Similarly, Fula does not have the sound [v]. When French words with [v] are borrowed, this sound is replaced (unpredictably) with one of [w,b,f] as in (5.5).

(5.5)

French		Fula	gloss
avocat	[avɔka]	awɔka	lawyer
civil	[sivil]	siwil	civil
verre	[vɛr]	wɛ:r	glass
avion	[avjɔ̃]	abijɔn	airplane
livre	[livr]	li:ba:r	book
vinaigre	[vinɛgr]	binɛ:gara	vinegar
élève	[elɛv]	ɛlɛf	student
mouvement	[muvmã]	mufmaŋ	movement
télévision	[televizjɔ̃]	tɛlɛfisjɔŋ	television

Since Fula does not have nasal vowels, French words with those sounds are borrowed with a sequence of oral vowel followed by nasal consonant. The nasal consonant is articulated at the same point of articulation as a following consonant; or, if there is no following consonant, the velar nasal [ŋ] appears.

(5.6)

French		Fula	gloss
bandit	[bãdi]	banⁿdi	gangster
canton	[kãtɔ̃]	kantɔŋ	canton
marin	[marɛ̃]	marɛŋ	sailor
changer	[ʃãʒe]	sans-u-dɛ	(to) change
gendarme	[ʒãdarm]	sanⁿdarma	policeman
ventilateur	[vãtilatœr]	wantilatɔr	fan

French consonant clusters at the beginning of a syllable are broken up by a vowel in words borrowed into Fula. The quality of this vowel is the same as that of the following vowel; or, if the second member of the cluster is a glide ([w] or [j]), a similar vowel ([u] or [i], respectively) is inserted.

(5.7)

French		Fula	gloss
briquet	[brikɛ]	birikɛt	lighter
classe	[klas]	kala:s	class
drapeau	[drapo]	darapɔ	flag
boisson	[bwasɔ̃]	buwasoŋ	drink
coiffer	[kwafe]	kuwa:f-a:-dɛ	coif (one's hair)
lieutenant	[ljøt(ə)nã]	lijɛtinaŋ	lieutenant

A word-initial cluster of [s] plus consonant is avoided by the insertion of a preceding [i], as in Fula *istati* "statue," from French *statue* ([staty]).

Syllable-final clusters in French words are also broken up by inserting a vowel. This vowel appears either between the consonants of the cluster or following the entire cluster, depending on which consonant of the cluster is a liquid ([l] or [r]).

(5.8)

French		Fula	gloss
contre	[kɔ̃tr]	kɔntɔr	against
filtre	[filtr]	filtir	filter
mètre	[mɛtr]	mɛ:tɛr	meter
table	[tabl]	ta:bal	table
carde	[kard]	karda	card (comb)
force	[fɔrs]	fɔrsɔ	force
course	[kurs]	kursi	course

These diverse ways of coping with French sounds and sound combinations that do not occur in Fula may seem complex, but a little reflection will show that they are quite conservative: in each case, as much of the content and organization of the French word is preserved as possible, within the framework of Fula sound patterns.

5.2   Can rules express phonological knowledge?

What is crucial for our purposes is the fact that these various systematic patterns of adaptation provide clear evidence that Fula speakers know the sound pattern of their language quite well. Since this knowledge governs the way foreign words are borrowed, there is no serious doubt that it forms part of the *I*-language system of speakers. It therefore behooves us to characterize that knowledge in a way that can account for the role(s) it plays.

But if our description of the phonological knowledge of Fula speakers takes the form of a system of rules relating underlying phonological forms to surface phonetic forms, it is not at all obvious that that requirement will be satisfied. For instance, French [v] has to become [f], [b], or [w] in Fula, because there are no voiced fricatives in the language. The independently motivated phonology of Fula itself, however, would not contain any rule turning /v/ into something else. For one thing, phonological representations of Fula words do not contain /v/, and so there is no need for a rule to convert it into something else; and there is no reason to believe that any other rule of the language would have this effect. The same is true for most of the other adaptations we have seen above.

The conclusion from this observation is that a system of "morphophonemic" rules does not properly represent the character of *I*-language in the phonological domain. The regularities of sound structure seem to have a reality whether or not the language can be argued to contain rules that modify its own forms so as to make them conform.

In some instances, such rules may exist: in particular, the combination of independently motivated morphological material may give rise to configurations that are at variance with the language's notion of what is "well-formed." For instance, clusters of consonants that are not otherwise possible can be formed by affixation; and when that happens, a rule inserts a vowel to break up the ill-formed sequence, as in (5.9).

> (5.9) a. /ɗɔjj-/ "cough" + /n/ "causative" ⟶ ɗɔjj-i-n "make cough"
> b. /ɓutt/ "(be) fat" + -ɗ-"inchoative" + -t "repetitive" ⟶ ɓutt-i-ɗ-i-t "become fat again !"

Clearly, the existence of rules such as that inserting [i] in the forms in (5.9) is motivated by (the need to conform as closely as possible to) the sound pattern of the language. We cannot, however, say that a speaker's knowledge of that pattern is comprehensively expressed by the set of rules that correct violations of it, since the range and existence of such rules is a largely adventitious side-effect of the range of morphological and other processes in the language that might give rise to otherwise ill-formed configurations.

Similar reservations about the adequacy of the rule-based form of description can be motivated in other ways, in a variety of languages. English, for example, is subject to a number of restrictions on consonant sequences, including those in (5.10).

> (5.10) a. Sequences of obstruent consonants must have the same value for voicing (e.g., the sequences *ts* or *zd* can occur within a word, but *tz* or *sd* cannot).[3]
> b. Clusters of "similar" coronal consonants within a single syllable (e.g., two sibilants, such as *šs*, or two coronal stops, such as *dd*) are prohibited.

---

[3] A very small number of exceptions to this generalization – words like *Aztec* – exist within morphologically simple forms, but there are no exceptions in word plus affix combinations. We disregard the exceptions here. In fact, they lose their exceptional character within a more detailed analysis than we have space to develop here.

These limitations on clusters can be related to the surface form taken by several productive morphological elements in English. For example, if we disregard "irregular" plurals such as those of (5.11a), the regular formation of the plural forms of nouns displays three phonetically distinct shapes, as in (5.11b).

(5.11) a. ox/oxen, radius/radii, woman/women, etc.
b. cats ([s]), dogs ([z]), horses ([əz])

It is natural to assume (see Anderson 1974, ch. 4, among many other discussions) that the English regular plural has a unitary basic shape /-z/. When suffixed to words ending in a voiceless obstruent, however, such as *cat*, or to a word ending in a sibilant such as *horse*, the resulting combination runs afoul of the restrictions in (5.10). To remedy this, the rules of (5.12) are generally assumed to form part of speakers' knowledge of English.

(5.12) EPENTHESIS: Insert the vowel [ə] between two adjacent sibilants in the same word.
DEVOICING: A voiced obstruent becomes voiceless after a voiceless obstruent.

These rules can be seen to yield the correct phonetic forms by way of the derivations in (5.13).

(5.13)

underlying:	/kæt#z/	dɔg#z/	/hɔrs#z/
epenthesis:	—	—	/hɔrs#əz
devoicing:	kæt#s	—	—
surface:	[kʰæts]	[dɔgz]	[hɔɹsəz]

These same rules can be seen to govern variation in shape in several other elements (as we have already noted above, in chapter 2), especially if the epenthesis rule in (5.12) is generalized so as to apply between two stops as well as between two sibilants.

(5.14) 3RD SG PRESENT OF VERBS: eat/eats, ride/rides, raise/raises
POSSESSIVES: Rick's [book], Fred's [book], Alice's [book]
CONTRACTIONS: Rick's, Fred's, Alice's [leaving now, left already]
PAST TENSE OF VERBS: pick/picked ([t]), raise/raised ([d]), wait/waited ([əd])

In these and many other cases, we can formulate a set of regularities of the language, and we see that the rules in our description serve to "enforce" those regularities when configurations arise that violate them.

But there are clearly problems in the claim that the knowledge involved is exhaustively characterized by these rules. For example, consider English *leak/leaked* vs. *drug/drugged*, as in the last set of forms in (5.14). We assume the basic form of the regular past ending is /-d/, as suggested by vowel-final verbs such as *delay/delayed*. The devoicing of the past tense ending in *picked*, *leaked*, etc. is clearly due to the regularity that English final clusters of obstruents must agree in voicing, as enforced by the devoicing rule in (5.12).

Now consider *leave/left, lose/lost*, and other similar verbs. These involve an alternative form of the past ending, one which we also find in *mean/meant*, *deal/dealt*, etc., and which we might represent as basic /-t/. But then in *left* (from /lijv#t/), *lost* (from /luwz#t/), we seem to have quite a different rule applying from the devoicing rule in (5.12): one that devoices the end of the **stem**, not the suffix consonant. Despite this difference in effect, though, the two clearly both enforce the same generalization: that of (5.10a). Somehow the grammar containing these rules is not actually capturing this overall regularity. This is a variation on the same kind of insufficiency we saw before in the ability of a language's rule system to account for patterns of adaptation in borrowing.

5.3   Constraint-based theories of phonological knowledge

Observations like those of the preceding subsection led phonologists to consider the possibility that a set of constraints on phonological form, rather than a set of rules converting one representation into another, would better represent the basic knowledge speakers have about sound structure. And in the early 1990s, this led to the development of a concrete theory known as Optimality Theory whose first full programmatic formulation was that of Prince and Smolensky 1993.

5.3.1   *Constraints* vs. *rules: patterns* vs. *effects*

A basic rationale for OT might be formulated as the claim that cross-linguistically valid regularities of phonological form are to be found in **output** configurations – that is, in the shapes of linguistic forms as they are pronounced – rather than in input (lexical) configurations or in the details of rules mapping one onto the other. The importance in particular of "cross-linguistically valid regularities" is of course that these are the most likely to derive from aspects of Universal Grammar (UG), and thus to be in some sense definitional of the language organ.

The approach followed by generative phonologists up to that point had been to proceed from an interpretation of the phonemic principle (4.4) to construct a system of underlying phonological forms. These have two related desiderata, as in (5.15).

>   (5.15) a. Abstract away from surface differences that are due to reg-
>   ularities of the language; and

      b. To the extent possible (i.e., except for cases of SUPPLETION), attribute the same phonological shape to a given linguistic element (word, morpheme) in all environments in which it appears.

The rules of the grammar then, exist (a) to state the regularities of sound structure in the language; and (b) to relate the abstract phonological forms of linguistic elements to their phonetic realizations in various contexts. The idea pursued by Prince and Smolensky and which has driven OT is that this approach is ultimately unproductive in satisfying the main goal of phonological theory: to provide a substantive definition of what constitutes a possible phonological system for a natural language. While it is obviously important to provide accurate descriptions of individual languages, the task of understanding UG requires us to provide a more general account of the content and organization of *I*-language.

Traditional generative phonology thinks of a grammar as a collection of rules, each of the form $A \rightarrow B/C\_\_ D$. Such a rule looks for input sequences of the form CAD and performs an operation of the form $A \rightarrow B$ ("A takes on property B") on them. But "[f]or this format to be worth pursuing, there must be an interesting theory which defines the class of possible predicates CAD (Structural Descriptions) and another theory which defines the class of possible operations (Structural Changes)." These theories have proven to be "loose and uninformative," and thus we should conclude that "the locus of explanatory action is elsewhere" (Prince and Smolensky 1993, p. 3).

The point here is that the rules themselves do not really seem to be very useful in arriving at generalizations about universal properties of phonological form. We can try to establish generalizations about what sorts of things rules can do, but all such theories seem to allow for the formulation of lots of things we "know" to be impossible. This suggests we should look elsewhere for explanations.

Furthermore, theories of rules have been limited to theories of **individual** rules. Even the best theory of the Structural Descriptions and Structural Changes of particular rules misses the overall nature of phonologies: that **sets** of rules have a coherence that cannot be seen in the individual rules themselves. As illustrated by the two rules for the pronunciation of consonant clusters in inflectional forms proposed above, devoicing can affect either the stem-final consonant or the ending itself depending on which form the ending has. These two rules are in principle quite independent of one another, but together clearly express a single regularity.

Now in the 1970s and 1980s there were a variety of proposals made to the effect that the basis of phonological rules was to be sought in their effects: that is, that there were various regularities of surface pattern that provided the

motivation for the differences between underlying and surface form that are expressed by individual rules. A language does not have an epenthesis rule because it likes epenthesis, but rather because as a result of this rule, it will avoid ill-formed clusters (as in English inflection, discussed above, or the rule of Spanish that avoids initial /sC/ by inserting an initial [e] in words like *España*). A language has assimilation rules not because of the way they work, but because as a result, all clusters will be homogeneous in some property.

Often it seems to be the case that a language has multiple rules, each of which by itself is only part of the picture, but which **taken together** have the effect that some pattern exists on the surface. Thus English assimilates voice progressively in inflection (/kæt + z/→[kʰæts]), but regressively in some other cases of inflection (*lose/lost*), as we have seen just above. The two formally quite different rules have one surface effect, a matter which we will take up in more detail below.

These "conspiracies" (a term introduced by Kisseberth 1970a, 1970b) seem to have a natural formulation as ways to satisfy some constraint on surface representations. Suppose we take this effect as the locus of explanation in phonology. Then we can attempt to develop a theory of how representational well-formedness determines the assignment of phonological structure: a theory of **constraints** and their interaction, as opposed to a theory of **rules**.

The nature of these constraints has been the subject of intense investigation in recent years. An important basic notion is that constraints are instantiations of universal aspects of sound structure – hence, they are the stuff of UG. Constraints address representational well-formedness (rather than the mechanics of converting one representation into another), and it is presumed that most of the content of this notion is due to the structure of the human language faculty, rather than to arbitrary interlinguistic variation.

A conceptually important difference between OT and related theories lies in the claim that constraints can be operative in a language even when they are not necessarily true (or satisfied) in every form. The members of a given set of constraints are typically in conflict, and not mutually consistent: satisfying one constraint may require the violation of another. The way a particular language resolves these conflicts is what characterizes its particular phonology as opposed to those of other languages.

We can make this concrete by suggesting that there are two fundamentally conflicting demands in sound structure:

> (5.16) MARKEDNESS: the tendency for phonetic forms to be pronounced in a simple, natural way (as determined in part by the nature of speech articulation, acoustics, and audition, and in part perhaps by more abstract cognitive factors – all aspects of the human language faculty).

> FAITHFULNESS: the tendency for properties that distinguish lexical elements from one another within a given language to be preserved in the phonetic realizations of those elements.

The notion of markedness certainly has a long series of antecedents. Attempts to incorporate it into generative phonology, however, had taken a form that effectively allowed the "unmarked" status of an element or configuration to figure in a grammar only to the extent it was true or completely satisfied. **Relative** markedness basically has no expression in systems such as that of Chomsky and Halle 1968: rules could be evaluated as "cheaper" to the extent they contributed to a universally unmarked set of possibilities, but this was essentially an all-or-nothing effect. OT, in contrast, allows for the possibility that a markedness effect can contribute to the sound pattern of a language even though some (perhaps even most) of the language's actual forms violate it.

Consider these issues with respect to an example. In terms of the places of articulation found in the world's languages, labials, dentals, and velars are all quite generally found, but labialized velars (e.g., $[k^w]$) are much less common. We could formalize this as a (markedness) constraint to the effect that labialized velars are prohibited:[4]

(5.17) $*k^w$

In a language like English, where there are no labialized velars, the effects of this constraint are absolute. We could express this by saying that "even if the lexical representation of an English word had a lexical labialized velar, it would be pronounced without velarization." Such a markedness constraint inevitably comes into conflict with the basic faithfulness property, expressed by a constraint to the effect that lexical values must be preserved. A language like English can then be described by saying that in such a language, the markedness constraint (5.17) takes precedence over (or "dominates") the faithfulness constraint (5.18).[5]

(5.18) IdentIO (Round)

In the Native American language Kwakw'ala (often called "Kwakiutl"), however, labialized velar stops are found in words like $[bəg^w anəm]$ "man" or $[k^w ag'uɬ]$ "Kwakiutl." We can account for this by saying that the same two

---

[4] The content of this statement is that a surface representation is disfavored to the extent it contains instances of rounded velar consonants.

[5] The content of this constraint is that a representation is disfavored to the extent underlying or input values of the property [Round] are not preserved in the output.

constraints apply to both languages, but that in Kwakw'ala faithfulness (5.18) dominates markedness (5.17) in this instance.

Actually, the facts about labialized velars are a bit more complicated than that. It is true that they are not common; but under some circumstances, they are actually preferred. In particular, when an adjacent vowel is round, the velar often is too. We might say, in fact, that it is dis-preferred to have a sequence of a vowel plus a consonant that **differ** in rounding. An approximation to this constraint might be (5.19):

(5.19) *[+syll,+round][−syll,−round]

Consider a language like Menomini (Bloomfield 1962), in which *k* following a round vowel is itself round (as in [okʷi:ˀsan] "his son"), but following a non-round vowel is not round (as in [meki:ˀs] "my son"). We could describe this by saying that in general, the markedness of labialized velars prevents their occurrence; but in the specific circumstance where they follow a rounded vowel, these occur to the exclusion of unrounded ones. We get this result by saying that the contextual markedness condition dominates the context-free one, and both dominate faithfulness.

Another possibility is illustrated by Kwakw'ala. In this language, we have both plain and labialized velars (*k'asa* "beat soft" *vs. xʷasa* "dance"). After the vowel [u], however, only [kʷ] appears. The element /-kas/ "really" appears without rounding in [gæɬa-kas] "really long" as opposed to rounded (after [u], a round vowel) in [əwu-kʷas] "really big." Here faithfulness dominates context-free markedness, but both are dominated by contextual markedness.

In English, Menomini, and Kwakw'ala, we have languages whose sound patterns differ in systematic ways with respect to the appearance of labialized velar consonants. Those differences in sound pattern are not easily expressed as differences in the content of the system of morphophonemic rules applicable to each language. We can, however, characterize the ways in which the knowledge of English, Menomini, and Kwakw'ala speakers differ in terms of the relative dominance of members of essentially the same system of constraints. The system of UG provides us with the relevant constraints, at least in some form. What differentiates one language from another (and thus, what individual speakers know about their language in the domain in question) is the way these constraints relate to one another. In other words, a specific language organ is described not in terms of a collection of rules, but rather in terms of the relative ranking of the constraints made available by UG.

Note that unrounding [u] would be another way for a language to avoid violating (5.19): to the extent this solution is not chosen, it must be prevented by an even higher ranking constraint (IdentIO(V)), requiring that the input features of vowels be preserved. If this outranks (5.17), then the violation of (5.19) will have to be repaired by rounding both (rather than unrounding both).

Constraints thus come in several flavors:

(5.20) MARKEDNESS constraints (the tendency for phonetic forms to be pronounced in a simple, natural way):

CONTEXT-FREE markedness constraints describe overall preferences for certain feature configurations over others within a single segment; and

CONTEXT-SENSITIVE markedness constraints describe preferences for certain feature configurations over others in combinations of segments.

FAITHFULNESS constraints (the tendency for properties that distinguish lexical elements from one another to be preserved in their phonetic realizations):

MaxIO constraints require that every element in the input have a correspondent in the output;

DepIO constraints require that every element in the output be the correspondent of some element in the input; and

IdentIO constraints require particular properties of output segments to be identical to those of the corresponding input segments.

We have as yet said nothing about just how a system of constraints (such as (5.17), (5.18), etc.) allows us to compute a surface form corresponding to a given input. In essence, this process consists in a comparison among all of the formally **possible** surface forms that might correspond to that input (a set of "candidates"), resulting in the selection of that candidate that best conforms to the system of ranked constraints. The grammar thus consists of two components, called GEN and EVAL. GEN operates on input representations to produce a set of candidates; these, in turn, are assessed by EVAL. The candidate with the highest degree of harmony (i.e., the one which violates highly ranked constraints to the smallest possible degree) is (by definition) **optimal**, and is thus chosen as the output.

When we investigate languages from this perspective, what we find is that the same set of constraints can describe a number of different systems, depending on their relation to one another. In any given language, the constraints are organized in a hierarchy, and then contribute to the determination of correct surface forms via principles of "harmony" that include those of (5.21).

(5.21) OPTIMALITY: An output is "optimal" when it incurs the smallest possible violation of a language-specific hierarchy of constraints.

STRICT DOMINATION: Any candidate which violates the highest-ranking constraint is eliminated, regardless of its evaluation by lower-ranking constraints, if candidates are available which do not violate the higher-ranking constraint.

How does GEN do its work? This is a matter of some dispute among practitioners of OT. One view is that GEN produces, for any input, the full range of possible well-formed expressions over the alphabet of phonological representations. This requires EVAL to be able to screen out vast masses of irrelevant candidates with particular focus on the few that are legitimate possibilities. While it has never really been shown how this is computationally possible with finite resources, something along these lines is commonly assumed in theoretical discussion.

Another possibility (one implicit in the notion that GEN "operates on input representations") is that GEN is smart enough to know, for a given input form, what forms could conceivably be at least possible output candidates. But that in turn requires that GEN incorporate some intelligence, mechanisms that sound suspiciously like a set of phonological rules. And of course if the same old set of rules turns out to be necessary as a (covert) part of the grammar, it is not obvious how different this system would be from that of classical generative phonology. These issues remain to be clarified, especially if OT is to be taken seriously as providing a model of how speakers bring what they know to bear on what they do, but at least the conceptual outlines of such a constraint-based theory are relatively clear.

Of course, apart from the constraint system provided by UG (whose internal ranking characterizes an individual language), a speaker's knowledge also includes information about individual linguistic forms: the LEXICON, a set of representations including phonological, morphological, syntactic, and semantic information. We will discuss the organization and content of the lexicon in chapter 7, but one strictly phonological issue in the structure of the lexicon forms an important aspect of OT. The goal of this theory is to characterize the phonological knowledge a speaker has of his or her language entirely in terms of a system of (ranked) constraints applying to **output** forms. It follows, therefore, that no constraints of this sort should crucially hold at the level of **input** forms. This notion (known as the hypothesis of the RICHNESS OF THE BASE) has quite interesting consequences for the form of our description.

For instance, in English, a language with no labiovelars, the absence of such segments follows entirely from the constraint ranking in (5.22).

(5.22) $*k^w \gg$ ("dominates") IdentIO(Round)

We do not need to say explicitly, in addition, that there are no underlying labiovelars: as we noted above, it would make no difference if such segments occured in inputs, since they would never survive into output forms. This suggests a general condition of LEXICON OPTIMIZATION: where a number of distinct inputs would all yield the same output, pick (as the lexical representation) the one whose output incurs the fewest violations. What that means in practice is that the input which is closest in its properties to the output excludes any of the others from the lexicon.

5.3.2   *An example: voice assimilation*

Throughout this discussion, we have presented as a basic motivation for constraint-based account of phonological knowledge the argument that the elemental units of that knowledge are sound **patterns** in language, not the specifics of the relation between underlying and surface forms. For a concrete example, let us return to the facts about English consonant clusters in inflected forms that we have already touched on several times above, and where the unity of formally distinct effects is perhaps clearer.

It is well known that clusters of obstruents differing in voicing are quite rare, and that most languages have ways of dealing with these when they would be expected to arise. Let us assume that voicing is specified by a property (or distinctive feature) ([Voice]) in obstruents. Voiced obstruents like [b,d,g,z] etc. will possess this property, while voiceless obstruents like [p,t,k,s] etc. will lack it. Then we can say that there is a general markedness constraint requiring clusters of obstruents to be uniform with respect to this feature.

> (5.23) AGREE(VOICE): If one member of a sequence of adjacent obstruent consonants has the property [Voice], every other member of the sequence should have that property as well.

This constraint, a part of UG, dis-prefers structures like those of (5.24), since in each case the property [Voice] is associated with only one member of the sequence to the exclusion of the other.

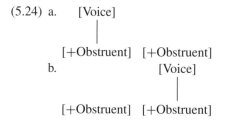

Let us see how we might invoke this apparatus to derive a familiar pattern of phonological variation (known as VOICING ASSIMILATION) found in English inflections such as the plural or past tense, as discussed above. For input /kæt + z/, /lajk + d/ we should prefer the output forms [kæts] and [lajkt]. The fact that the lexical value of voicing is not generally preserved here suggests that a faithfulness constraint must be being violated. Let us call it IdentIO(Laryngeal).

> (5.25) IDENTIO(LARYNGEAL): Consonants should be faithful to input laryngeal specifications.[6]

A constraint like (5.25) actually stands for two subcases: on the one hand, input specifications should be preserved; and on the other, output specifications should reflect input. Jointly, these two aspects of (5.25) have the effect that input specifications of [Voice] should correspond exactly with those in the output. Clearly, since input specifications of [Voice] are *not* in fact always reflected faithfully in the output (e.g., the final voiceless segments of *cats, liked* correspond to segments that are voiced in the input), some other constraint must outrank (5.25) in the English constraint hierarchy. The relevant constraint which has this effect, of course, is Agree(Voice), (5.23).

But that does not determine a unique output form. Corresponding to inputs such as /lajk+d/, for example, both [laikt] and [lajgd] would satisfy (5.23), each incurring a single violation of (5.25) and otherwise the same. What aspect of the grammar of English, then, results in the fact that we prefer [laikt] over [lajgd] as the realization of /lajk+d/?

The answer to this is probably to be sought in more general considerations in UG. In the languages of the world, voiceless obstruents are much commoner than voiced ones, and while it is quite rare for a language to make use of voiced obstruents without matching voiceless ones, the opposite is not at all unusual. This suggests that overall, the property of voicing is dis-favored in obstruents, a fact that we could represent as (5.26).[7]

> (5.26) *VOICED OBSTRUENT: avoid voiced obstruents.

Since English obviously has voiced obstruents, this constraint must be outranked by others, such as (5.25) which requires the preservation of input values if possible. But in comparing [lajgd] and [lajkt] as possible outputs corresponding to /lajk+d/, we saw that each incurs exactly one violation of (5.25) – the stem-final consonant in one case, and the affix in the other, but each with the same overall value, a violation forced by the higher ranked (5.23). Since these

---

[6] Including, among others, [Voice], a (possibly complex) property characterizing the activity of the vocal folds.

[7] This is presumably related to the articulatory fact that airflow conditions during the production of obstruent consonants are such as to inhibit vocal fold vibration, and some additional gesture is necessary if voicing is to be maintained under these circumstances. Vowels and sonorant consonants, in contrast, are articulated in such a way that vocal fold vibration is a normally expected concomitant, and indeed some additional gesture is necessary in these sounds if voicing is to be inhibited. Here part of the content of UG can be grounded in – though probably not mechanically deduced from – properties of the speech production system.

two are thus tied with respect to their faithfulness to the input, the choice between them falls to (5.26), which tells us to prefer [lajkt] over [lajgd] since the
former contains no voiced obstruents.

If we were to formulate this effect in terms of a rule, it would look something
like (5.27).

(5.27) [+Obstruent] → [−Voice]/[−Voice]+ ___

Such a rule would quite adequately express the fact that underlyingly voiced
affixes are devoiced when added to a stem ending in a voiceless segment. We
can show, however, that it would not suffice to describe the knowledge about
voicing assimilation which English speakers bring to bear in determining the
forms of their language.

As we mentioned above, English regular verbs form their past tense (and
past participle) by adding a uniform ending whose basic shape appears to be
/-d/ (although it also appears as [t] or [ɨd] when required by the shape of
the stem). Among the classes of irregular verbs, however, we find a number
(e.g., *learn/learnt*, *burn/burnt*, *mean/meant*, *deal/dealt*) which involve a similar
but distinct ending whose basic shape appears to be /-t/. This ending shows a
different pattern of assimilation from the "regular" /-d/: instead of altering
the shape of the ending to assure compliance with a requirement that voicing
be uniform in clusters, in this case it is the stem that changes, in verbs like
leave/left, *lose/lost*. Notice this direction of assimilation is also what we need
for derived forms such as *describe/descriptive* (cf. *retain/retentive* for the form
of the ending), *absorb/absorption*, *five/fifth*, etc.

The rule in (5.27) is not adequate to describe this situation, although we can
easily formulate a rule that is.

(5.28) [+Obstruent]→[−Voice]/ ___ +[−Voice]

(5.28) is clearly a different rule from (5.27), formally quite distinct despite the
fact that both are basically ways of enforcing a single regularity. Such duplication, where we need multiple formally unrelated rules to express a single
generalization, seems quite unsatisfactory if our aim is to describe the knowledge a speaker of English has about the language.

But now notice that this redundancy or duplication can be eliminated if we
base our account on constraints rather than rules. To deal with outputs such as
[left] corresponding to input /lijv+t/,[8] we do not in fact have to add anything
to the constraint system as we have elaborated it above. As we saw, this system
will prefer outputs with uniform voicing to ones that are strictly faithful to their

---

[8] In accounting for these verbs, we must obviously also include an explanation of the alternation
in the stem vowel ([ij]↔[ɛ]), but that issue is orthogonal to the one involving voicing which we
are discussing here.

input values; it will also prefer **de**voicing (either regressively, right-to-left, or progressively, from left-to-right) and not voicing as the optimal way to achieve this, given the general markedness constraint (5.26).

In fact, the same constraint system also describes yet another way of enforcing the same overall regularity. In Swedish, we find bidirectional spreading of voicelessness, as in the examples of (5.29).

(5.29) a. hög "high"; högtid [hœkti:d] "festival"
   b. viga "to marry"; vigsel [viksəl] "marriage"
   c. dag "day"; tisdag [tista] "Tuesday"
   d. skog "forest"; skogsbrand [skoksprand] "forest fire"
   e. äga "to own"; ägde [ægdə] "owned"

In this case, the assimilation may go in either direction, but we see that whichever segment is altered, the result is to prefer a (uniformly) voiceless cluster to a (uniformly) voiced one. We derive this result again by saying that agreement in voicing (5.23) outranks laryngeal faithfulness (5.25), while (5.26) tells us that (other things being equal) it is better to devoice both than to voice both as a way of ensuring homogeneity of voicing in a cluster.

The constraint-based approach thus allows us to describe three rather different patterns of voicing assimilation (progressive, regressive, or bi-directional) as instances of the application of the same underlying knowledge, knowledge which we can attribute in substance to constraints provided by UG (and ranked within the particular grammars of individual languages). Notice further that even if English did not have any actual alternations in voicing at all, this knowledge could still play a role in the adaptation of borrowed words: we predict that where such words are borrowed into a language with such a constraint hierarchy, clusters that differed in voicing in the original language should be replaced by uniformly voiceless ones as a part of the nativizing process.

5.4   The extension of constraint-based description

In the sections above, we have explored some reasons to believe that a system of constraints implemented in the general way proposed by OT may provide a more accurate description of the content of a speaker's linguistic knowledge than a system of rules that specify the mechanics of converting input to output forms. The replacement of rule-based theories by constraint-based ones is certainly not complete (even in phonology), and many other details of the architecture of the language faculty remain to be explored in order fully to understand the nature and role of such constraints. Nonetheless, it is fair to say that the bulk of research in phonology at present is being conducted within this general framework; and furthermore, that the replacement of rules by constraints has followed from a greater appreciation of the demands of a theory that purports to offer a description of speakers' knowledge, not just of the forms speakers employ.

It is natural, then, to ask whether this result is confined to the study of phonology. In fact, recent years have seen a number of efforts to apply the analytic methods of OT as practiced by phonologists directly to syntactic problems: see papers in Barbosa et al. 1998 and Dekkers, van der Leeuw, and van de Weijer 2000, among others. But regardless of whether the specifics of theoretical apparatus transfer literally from one domain of linguistic structure to another in this way, there is a more general trend of which OT is a part, which is certainly relevant to areas other than phonology.

Just as generative phonology was originally focused on the notion of rules as they describe the specifics of how one representation is related to another, so generative syntax originally concentrated on rules (transformations) describing specific constructions in specific languages (the passive in English, causatives in Turkish, etc.). In the 1980s, however, talk of such specific rules came to be replaced by talk of more general principles and parameters of grammatical structure, notions not specific to any particular construction but rather characteristic of syntactic form overall.

Along lines like those pursued in chapter 3, exploration of the properties of Binding Theory, Case Theory, etc. led to greater explanatory depth in syntactic theory as a general account of the human language capacity. Most current work in syntax seeks general properties of linguistic structure from which the specifics of individual constructions follow, rather than the other way around. Though much of the concrete theoretical apparatus of the resulting theories differs signficantly from that of OT, the two can be seen as intellectually similar responses to the challenge of characterizing the human language faculty, and both are opposed to earlier *E*-language-oriented attempts to characterize directly the external phenomena of language.

There is no obvious reason to believe *a priori* that sound structure and syntactic structure are governed by exactly the same sorts of principle, but it is relatively clear by now that knowledge of language is better characterized by systems of principles, parameters, and constraints than by construction-specific (or configuration-specific) rules of transformation. In that sense, OT is simply one instance of a broad class of theories that have arisen as a result of the shift from *E*-language to *I*-language as the object of inquiry in linguistics.

6   Phonetics and the *I*-linguistics of speech

Our knowledge of a language is determined by the language organ we develop
as a child on the basis of exposure to utterances in that language, and includes
what we know about contrasts, relations, and regularities within the set of
linguistic objects. Obviously, though, it also includes what we know about the
objects themselves. The structure of that knowledge is described by a theory of
representations of the various sorts of object that form parts of our language.
Seeing the foundation of these representations as an aspect of our knowledge
(an *I*-language point of view) has somewhat different consequences from seeing
them as based purely on externally determined properties, part of *E*-language.
There may be much formal similarity between the actual representations that
result from these two differing perspectives, but the conceptual content is still
quite distinct.

   In this chapter, we address the nature of the representations that seem to
be most obviously and irreducibly based on observable, physically measurable
properties: phonetic representations. We argue that when phonetics is seen as
genuinely part of language, rather than a subpart of physics or physiology,
the resulting conception of "phonetic representation" (while still recognizable)
differs in a number of important ways from what is often taught (or more
accurately, assumed) in standard textbooks.

6.1   Representations and the study of sound structure

Most linguists assume, as we argued in chapter 4, that the principles of sound
structure in a given language mediate between a PHONOLOGICAL REPRE-
SENTATION that indicates all and only the properties of an utterance in terms
of which it contrasts with other utterances in that language, and a PHONETIC
REPRESENTATION that provides a language-independent characterization of
its pronunciation.

   The nature of phonological representations has occasioned a great deal of
discussion and a vast literature. Some of the most radical proposals within OT
have argued that representations of any sort other than surface phonetic ones
are redundant, but the linguistic significance of **some** sort of phonological

representation for linguistic items and utterances has generally not been in doubt. Many readers may be surprised to learn, though, that the status of phonetic representations themselves in linguistic theory has not always been quite so clear.

To be sure, there has often been some question about the extent to which phonetics is properly part of linguistics at all. If this kind of investigation of the articulatory, acoustic, and perceptual properties of concrete acts of speaking is essentially a matter of more and more precise measurement of physiological, physical, and neurological events, it seems to have little to do with linguistic structure *per se*, especially if we construe the latter as primarily cognitive in its basis. Phonetics would have the status of an auxiliary discipline – overlapping with, but properly included within, physics, physiology, and the neurophysiology of the auditory system – that simply described the externally observable properties of the abstract objects with which linguistics is concerned. As Trubetzkoy (1939) put it, "phonetics is to phonology as numismatics is to economics."

We argued in section 4.1 of chapter 4 that the kind of representation generally called "phonetic" is a significant abstraction from the raw physical facts. Nonetheless, few would question the premise that acts of speaking do have some observable properties, and that the business of phonetics is to settle the facts of the matter as to what these are, as far as the language system is concerned. Relevant results of such observations can then be presented in some appropriate form, and who could question that such a "phonetic representation" describes the things phonologists have to account for?

Leonard Bloomfield, in contrast, argued that there is no linguistic significance to phonetic representations (cf. Anderson 1985, pp. 262ff.). His point was that insofar as these deviate in any way from a full physical record of the speech event (such as might be provided by a tape recording, supplemented with cineradiographic and other records of the articulatory details), they represent an arbitrary selection of some properties to the exclusion of others and cannot be said to be based on theoretically interesting principles. As such, they serve more as a record of biographical details about the phonetician (what properties he or she has learned to record and what to omit) than as a theoretically significant record of a linguistic event. Somewhat similar objections have been revived (on different grounds) in an updated form by Pierrehumbert (1990).

Bloomfield's objection is a very serious one, and one to which linguists have not always devoted enough attention – if only to be clear in their own minds about why they reject it. Why, after all, **should** we attribute to some particular subset of the physical properties of utterances the status of a fundamental characterization of language? The essential nature of language is that of a system of tacit knowledge as represented by the language organ, an aspect of the organization of the mind and the brain. In that light, the selection of some external properties of linguistic utterances as systematic to the potential exclusion of others requires at least some justification.

In this chapter, we will defend the claim that there is a significant notion of "phonetic representation," one that is distinct both from a phonological representation and from a complete physical record of a speech event. This is part of our *I*-language system, and thus it merits the attention of linguists. The kind of representation to which we wish to attribute this status, however, is at least at first blush rather different from the sort of thing linguists typically teach their students to produce in a beginning phonetics course.[1]

Let us begin by asking about the factors that contribute to determining the physical properties of an act of speaking. A talker, let us assume, has something to say and initiates a sequence of gestures of the vocal organs which affect the surrounding air and are thus conveyed, perhaps, to the ears of potential listeners. Any particular speech event of this sort can be regarded as resulting from the interaction of a number of logically distinguishable aspects of the system that implements that intention:

a. The talker's intention to produce a specific utterance (i.e., the properties that characterize the particular linguistic items – words, etc. – that compose it);

b. The fact that the utterance is produced by a speaker of a particular language (i.e., patterns of neuromuscular activity characteristic of the sound pattern of the particular language being spoken);

c. The fact that the utterance is a speech event (i.e., that its production invokes neurophysiological and motor control mechanisms that are brought into play in speech in general, as opposed, for instance, to the control regimes that are relevant to swallowing, breathing, etc.); and

d. The physical and physiological properties of the speech apparatus, the acoustics of such systems, etc.

Since we can decompose speech into its articulatory, acoustic, and perceptual aspects, we might envision (at least) three separate representations, one in each domain. Alternatively, we might seek a single representation that unifies all of these sorts of property in terms of one set of independent variables. Without going into the matter in more detail here, we should make it clear that we are quite persuaded by the arguments of advocates of a Motor Theory of Speech Perception (see Liberman and Mattingly 1985, Mattingly and Studdert-Kennedy 1991 for discussion) to the effect that the primes of phonetic specification lie in the articulatory domain, and not (directly) in the acoustics or in perception. This decision goes against much work in automated speech recognition, for example, which tends to be resolutely grounded in a "bottom up" approach to recovering linguistic structure on the basis of the structure of the acoustic signal alone.

Even granting the apparent difficulties that arise in the effort to specify an architecture for perception that implements a motor theory, we think that the

---

[1] Another recent proposal involving a notable expansion of the notion of "phonetics" beyond the traditional is that of Kingston and Diehl 1994. The analyses and proposals of these authors are in some ways similar to the point of view presented below, though they differ in other technical and substantive respects that we do not go into here.

problem for those who would model perception is to find a way to implement such an architecture. The tendency in much technologically oriented work on speech perception and recognition is rather to retreat into the notion that somehow the invariants must be out there in the acoustics if we will only keep looking, because perception would be more straightforward if they were. This is simply another example, we feel, of the drunk who persists in looking for his keys under the streetlight because the light is best there. We could refine our view of just what a Motor Theory is, but for present purposes that is not really necessary. Our reason for bringing the matter up at all is simply to be explicit about the assumption that it is articulatory activity that we wish to characterize.

6.2   A linguistic basis for phonetic representation

Returning to the problem of justifying the attribution of linguistic significance to a phonetic representation, suppose that we could arrive at a representation of the speech event that met the conditions in (6.1), one which characterizes all and only those aspects of it that are under the control of the linguistic system (as opposed to those that are language-independent consequences of other factors). We submit that this could then be said to be genuinely linguistic, rather than accidental and external, and to furnish an appropriate notion of "phonetic representation" for inclusion in linguistic theory. Such a representation would clearly describe speech events from the point of view of the language organ.

> (6.1) A phonetic representation characterizes all **and only** those aspects of a speech event that are under linguistic control, in the sense of being managed by the system of linguistic knowledge that the talker brings to bear in performance.

That means that we certainly want to include indications of properties that distinguish utterances from one another within a language. We also want to include indications of non-contrastive properties of an utterance that are under the control of the specific linguistic system within which it is produced – an indication, for example, of whether the occlusion of utterance-final stop consonants, or of stops in clusters, is released or not (recall the discussion of unreleased stops in Korean in chapter 4). This property seems not to be used contrastively in any language. That is, there is apparently no language in which, for instance, [tap] and [tap˹] might be distinct words. Despite this, it is still the case that languages can differ from one another in terms of it (cf. Anderson 1974), which means it is manipulated by the systems of individual languages.

On the other hand, we want to omit many things which we could, in principle, measure and record. By and large, for example, we can neglect the activity of the epiglottis in speech – not because it is completely inactive (it is not) or because its position has no auditory consequences (also untrue), but rather because, as far as we can tell, epiglottal activity is not something we manipulate *per se*, a dimension which is controlled differently in some languages than in others.

This is perhaps a controversial thing to assert, but let us be clear on why: some phoneticians have reported that in some languages epiglottal activity **is** manipulated for linguistic purposes. But in the absence of clear support for such claims, we would want to exclude the epiglottis from phonetic representation in spite of its physiological and acoustic importance unless and until it can be shown that epiglottal activity is independent of other articulatory events, events which correspond to dimensions of irreducible linguistic importance.

What we seek, then, is a representation of all **and only** those aspects of a speech event that are under linguistic control, in the sense of being managed by the language organ: the system of linguistic knowledge that the talker brings to bear in performance. Another way to put this is to say that we want to characterize everything in the talker's linguistic intention, as opposed to aspects of the event that follow from the physical, neurophysiological, and other extra-linguistic properties of the apparatus that is employed in talking. Providing such a representation would respond substantively to Bloomfield's objection, by grounding the properties attributed to it in their role in the cognitive system that constitutes our linguistic knowledge. It would certainly be distinct from a full physical record of the speech event, since it would explicitly abandon the attempt to describe everything that is true of this event in favor of a description of everything that is linguistically determined about it.

One particular view of language in which the place of such a representation is clear is that of Chomsky's recent MINIMALIST analyses (Chomsky 1995). In that approach, there are only three significant kinds of representation. Postponing one of these, the nature of lexical items, for chapter 7, the two key representations are the interfaces to sound, on the one hand (PHONOLOGICAL FORM, or PF), and to meaning, on the other (LOGICAL FORM, or LF). The first of these is intended to characterize all and only the aspects of an utterance's form that are managed by the linguistic computational system, and it must be (exactly) adequate to serve as an interface to the language-independent systems of articulation and perception. PF in these terms is exactly the representation we seek.

6.2.1 *Measurable but "unintended" effects*

It is, however, far from simple to construct such a representation. Disentangling the properties of the speech event that are due to linguistically formed intention from those that are due to the physics and physiology of the vocal apparatus, or to general motor control mechanisms that are operative in speech, is far from trivial. Particular properties certainly do not come labeled as to their source, and there are few generally applicable diagnostics in this area that can be applied directly to observations of physical events of speaking.

Pitch microcontours   We have said that the range of distinctions that separate linguistic elements from one another in a given language is a matter that should be resolved in the phonological representations characteristic of that language. However, the way in which particular phonological distinctions are realized phonetically is also a part of the phonology of the language. Phonetic representation must therefore provide us with a range of descriptive properties adequate to differentiate languages from one another in these terms. As a special case, we must also be able to discriminate between, on the one hand, phonetic differences that correspond to different ways in which the vocal apparatus is controlled in distinct languages, and on the other, differences that correspond to the fact that some dimension which is specifically controlled in one language is left to the unguided control of the speech apparatus itself in another. In the first case, the grammars of the two languages in question differ in the way they specify the phonetic realization of the property in question. In the second case, the grammars differ in that one provides specific instructions for this realization, while the other leaves it unspecified, under the control of the speech apparatus.

Presystematically, here is the sort of distinction we wish to make: particular phonetic phenomena may be represented in the grammars of some languages but not others. Consider the fact that in general, vowels following syllable-initial voiced obstruents begin at a somewhat lower pitch than their target value, and rise to that value over a relatively short period of time. Following voiceless obstruents, vowels begin on a slightly elevated pitch and fall to their target values.[2] The basis of this effect might be the following: in order to overcome the fact that the aerodynamic conditions for vocal fold vibration are less than optimal when an obstruent constriction exists in the supra-laryngeal vocal tract, a compensatory internal adjustment of vocal fold elasticity or stiffness is a common accompaniment of voiced obstruents. Correspondingly, voiceless consonants are often accompanied by a stiffening that ensures the lack of vibration during their closure period. We do not need to understand the precise basis of the effect, however, to be sure that there is one: the testimony of the world's languages is quite adequate on that score.

It is not hard to show that the vocal fold stiffness adjustments accompanying consonants are logically and phonologically independent of the dimensions of specification of vowel pitch. Nonetheless, such gestures associated with consonants have consequences for the rate of vibration, when, at some point shortly after the release of the occlusion, it occurs. This is a matter of the physics and physiology of the structures brought into play in speech production. On the other hand, we might well see the actual time course of the pitch contour between the consonant release and the following vowel as characteristic of the baseline control regime of the vocal organs as this applies in speech. The stiffness or

---

[2] See Lehiste 1970 for a review of the classic literature establishing these facts.

slackness of the folds disappears with some particular latency and elasticity, and it seems reasonable to attribute the particular contour of pitch that results in a language like, say, English to general mechanisms of speech motor control, not to the grammar of English.

In general, we find essentially the same pitch contours in post-consonantal vowels across many languages. In some languages, however, such as Yoruba and Thai, where tone is linguistically significant, we find that the pitch contours of post-obstruent vowels are much sharper. We might suggest that in these cases, the language specifies an independent compensatory gesture that has the effect of bringing the vowel to its intended (and significant) pitch value more rapidly than in English. Compare the contours in figure 6.1. In English, as represented by the graphs in figure 6.1a, we see that there is still a difference in pitch in the vowel following a voiced consonant (e.g., [b]) as opposed to a voiceless one ([p]) more than 100 millseconds after the stop release. In Yoruba, on the other hand, there are three contrastive tonal levels. We see in figure 6.1b that a vowel following voiced *vs.* voiceless consonants displays the same (high, mid, or low) pitch value within roughly 50 milliseconds after the stop release (slightly longer in the case of a high tone, but still sooner than in the non-tonal language English). Hombert (1976, p. 44) argues "that there is a tendency in tone languages (which does not exist in non-tonal languages) to actively minimize the intrinsic effect of prevocalic consonants."

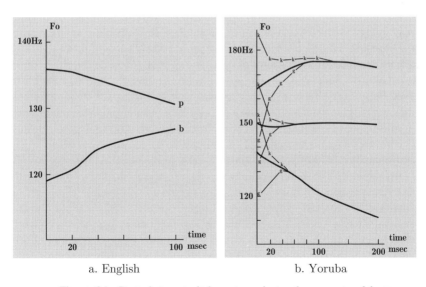

a. English   b. Yoruba

Figure 6.1 Post-obstruent pitch contours in tonal *vs.* non-tonal languages (from Hombert 1976)

We suggest that Yoruba phonetic representations thus should specify the presence of this property, which we can distinguish from matters of general physics and physiology (including the fact that the vowel pitch deviates at all from its target initially) as well as from matters of general speech motor control (such as the time course of pitch change that occurs, other things being equal). What matters is that in Yoruba, other things are not in fact equal. Phonetic representations in this language have to indicate a language-specific compensatory gesture that is part of its system, part of what the language organ of Yoruba speakers determines. Phonetic representations in English, on the other hand, ought not to say anything about the post-consonantal pitch contours: the contours that we can observe physically are a matter simply of the vocal organs, not of the language organ.

Vowel length effects   In the case of English post-consonantal pitch contours, we can see how we want the answer to turn out, but in the general case there are many questions whose answers are not self-evident about what does and does not belong in a phonetic representation. A first problem, noted in Fowler 1990, results from the fact that not all of what is systematically carried out in speaking is due to linguistic intention. We might hope that any pattern which occurs in some languages but not in others must surely be under linguistic control, and thus suitable for inclusion in our phonetic representation. This is, in fact, a very standard form of argument in the linguistic phonetic literature.

Fowler (1990) points out, though, that this apparently obvious diagnostic may fail us. She notes that one of the most often cited phonetic regularities in the literature is the fact that, in most languages, vowels are shortened by ca. 20–30 milliseconds before voiceless obstruents as opposed to the duration they show in other environments. In a few languages (cf. Anderson 1981 and references cited there) this effect is suppressed, and vowels display the same durations regardless of the nature of a following consonant. In English, on the other hand, the difference in length between vowels before voiced and voiceless consonants is considerably exaggerated, and (in contrast to the case in most others) well above the threshold of perceptibility.

In languages like Saudi Arabic where the expected contextual vowel length difference is apparently suppressed, it is necessary to indicate this as a fact about the linguistically governed intentions of speakers. This is so despite the fact that the result is no difference at all in vowel duration regardless of context. And, of course, it is also necessary to indicate in a representation of English utterances that vowels are considerably longer in voiced environments than would otherwise be expected. But what about the languages that simply show the expected small differences? Fowler argues that in fact these differences arise as a mechanical consequence of the different dynamics of closure gestures in voiceless as opposed to voiced obstruents: the talker "intends" the same thing with respect to the vowels in both cases, but the implementation of that intention leads to an unintended consequence as a result of the coordination of the vowel and consonant gestures. In this case, then, the phonetic representations of vowels ought to be uniform, despite the fact that acoustically the vowel portions of utterances differ quite systematically by 20–30 milliseconds, depending on the environment. Paradoxically, vowels of equal duration may thus come to be specified differently (the Saudi Arabic case) while ones of different duration will not differ in their phonetic representation where the differences are not intended *per se*. On the other hand, where the durational differences considerably exceed what can be attributed to the mechanical effects (as in the English case), we must again indicate the presence of some specific phonetic intention responsible for this.

Laryngeal specifications in Korean   The differences we observe across languages in the duration of vowels suggest the possibility that some of the observable properties of phonetic elements may result not from our active articulatory intentions, governed by the language organ as properties of a particular language, but rather as consequences of the necessities associated with other articulations. This notion has been discussed in the phonetic literature by Patricia Keating (1988) as a matter of UNDERSPECIFICATION.

Keating begins from the premise that parameters of a segment that are predictable should be unspecified in a phonological representation indicating contrasts, i.e. that **phonological** representations, at least, are underspecified in the sense that not all segments have specified values for all possible properties. This is thus a version of the "incompletely specified" view of phonological representations discussed earlier in section 4.2.1. She goes further, however, in suggesting that under some circumstances such underspecification may persist into the phonetics. It may be the case, that is, that the values assumed along some dimension during some period of an utterance result not from any linguistically governed property of that part of the utterance, but simply from interpolation, as a result of the exigencies of getting from where you were to where you have to be. The spirit of such phonetic underspecification is entirely consistent with the view being developed here.

For example, Korean (cf. Kagaya 1971) contains three series of stops: "voiceless aspirated" stops, followed by a puff of breath as in for the [pʰ] in English *pit*, as opposed to "unaspirated" ones like the [p] of *spit*; and "voiceless glottalized" ones, associated with a simultaneous constriction of the vocal folds. Two of these, the voiceless aspirated and the voiceless glottalized, clearly have characteristic properties: in the one case, a spread glottis gesture (which is what produces the puff of breath) and in the other, a constriction of the glottis. The remaining series, however, is what interests us.

These sounds are described as voiceless unaspirated initially, but voiced intervocalically. Measurement of the time course of opening of the glottis (Kagaya 1971) during their production suggests that the voicelessness in initial position is actually a gradual transition from the open glottis position associated with the neutral position for speech in that environment to the approximated position required for the following vowel; and that intervocalic voicing represents merely the maintenance of the position appropriate to the consonant's surroundings. The "unaspirated" stops, then, have no value of their own for the position of the larynx: they are phonetically underspecified for this property.

Vowel quality differences   Identifying real instances of phonetic underspecification may in fact be quite difficult, since the mere fact of apparent predictability does not suffice to distinguish our linguistic intentions from the baseline behavior of the systems employed in speech. Sometimes properties that may seem thoroughly predictable nonetheless look as if they have linguistically enforced target values. Boyce, Krakow, and Bell-Berti (1991) argue that for some speakers, at least, there is apparently an articulatory target for the property of lip rounding, under the control of the language organ even for segments like [t] where this would seem to be particularly irrelevant and thus most likely to follow from interpolation.

Fowler (1990) suggests that in some cases, what appears to be a gestural target may in fact follow from the assumption that the speech apparatus tends to return to the neutral position for speech insofar as it is otherwise unoccupied, and some apparent deviations from straightforward interpolation may result from this effect rather than from an active articulatory target. Sorting out these hypotheses is not easy. Nonetheless, even though many apparently predictable properties may turn out to be actively determined after all, it seems eminently plausible that a number of examples will remain in which some articulatory phenomenon results not from phonetically controlled gestural intentions but rather as consequences of interpolation between other, surrounding gestures.

An interesting case in which we can ask how much of what is articulated is actually a part of the (*I*-language) grammar concerns the vowel systems of languages with very few contrasting segments.

Anderson (1978) takes up a proposal originally due to Aert Kuipers (1960) concerning the Circassian languages, particularly Kabardian. This language has a full range of vowel types (including [i,e,a,o,u], etc.), and a listener with no knowledge of the language would notice nothing unusual about its vowels. On closer inspection, however, it turns out that in Kabardian, the actual quality of a vowel in any given position in a word is almost completely predictable from its surroundings. That is, both [i]s and [u]s occur in Kabardian words, for example, but [i] only occurs where adjacent to certain consonants, and [u] only adjacent to some others. The two are in COMPLEMENTARY DISTRIBUTION in that there are no environments in which we might potentially find either sound, with the difference between them serving as the basis of a contrast between words. Furthermore, the consonants surrounding [i] *vs.* [u] are not arbitrary: those favoring [u] are ones whose articulation is similar to that of an [u] in involving lip rounding and a relatively retracted tongue position, while those favoring [i] involve no rounding, but a relatively high, front tongue body position. Similar observations can be made for the environments in which the other phonetic vowels are found.

These facts suggest that in Kabardian, the wide phonetic variety of vowels corresponds to little or no difference in linguistic intention: essentially, the vowels consist of a vocalic transition from the position of a preceding consonant to that of a following one. In any given environment, there are in general only two possibly distinct qualities that can occur, which we can differentiate by saying that the transition is made with or without an accompanying deflection of the tongue body downward. The presence or absence of this deflection is thus the only way in which the articulation of one vowel differs from that of another *per se.*

This kind of analysis was examined more deeply by John Choi (1992). Choi explored a variety of possibilities quite closely, and examined articulatory and acoustic data on languages of this type. One such language which he analyzed in detail is Marshallese. Choi concluded that the front–back dimension in the realization of Marshallese vowels does not correspond to anything that is under independent linguistic control: no gesture of fronting or backing intervenes in the relatively smooth transition from preceding to following tongue body position as determined by the surrounding consonants, although tongue height is independently controlled. This state of affairs is thus intermediate between the almost completely underspecified vowels of Kabardian and a fully determined system.

When is a "schwa" not a [ə]? Even in less "exotic" languages, we may find support for the conclusion that certain vowels are phonetically underspecified despite the fact that they are pronounced in a particular way. In particular, reduced vowels (e.g., those of unstressed syllables in English, where there are many fewer possible vowel qualities than in stressed syllables) may have some surprises in store for us as far as their phonetic content is concerned. Browman and Goldstein (1992c) examined the production of schwa (the vowel in the first syllable of *tomato*) in English, with the expectation that this would prove to have no distinct articulatory target associated with it. In fact, the acoustic character of the vowels we transcribe as [ə] varies considerably as a function of the vowels in surrounding syllables (and to some extent, of adjacent consonants). English schwa is generally the result of a principle of reduction which neutralizes other differences in vowel quality under given conditions, especially absence of stress: compare the final syllables of *relate*, *compare*, *precede*, where there is a stress, with the corresponding syllables in *relative*, *comparable*, *precedence*, where that stress does not appear. Since the thing that seems to distinguish schwa from the other vowels of English is precisely its **lack** of potentially contrastive properties, it might be logical to expect it to have few or no positive properties of its own.

Nonetheless, Browman and Goldstein found evidence that schwas produced by English speakers in certain environments do indeed have a target associated with them: [ə] in /pVpəpVp/ (e.g., [pipəpip]) has an articulatory target in the middle of the English vowel space (Browman and Goldstein 1992c), a sort of average of all of the other vowels, but they observe a distinct gesture deflecting the tongue body toward this position in the transition from a preceding vowel's articulation to that of a following one. The [ə] target frequently has little or no direct acoustic consequence (beyond what we would expect of a smooth, targetless transition), but it is apparently present nonetheless in the speaker's intention.

Interestingly, though, a later study (Browman and Goldstein 1992b) showed that while schwas in syllables within lexical items display this kind of articulatory target, schwas that appear epenthetically before the productive inflectional endings of the language may well be targetless after all. Thus, in "If Nita'd even KNOWN . . ." the underlined schwa shows a distinct lowering of the tongue dorsum, but in "It's needed even NOW . . ." there is little or no such lowering. This suggests that the "schwas" in such endings, though often acoustically indistinguishable from other schwas, nonetheless correspond not to the speaker's intention to produce a specific vowel, but rather to a dynamic effect in articulation whereby two similar gestures are sequenced in time so as to separate them, resulting in a brief interval whose only relevant property is the duration of the gestural offset. *Nita'd* thus contains two real, phonetic vowels, while *needed* contains only one, plus an additional vocalic interval that arises as a consequence of the need to separate the two *d*s.

In all of these cases, we have portions of the speech event that bear properties which we could perfectly well measure, and record, and which may correspond closely to properties that are clearly linguistic in other cases; but for which a case can be made that in **these** instances, they correspond to nothing specific in the speaker's intention. There is thus a clear difference in the extent to which the same *E*-language facts correspond to something present in the *I*-language of a given speaker, depending on the language. In a principled phonetic representation of the sort we are interested in here, then, we ought to omit them in the case where they are not in fact governed by the language organs of speakers of the relevant languages; but it does not appear that we can always determine that fact directly from examination of the physical facts alone.

6.2.2   *Intended effects hidden from observation*

We must, furthermore, cope with the fact that not all of what we intend in speech is actually realized physically (articulatorily and/or acoustically). Lindblom's "H&H" theory (Lindblom 1990), for example, suggests that the phonetic characterization of phonetic elements might be in terms of a "hyper-articulated" form whose actual implementation within a larger context may be (indeed, generally is) incompletely achieved by virtue of other properties of the context.

This notion is further supported by Johnson, Flemming, and Wright (1993), who provide evidence that listeners identify vowels in terms of extreme, hyper-articulated targets rather than by their actual values. When asked to select the simple vowel that best corresponds to a vowel in a word in running speech, that is, they choose a "pure" quality rather than one closer to the actual physical signal they have just heard. Here we have a variant of the traditional notion of "undershooting the articulatory target," the point being that there is good reason to believe that the talker's actual phonetic intention, as well as the listener's interpretation of the event, is characterized by an ideal target and not by its undershot (or "hypo-articulated") realization.

The most direct sort of argument for this general conclusion is provided by facts of casual speech cited by Browman and Goldstein (1990b). They observed that in relatively casual pronunciations of sequences such as *must be, ground pressure*, "phonetically" [mʌsbi], [graʊmprɛšɚ], there is apparent "loss" of the segments [t] and [d]. X-ray microbeam studies, however, reveal that an alveolar stop closure is actually made in each of these cases. It has no acoustic consequences, though, since it is (more or less) completely concealed by its overlap with the labial closure of the following [b] or [p]. The presence of the stop in the speaker's *I*-language representation is confirmed by the articulatory data, even though this has no reflex in the actual signal, and thus would not be present in a traditional (*E*-language) phonetic representation.

In many forms of English, final stop consonants are lost in certain environments in fluent speech: thus, *mist* may be pronounced as [mɪs]. It is natural to ask whether the same sort of gestural "hiding" is responsible for this. The phenomenon of variable final stop deletion in English is clearly very complex and related to a number of conditions.[3] In some instances, such as the loss of final stops in morphologically simple ("monomorphemic") forms before pause (e.g., the pronunciation of *mist* just cited), it is clear that gestural reduction rather than hiding must be at work, since there is no other gesture in the environment which could be said to overlap with the final [t] so as to obscure it. We must conclude that for such speakers, the reduction of the [t] in this case must be due to an *I*-language principle of phonetic realization.

---

[3] Guy (1991a, 1991b) provides a summary of what is known about this variation, and Kiparsky (1993) suggests an account in terms of OT of the range of systems that have been found.

Potentially, there is further empirical evidence to be found for Browman and Goldstein's proposal: the gestural overlap account suggests that varying degrees of overlap ought to be found in a wide enough sample of speech, while the traditional (deletion) story is only up to describing variable probabilities for a categorical process deleting (or retaining) the stop. These considerations should not obscure the point of the example for our purposes, however: in at least some instances a gesture is actively intended, and indeed accomplished, despite the fact that other conditions interact with it so as to deprive it of any audible effect.

Such a gesture is obviously part of our intention, and surely appears in the instructions to the vocal apparatus (i.e., in PF, the *I*-language phonetic representation), despite the fact that it is quite undetectable in the acoustic event. Obviously, then, such a phonetic representation is not at all a neutral observation language for speech, simply reflecting physically measurable properties of the sounds produced. Instead it is a rather abstract and theoretical articulation of our understanding of what is orderly and coherent about speech events from the point of view of the dimensions controlled by the system of language, the language organ.

6.2.3   Discreteness of phonetic dimensions

Let us return to the issue of whether phonetic transcription is in fact a coherent notion that ought to play a role in linguistic theory. A recent argument that it is not is due to Pierrehumbert (1990), whose objections are based on the fact that traditional phonetic transcriptions are discrete and categorial (e.g. symbols of the INTERNATIONAL PHONETIC ALPHABET, or IPA), but there are several ways in which this fails to reflect linguistic reality:

a. effacement of segments in reduction (and epenthesis, such as the oral stop in nasal+fricative clusters) is a matter of "less and less" (or "more and more"), not "something *vs.* nothing";

b. language-specific variation may involve continuous detail, so there is no (finite) list of possible sounds;

c. gradient (but systematic) phenomena such as intonation and laryngeal lenition (Pierrehumbert and Talkin 1992) require attention to hierarchical organization, not just fine transcription;

d. phonetic details, as opposed to (categorical) phonological contrasts, are out of awareness, and thus not "cognitive."

There is some cogency to these complaints about phonetic representations of the sort phoneticians teach beginning students to produce, but their force is to show that this needs to be revised, not abandoned. We adopt here the gestural perspective of Articulatory Phonology (Browman and Goldstein 1990a, 1990b, 1992a, and elsewhere), on which the properties we specify correspond to dynamic **gestures** of the vocal organs, aspects of what a speaker intends to do in speaking (as opposed to frameworks based on describing static articulatory configurations or targets). Recall from chapter 4 that the representation of speech as a sequence of discrete, static segments is after all a theoretical idealization, warranted essentially by the insight it can bring to the study of sound in language. To the extent that that picture actually interferes with a coherent view of the relation between *I*-language structure and the implementation of speech, it needs to be replaced with a view that is more appropriate to its subject matter.

The gestural view provides us with a language for describing some of these phenomena, and for responding to the substance of the objections raised by Pierrehumbert. Browman and Goldstein's model is not the only one that might serve for this purpose: the "C/D" model proposed by Fujimura (1994), for instance, has somewhat similar goals but interestingly different dynamic properties. This diversity suggests that there are quite genuine empirical issues involved in the determination of the properties of an appropriate phonetic representation, but that these issues are independent of the logical basis of phonetic representation as a characterization of the talker's intentions. This is surely a desirable result (if not a very surprising one).

In responding to Pierrehumbert's points, important advantages derive from the fact that the gestural representations of Browman and Goldstein do not have the exclusively categorial and segmentalized character of traditional transcriptions. Instead, gestures have magnitudes and temporal extent which are (at least in part) subject to specification and manipulation by the principles of individual linguistic systems. The representational vocabulary of *I*-language, on this account, thus includes some aspects of speech dynamics, as is apparently required, and not simply the description of a sequence of static configurations. Furthermore, the overall organizing principles of gestural synchronization and sequencing, and the description of the time course involved in the transition between distinct gestures, are also (at least in principle) parameterizable as a property of particular linguistic systems, thus determined as a property of individual language organs. This sort of specification of the overall system of gestural realization in a given language can be understood as something like a formalization (in part) of the traditional impressionistic notion of the "base of articulation" of the language (including statements like "French is spoken in the front of the mouth," etc.).

6.2.4   Timing effects

On the basis of what we have seen, let us assume that the language organ deals with phonetic specifications in terms of intended gestures, rather than (as in much traditional terminology) semi-snapshots of ideal articulatory configurations or an acoustically based parameterization of speech events. An important component of gestural representations is the fact that they bring a non-discrete notion of time into consideration, in ways that traditional phonetic representations based on sequences of individual independent phonetic segments do not. Once non-discrete phenomena based on the detailed time course of speech are taken into account, the problems of isolating those dimensions of control that are under the control of linguistic intention (that is, that are part of *I*-language) and of identifying the range of specifiable variation along those dimensions becomes even more difficult. It must be stressed that phonologists – the people most concerned about language-particular characterization – have no serious descriptive language for low-level temporal dynamics, let alone an articulated theory of the independent variables in this domain.

In fact, phonologists have generally had little to say about the details of speech timing. Phoneticians know a lot about the time course of speech events, but phonologists have until quite recently worked hard to develop models in which there is literally no place for the details of time course: phonological elements are points in time that can succeed one another but that do not have duration, magnitude, elasticity, and so on. A widespread (but completely unsubstantiated) assumption among phonologists is that it is precisely in this domain that we can attribute everything we observe to the (language-independent) mechanics of speech articulation.

But of course the increased information content of non-discrete gestural representations potentially comes at a high price: it provides us with **too much** freedom in its raw form. In order to isolate the linguistically significant degrees of freedom in the domain of the time course of speech, we must separate the dimensions of rhythm and timing that are under the control of the language organ from the background dynamic properties of the articulatory system.

It seems clear that there are **some** important language-particular components to the determination of speech rhythm and timing: that is, there are properties of this sort that differentiate languages from one another, as anyone can testify who has vaguely heard a conversation across a crowded room and recognized immediately that the speakers involved must be, say, Dutch, though without actually picking up a single word. See Beckman, Edwards, and Fletcher (1992) for some discussion. And if these factors have a language-particular component, they must be reflected in phonetic representations of the sort we seek. But until we have phonological models that take time course seriously, we have quite literally no principled way to talk about what might be language-particular about speech dynamics. Such models are in fact beginning to emerge,[4] but the problem has not, perhaps, received the attention it deserves from phonologists.

---

[4] See Byrd and Saltzman 1998 and Byrd et al. 2000 for one approach to a phonological model of speech dynamics.

And of course, until we know what aspects of speech organization are subject to language-particular determination, we do not know what we need to have a principled theory of in order to describe this aspect of the language organ.

Introduction of an appropriate specification of rhythmic and temporal effects into the description of the aspects of speech that fall under linguistic control is thus an important refinement of the range of problems to which phonologists should attend. We have assumed above that the form this might take is simply a specification of appropriate aspects of the time course of particular gestures in speech, but there is another aspect to the problem. Not only can the implementation of particular gestures over time fall under linguistic control, but independent of this, their synchronization and relative organization can provide yet another dimension of possible variability. Browman and Goldstein and their colleagues (Browman and Goldstein 1998, Browman et al. 1998) develop this point in suggesting that otherwise comparable gestures in English and Tashlhiyt Berber, for example, differ in their "bonding" or relative synchronization more than in their individual component timings. These ways of describing timing relations need further refinement and application to a variety of language types.

6.3   Speech microprosody: a research program

A greater understanding of the ways in which languages can differ in their overall patterns of speech rhythm and timing requires much more study of speech microprosody: the low-level dynamics of pitch, intensity, and a variety of measures of the temporal control of articulation within and below the level of syllables. The problem in this investigation is to hold physical and phonetic factors (roughly) constant, while varying control of the prosodic system (in a rather general sense of "prosody") within an individual language.

One possibility which can be exploited is that of comparing ordinary native speakers of (e.g.) English with speakers who have a good command of the language, but a "foreign accent." A plausible hypothesis is that prosody is the hardest thing to learn, partly because it cannot be taught (since we do not know how to articulate our knowledge of it) and partly because in general we are not even aware of it. As we will note below in chapter 9, prosody is apparently controlled by the language organ at a very early stage of the language acquisition process – even before the appearance of the first words in the child's production. A similar point is argued at length by Locke 1993. Although this is surely not all of the story, one large component of a "foreign accent" is likely to be prosodic anomaly. On the other hand, these speakers are still perfectly normal with respect to the basic phonetic mechanisms underlying articulation; and so we can assume that ways in which they deviate from the patterns evidenced by ordinary native speakers will reveal differences in the cognitive system controlling the dynamics of articulation, and thus aspects of the dimensionality of that system.

But there are several other populations of interest where we can hope to find anomalies *vis à vis* normal prosody. One of these is a class of clinically brain damaged patients who display what is called Acquired Foreign Accent Disorder.[5] These are people who (sometimes only for a relatively short period) during recovery from cerebral insult (strokes and other sources of brain damage) are perceived to have acquired an accent – typically that of a language to which they have never been exposed. A notable example from the literature (Monrad-Kröhn 1947) is a Norwegian woman during the Second World War who was perceived to have a German accent following head trauma (sustained, ironically, in a German bombing attack), and who was subsequently ostracized in her village on this account, when in fact she had never had any exposure to spoken German. Some rather similar symptoms can occasionally be induced by electrical stimulation of areas of the cortex in epileptic patients undergoing exploratory investigation of anatomical brain function prior to surgery intended to relieve intractable seizures.

Examination of the phonetic details of the speech of such patients suggests that in general, whatever they are doing, it bears little or no specific resemblance to the speech of genuine foreign accented (normal) speakers. Furthermore, attempts to characterize what these patients are doing wrong in terms of segmental articulations seem to fail (or at least to be quite insufficient). Their similarity to foreign accented normal speakers lies in the fact that while they get (most of) the segmental phonology right, their prosody seems to be disordered.

Our hypothesis here is that the cognitive deficit underlying "acquired" foreign accents is – or at least often involves – impaired control of rhythm and timing, the prosodic organization of the native language. When prosody sounds wrong, but the speech is still basically segmentally correct and intelligible, other speakers perceive this as a "foreign accent." This is thus a circumstance in which the language organ's control of speech prosody is disrupted, and comparison of these patients with normal speakers provides another potential basis for exploring the properties of the system itself.

Studying both natural and acquired foreign accents in comparison to the prosody of normal speech gives us two somewhat different windows on the question of what aspects of prosodic organization are part of the linguistic system, such that control of them could be lost (or fail to have been correctly

---

[5] Some references on this topic include Graff-Radford et al. 1986, Blumstein et al. 1987, Kurowski, Blumstein, and Alexander 1996, and Carbary, Patterson, and Snyder 2000. The interpretation of this disorder as one of a prosodic, rather than segmental, nature, as suggested below, has come to be fairly widely accepted, though details vary considerably among both patients and researchers. A particularly useful review with respect to this issue is provided by Berthier et al. 1991.

acquired). There is also another kind of population that would be of interest: subjects in which a disorder exists that affects the system of articulation in general, rather than the cognitive systems that provide the instructions for control of articulation. The reason to look at this as well is to disentangle systematicities that are, as it were, "post-PF" (i.e., implementational matters external to the *I*-language organization of speech) from those that represent dimensions of variation in a cognitively significant phonetic representation.

At least two such populations are potentially available for study, both involving subcortical damage that results in speech disorders. In cerebellar lesion patients with ataxic dysarthria, we find a perceived speech rhythm impairment, without (in general) corresponding impairment to higher level language functions. Somewhat similar symptoms are displayed by some early AIDS patients in whom subcortical degenerative damage has occurred. Our hypothesis is that the deficit in these patients is in the system responsible for general control and organization of rhythmic speech movements (cf. Keller 1987). Theirs is a problem in the general phonetics of prosody, not the language-specific cognitive system.

These populations can be studied with respect to standard acoustic measures of timing, the time course of acoustic intensity and pitch, and also with articulatory measures (e.g., the time course of jaw movement, ultrasound studies of tongue movement, and other articulatory variables) as possible, depending on the conditions of access to individual subjects. The hope is that comparing these talkers along these dimensions will give us insight into what aspects of normal performance are attributable to what aspects of the overall speech and language system. Such investigations are still in early stages of development[6] – there are major problems of principle and experimental design yet to be resolved, and few concrete results. The purpose of bringing up this work at all is simply to propose a methodology for gathering the sort of information we will need in order to arrive at an improved understanding of those dimensions of speech rhythm and timing that are part of the system of *I*-language, and which thus ought to be recognized as components of a linguistically significant phonetic representation.

6.4   Conclusion

If we take the lessons of the sections above to heart, the representation we arrive at for "PF" – the interface of the language organ with the mechanics of articulation[7] – is quite distant from the sort of fine phonetic transcription

---

[6] See Boatman et al. 1994.

[7] The same representation is also appropriate as the interface between the langauge system and perception, if something like the Motor Theory referred to above is correct, as we presume.

using symbols of the IPA (or some other, similar system) which most current linguists learned as students (and generally continue to teach). An accurate PF representation:

a. fails to indicate some properties that are perfectly true, measurable, and systematic about utterances, insofar as these are the consequences, not specifically intended, of other aspects of speech;

b. indicates gestures that **are** intended even under circumstances where those gestures do not have their intended auditory (or perhaps even articulatory) effect;

c. specifies gestures with associated temporal dynamics, and not just timeless points, and which are related in hierarchical ways;

d. indicates gradient temporal relations rather than mere succession;

e. indicates gradient gestural magnitudes and not only categorical presence *vs.* absence; and

f. indicates the overall pattern of articulatory dynamics within which the gestural intentions of the talker are realized.

A representation with these characteristics obviously cannot be taken to be the kind of physical observation language phonetics is often presumed to provide. It is rather a description of the cognitively real (though largely unconscious) representations that underlie speech motor control and that are in some sense recovered in perception. Despite its non-traditional character, it does seem to serve the larger goal of characterizing what is linguistically significant about the facts of speech. It is neither a full physical record of speech events, nor a restricted characterization of the minimal distinctive core that distinguishes higher-level linguistic elements from one another. As such, it serves as the output (or perhaps better, as the implicature) of the sound-structural regularities of a language. We claim that these are the things that ought to be demanded of a "phonetic representation" by those for whom such a notion finds its significance in the theory of language and the mind, rather than in physics or physiology. That is, it is an appropriate way of characterizing PF, the connection between the language organ and the organs of speech and hearing.

7   Morphology

If you ask a naive person-in-the-street – the kind of person the British call "the man on the Clapham omnibus" – what the central thing is that has to be learned in order to "know" a language, the chances are that a major part of the answer will be "the words of the language." This notion that the words of a language are the essence of its identity is reinforced by standard language courses, which devote great attention to the systematic presentation of vocabulary. Indeed, much of what passes for "grammar" in many language courses is actually a subpart of the theory of words: what has to be learned about things like conjugation and inflection is first and foremost how to form inflected words. Compared with the effort usually devoted to drilling vocabulary and word formation, the amount of attention devoted to exemplifying the uses of the various forms and providing usage notes is usually quite limited, and the space given to fundamental matters of syntactic structure virtually none at all.

So if the set of words is such an important property of, say, English, how do we determine what that set is? A standard answer is provided by a dictionary (though that, of course, simply puts the problem off by one step: how did the dictionary makers know what to include?). Most speakers behave as if the question "Is [such and such] a word of English?" has a determinate answer, but if so, the dictionary probably does not provide that answer, at least in the general case. For instance, *overlook* "disregard" is clearly a word of English, and is recognized as such in dictionaries, but what about *overlookable* "subject to being disregarded"? Surely this is also a word of English, though it will not be found in any of the standard dictionaries, even the *Oxford English Dictionary*. And this ignores the fact that new words enter the language all of the time: if a word like *frobnicate* "to manipulate or adjust, to tweak" did not exist prior to the second half of the twentieth century, how did that change? And why, as soon as we recognize *frobnicate*, do we have no trouble at all accepting *prefrobnicate* "to manipulate or adjust something prior to performing some other operation on it"? Clearly a dictionary of a language **reflects** the language's words, but equally clearly no dictionary can be taken as a **definition** of what constitutes a word of the language.

Linguists generally think of the LEXICON of a language as a component of its grammar separate from its syntax and its sound system, the component that provides an account of the words whose organization into phrases, clauses, etc. is given by the syntax and whose pronunciation is specified by the phonology and the phonetics. Beyond this, however, there tends to be rather a lot of vagueness about just what sort of system the "lexicon" is.

Our argument in this chapter is that the standard construal of the lexicon as primarily an inventory derives from the conception of language as *E*-language. The deficiencies and lacunae in that view suggest the need to replace it with an *I*-language idea, that of the lexicon not as a list but as a form of knowledge – a component of the language organ.

7.1   The lexicon

Mark Aronoff (1988) points out that there are a number of distinct senses that can be (and have been) assigned to the notions "lexicon" and "lexical," including on the one hand that of the locus of idiosyncrasy in language, and on the other that of a collection of all of the items that belong to "open" or "major" word classes (typically nouns, verbs, and adjectives).

The first of these conceptions is usually associated with Leonard Bloomfield, who said that

A complete description of a language will list every form whose function is not determined either by structure or by a marker [a "function word," or closed-class item characteristic of some grammatical structure]; it will include, accordingly, a *lexicon*, or list of morphemes, which indicates the form-class of each morpheme, as well as lists of all complex forms whose function is in any way irregular. (Bloomfield 1933, p. 269)

The "morphemes" of a language are supposed to be the smallest discrete pieces into which words can be broken that constitute irreducibly arbitrary associations of form and meaning. Thus, *overlook* consists of two morphemes *over* and *look* because each of these parts has a more or less distinguishable meaning, and the meaning of the word as a whole is built on those partial meanings, but there is no separable meaning to smaller parts (e.g., *o*, *ver*, *loo*, etc.). Larger constructions containing several morphemes appear in Bloomfield's lexicon to the extent their properties are not entirely those that would be projected from those of their components together with the rules of the grammar.

If this notion is taken literally, the lexicon in this sense

is incredibly boring by its very nature. It contains objects of no single specifiable type (words, VPs, morphemes, perhaps intonation patterns, and so on), and those objects that it does contain are there because they fail to conform to interesting laws. The lexicon is like a prison – it contains only the lawless, and the only thing its inmates have in common is lawlessness. (Di Sciullo and Williams 1987, p. 3)

In contrast to this notion, Aronoff shows that the notion of the lexicon as an inventory of "members of a major lexical category" is presumed in much writing on generative grammar. Evidently these two conceptions are not coextensive: on the one hand, some idiosyncratic items (including both members of the set of grammatical items like determiners, pre- or post-positions, etc.; and idiomatic phrasal constructions) are not members of open word classes; and on the other, many words that are members of the classes noun, verb, and adjective (or whatever the correct set might be) will, in many languages, be completely compositional formations composed of more than one morpheme, such as *overlookability*. Ignoring these differences, the *a priori* interest of the lexicon defined in either way is not self-evident.

What these two ways of construing the notion of "lexicon" have in common is that they are both kinds of list. Perhaps by analogy with dictionaries in the real world, it seems often to be taken for granted that the lexicon is a kind of set or database.

Now of course no one would take seriously the notion that the "syntax" of a language is a list of its sentences (whether the unpredictable ones or all those of some given type), or that the "phonology" is a list of sound combinations. Both of these aspects of grammar are generally construed as kinds of knowledge speakers have about their language: in the one case, knowledge of the patterns by which words can be organized into larger structures, and in the other, knowledge of how sound units of various sorts combine and the modifications they undergo within such larger combinations. These are all components of our language organ, which develop in particular ways on the basis of our exposure to data characteristic of a given language. It seems productive to interpret the "lexicon" of a language in a similar sense as, roughly, "the knowledge a speaker has of how words can instantiate positions in a syntactic structure."

When construed in this *I*-language fashion, the lexicon is not just a list of items. Of course, much of what we know about the words of our language does have the character of individual and rather local stipulations, like "*cat* is a noun pronounced /kæt/ and meaning 'a carnivorous mammal (Felis catus) long domesticated and kept by man as a pet or for catching rats and mice.'" But in addition, a speaker's lexical capacity must also include a system of rules or principles by which words are related to one another, insofar as these relations are (at least partially) systematic and thus part of what we know about words, *qua* speakers of a particular language. Such regularities are also implicated in describing the formation of new words not hitherto part of a speaker's explicit knowledge of the language but implicit in its principles of word formation. Even when a language has a rich set of general principles for forming new words, it is typically the case that the question of whether or not a given possible word is also an actual one remains a lexical issue – not, say, a syntactic one.

It is not immediately clear that a notion of "lexicon of language L" in the *E*-language sense of "the set of words of L" is conceptually well formed, or that it would be particularly interesting even if it were. Given potential sound/meaning correspondences, speakers can assign interpretations to these, such as "a word of my language that I have heard before," "a word that I can't recall having heard, but which probably means [such and such]," "a word I've heard before, and that has something to do with a part of a boat, but I don't really know what part," "a word I don't know, that sounds like it has something to do with [such and such], but I can't tell exactly what," "surely not a word of my language," etc. These are all aspects of the set of principles a speaker controls, and it is the study of those principles that ought to be primary in the study of lexical knowledge.

It seems quite unlikely that any particular list of specific forms, however annotated, can be formulated so as to express the same information. The fact that much of our knowledge of the lexicon is rather specific to individual words may seem to give it such a list-like character overall, but this is probably illusory. Much the same problems arise in studying the lexicon from the point of view of its extension (i.e., as a list of words) that arise in studying other aspects of language extensionally rather than as systems of knowledge.

The knowledge that speakers have of a language's lexicon probably applies over a superset of both notions discussed by Aronoff. Idiosyncratic things that speakers know about particular words are certainly "lexical," as are the properties of idiomatic units larger than the word. Similarly, the lexicon comprehends our knowledge of the words that can fill major lexical categories, whether these are related in completely (or only partially) compositional ways to "simpler" words or are themselves irreducible lexical primes. But while both of these kinds of knowledge can be presented in the form of lists, no particular list can be taken to exhaust the content of the knowledge that is the lexicon. For instance, speakers can certainly apply their knowledge to provide analyses of parts of unfamiliar potential words, analyses that may be insufficient to assign a structure to the entire word (just as, in syntax, speakers may be able to assign structural descriptions to only some parts of a sentence that is not fully grammatical).

Central to our knowledge of language in this area, as in others, is the notion of rule-governed regularities. In the discussion below, we will speak of these as Word Formation Rules, but we should bear in mind the lesson of chapter 5 that there may be quite different ways to express such things. Only further investigation can show whether, for instance, a system of hierarchically organized constraints might not provide a more satisfactory account of this component of the language organ.

7.2   Words and "morphemes"

We would like, then, to replace "externalist" points of view that construe the lexicon of a language as a collection of individual lexical items with a conception of the lexicon as a particular form of knowledge of the language – knowledge about its words and their relations with one another, part of a person's grammar and properties of the language organ. Let us start from the nature of words: we can agree that what we know about a particular word in and of itself can be represented as an association among several distinct sorts of information. A LEXICAL ITEM, then, is an association of SOUND (phonological form) with SYNTAX (morphosyntactic properties) and MEANING (semantics).

This conception of words as associations is, of course, a version of the Saussurean notion of words as SIGNS: the minimal units in language that connect form (sound, or in the case of signed languages, gesture) with content (meaning). A minimal sign, like "*cat*"={/kæt/, noun, CAT}, displays an irreducible connection among these properties. As far as the syntax is concerned, these can be taken to be the atoms of linguistic structure.

Now if all words were like *cat* there would be very little left to do but list them, but it quickly becomes apparent that this is not the case. And apart from the question of whether all words are signs in just this sense, we can also ask the converse: are all signs words? That is, do *parts* of words – "morphemes" in traditional terms – have the logical structure of signs?

This question comes up because of the fact that not all lexical items are equally arbitrary: some are **partially motivated** (de Saussure 1974) in that they are related to other lexical items. We saw that above, in considering the word *overlook*: some proper subparts of the meaning of this word are associated with proper subparts of its form (*over*, *look*) in a way that would contradict the notion of signs as irreducible if signs and words were the same thing. The relation of *overlook* to *over* and to *look* is not just a connection among three items that happen (independently) to be words of English: there are things shared among these words of a sort that do not apply to other sets (e.g., *cat*, *cake*, *hat*) that show some overlap in form.

How are we to explicate this notion of partial motivation, and in general the idea that some words are **related** to one another? The traditional notion of the morpheme is driven in large part by this question. Within structural linguistics, the morpheme was proposed as the "real" locus of the irreducible sign relation. Some words of course consist of only a single morpheme on this view (*cat*, *look*), while others are composed of more than one (*overlook*, which contains the same morpheme as *look* plus the same morpheme as that occurring alone in the word *over*). In some languages, the number of such pieces within a word can get really very large. Some examples from languages that are particularly noted for this are given in (7.1).[1]

---

[1] "*Eskimo*" is a name to be avoided, since (like the names of many other groups around the world) it was assigned to the people involved by speakers of another language, and is considered offensive. In this case, the word "*Eskimo*" was apparently supplied by speakers of an Algonquian language who served as guides to early French and English speaking explorers. It means roughly "people who eat really disgusting stuff."

(7.1) WEST GREENLANDIC ("ESKIMO")

tusaanngitsuusaartuaannarsiinnaanngivipputit

you simply cannot pretend not to be hearing all the time

SIBERIAN YUPIK

avelghaghtesnaanghisaghqaqsaghanka . . .

I am supposed to prevent them from missing it (school) in the future, but . . .

GERMAN

Lebensversicherungsgesellschaftsangestellter

life insurance company employee

Some morphemes (traditionally called "free") can appear alone as words, while others (traditionally called "bound," such as *pre-* in *prefrobnicate*) are always part of larger constructions, where their status as morpheme units is based on the fact that they make (roughly) the same contribution to form and to meaning in each of the more complex words in which they appear. In these terms, we could define the notion of MORPHOLOGICAL RELATEDNESS as follows: words are related insofar as they share a common morpheme (or morphemes). A word W_1 is derived from another word W_2 if (and only if) $W_1 = W_2 + \mu$ for some morpheme μ (disregarding order).

This leads to a formulation like the following of the relation between words that share morphological material:

$$(7.2) \quad \left\{ \begin{array}{c} \text{/ınflejt/} \\ [_V\_\_NP] \\ \text{INFLATE} \end{array} \right\} + \left\{ \begin{array}{c} \text{/əbl/} \\ \text{Adj} \\ \text{ABLE TO BE} \\ [_V\_\_]\text{ED} \end{array} \right\} \Rightarrow \left\{ \begin{array}{c} \text{/ınflejtəbl/} \\ \text{Adj} \\ \text{ABLE TO BE} \\ [\text{INFLAT}]\text{ED} \end{array} \right\}$$

$$\text{"inflate"} \quad + \quad \text{"-able"} \quad \Rightarrow \quad \text{"inflatable"}$$

Here we have a complex word (*inflatable*) representing a collection of properties including sound (the phonological representation, /ınflejtəbl/), the morphosyntactic property of being an adjective, and (what we frankly admit is little more than a stand-in for) meaning.[2] The diagram indicates that the properties of this complex word can be regarded as composed from corresponding properties of its component parts (*inflate* and *-able*) in a straightforwardly additive fashion.

If this picture is viewed seriously as a claim about how words are constructed in a speaker's mental grammar, by his language organ, and not simply as a

---

[2] We have essentially nothing to say in this book about semantics, the study of meaning, but that certainly does mean we think this is unimportant, or not related to the nature and structure of the language organ. This omission simply reflects the limitations of our own research competence. The work of Ray Jackendoff, for instance (including Jackendoff 1983, 1990 among others) sheds important light on the way the language organ associates linguistic form with meaning. Representations in small capitals are intended to refer to elements of meaning: while these are not quite as arbitrary as they may appear, we will not attempt to defend claims about them here.

kind of metaphor, it has some rather strong consequences. Some of these are the following. (a) Since the relation between a (complex) word and another from which it is derived consists exactly in the addition of another minimal sound–meaning complex, sign composition must always be strictly monotonic (additive, concatenative). (b) Since the basis of the sign is the indissoluble unity of sound and meaning (and (morpho)syntax), there should be a one-to-one association between form elements and content elements. That is, every chunk of form ought to correspond to exactly one chunk of meaning, and *vice versa*. Exceptions to this are unsystematic instances of accidental homophony or synonymy. (c) Derivational relations are **directional**, in the sense that (all of the) properties of the base form are presupposed by a derived form that involves an additional marker. We will examine in turn each of these implicit empirical claims of the morpheme-based theory of lexical structure, and conclude that none of them are consistent with the facts of natural language in general. This will lead us to the conclusion that the lexical component of the language organ should be viewed as a system of rule-like relations among words, rather than just an inventory of minimal signs (the morphemes).

It should be stressed that the notion that words are exhaustively composed of morphemes, and that the theory of word structure is essentially a kind of "syntax of morphemes," has a long history in linguistics, and a good deal of initial appeal. Nonetheless, we suggest that this is essentially an *E*-language notion that ought to be replaced by a somewhat different conception if the structure of the language organ is to be properly understood.[3]

7.2.1   *Monotonicity in word formation*

The first consequence of the morpheme-based view that we will consider is the claim of monotonicity: the idea that a derived word consists of its base with some additional material added. If complex words are just simpler stems with the addition of (one or more) sound–meaning complexes, we should find that derived words always contain their bases as a proper subset, in terms of form, meaning, and morphosyntax. We will see, however, that the relations we find in natural languages are actually more complicated than that.

Problems of morpheme form   As far as word shape is concerned, it has been clear at least since such work as Hockett 1947 that not all morphology is monotonic (i.e., some morphology is "non-concatenative"). Following the analytic tradition initiated by Hockett's paper, the consequences of this observation are frequently obscured by giving descriptive names to the kinds

---

[3] Again, the work of Jackendoff, especially Jackendoff 1975, furnishes important precedents for the ideas developed here.

of case that pose problems, providing the illusion that these have somehow been solved. In fact, though, they present a solid core set of cases in which a morphological relation between two forms is not signalled by the addition of new material, as the morphemic view would require.

One large group of examples of this sort can be collected as instances of APOPHONY, or relation by replacement. English pairs such as *sell/sale, sing/song, blood/bleed, food/feed*, etc., as well as the familiar examples of *man/men, woman/women, mouse/mice*, etc., indicate relations such as those between a verb and a corresponding noun or between singular and plural by **changing** the main stressed vowel, not by adding an affix of some sort. In some languages, such as the Semitic languages Arabic and Hebrew, replacive operations of this sort (e.g., Modern Hebrew *semel* "symbol," *simel* "symbolize"; *xašav* "think," *xišev* "calculate," etc.) can be treated as the association of a basic set of consonants with one word pattern or another (see McCarthy 1981), but this analysis has no appeal for English examples like those above.

Other apophonic relations involve consonants, rather than vowels, and are sometimes called instances of MUTATION (as opposed to "Ablaut" or "Umlaut" where vowel changes are concerned). Consider English pairs such as *believe/belief, prove/proof, speak/speech, bath/bathe, breath/breathe, glass/glaze* "provide with glass." Again, the relations involved are signalled (in the modern language, at least) not by the addition of some marker, but rather by a change from one consonant to another.

Some languages (though not English) go so far as to indicate a class of derived words not by adding material to a base, but rather by subtraction. An interesting class of nouns is derived from verbs in Icelandic by deleting the final *-a* that marks the infinitive: thus, *hamr* [hamr] "hammering" from *hamra* [hamra] "to hammer"; *pukr* [pü:kr] "concealment" from *pukra* [pü:kra] "make a secret of." One might think that the infinitive is here derived from the (shorter) noun form by adding the ending *-a*, but we can see that that is not the case from the vowel length in forms like *pukr* [pü:kr]. The fact that this vowel is long appears to contradict the rules for vowel length in Icelandic; but it makes sense in terms of the form of the untruncated infinitive ([pü:kra]). Forms derived from this infinitive preserve its vowel length, but this explanation requires us to assume that *pukr* is derived from *pukra* – by deletion of the final *-a*.[4]

Problems of morpheme content   The cases above, and similar types as discussed in Anderson 1992, make it clear that morphological complexity is not always represented in an additive way as far as word form is concerned. As already noted, such examples have been well known for some time, and

---

[4] See Orešnik and Pétursson 1977, Kiparsky 1984 for details and discussion.

a number of efforts have been made to accommodate them within theories of word structure. What is rather less familiar, however, is the fact that the same conclusion holds for the semantic and morphosyntactic dimensions of word formation. Here too it is not hard to see that word formation cannot in general be monotonic, as required by the morpheme model. That is, the syntax and/or the semantics of a complex form may not be just an additive function of its pieces. Actually, we can see something like that even in the case of *inflatable*: the syntactic properties of this word show little or no reflex of those of the underlying verb. We might suggest that they are somehow still there, but are just covered up by the over-riding syntax of being an adjective. Other examples do not seem to be as simple, though.

Subtractive semantics. An example of semantically non-monotonic morphology is provided by a category of verbs in Icelandic traditionally known as "middle voice" forms (Anderson 1990). These are built by adding a suffix *-st* to a basic verb, and as far as their form is concerned, they are quite unexceptional. The suffix itself represents a fossilized form of what was originally (that is, earlier in the history of the language) a reflexive pronoun attached as an enclitic to the verb, but that connection has now been lost. There is no reason to believe that in contemporary Icelandic the *-st* is in any syntactic sense a pronoun rather than simply a suffix appearing in a large number of verbs. One might think this is a perfectly ordinary "morpheme," but the problem is that the relation between the basic and derived verbs is subtractive: typically, one of the arguments of the basic (transitive) verb, together with the semantic relation associated with it, is simply absent from the derived verb. Consider the pairs of verbs in (7.3).

(7.3)	gleðjast	"rejoice"	gleðja	"gladden (trans)"
	kveljast	"suffer"	kvelja	"torture (trans)"
	lýjast	"get tired, worn out"	lýja	"tire (someone) out"
	hefjast	"begin (intrans)"	hefja	"begin (trans)"
	opnast	"open (intrans)"	opna	"open' (trans)"
	finnast	"exist, be to be found"	finna	"find"
	heyrast	"be audible"	heyra	"hear"
	týnast	"be, get lost"	týna	"lose"
	ágoggast	"(of a fish) be hooked"	gogga	"catch with a hook"

The morphology here is clearly additive in form. Could we think of it as additive in content too? In logical terms, we might think of the semantics as adding an operator that binds the Agent argument in semantic representation, along the lines of (7.4).

$$(7.4) \quad \left\{ \begin{array}{c} \text{/kvelja/} \\ [_V\_[NP]] \\ (\text{CAUSE}\ x, \\ (\text{BECOME TORTURED}, y)) \end{array} \right\} + \left\{ \begin{array}{c} \text{/st/} \\ V \\ \exists x\,(\text{CAUSE}\ x, P) \end{array} \right\}$$

$$\text{"torture"} \qquad\qquad + \qquad\qquad \text{"-st"}$$

$$\Rightarrow \left\{ \begin{array}{c} \text{/kveljast/} \\ \text{Adj} \\ \exists x\,(\text{CAUSE}\ x, \\ (\text{BECOME TORTURED}, y)) \end{array} \right\}$$

$$\text{"suffer"}$$

In (7.4), the "meaning" of the element *-st* is that where the meaning of the base includes the notion that some participant CAUSES some state of affairs, the causer is some indefinite agent that need not be explicitly mentioned. Thus, when the subject of the verb *kveljast* "suffers," what that means is that this individual comes to be tortured by some person or persons unknown.

But saying this makes an incorrect prediction: it predicts that in the interpretation of the derived (*-st*) verb, there is an implied generic or other agent responsible for the patient's state, and this is simply false. Verbs of this sort in Icelandic do not necessarily have any such interpretation. When an Icelander suffers, s/he doesn't need to feel there is someone or something to blame it on. Compare this with the rather similar English passive form in (7.5a).

(7.5) a. During their captivity, Kim and Sandy were tortured (by thoughts of home and family).

     b. When called on in class, Terry always looks tortured (by insecurity).

When no explicit agent is given (for instance, in a *by* phrase), a sentence like (7.5a) still carries the implication that there was some cause for the suffering, even if only mental; and this cause can be made explicit. Even in the adjectival form (7.5b), the source of the suffering, though not as strongly implied as in the verbal form, **can** be made explicit. In Icelandic, however, there is no possibility of adding an *af* phrase (the equivalent of an English *by* phrase, used with true passives to indicate an agent), and there is no necessary implication that the suffering has a determinate cause. Any such source can only be mentioned in the form of an adverbial adjunct phrase.

(7.6) a. *Jón   kveljast   af   tannpínu
          John   is-tortured   by   toothache
          John is tortured by toothache

     b. Jón   kveljast   (í   tannpínu)
          John   suffers   from   toothache
          John suffers (from toothache)

English passives thus have a place for reference to a causer – a place that may be represented explicitly (with a *by* phrase), or implicitly, through the introduction of a non-specific or indefinite semantic operator. Icelandic *-st* verbs, in contrast, do not involve such reference (even though ordinary passive forms in Icelandic do, like English). The right semantic analysis of the relation between the basic and the *-st* verbs in (7.3) must therefore involve not the binding (by an abstract or impersonal operator) of an agentive argument, but rather the omission of the entire layer of semantic structure associated with agentivity. Semantically, the verbs that serve as bases for this formation have the schematic form in (7.7).

(7.7) (CAUSE x, (BECOME (P y)))

That is, "(subject) causes (object) to become tired, miserable, started, open, etc." The addition of the ending *-st* has the effect of deleting the highest predicate (CAUSE x,y) from this structure. This means the corresponding argument disappears from the syntax, so that a basic transitive verb becomes intransitive; and also that the role played by this argument is no longer present in the semantics of the derived verb. In modern Icelandic, "suffering" is not a matter of *being tortured by someone/something*, even though such a meaning may well provide the etymology of the word.

What does this mean? Simply that there is no way to describe the verbs in (7.3) as being related by the addition of a "morpheme" *-st*, because there is no way to characterize this morpheme's contribution to meaning as the addition of something to the meaning of the base verb. The **relation** between the two columns of (7.3) is relatively straightforward: speakers know that when a given verb involves causation of this sort, a related verb ending with *-st* may describe the same resulting state, but without reference to its causation. This *I*-language characterization, however, has no clear correspondent in terms of the *E*-language conception of words as built by combining morphemes.

This example is actually typical of a large class of cases. In many languages, we find some morphological element that converts transitive verbs to intransitives, often with no remaining trace (in the form of "understood" material) of the missing argument(s). The subtractive nature of this operation is usually concealed by grammar writers, who give the element in question a superficially additive interpretation "DETRANS" or the like. But we must not lose sight of the fact that the actual content of "DETRANS" may be precisely the suppression of some part of the base verb's content – an operation just like that of phonological subtraction (truncation), when Icelandic *pukra* "make a secret of" becomes *pukr* "concealment."

Subtractive morphosyntax. We turn next to a case that also involves "subtractive" operations as the concomitant of a derivational relation, but where the subtractive operation in question alters the **syntactic** information in the lexical items affected.

English has a large array of nominals formed with the ending *-er*, many of which are derived from related verbs. An interesting point about these concerns the extent to which the nominal does or does not appear associated with the same arguments as the basic verb. Hovav and Levin 1992 distinguish two classes of *-er* nominals: some (typically with an agentive interpretation) inherit the argument structure of the base verb, while others (typically with an instrumental interpretation) do not. Consider, for example, two senses of the noun *wrapper* in relation to the syntax of the base verb *wrap*, as illustrated in (7.8). Here the difference in prepositions reflects a difference in argument structures, a variation that is associated with the difference between agentive and instrumental readings of the nominal.

(7.8) a. The best job for Fred would take advantage of his experience as a wrapper {of/*for} presents in fancy gold paper at Tiffany's.
b. The best use I can think of for *The New York Times* is as a wrapper {for/*of} fish that didn't keep well overnight.

Note that, in association with nominals, *of* marks complement arguments (as in (7.8a) – see similar examples in chapter 3), while various other prepositions (like *for* in (7.8b)) mark adjuncts.

Hovav and Levin draw an analogy with two types of derived nominals, distinguished by Grimshaw (1990) among others:

(7.9) a. The examination (of/*for the graduating seniors) lasted three hours.
b. The examination/exam (for/*of prospective students) was three pages long.

"Event"-derived nominals such as (7.9a) refer to events, and they can take complements, as the possibility of (7.9a) with *of* shows. Non-event-derived nominals such as (7.9b) refer to objects, results of actions, etc. rather than events, and these do not take complements, as the **im**possibility of (7.9b) with *of* rather than (the adjunct-marking) *for* shows.

Hovav and Levin propose to unify the differences found in (7.8) and (7.9) in the following way. They suggest that the **syntax** of basic verbs like *wrap*, *examine* includes a reference to an event (of *wrapping*, *examining*).[5] Both in the *-er* cases (7.8b) and the others (7.9b), the derived word involves a change in the "event" position, as a correlate of the derivational relations illustrated

---

[5] We do not attempt to justify this analysis here, but refer the reader to Hovav and Levin's work for the motivation and details.

by (7.8b) and (7.9b). The relations illustrated by (7.8a) and (7.9a), in contrast, involve the same formal marker, but quite different semantics; and here the argument structure of the basic verb, including its "event" argument, are preserved in the derived noun.

If this account is correct in its essence, it provides an example of "subtractive" morphosyntax in association with "additive" phonological marking: the formation of instrumental and non-event-derived nominals involves the deletion of syntactic argument structure with respect to the properties of the base verb. Again, this makes sense if we think of the derivation of one lexical item from another as based on a RELATION which is part of the *I*-language that develops as the language organ of speakers of (in this case) English. It is much harder to understand if we attempt to represent this part of the language by an *E*-language-based inventory of morphemes.

Derivation involving semantic or syntactic change. In some cases of apparent subtraction, it is at least logically possible that the relation is actually monotonic (additive), and we have simply gotten the direction of derivation wrong: perhaps the shorter form is actually the base, with the longer one derived from it (by addition) rather than *vice versa*. We now consider more complex examples, where the derived form is **changed**, rather than being added to or truncated. In these cases, playing with the question of which form is the base is not really an option, since the relation in question cannot be construed as additive in either direction.

Derivation with morphosyntactic (and/or semantic) *Abwechslung* (rather than monotonic addition of material) is illustrated by a quite productive relation in the Australian language Warlpiri (Nash 1986, Laughren 1988). In this language, transitive verbs can be associated with either of two case-marking patterns on their subject and object arguments, with a difference in meaning.

Warlpiri is an ERGATIVE language. This refers to a pattern of case marking on the arguments of verbs which differs systematically from that found in, say, German or Latin, where subjects appear in the nominative (nom) case and direct objects (usually) in the accusative (acc). In an ergative language, the subject[6] of a TRANSITIVE verb is marked with a special case, called the ERGATIVE (erg), while the subject of an intransitive verb appears in a different form, called the ABSOLUTIVE (abs). In the basic clause pattern of Warlpiri, as in most ergative languages, the (direct) object is marked with the absolutive case (the same form that appears on the subjects of intransitive verbs).

---

[6] There is an extensive literature on the structure of "ergative" languages, and a major point of contention is the nature of grammatical relations within basic clauses in such a language. Since the resolution of those issues does not concern us here, our use of "subject" and "object" in referring to Warlpiri can be be taken as presystematically referring to the arguments that would correspond to the subject and object of a literal translation of the sentence into English.

Most transitive sentences, however, have an alternative form in which the object is in the DATIVE (dat) case. When the object takes this form, there is also a special interpretation: the object is interpreted as less completely or directly affected by the action than in a corresponding sentence with an absolutive object. This replacement of erg+abs marking by erg+dat is thus associated with a semantic distinction which is also found in many other languages, though the way in which it is formally indicated may be somewhat different. For instance, in English many transitive verbs can appear either with a direct object, or with an object marked with a preposition, as in the sentence pairs in (7.10). The second sentence of each pair implies a less comprehensive effect on the object.

(7.10) a. i. Every night, I read *War and Peace* to my wife.
            ii. Every night, I read from *War and Peace* to my wife.
        b. i. I can't believe my own cousin shot me!
            ii. I can't believe my own cousin shot at me!

Without attempting to give a comprehensive account of these differences,[7] for present purposes we need only attend to the fact that in Warlpiri, two distinct morphosyntactic patterns are associated with two semantically distinct interpretations of sentences involving what appears to be the same basic verb. In the pairs of Warlpiri sentences below, we have an alternation between the two case frames (erg+abs *vs.* erg+dat) that is associated with a shift from "basic" to "incompletive" or "partitive" semantics.

(7.11) a. i. Yarla-rna   pangu-rnu   ngajulu-rlu
               yam(abs)-1sg   dig-past   1sg-erg
               I dug (up) yams
           ii. Yarla-ku-rna-rla   pangu-rnu   ngajulu-rlu
               yam-dat-1sg-3dat   dig-past   1sg-erg
               I dug for yams
        b. i. Walya-rna   pangu-rnu   ngajulu-rlu
               earth(abs)-1sg   dig-past   1sg-erg
               I dug the earth
           ii. Walya-ku-rna-rla-jinta pangu-rnu   ngajulu-rlu
               earth-dat-1sg-3dat-dd dig-past   1sg-erg
               I dug at the earth

Although there is no relevant overt affix present on the verb in (either alternant of) these forms, they are nonetheless quite typical of the sort of relation we see in many languages between semantically similar verbs, appearing with two distinct case-marking patterns, as in the English examples we saw above in

---

[7] See Anderson 1988 among much other literature for some discussion.

(7.10). The English expressions that gloss the examples in (7.11) – *dig yams*, *dig the ground* vs. *dig for yams*, *dig at the ground*, etc. – illustrate the same kind of contrast.

It happens that the (quite systematic, familiar and productive) relation between these two patterns is not marked in Warlpiri by an overt verbal affix, but in various other languages (including one to which we will turn shortly, West Greenlandic) entirely comparable relations are overtly marked. We assume that the relation between these two patterns in Warlpiri, as in languages where there is an overt affix, is appropriately established in the lexicon, since there are two distinct morphosyntactic behaviors correlated with a difference in meaning.

There have been a number of proposals in the literature as to how to express the difference between the members of such pairs. Mary Laughren (1988) makes an interesting suggestion about the Warlpiri case. She suggests that the affected verbs have a semantic interpretation involving more than one layer of structure, and that the morphosyntactic relation is correlated with a reorganization of those layers.

(7.12) a. i. [$_V$_[erg][abs]], "I GOT YAMS *by* I DIG"
          ii. [$_V$_[erg][dat]], "I DUG *in order to* I GET YAMS"
       b. i. [$_V$_[erg][abs]], "I BROKE UP EARTH *by* I DIG"
          ii. [$_V$_[erg][double-dat]], "I DUG *in order to* I BREAK
              UP EARTH"

If Laughren's account is more or less on target, we have an example of what we might call "semantic metathesis"[8] as the concomitant of a lexical relation. That is, the relation between two lexical variants of the same verb involves no phonological change, but only the morphosyntactic replacement of one case frame by another, and the reorganization of subordination relations within the logical conceptual structure that represents the verb's semantics.

A somewhat different take on a very similar construction is provided in an interesting paper by Maria Bittner (1987). In West Greenlandic (an "Eskimo" language), the "object-demoting" or anti-passive construction is overtly marked – there are at least five different suffixes, in fact, that have this effect. Bittner argues, contrary to previous accounts, that these affixes are in fact independent. But what interests us is the change in the morphosyntax of case marking that accompanies each of the affixes.

We illustrate first with some simple cases, to show the form of the alternation. The first member of each pair in (7.13) is formally transitive, while the second is intransitive and "anti-passive" (AP) with a complement in the instrumental case (inst).

---

[8] METATHESIS is a change whereby two elements switch position, without otherwise changing their form. An example is provided by English dialects in which the verb *ask* is pronounced [æks].

(7.13) a. i. Jaakup   ujarak   tiguaa.
            Jacob-erg   stone-abs   he-took-it
            Jacob took a/the stone.
      ii. Jaaku   ujaqqamik   tigusivuq.
            Jacob-abs   stone-Inst   he-took-AP
            Jacob took a/the stone.
   b. i. Jaakup   illu   taanna   sanavaa.
            Jacob-erg   house-abs   this-abs   he-builds-it
            Jacob built/was/is building this house (and may have
            finished it).
      ii. Jaaku   illumik   taassuminnga   sanavug.
            Jacob-abs   house-inst   this-inst   he-builds-AP
            Jacob was/is building this house (and hasn't finished).

More interesting differences show up when the sentence contains various logical operators. When that happens, Bittner suggests that a semantic difference appears which corresponds to the scope in a conceptual representation of some logical variable.

(7.14) a. i. Atuartut   ilaat   ikiurtaraiqarpara.
           of-students   one-abs   I-must-help-him/her
           I must help one of the students (namely, Nanuq).
           $\equiv \exists x[x$ is one of the students and I must help $x]$
      ii. Atuartut   ilaannik   ikiuisariaqarpunga.
           of-students   one-inst   I-must-help-AP
           I must help one of the students (but it doesn't matter which one).
           $\equiv$ It is necessary that $(\exists x[x$ is one of the students and I help $x])$
   b. i. Jaakup   siumukkurmiuq   ajugaassasuraa.
            Jacob-erg   member-of-"Siumut"-abs   he-believes-he-will-win
            Jacob believes a member of "Siumut" will win.
            $\equiv \exists x[x$ is a member of "Siumut" and Jacob believes $(x$ will win$)]$
      ii. Jaaku   siumukkurmiumik   ajugaassasurinnippuq.
           Jacob-abs   member-of-"Siumut"-inst   he-believes-will-win-AP
           Jacob believes a member of "Siumut" will win.
           $\equiv$ Jacob believes $(\exists x[x$ is a member of "Siumut" and x will win$])$

The difference between members of the pairs in (7.14) is comparable to a well-known ambiguity that appears in "intentional" contexts, as illustrated by the two senses of *John wants to marry a Norwegian*: either (a) there is some particular Norwegian, namely Sigrid, that John wants to marry; or else (b) his interest is motivated by his desire to get a Norwegian passport, so he will settle for any marriageable Norwegian who might be available. Similar phenomena have been pointed out in a number of languages, including Finnish, Basque, Polish, and others. A Finnish example is provided in (7.15).

(7.15) (Finnish)
    i. Matkustajat   ovat   jo   laivassa.
       passengers-nom are   already on-ship
       The passengers are already on the ship.
       $\equiv \exists x[x$ a group of passengers and already (x is on the ship)]
   ii. Laivassa   on   jo   matkustajia.
       on-ship   is   already passengers-Part
       There are already passengers on the ship.
       $\equiv$ already ($\exists x[x$ a group of passengers and x is on the ship])

To accommodate these examples, Bittner (1987, p. 230, paraphrased) proposes what she calls the "Scope Generalization": where the basic casemarking pattern of a language involves interpretations with certain logical operators taking wide scope, an alternative case-marking pattern may be associated with interpretations where those operators may (or must) take narrow scope.

Of course, in order to make the descriptions of Warlpiri, West Greenlandic, etc. suggested above into fully formal accounts, we would need to have a much more explicit theory of logical conceptual structure. But assuming the general plausibility of Laughren's and Bittner's analyses, it seems that the lexical relation between basic and anti-passivized verbs in Warlpiri and West Greenlandic involves an operation of rearrangement on these structures, rather than the simple addition of new material.

The reader who has struggled this far through the exotica of the last few pages may well be wondering what these data have to tell us about the nature of the language organ. The answer is that, from the variety of considerations adduced above, we conclude that derivational relations are not in general monotonic in character. They may involve subtractive or replacive operations on the morphosyntactic and/or semantic content of an item, as well as on its phonology. The importance of that fact is that it shows us that our knowledge of words cannot be reduced to a list or inventory of words or morphemes: rather, the language organ must deal in more general relations among words that are not reducible simply to the presence *vs.* the absence of meaningful elements. This is perfectly natural on the *I*-language view of our subject matter, of course, but it also reinforces that picture.

7.2.2   *The solidarity of form and content*

We turn now to the question of whether recurring elements of word form are consistently and uniformly associated with recurring elements of word content, and *vice versa*. That is, do word classes defined by form correspond one-to-one with those defined by meaning (or function)?[9] When we look seriously at this issue, we see that a single formal marker typically goes with a particular derivational content, and *vice versa*, but this is not true in general, so we must separate the two kinds of relation. This point has been made in great detail by Robert Beard (1995); see also work by Arnold Zwicky and Richard Janda, and much earlier, by Franz Boas.

The categories of word form and word content may fail to be isomorphic in both directions. On the one hand, we often find a single function which is represented by several forms. Consider the formation of English "action nominals" (*destruction, settlement, arrival, laughter*, etc.) as an example. Most verbs have such a nominal, and **only** one: if there is more than one, there is semantic specialization, as in the difference between *recital* and *recitation*. The class of action nominals is functionally unitary, but the forms are quite diverse. However, the fact that these multiple potential forms are mutually exclusive shows the significance and underlying unity of the class.

Another example is furnished by the *binyan* system of Semitic languages such as Arabic and Hebrew. There is a limited set of fixed word structural patterns (made up of syllable structure together with associated vowels) in such a language, and the same lexical material (represented by a set of – typically three – consonants) can be associated with various of these. Each pattern has a typical semantic correlate, but in some cases very similar semantics can be associated with more than one pattern. An example is furnished by the two Arabic[10] causative forms ʕallam "teach" and ʔaʕlam "inform." Both are causatives of the basic verb ʕalim "know," and thus provide an example in which the same function can be associated with more than one formal characteristic.

On the other hand, a single form can also be used to represent several distinct functions. For instance, in the formation of nominals in English, the ending *-er* is associated with agentives (*trainer, writer*) and instruments (*wringer, mixer*) derived from verbs, as well as other forms derived from nouns meaning "person connected with (N)," such as *roomer, second-grader, honeymooner, carpetbagger, footballer, Londoner, Pittsburgher*; nouns referring to non-humans, somewhat parallel, such as *ten pounder, freighter, tanker, Nor'easter*, etc.; nouns from numbers, like *fiver, forty-niner, (seventy-)sixer*, etc. The formally unitary class of nouns in *-er* is thus functionally quite diverse.

[9] The assumption that they do underpins what Bazell (1952), in discussing American Structuralist theory of the 1950s, called the "Yale morpheme," one of his canonical instances of the "Correspondence Fallacy" (the assumption that structure in one domain will be isomorphic to structure in another). The reference here is to the fact that linguists at Yale such as Bernard Bloch, Rulon Wells, and others were particularly prominent in the development of a picture of morphological structure closely analogous to the then-prevalent view of phonology based on biunique phonemes, as sketched in chapter 4.

[10] In the transcription of Arabic forms here, [ʕ] is a fricative consonant produced with a constriction in the pharyngeal region, while [ʔ] is the somewhat more familiar glottal stop.

Much the same can be said, again, for the formal patterns of Semitic morphology. Arabic verbs in the $C_1aC_2C_2aC_3$ pattern, for example, include both intensives (e.g. *qattal* "massacre"; cf. *qatal* "kill"), and causatives (e.g. *ʕallam* "teach"; cf. *ʕalim* "know"). While the pattern presents a single category of word form, that category is associated with quite different content in different instances.

These facts suggest that within the lexicon of a language, we need to recognize a collection of formal classes (like -*er* nouns), and a collection of content-based classes (like "derived nominals"), independently of one another. Typically a given form-based class will be largely coextensive with a particular content-based class (or at least with a small number of these), and *vice versa*; but since the two have independent bases, there is no need for the structure of the two domains to map onto one another in any simple way.

Let us take a look at one such content-based class, to see how it is related to formal structure. English contains a great many "agent nouns" derived from verbs, such as [N [V bake]-r], [N [V preach]-er], etc. Some other agent nouns appear to end in -*er*, but not an -*er* which has been added to a more basic verb: rather, if there is a related verb, it is homophonous with the noun, and should probably be regarded as derived from it, as in the cases of [V [N butcher]], [V [N huckster]], and (perhaps) [V [N minister]]. In yet other cases, the noun ends (phonetically, at least) in the same way as other agent nouns, but there is no related verb at all: [N carpenter], [N soldier], [N janitor], [N bursar]. We also have agent nouns that apparently display the same ending, but where the related word that serves as the base is another noun, rather than a verb: *messenger, adulterer, lawyer, astronomer, furrier, clothier, hatter*, etc.

The sources of agent nouns in -*er* can thus be quite diverse, but that is not at all the end of the story. Other nouns seem to be just as validly "agent nouns" in terms of their content, but do not display -*er* at all: *poet, musician, artist, linguist*. Many such nouns are related to verbs in the language, but where such a non-*er* agent noun exists, the expected regular formation with -*er* added to the verb is not well-formed: cf. *cook* (**cooker* in the sense "one who cooks": cf. Kiparsky 1982), *judge* (**judger*), *student* (**studier*), *representative* (**representer*), *correspondent* (**corresponder*).

Notice that these regular forms are not blocked *per se* as possible words: in fact, *cooker* exists, at least in British English, but as an instrumental (meaning "oven"), rather than an agentive. The regularity is rather that once a verb is associated with one action noun in the lexicon, we cannot create another synonymous action noun for that verb by applying the regular process. This is quite parallel to the fact that a single verb has a single associated action nominal, as we observed above, though this may come from any one of a wide range of formal types. The same form can be employed for two different functions – e.g. *wrapper*, which can be either an agent or an instrument – but not *vice versa*.

This complementarity establishes the significance of the content-based classes within the lexicon of a language, and also shows us that the nature and content of these classes cannot in general be equated with any particular formal marker. Again we see that a speaker's knowledge of the lexicon of a language cannot be equated with a list of sign-like items.

7.2.3   Directionality in word formation

We usually think of derivation as a process that leads from base to derived form, and thus has an inherent directionality. That is suggested naturally by the notion of derivation as **adding** a morpheme to a base. But once we take the classes that are involved in derivational relations seriously, we see that that is not necessary: relations between lexically significant classes might have no relevant directionality at all.

An example of this state of affairs is presented by the verbal system of West Circassian (Dumézil 1975). In these languages,[11] transitive verbs with the canonical shape /C(ə)/ are commonly related to intransitives with the shape /Ce/, where the consonants are the same in such semantically related pairs, and only the vowel differs. In some cases (e.g., 7.16a,b), it seems plausible that the transitive meaning is the more "basic" one, while in others (e.g., 7.16c,d) it would seem to be that of the intransitive that has this status.

(7.16) a. se-tχe "I write (intrans)"; zə-tχəʎ se-tχə "I write a letter"
         b. š°əzə-r me-ṭhač''e "the woman washes, does the dishes (intrans)";
             š°əzə-m šəq°ə-r ye-ṭhač''ə "the woman washes (trans) the dishes"
         c. me-laž'e "he works"; yə-χate ye-lež'ə "he works his garden"
         d. ma-k°'e "he goes"; mə-ɣ°eg°ə-r ye-k°'ə "he goes this road"

In such a system, there is no independent motivation for thinking of either the transitive or the intransitive form as "derived from" the other, though there is a clear, systematic and productive relation between the two.

Another similar example is provided by the gender system of the African language Maasai (Payne 1998). In this language, every noun belongs to one or the other of two genders, masculine or feminine.[12] Each gender has an associated prefix. There are systematic connections between the two, but the relation is such that where there exist pairs of words differing only in gender, it can go

---

[11] In terms of the number of distinctions they show among consonants, the West Circassian languages are among the most elaborate in the world. The reader for whom the transcriptions below seem like gibberish should not be concerned, since these details of pronunciation are not material to the point at issue.

[12] We ignore here a separate "gender" which applies only to one or two locative words.

either way, in the sense that either the masculine form or the feminine might be taken as basic depending on the example.

The simplest cases are those in which the relation is perfectly symmetric; and those in which only one gender is possible.

(7.17) a. *ɛnk-apʋtánì* "wife's mother"; *ɔl-apʋtánì* "wife's father"
b. *ɛ-mɔ́dáí* "female fool"; *ɔl-módáí* "male fool"
c. *ɛnk-áí* "God"; **ɔlk-áí*
d. *ɛ-mɛná; *ɔl-mɛná* "contempt"

In other cases, however, it appears that the feminine is basic, and the masculine derived.

(7.18) a. *en-kíné* "goat; female goat"; *ol-kíné* "male goat"
b. *ɛn-kɛ́ráí* "child (either gender)"; *ɔl-kɛ́ráí* "large male child"
c. *ɛnk-anáshè* "sister"; *ɔlk-anáshè* "very large sister (pejorative)"
d. *en-tít!o* "girl"; *ol-tít!o* "large, shapeless hulk of a woman (pejorative)"
e. *en-kitók* "woman"; *ol-kitók* "very respected man"

In a number of other cases, there is a relation of relatively small/relatively large between the two forms, and in these instances the feminine seems secondary with respect to the masculine.

(7.19) a. *ɛn-dóínyó* "hill"; *ol-dóínyó* "mountain"
b. *ɛnk-álɛ́m* "knife"; *ɔl-álɛ́m* "sword"
c. *ɛnk-aláshè* "weak brother (pejorative)"; *ɔl-aláshè* "brother"
d. *ɛnk-abáánì* "female or small doctor, quack"; *ɔl-abáánì* "(male) doctor, healer"
e. *ɛn-dɛkɛ́t* "ineffectual curse"; *ɔl-dɛkɛ́t* "curse"
f. *ɛ-lɛ́ɛ* "man (pejorative)"; *ɔ-lɛ́ɛ* "man"

It seems that in this instance, we should recognize a basically symmetric relation between the two genders:

$$(7.20) \quad \left\{ \begin{array}{c} \textbf{feminine} \\ \text{(female, relatively small)} \\ /\text{E}(n)\text{-}/ \end{array} \right\} \Leftrightarrow \left\{ \begin{array}{c} \textbf{masculine} \\ \text{(male, relatively large)} \\ /\text{o}(\text{l})\text{-}/ \end{array} \right\}$$

In some cases, basic items have the same status (but different sense) in either class. In other cases, the lexical item has a "basic" gender, and a shift in either direction may imply a pejorative value. There is still no sense in which one of the genders is in general derived from the other, however.

The theme being developed here should be familiar by now. *E*-language-based views have assumed that the lexicon of a language can be characterized by a set of items (signs) whose properties of sound, meaning, and morphosyntax can be identified in the utterances of speakers. In contrast, we see, the "lexicon" of a language is based on relations among items that are not reducible to the mere presence or absence of individual meaningful signs. It is the systematicities of these relations that the language organ must accommodate. Eventually, of course, we must ask how much of this structure is due to properties of Universal Grammar (UG) and how much variation exists among individual languages; and how, where such variation exists, the properties of the language faculty allow it to be derived from the data available to the child learning a specific language. Before such questions can even be contemplated, however, we must have an adequate view of what the basic content of lexical knowledge must consist in.

7.3   Productivity

Let us summarize what seems to be true about our knowledge of words from what we have seen thus far. First, it is quite impossible to maintain that that knowledge takes the form of a list of full words we have learned individually. In fact, we could not possibly have just memorized a list of all the complex words – certainly not in languages like West Greenlandic or Siberian Yupik, where much of the expressive power of the language is built into the system that forms new words, so the creative aspect of language is not limited to the syntax. Indeed, this is also the case for German or English.

A list would not represent our knowledge for several reasons. First, we can clearly make new compounds (e.g., *PlayStation*, *ThinkPad*, *earbud* [part of a hands-free cell phone]) and derived words (*prefrobnicate*, *overlookable*), and at least the first time we use them, such forms would not be on the list. Secondly, in languages with extensive inflectional paradigms (such as Finnish, Hungarian, and many others), every lexical item may have thousands of inflected forms, many of which a given speaker might never have encountered for a particular word, but which can all be produced and recognized when required. We recognize new inflected forms of words, and may not even know whether we have ever seen them before. We can even provide such forms for nonsense words (as in *Jabberwocky*). Most generally, such a list does not take advantage of or express our knowledge of systematic regularities that may be more complicated than what can be expressed merely as the addition of a "morpheme"; and there are a great many such regular relations to take advantage of among the words we know. All of this suggests that our knowledge of words is better represented by something more like a system of rules than (just) a list. Of course, we have to have a list of the irreducible bits – the fact that [k^{h}æt] is a noun that means "cat," for instance – but we also have to have a system of rules or the like to represent our knowledge that expresses – and indeed goes well beyond – the ways in which these bits are combined.

A standard, if incomplete, response to this is to treat word structure as analogous to syntax. We could say that the list is a list of word structure components, or morphemes, and that complex words are formed by combining and recombining these elements. That approach allows us to express the possibility of forming new words (from known elements), but it also makes a number of concrete predictions about the kinds of relation we ought to find among words, and as we have seen in the preceding sections, those predictions (monotonicity, solidarity of form and content, directionality) are often not satisfied.

An alternative to the strictly morpheme-based theory is to treat our knowledge of words as knowledge of systematic *classes* of lexical items, together with the systematic relations among them. For instance, we know that there is a large class of adjectives in English ending in *-able* (sometimes spelled *-ible*), each of which has a meaning involving roughly "ABLE TO BE (something)ED" (*inflatable*, *navigable*, *potable*, etc.). Many of these are related to other words, verbs whose meaning is more or less the "something" in that formula, and whose shape is similar (but not necessarily identical) to the rest of the *-able* word (*inflate*, *navigate* – but not *pote*). Word knowledge includes both knowledge of the regularities of form and meaning that characterize such classes and knowledge of the relations among them.

Derivational relations can be expressed by rules that operate over the lexicon, relating one class of lexical items to another: for instance, "given a transitive verb, the same shape extended by /əbl/ corresponds to an adjective with the meaning ABLE TO BE verbED." The relations involved (often) have the character that they can be used to support the positing (or creation) of new lexical items: given an appropriate verb (e.g., *frobnicate*), we can construct *prefrobnicate*, and given that, we can further produce an adjective *prefrobnicatable* "able to be manipulated or adjusted prior to the performance of some other operation." Each form follows from our knowledge of the relationships among lexical classes.

On the other hand, some instances of derivational relations are only partial, serving as a reconstruction at a finer granularity of Saussure's notion of the "partially motivated sign." For instance, we recognize that *potable*, *ineluctable*, *eligible*, *possible*, *probable*, *credible*, etc. are also members of the class of *-able* words, because they have the right form and sense even though there is no more "basic" word from which they could be derived by adding the suffix *-able*.

We have also seen that the important class of agent-nominals in English includes not only words ending in *-er*, some of which (e.g., *baker*) are related to simple verbs and some of which (e.g., *butcher*) are not, but also others that do not have that shape (e.g., *cook*). The membership of these latter in the relevant class is confirmed by the fact that their presence obviates the formation of new words that might seem to be perfectly regular (e.g., the impossible *cooker* "one who cooks").

We can clearly see that our knowledge of lexical relations can be more or less exhaustive. This is known in the literature on morphology as the issue of "productivity": the formation of new adjectives in -*able* from verbs is essentially completely productive, but the relation between *spit* and *spittle* is essentially limited to this pair (and perhaps *prick/prickle*) in modern English, since there is no reason to assume any relation at all between such superficially similar pairs as *cod* and *coddle*. Many other connections fall somewhere in between, applying in a number of instances but not really providing a warrant for novel creations.

At least a lot of what goes by the name of productivity in the study of morphology is probably a reflection of the extent to which what we know about lexical relations determines the properties of new instances. That is, the properties of a class may sometimes be sufficient to allow us to predict all of the characteristics of a potential new member, but in other instances the internal diversity of the class might leave much underdetermined.

A case where our knowledge is clearly only partial, and where the relation in question is only marginally productive, is that of English adjectives in *a*-: e.g., *ablaze, abroad, aground, afoot, afield, ajar, alight, asleep, askew, astride, aspread, awash, aghast*, etc. These are derived from verbs (e.g., *ablaze*), nouns (e.g., *afield*), or other adjectives (*abroad*). Some do not correspond to more "basic" stems from any class: *ajar, aghast* (but *ghastly*?). The class of these adjectives displays a sort of family resemblance semantically, but no consistent semantics: Marchand (1969) suggests that they mean "in a state or position of . . . ," but that is not interestingly distinct from what we could say about the class of adjectives as a whole. And of course the conclusion we can draw is that our inability to make up new adjectives of this class – the lack of productivity of "*a*- adjectives" – follows from the fact that the existing relations do not provide enough limitations to determine what such a word would mean: if we were to coin the word *awalk*, we would not know what use to put it to.

Much derivational morphology is lexically isolated in this way. Aronoff (1976) suggests that **productivity** might be reduced, when properly understood, to the transparency of a derivational relation. Relations are more or less productive depending on how completely they determine the properties of a potential word as a function of those of an existing base, an account which clearly rests on a conception of word structure as an elaborate and articulated kind of knowledge, rather than just a set of basic elements together with rules for combining them. Surely **some** account of the differences among word formation patterns in terms of their productivity is necessary as part of a description of what a speaker knows about a language, and it seems inevitable that any such account will need to be based on the *I*-language notion of word structure relations, rather than on the *E*-language notion of an inventory of signs.

7.4 Conclusions about lexical organization

A number of consequences follow from the discussion in this chapter for our understanding of lexical relatedness. First, of course, we must avoid thinking of the "lexicon" as a static list – either of full words or of morphemes. Second, we must recognize that while similarities of form are quite typically associated with similarities of meaning, the two are not as solidary as the picture of the Saussurean sign (or the structuralist morpheme) might lead us to hope. The need to analyze the two separately, while treating the connections between them as another complex dimension of word structure, goes back at least to the proposal of Franz Boas (1911) to distinguish "grammatical processes" from the "ideas expressed by grammatical processes." The "processes" Boas had in mind correspond to formal characteristics, including both affixal and non-affixal markers; the "ideas" correspond to the semantic content of morphological classes. The two are not necessarily associated one-to-one, and a coherent analysis of word form must not assume that they are.

A modernized version of Boas' picture distinguishes "derivation" in the abstract sense of relations among lexical subclasses, each characterized by various substantive properties, from the formal expression of these relations. Perhaps the most explicit form of this position is the "Separation Hypothesis" of Robert Beard (1995), but a number of variations have appeared in the linguistic literature of recent years. The central point of these is the need to recognize a class of relations among existing lexical items, rather than just rules for building new items (a notion introduced to the generative literature by Jackendoff 1975).

Such a move also requires us to give up on what Bazell called "Yale morphemes" as minimal signs (see note 9 above). Instead of thinking of derivation as the addition of a morpheme, we should think of it as a bundle of phonological, semantic, and morphosyntactic mappings among lexical classes. Often, of course, these will be coherent in the sense that a given phonological effect will be primarily associated with unique, specific semantic and morphosyntactic effects. But not always.

When we look at the full range of relations established in word formation, we get a very different picture of what "lexical relatedness" can consist in from the one that has dominated the field for many years. The resulting picture is quite different from what theories based on morpheme combination – at least in any serious sense – would suggest. If we think of language, and especially the lexicon, in *E*-language terms as an inventory or collection of signs that can be combined, the morphemic view seems self-evident. But if we think of the lexicon as a kind of knowledge, it seems equally obvious that it might be partitioned in the various ways we have seen: knowledge of form, of meaning, of grammatical properties, etc. – and that the connections among these might be only partial. Thus, the shift from a morpheme-based view of derivation to a more complex relational one goes along with a shift in the nature of linguistics from a focus on items and the properties of a collection of linguistic **objects** to a focus on language as a cognitive system, and a kind of knowledge.

We are really only at the beginning of an understanding of how the language organ accommodates and organizes knowledge of words and their relations with one another, and of how principles of UG both limit and enable the kinds of things that can occur in particular languages. We have not even begun to address issues such as those raised in chapter 5, concerning whether a system of rewriting rules is the most appropriate way to formulate a description of the systematicities of *I*-language in this domain.

It seems self-evident that there is much more variation among languages in their lexicons than elsewhere in grammar, but perhaps, once the contribution of UG to lexical structure is properly understood, that will turn out to be illusory, just as it has turned out that languages are much more similar in their syntactic organization than was once thought. Any approach to such problems, however, must start from a clearer picture of just what lexical structure involves than is provided if we concentrate simply on the identification of a collection of irreducible basic signs: a "lexicon" in the sense of a "dictionary."

8   Language change

In chapter 1, we saw how nineteenth-century linguists promoted the rise of linguistics as a distinct discipline, thinking of texts as the essential reality and taking languages to be entities "out there," existing in their own right, waiting to be acquired by speakers. For them, languages were external objects and changed in systematic ways according to "laws" and general notions of directionality. They focused on the products of human behavior rather than on the internal processes that underlie the behavior, dealing with *E*-language rather than *I*-language. By the end of the nineteenth century, the data of linguistics consisted of an inventory of sound changes but there were no general principles: the changes occurred for no good reason and tended in no particular direction. The historical approach had not brought a scientific, Newtonian-style analysis of language, of the kind that had been hoped for, and there was no predictability to the changes – see section 1.2. The historicist paradigm – the notion that there are principles of history to be discovered – was largely abandoned in the 1920s, because it was not getting anywhere.

In sections 8.3 and 8.4 we shall ask what kinds of accounts of language history we can give if we take a more contingent, *I*-language-based approach. Following our general theme, we shall shift away from a study of the products of behavior toward a study of the states and properties of the mind/brain that give rise to those products. This will enable us to link language change closely to childhood acquisition and to offer different kinds of explanation, which are more satisfactory. Before we do that, however, we shall consider more recent, twentieth-century work, which perpetuates aspects of nineteenth-century thinking and pursues *E*-language approaches to explaining how languages change.

8.1   Long-term directionality in the twentieth century

Nineteenth-century linguists viewed languages changing as objects floating smoothly through time and space, and that image continued to be adopted throughout the twentieth century. Despite the move away from historicism in the 1920s, linguists resumed the search for historical principles in the latter decades of the twentieth century. In the 1970s much work recast the notion of "drift," originally due to Sapir (1921, ch. 7). Sapir dealt with long-term change by postulating drifts. A drift represented the unconscious selection of those individual variations that are cumulative in some direction. So he attributed the replacement of English *whom* by *who* to three drifts:

a. the leveling of the subject/object distinction;
b. the tendency to fixed word order;
c. the development of the invariant word.

Sapir was concerned that in positing a "canalizing" of such "forces" one might be imputing a certain mystical quality to this history. Certainly the modern work confirms that fear. Robin Lakoff (1972), for example, examined changes in various Indo-European languages which yield a more "analytic" surface syntax, and she sought to combine Sapir's three drifts into one. The phenomenon cannot be described, she pointed out, by talking about individual changes in transformational rules or other aspects of a grammar:

Rather, it must be described as a meta-condition on the way the grammar of a language *as a whole* will change . . . Speaking metaphorically, it instructs the language to segmentalize where possible . . . It is not at all clear where this meta-condition exists: neither as part of a grammar nor as a universal condition on the form of grammars. It is not clear how a constraint on change within one language family, a constraint which is not absolute but which is nevertheless influential, is to be thought of. But there is no other way to think of these things: either there is such a meta-condition, whatever it is, or all the Indo-European languages have been subject to an overwhelming series of coincidences. (Lakoff 1972, pp. 178, 192)

If the explanation is admittedly incoherent, then maybe the fallacy is in requiring a principled explanation for such a large-scale change taking place over such a long period. What is wrong with a series of independent events? Why should we believe that a meta-condition is needed to explain these changes?

Only slightly less mystical is the approach to drifts based on Greenberg's (1963) word order typologies. This distinguishes "transitional" and "pure" language types, which are defined universally in terms of hierarchically ranked word-order phenomena. Languages change from one pure type to another by losing/acquiring the relevant orders in the sequence specified by the hierarchies. Again, the unit of change is taken to be a language, an object "out there" which can be described independently of its speakers.

A pure subject–verb–object language, for example, has verb–object order, auxiliary–verb, noun–adjective, and preposition–NP/DP; and these orders are ranked in some hierarchy. A subject–object–verb language is essentially the mirror image and has the opposite orders: object–verb, verb–auxiliary, adjective–noun, and NP/DP–postposition, etc. If a language changes from the object–verb type to the verb–object type, it acquires all of the new orders in the sequence prescribed by the hierarchy: first verb–object, then auxiliary–verb, and so on. The hierarchy is the substance of a historical law which stipulates how a language of one type changes to a language of a different type.

This raises the question of how a child attains a language which is exactly halfway between the subject–verb–object and subject–object–verb types; how does she know whether this is a subject–verb–object language changing to subject–object–verb or *vice versa*? How does she know that her generation must push the language a little towards, say, the subject–verb–object type? It seems that the only conceivable answer is to postulate a racial memory of some kind, such that the child knows that this is a subject–verb–object language changing towards subject–object–verb. This is presumably what Robin Lakoff had in mind in postulating a "meta-condition on the way the grammar of a language as a whole will change."

Sapir stressed that whether or not an individual change is part of a larger drift, its cause must be found locally, thereby avoiding the mystical quality that he warned against or the need for racial memories. The replacement of *whom* by *who* is part of the general drift towards invariable words and the loss of the case system, but Sapir nonetheless isolated four reasons for this particular change: first, *whom* was felt not to belong to the set of personal pronouns, which have distinct subject/object forms, but to a set of interrogative and relative pronouns, which show no such distinction; second, the emphatic nature of interrogative pronouns militates in favor of their invariableness; third, an objective form rarely occurs in initial position; and fourth, [hu:m] was alleged to be phonetically clumsy before the alveolar stops of *do* and *did*. We are not interested here in the validity of this account, but rather in the form that Sapir felt an explanation should take: local reasons for the change suffice to account for it. This is very different from the ideas of the 1970s typologists, who argued that notions like the subject–object–verb to subject–verb–object continua constituted diachronic explanations (Vennemann 1975); for them, the drift was the explanatory force, rather than being something which required explanation, and no local causes were needed.

The typologists remain faithful to the methods of the nineteenth century. They retain the same kind of historical determinism, believing that a language of one type changes inexorably to a language of another type; and they deal with the products of the language capacity rather than with the capacity itself, like their nineteenth-century predecessors. The goal remains one of finding "straightline explanations for language change" (Lass 1980), generalizations which would hold of history. And they are no more successful.

A recent variant on this approach offers historicist accounts in a biological, evolutionary guise. Bauer (1995) argued that Latin was a thorough-going left-branching language, which changed into a thoroughgoing right-branching system in French. Where Latin has a head to the right of its complement (*exercitum duxit* "he led the army," *deorum munus* "gift of the gods," etc.),

French has its head to the left (*il conduisit l'armée* "he led the army," *le don des dieux* "the gift of the gods"). She explains the change through "an evolutionary concept of language change: . . . languages evolve in the direction of features that are acquired early" (Bauer 1995, p. 170). She says that "Latin must have been a difficult language to master, and one understands why this type of language represents a temporary stage in linguistic development" (Bauer 1995, p. 188), but she gives no reasons to believe this and she gives no reason why early languages should have exhibited structures which are hard to acquire.[1] If a diachronic change is "adaptive," one needs to show how the environment has changed in such a way that the new phenomenon is adaptive in a way that it wasn't before. However, proponents of this kind of evolutionary explanation do not do this; instead, they set up universal "tendencies" by which any change is "adaptive," such as a tendency for left-branching languages to become right-branching, and, like the typologists, they postulate inexorable, historical tendencies as explanatory forces.

Another line of work, again focusing on how languages change in some global fashion, has similarly emphasized the alleged unidirectionality of change. Accounts of "Grammaticalization" also treat languages as external objects "out there," subject to change in certain inevitable ways. Grammaticalization, a notion first introduced by Antoine Meillet in the 1930s, is taken to be a semantic tendency for an item with a full lexical meaning to be bleached over time and to come to be used to mark a grammatical function. Such changes are said to be quite general and unidirectional; one does not find changes proceeding in the reverse direction, so it is said.

We shall discuss an instance of grammaticalization in section 8.3 and there are many examples that have been described this way in the literature (for a survey, see Hopper and Traugott 1993). One which is often cited concerns negative markers in French. In Old French, the negative particle *ne* was often reinforced with an appropriate noun. With motion verbs, *ne* was reinforced with the noun *pas* "step." Over time, *pas* began to occur even where there was no motion, and eventually some reinforcing noun became effectively obligatory. As a result, the reinforcing nouns like *pas* (others were *point* "point," *mie* "crumb," *gote* "drop") underwent grammaticalization from noun to negative particle.

Grammaticalization is a real phenomenon, but it is quite a different matter to claim that it is general and unidirectional, or an explanatory force. If there were a universal tendency to grammaticalize, there would be no counter-developments, by which bound forms become independent lexical items (affixes becoming clitics or independent words – we mention an example of this later in this chapter,

---

[1] The same logic, another throwback to nineteenth-century thinking, shows up in the evolutionary explanations of Haspelmath 1999b; see the commentary on this paper by Dresher and Idsardi 1999.

when we point to genitive endings in -*es* in Middle English being reanalyzed as *his*, yielding genitives like *Christ his sake, Mrs Sands his maid*). In our view, when grammaticalization takes place, it is **explained** when one points to local factors which promoted the new grammar; these would be new triggering experiences, changes in cues, or what Kiparsky (1996) calls the "enabling causes."

Grammaticalization, while interesting as a **phenomenon**, is not an explanatory force. We have no well-founded basis for claiming that languages or grammars change in one direction but not in another, no basis for postulating historical algorithms mapping one kind of grammar into another kind ($G_x \rightarrow G_y$). The fact that we observe locative case endings coming to be used with partitive force in some language does not mean that it cannot be otherwise. Van Gelderen 1997, Janda 2001, Joseph 2001, Newmeyer 1998, ch. 5, and others offer careful studies showing changes which run counter to grammaticalization, "degrammaticalization," where affixes or minor categories become full lexical items.[2]

If we observe a lexical verb being reanalyzed as a functional category in a given language, we need to seek a local cause, rather than invoke principles of history as explanatory forces.[3] Those that have been invoked do not work and, if they did, they would themselves need deeper explanation . . . unless one believes that Clio, the muse of history, or some other unseen hand is directing human events. The work we have surveyed in chapter 1 and in this section sees languages following historical laws in order to change from one type to another. The search for principles which require that a particular type of system change historically into another type was no more successful in the late twentieth century than it was in the nineteenth, not surprisingly; and all such accounts view languages as objects "out there," external to individual speakers, *E*-languages.

8.2   Grammars and time

If we switch our perspective from language change to grammar change, from *E*-language to *I*-language, from the products of the language system to the

---

[2] Janda 2001 offers many references. He also has good critical discussion of how fundamental the issue of unidirectionality is for grammaticalizationists and how cavalier some of them have been in dismissing changes which appear to run counter to their predispositions. Imperious blanket denials that such changes occur, as in the writings of Haspelmath (1999a, 1999c), do not remove them from history. Newmeyer (1998, ch. 5) provides an excellent general discussion of grammaticalization and examines studies which use reconstructions as **evidence** for "grammaticalization theory," despite the fact that it was **assumed** in the very reconstruction.

[3] Nor is it appropriate to explain the change by invoking some principle of UG which favors the new grammar (*pace* Roberts 1993; see Lightfoot 1999, section 8.3 for discussion).

system itself, we explain grammatical change through the nature of the acquisition process, as we indicated in chapter 2. A grammar grows in a child from some initial state (Universal Grammar, or UG), when she is exposed to primary linguistic data (PLD) (schematically, as in (8.1)). So the only way a different grammar may grow in a different child is when that child is exposed to significantly different primary data.

(8.1) primary linguistic data (Universal Grammar → grammar)

There is more to **language** change, a phenomenon of social groups, than just **grammar** change, a phenomenon of individuals. Grammar change is nonetheless a central aspect of language change, and it is (naturally enough) intimately related to other aspects of language change. The explanatory model is essentially synchronic and there will be a local cause for the emergence of any new grammar: namely, a different set of primary linguistic data. Time plays no role and there are no principles which hold of history.

St. Augustine held that time comes from the future, which does not exist; the present has no duration and moves on to the past, which no longer exists. Therefore there is no time, only eternity. Physicists take time to be "quantum foam" and the orderly flow of events may really be as illusory as the flickering frames of a movie. Julian Barbour (2000) has argued that even the apparent sequence of the flickers is an illusion and that time is nothing more than a sort of cosmic parlor trick. So perhaps linguists are better off without time, without attributing intrinsic properties to history.

Let us consider the kinds of explanations that are available if we view grammars as elements of cognition, language organs in individual brains, and then ask whether we can or should be more ambitious. In the next section we shall illustrate a different strategy in considering an instance of grammaticalization, a set of changes affecting modal auxiliaries in English, offering local causes for the various changes and not invoking any general tendency to grammaticalize as an explanatory force.

8.3   English auxiliary verbs

English modal auxiliaries like *can, could, may, might, will, would, shall, should,* and *must* differ from ordinary verbs in their distribution. A modal auxiliary is fronted in a question, but a verb like *understand* is not (8.2a); a modal occurs to the left of a negative particle, unlike a verb (8.2b); a modal does not occur with a perfective (8.2c) or present participle (8.2d), unlike a verb; a modal does not occur in the infinitival complement to another verb (8.2e), nor as the complement of another modal (8.2f), unlike a verb like *try*; and no modal may occur with a complement DP, whereas some verbs may (8.2g).

(8.2) a. i.   Can he understand chapter 4?
          ii. *Understands he chapter 4?
      b. i.   He cannot understand chapter 4.
          ii. *He understands not chapter 4.
      c. i.   *He has could understand chapter 4.
          ii. He has understood chapter 4.
      d. i.   *Canning understand chapter 4 . . .
          ii. Understanding chapter 4 . . .
      e. i.   *He wanted to can understand.
          ii. He wanted to try to understand.
      f. i.   *He will can understand.
          ii. He will try to understand.
      g. i.   *He can music.
          ii. He understands music.

The distribution of these modal auxiliaries is peculiar to modern English. For example, the French verb *pouvoir* "can" behaves the same way as a regular verb like *comprendre* "understand" with respect to movement in a question (8.3a) and negation (8.3b). Unlike *can*, *pouvoir* may occur as a complement to another verb (8.3c), even to another modal verb (8.3d), and may take a clitic direct object (8.3e), and to that extent it behaves like ordinary, common-or-garden verbs in French. In French grammars, the words which translate the English modals, *pouvoir*, *devoir*, etc., walk like verbs, talk like verbs, and are verbs, just like *comprendre*.

(8.3) a. i. Peut-il   comprendre   le chapitre?
             can-he   understand   the chapter
             Can he understand the chapter?
         ii. Comprend-il   le chapitre?
             understands-he   the chapter
             Does he understand the chapter?
      b. i. Il   ne   peut   pas   comprendre   le chapitre.
             he   NEG$_1$ can   NEG$_2$ understand   the chapter
             He cannot understand the chapter.
         ii. il   ne   comprend   pas   le chapitre.
             he   NEG$_1$ understands NEG$_2$ the chapter
             He doesn't understand the chapter.
      c.   Il   a   voulu   pouvoir   comprendre   le chapitre.
             he   has   wanted   to be able   to understand the chapter
             He wanted to be able to understand the chapter.
      d.   Il   doit   pouvoir   comprendre   le chapitre.
             he   must   to be able   to understand   the chapter
             He must be able to understand the chapter.

e.   Il   le   peut.
       he   it   can
       He can (do) it [e.g., understand the chapter].

Furthermore, not only may languages differ in this regard, but also different stages of one language. Sentences along the lines of the non-existent utterances of (8.2) were well-formed in earlier English. If the differences between Old and modern English were a function of separate features with no unifying factor (Ross 1969), we would expect these features to come into the language at different times and in different ways. On the other hand, if the differences between Old and modern English reflect a single property, a categorical distinction, then we would expect the trajectory of the change to be very different. And that is what we find. If the differences between *can* and *understand* were a function of the single fact that *understand* is a verb while *can* is a member of a different category, inflection (I), then we are not surprised to find that (8.2ci), (8.2di), (8.2ei), (8.2fi), and (8.2gi) dropped out of people's language in parallel, at the same time.

In Middle English *Kim can understand the chapter* had the structure (8.4a) and in present-day English (8.4b). If in present-day English *can* is an I element, as in (8.4b), then one predicts that it cannot occur to the left of a perfective or present participle, as in (8.2ci), (8.2di) (those participial markers are generated in Spec VP), that it is mutually exclusive with the infinitival marker *to* (which also occurs in I) (8.2eii), that there may only be one modal per VP (8.2fi), and that a modal may not be followed by a complement DP (8.2gi). Simply postulating the structure of (8.4b) accounts for the data of (8.2c–g) in present-day English. Earlier English had structures like (8.4a), where *can* is a verb and behaves like *understand*.

(8.4) a. Middle English

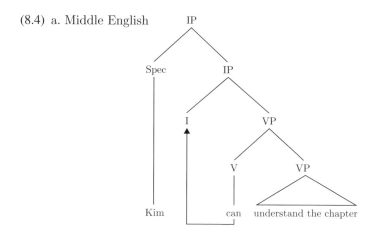

b. Present-day English

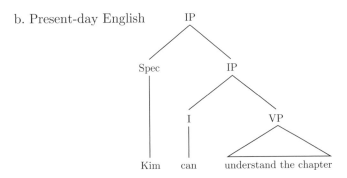

If we attend just to changing phenomena, the historical change between Middle and present-day English consists in the **loss** of various forms, not in the development of new forms; people ceased to say some things which had been said in earlier times. Before the change, all of the utterances in (8.2c–g) (we return to (8.2a–b) in a moment) might have occurred in a person's speech, but later only those forms not marked with an asterisk. That fact alone suggests that there was a change in some abstract system. People might start to use some new expression because of the social demands of fashion or because of the influence of speakers from a different community, but people do not cease to say things for that sort of reason. There might be an indirect relationship, of course: people might introduce new expressions into their speech for external, social reasons, and those new expressions (e.g. analogues to (8.2aii) and (8.2bii) with the periphrastic *do*: *Did he understand chapter 4?*) might entail the loss of old forms, but one needs an abstract system in order to make such a link. Changes involving only the loss and obsolescence of forms need to be explained as a consequence of some change in an abstract, cognitive system. This methodological point is fundamental.

If one focuses on the final disappearance of the relevant forms, one sees that they were lost at the same time. The most conservative writer in this regard was Sir Thomas More, writing in the early sixteenth century. He used many of the starred forms in (8.2c–g) and had the last attested uses of several constructions. His grammar treated *can*, etc. as verbs in the old fashion (8.4a), and the fact that he used **all** the relevant forms and his heirs none, suggests that his grammar differed from theirs in one way and not that the new grammars accumulated unrelated features. The uniformity of the change suggests uniformity in the analysis, and that tells us about people's language organs. There was initially a single change, a change in category membership: *can*, etc., formerly verbs which moved to I in the course of a derivation, came to be analyzed as I elements (8.4b). The fact that there was a single change in grammars accounts for the bumpiness: several phenomena changed simultaneously.

The change in category membership of the English modals explains the catastrophic nature of the change, not in the sense that the change spread through the population rapidly, but that phenomena changed together. The notion of change in a grammar is a way of unifying disparate phenomena, taking them to be various surface manifestations of a single change at the abstract level. Anthony Kroch and his associates (see Kroch 1989, for example) have done interesting statistical work on the spread of such changes through populations of speakers, showing that it is the grammars which spread: competing grammars may coexist in individual speakers for periods of time. They have shown that the variation observed represents oscillation between two fixed points, two grammars, and not more random oscillation in which the **phenomena** vary independently of each other. In addition, we now have computer models that simulate the spread of grammars through populations of speakers, exploiting the methods of population genetics (Niyogi and Berwick 1997, Briscoe 2000, Niyogi 2002, Yang 2002).

So much for the nature of the change, a change in people's grammars. Now let us ask why this change took place. Under the cognitive view of grammars, we do not appeal to historical forces as explanations. The cause of the grammatical change can only be earlier changes in PLD; there must have been differences in what people – in particular, children – experienced. In this instance, there were two such changes.

First, the modal auxiliaries became distinct morphologically, the sole surviving members of the preterite-present class of verbs. Here is how that happened. In early English, there were many verb classes, and the antecedents of the modern modals were preterite-presents. The preterite-presents (so-called because their present tense forms had past tense or "preterite" morphology) were distinct in that they never had any inflection for the third person singular, although they were inflected elsewhere: *þu cannst* "you(sg) can," *we cunnan* "we can," *we cuðon* "we could." Nonetheless, they were just another class of verbs, one of many, and the forms that were to become modal auxiliaries belonged to this class, along with a number of other verbs which either dropped out of the language altogether or were assimilated to another more regular class of verbs. For example, *unnan* "grant" was lost from the language and *witan* "know" simply dropped out of the preterite-present class, coming to be treated like non-preterite-presents. After the simplification of verb morphology, verb classes collapsed and the only inflectional property of present tense verbs to survive was the *-s* ending for the third person singular, and the preterite-present verbs had always lacked that property. The preterite-presents did not change in this regard, but a great mass of inflectional distinctions had disappeared, and now the preterite-presents were isolated; they looked different from all other verbs in lacking their one morphological feature, that *-s* ending. And the surviving preterite-presents were the elements which would be recategorized as I items.

The morphological distinctiveness of the surviving preterite-presents, the new modals, was complemented by a new opacity in their past tense forms. The past tense forms of the preterite-present verbs were phonetically identical in many instances to the subjunctive forms and, when the subjunctive forms were lost, past tense forms survived with subjunctive-type meanings rather than indicating past time reference. While *loved* is related to *love* pretty much exclusively in terms of time reference in present-day English, the relationship between *can* and *could* is sometimes one of time (8.5ai) and sometimes has nothing to do with time (8.5aii). And *might* is never related to *may* in terms of time in present-day English (8.5bi,bii); in earlier times, *might* did indicate past time (8.5biii) but the thought of (8.5biii) would need to be expressed as *might not have intended* in present-day English. So *might, could, should,* etc. came to take on new meanings which had nothing to do with past time, residues of the old subjunctive uses; that is what we mean when we say that the past tense forms became semantically opaque.

(8.5) a. i.   Kim could understand the book, until she reached page 56.
       ii. Kim could be here tomorrow.
     b. i. *Kim might read the book yesterday.
       ii. Kim may/might read the book tomorrow.
       iii. These two respectable writers might not intend the mischief they were doing. (1762 Bp Richard Hurd, *Letters on Chivalry and Romance*, 85)

As a result of these two changes, the preterite-present verbs came to look different from all other verbs in the language: they were morphologically distinct, and also their past tense forms did not have the meanings associated with the past tense of real verbs. UG provides a small inventory of grammatical categories and elements are assigned to a category on the basis of their morphological and distributional properties. Consequently, morphological changes entail new primary linguistic data: after the morphological changes occurred, children heard different things, and these new PLD may trigger new category distinctions. In this case, we know that, following the morphological changes, the surviving verbs of the preterite-present class were assigned to a new grammatical category, and that change was complete by the early sixteenth century. The evidence for the new category membership is the simultaneous loss of the phenomena we discussed in (8.2c–g).

There were two stages to the history of English modal auxiliaries (Lightfoot 1999, ch. 6). First, a change in category membership, whereby *can*, etc. ceased to be treated as verbs and came to be taken as manifestations of the I category; this change affected some verbs before others, but it was complete by the sixteenth century. Consequently, for a sentence like *Kim can sing*, early grammars had structures like (8.4a), where *can* is an ordinary verb which sometimes moves to

I, but later grammars had structures like (8.4b), where *can* is an I item, drawn from the lexicon and merged into a structure as an instance of I. As a result, sentences like (8.2ci–gi) dropped out of the language and no longer occurred in texts.

The second stage was that the grammars of English speakers lost the operation moving verbs to a higher I position (e.g., in 8.4a). This change was completed only in the eighteenth century, later than is generally supposed (Warner 1997). At this point, sentences with a finite verb moved to some initial position (8.2aii) or to the left of a negative (8.2bii) became obsolete and were replaced by equivalent forms with the periphrastic *do*: *Does Kim understand this chapter? Kim does not understand this chapter*, etc. Also sentences with an adverb between the finite verb and its complement became obsolete: *Kim reads always the newspapers*. This change has been discussed extensively and Lightfoot (1999, section 6.3) argues that it was caused by prior changes in PLD, most notably the recategorization of the modal verbs just discussed and the rise of periphrastic *do* forms (above). These changes had the effect of greatly reducing the availability of the relevant cue, $[_I V]$, i.e. a verb occurring in an I position.

The two changes are, presumably, related in ways that we do not entirely understand: first, the Inflection position was appropriated by a subclass of verbs, the modal auxiliaries and *do*, and the V-to-I operation no longer applied generally to all tensed clauses. Somewhat later, the V-to-I movement operation was lost for all verbs other than the exceptional *be* and *have* (see below) and I was no longer a position to which verbs might move. We pass over the details of this change here, in order to discuss something else.

An intriguing paper by Anthony Warner (1995) shows that there is a third stage to the history of English auxiliaries, involving changes taking place quite recently affecting the copula *be*, and this turns out to be of current theoretical interest. It has often been observed that VP ellipsis is generally insensitive to morphology. So one finds ellipses where the understood form of the missing verb differs from the form of the antecedent (8.6).

(8.6) a. Kim slept well, and Jim will [sc. sleep well] too.
 b. Kim seems well behaved today, and she often has [sc. seemed well behaved] in the past, too.
 c. Although Kim went to the store, Jim didn't [sc. go to the store].

There is a kind of sloppy identity at work here. One way of thinking of this is that in (8.6a) *slept* is analyzed as $[past+_V sleep]$ and the understood verb of the second conjunct accesses the verb *sleep*, ignoring the tense element. However, Warner noticed that the verb *be* works differently. *Be* may occur in elliptical constructions, but only under conditions of strict identity with the antecedent form (8.7). In (8.7a,b) the understood form is identical to the antecedent, but not in the non-occurring (8.7c,d,e).

(8.7) a. Kim will be here, and Jim will [sc. be here] too.
  b. Kim has been here, and Jim has [sc. been here] too.
  c. *Kim was here, and Jim will [sc. be here] too.
  d. *If Kim is well behaved today, then Jim probably will [sc.be well behaved] too.
  e. *Kim was here yesterday, and Jim has [sc. been here] today.

This suggests that *was* is not analyzed as [past + ᵥ*be*], analogously to *slept*, and *be* may be used as an understood form only where there is precisely a *be* available as an antecedent; not *was* or *is*, but just *be*, as in (8.7a). Similarly for *been*; compare (8.7b) and (8.7e). And similarly for *am, is, are, was, were*.

Warner goes on to note that the ellipsis facts of modern English were not always so and one finds forms like (8.7c,d,e) in earlier times. Jane Austen was one of the last writers to use such forms and she used them in her letters and in speech in her novels, but she did not use them in narrative prose (8.8a,b). These forms also occur in the work of eighteenth century writers (8.8c), and earlier, when verbs still moved to I (8.8d).

(8.8) a. I wish our opinions were the same. But in time they will [sc. be the same]. (1816 Jane Austen, *Emma*, ed. by R.W. Chapman, London: OUP, 1933. 471)
  b. And Lady Middleton, is she angry? I cannot suppose it possible that she should [sc. be angry]. (1811 Jane Austen, *Sense and Sensibility*, ed. by C. Lamont, London: OUP, 1970. 237)
  c. I think, added he, all the Charges attending it, and the Trouble you had, were defray'd by my Attorney: I ordered that they should [sc. be defrayed]. (1740–1 Samuel Richardson, *Pamela*, London. 3rd edition 1741. Vol. II, 129)
  d. That bettre loved is noon, ne never schal. (*c.* 1370 Chaucer, *A Complaint to his Lady*, 80. "So that no one is better loved, or ever shall [sc. be].")

These forms may be understood if *were* in (8.8a) was analyzed as subjunctive +*be* and the *be* was accessed by the understood *be*. In other words, up until the early nineteenth century, the finite forms of *be* were decomposable, just like ordinary verbs in present-day English. This is what the ellipsis facts suggest.

Warner then points to other differences between present-day English and the English of the early nineteenth century. Present-day English shows quite idiosyncratic restrictions on particular forms of the verb *be*, which did not exist before the late eighteenth century. For example, only the finite forms of *be* may be followed by *to*+infinitive with a modal sense of obligation (8.9a); only *been* may occur with a directional preposition phrase, effectively meaning "gone" (8.9b); and *being*, unlike any other form of *be*, has a special restriction that it does not permit an *ing* complement (8.9c).

(8.9) a.   i.   Kim was to go to Paris.

        ii. *Kim will be to go to Paris.

    b.   i.   Kim has been to Paris.

        ii. *Kim was to Paris.

    c.   i.   I regretted Kim reading that chapter.

        ii.   I regretted that Kim was reading that chapter.

       iii. *I regretted Kim being reading that chapter.

Restrictions of this type are stated in the lexicon and these idiosyncrasies show clearly that *been*, *being*, etc. must be listed as individual lexical entries, because they have individual peculiarities. However, these restrictions are fairly new in the language and we find forms corresponding to the non-occurring sentences of (8.9a–c) through the eighteenth century:

(8.10) a.   You will be to visit me in prison with a basket of provisions; ... (1814 Jane Austen, *Mansfield Park*, ed. by J. Lucas, Oxford: Oxford University Press, 1970. 122)

     b.   I was this morning to buy silk. (1762 Oliver Goldsmith, *Cit W*: 158 (meaning "I went to ... ," not "I had to ... "))

     c.   Two large wax candles were also set on another table, the ladies being going to cards. (1726 Daniel Defoe, *The Political History of the Devil*, Oxford: Talboys, 1840. 336)

     d.   ... he being now going to end all with the Queene ... (1661 Samuel Pepys, *Diary* II 129.1(30 June))

     e.   One day being discoursing with her upon the extremities they suffered . . . (1791 Daniel Defoe, *Robinson Crusoe*. Vol. II, 218)

     f.   ... and exclaimed quite as much as was necessary, (or, being acting a part, perhaps rather more,) at the conduct of the Churchills, in keeping him away. (1816 Jane Austen, *Emma*. 145)

     g.   Their being going to be married. (1811 Jane Austen, *Sense and Sensibility*, ed. by R.W. Chapman, Oxford: Oxford University Press, 1923. 182)

     h.   The younger Miss Thorpes being also dancing, Catherine was left to the mercy of Mrs. Thorpe. (1818 Jane Austen, *Northanger Abbey*, ed. by R.W. Chapman, Oxford: Oxford University Press, 1923. 52)

Warner concludes that after the change

was continues to carry the information that it is third singular past finite indicative. The point is that it does not do so as a consequence of inflection or inflectional relationships, but is essentially monomorphemic. The relationship *was:be* becomes fundamentally different not only from regular verbs *loved:love*, etc. but also from that of irregular or suppletive verbs (*slew:slay, went:go*), which are in some sense essentially compositional, as the contrast of behavior in ellipsis shows. (Warner 1995, p. 538)

Whether the change affects *be* alone or also *have*, it is clearly restricted to a very narrow class of lexical items. The analysis, however, reflects quite general properties and the change relates to the matter of category membership. Forms of *be* cease to be analyzed as a verb with the usual morphological structure and came to be listed in the lexicon atomically with no internal structure.

Words are stored in different ways in the mental lexicon. Irregular words are stored individually, while words formed by a regular, productive process are not. The various forms of *be* are listed individually in the lexicon, like *mice* and *men*, and they are not composed by productive lexical processes. Our conclusion, then, is that *was, been*, etc. have no internal structure and occur in the lexicon as unanalyzed primitives. In that case, computational operations like those involved in ellipsis may access atomic forms like *was* or *been* but not any internal structure along the lines of [past+*be*], because they do not exist.

Grammars have quite small sets of categories and individual lexical items are assigned to one or other of these categories. Evidence suggests that items are assigned to grammatical categories on the basis of their morphological properties. If a given item becomes morphologically distinct from other items in its category, then it is liable to be assigned to a new category. This is what was involved in the earlier changes involving the modal auxiliaries, formerly preterite-present verbs. As a result of changes affecting the preterite-present class of verbs and the subjunctive mood, these items became morphologically and semantically distinct from other verbs and were assigned to a new category, I(nflection), as we just saw. Similarly with the changes affecting *be* in the eighteenth century.

If we ask why this third change took place, we get some insight into the grammatical property involved. Again, the only explanation available to us must derive from earlier changes in PLD, in people's linguistic experience. The change in the internal structure of *be* forms was preceded by two other changes.

First, the operation moving verbs to an I position, V-to-I, was finally lost in the eighteenth century, as manifested by the obsolescence of sentences like (8.2aii) and (8.2bii). The loss of V-to-I movement further distinguished the modal auxiliaries from verbs, with the modals continuing to occur in the old I positions, clause-initially and to the left of a negative. Unlike modals in other respects, *be* patterns with them in this regard and not with verbs: *Is she happy?* and *She is not happy.*

Second, the pronoun *thou* and the accompanying inflectional forms in *(e)st* were lost from informal spoken English in the eighteenth century. *Thou* had the use of French *tu*, directed to children, intimates, and inferiors. It was lost for social reasons, as speakers abandoned a linguistic manifestation of these social distinctions. The obsolescence of *Thou shalt, Thou shouldest*, etc. removed the last inflectional property of modal verbs which was shared with ordinary verbs.

Modals had become very different from verbs in the course of changes that we have linked to their change in category, completed by the sixteenth century. They ceased to have non-finite forms, ceased to have mood and tense forms, ceased to have complements, etc; all of which showed that they were recategorized as I elements. The loss of the second person singular forms constituted a further step in this bifurcation: the last remaining inflectional commonality shared by modals and ordinary verbs was lost. This last change also affected the verb *be*, which had shown no symptoms of the category change affecting the modals: *be* did not lose its non-finite forms in the way that *can* did, nor did it lose its mood and tense forms, nor its ability to be followed by a complement. Now, however, forms of *be* became distinct from ordinary verbs in that they continued to move to I and on to C, while main verbs lost this ability, and they did not look like verbs any more in terms of their finite inflectional properties.

The first of these changes affected all verbs – they ceased to move to I – and the second change affected all verbs and (modal) elements generated in the I position. Neither change affected *be* in particular, but their effect was to single out *be* and make it less like a verb. As a result of these changes, *be* differed from verbs in that it could occur in (structurally) high functional positions like I and C, and it lacked the only morphological properties characteristic of verbs, the universal third person singular marker in *s* and the usual past tense *ed* marker.

It is plausible that these were the changes which led children to treat *be* differently. *Be* was once a verb, but now it ceased to look like a verb and ceased to have the internal structure of a verb. Nor was it an I element: *be* did not undergo the category change that the modals underwent by the sixteenth century and it was never associated intrinsically with the (finite) I position in the way that modals are, and continues to occur in non-finite contexts (*I want to be happy*, *Being happy is a good thing*, *Be happy!*, etc). This shows that the finite forms of *be* move to I and are not base-generated there like the modals. In the eighteenth century verbs ceased to move to I but the finite forms of *be* continued to do so. As a result, *be* no longer walked like a verb and no longer talked like a verb. The evidence suggests that, in addition, in the nineteenth century *be* ceased to show the paradigmatic properties of verbs. *Be* was no longer categorized as a verb; instead, its inflectional paradigm was individually specified as a series of lexical items, stored individually in the mental lexicon. This was the grammatical change.

Forms of *be* (and similarly verbal forms in French) are fully formed by lexical operations but verbs in English are bare, acquiring affixes via the syntax, when syntactic features are realized on the verb. Before that takes place, the abstract *sleep* of *slept* is identifiable as a distinct unit and therefore is an appropriate antecedent for ellipsis in (8.6a) *Kim slept well, and Jim will [sc. sleep well] too.* This reveals how elements are stored in the mental lexicon: *is* is stored in just that form while *slept* is stored as $_V$*sleep* with the form *slept* created morphologically by the attachment of an affix. If all verbs were treated the same way, as in Chomsky 1995, there would be no obvious way to make the distinction between those which may be antecedents for ellipsis under conditions of sloppy identity (*sleep*, etc.), and those which may not (*is*, *are*, and other forms of *be*).

Lasnik (1999, ch. 5) drew a similar distinction between "affixal" and "featural" verbs and keyed the distinction to whether the verb moves: if a verb moves in the syntax (e.g., *be* forms and all finite verbs in French), then it already has its inflectional features attached when it is merged into the syntactic structure and is "featural," but if a verb does not move to a higher inflectional position, then it is "affixal" and has affixes lowered onto it in the syntax. However, this correlation is not general and there is more to the story than this. Modal elements are featural and are generated in I, not moving there. Finite *be*, on the other hand, clearly moves to I, because *be* may also occur in other, non-finite positions if I is filled with a modal (8.11).

(8.11) Kim might still be reading that chapter.

So forms of *be* (and *have*) move to I; they are and always have been featural. They have always moved to I at all stages of their history but it was only in the late eighteenth century that they came to be stored atomically and developed the odd properties discussed here. We conclude that if a verb is featural, it moves to I. However, a featural item may be base-generated in I (modern modals) and may or may not be stored atomically: *was* is not a verb and it is stored atomically in modern grammars.

What is important about this story is that, while the changes we have discussed only involve the verb *be*, they have the hallmarks of grammatical change. There are several surface changes, all involving *be*, which can be attributed to one analytical notion. The changes reflect quite general properties of the grammar. One can identify the structural property which is relevant and we can tell a plausible and rather elegant story about why and how the grammatical change might have come about. We distinguish how items are stored in the lexicon.

We see, again, that morphology has syntactic effects. It is particularly important in defining category membership; children assign items to categories on the basis of their morphology. We have explained the third change by pointing to changes in the trigger experience which led to the new morphological structure of *be* forms. Those changes in the trigger are a function of prior grammatical shifts, relating to the change in category membership of the modal auxiliaries and the loss of V-to-I movement; there are links among the three changes and we have another domino effect. Again we have local causes and we do not need to appeal to internal motivating factors.

While morphology clearly influences category membership, one finds a stronger claim in the literature. It is sometimes argued that richly inflected languages differ in a fundamental, global way from poorly inflected languages like English, Swedish, and Chinese. In this context, it might be argued that grammars with rich inflectional systems, like those of French speakers, list forms individually in the lexicon and do not form them by general operations. On the analysis offered here, this would entail that there would be no bare forms available to syntactic operations and one would find various lexical restrictions on particular forms, as we saw for *be* in present-day English in (8.10) above. In grammars like those of present-day English speakers, involving fewer inflectional distinctions, there are fewer individual listings. Plural nouns in *s* and third person singular forms of verbs in *s* are composed in the syntax through the affixal realization of featural content, and they are not listed in the lexicon fully formed. As a result, the bare form of the noun and of the verb, shorn of its affixal ending, is available to various grammatical operations and it is not possible to state lexical restrictions on particular third person singular forms.

However, the material of this section shows that this is not correct and it suggests that the way items are stored in the lexicon is neither a function of movement nor a simple function of morphological richness. Verbs and *be* could occur in ellipses without strict identity with their antecedent up until the nineteenth century. This suggests strongly that their forms were not stored atomically, even though they were richly inflected in the early stages of the language; instead, they were formed by operations applying internal to the lexicon. Consequently, we conclude that the way elements are stored in the lexicon has many syntactic consequences, but that distinction represents variation which is independent of whether an item moves to an Inflection position and independent of whether an item is richly inflected.

In affecting a narrow class of words, the third change described here is small scale. It can be understood in terms of prior changes, including the highly contingent loss of *thou* forms, and it reflects ways in which items may be stored in the mental lexicon. It is a function of earlier changes.

In this section we have tracked some changes affecting the English modal auxiliaries, changes which might be labeled "grammaticalization." We have shown local causes for each of the three changes in grammars (the new category membership of the modal auxiliaries, the loss of V-to-I movement, and the new atomic lexical forms *was*, etc.), taking grammars to be individual, internal systems existing in individual brains. There was nothing inevitable about these changes: the equivalent words in French and Swedish did not undergo parallel changes, because there were no parallel local causes. Grammaticalization theory has nothing to say about small-scale changes like these, nor does it tell us why Swedish and French have not behaved like English. The problem with postulating general historical tendencies is that they are too "Cyclopean" (to adopt a useful term from Calvert Watkins' (1976) critique of typological analyses) and too gross to be enlightening, and they predict that languages should undergo parallel historical changes.

If changes in category membership are relatively common (whatever that means), they still need local causes. Identifying local causes enables us to understand the details of the change, as we have illustrated here. This case study suggests that category changes may result from morphological changes. Not many of the world's languages have a richly recorded history, but many that do have undergone morphological simplification, sometimes with category changes. If our historical records included languages with increasing morphological complexity, we would be in a stronger position to relate morphological and categorial changes. However, given the records that we have, we can see the precariousness and uselessness of seeking to explain categorial changes by general historical tendencies.

8.4   Syntactic effects of the loss of case

In chapter 3 we sketched a theory of abstract Case, which determines the positions in which DPs may be pronounced, extending the traditional notion of morphological case. DPs occur as the subject of a finite clause (*they left*), as a specifier of a larger DP (*their book*), or as a complement to a verb or a preposition (*read them, look at them*). Our abstract Case seems to be related to the overt, morphological case studied by earlier grammarians, and one can probe that relationship by examining what happens syntactically when a morphological case system is eroded and eventually lost.

In this section we shall examine some curious syntactic effects resulting from the disappearance of the morphological case system in English. The loss of morphological case will enable us to understand to a significant degree the hitherto mysterious emergence of new "split genitives" in Middle English. What strikes us is the tightness of the explanation, the way in which one element of Case theory explains the details of the development. We shall see that if one part of a child's linguistic experience changes, namely the transparency of the case morphology, then other things must also change in the grammars which emerge.[4]

The Case theory we adopt links Case to thematic roles. Thematic roles define the semantic relationship of DPs to a head. In (8.12a) the subject DP is an Agent, in (8.12b) a Theme, in (8.12c) a Location, and in (8.12d) an Instrument. These

---

[4] The loss of morphological case is discussed more fully in Lightfoot 1999, ch. 5, from which this study is drawn, with some revisions.

thematic roles are a function of the meaning of the verb and are "assigned" by the verb, so the DPs are thematically linked to the verbs. In a sentence like *Kay drove to New York*, *New York* is thematically linked to the preposition *to* and not to the verb *drove*; in a phrase *John's mother's house*, the DP *John's mother* is thematically related to *house* but the smaller DP *John* is thematically related only to *mother*.

(8.12) a. [DP The striker] kicked the defender.
     b. [DP The striker] received the award.
     c. [DP The Indian Ocean] surrounds Madagascar.
     d. [DP The wind] blew the door open.

If UG stipulates that heads may assign Case to the left or to the right in accordance with the head-order parameter, as we indicated in chapter 3, one is not surprised to find Old English nouns assigning Case to the left **and** to the right. There is good reason to believe that the head-order parameter was shifting in late Old English: one finds verbs preceding and following their complement, object–verb order alternating with verb–object. There is independent evidence that OE nouns assigned genitive Case not only to the left (8.13a) but also to the right (8.14b). One finds possessive–head order alternating with head–possessive. Old English has a very simple analysis. It is more or less a direct manifestation of this UG theory of Case: nouns assigned Case to the left and to the right, and only to DPs with which they were thematically related, as we shall see. Case was assigned in that fashion and then was **realized** on both sides of the noun with the morphological, genitive suffix. *Lof* assigns a thematic role to *god* in (8.13ai) and *lufu* to *god* and *mann* in (8.13bi).

(8.13) a. i. Godes lof "praise of God" (Ælfric)
        ii. Cristes læwa "betrayer of Christ"
     b. i. Lufu godes and manna "love of God and of men"
           (Ælfric, *Catholic Homilies* ii, 602.12)
        ii. Ormæte stream wæteres "huge stream of water"
           (Ælfric, *Catholic Homilies* ii, 196.5)

If Old English nouns assigned Case to the left and to the right, and if in both positions it was realized as a morphological genitive, then one is not surprised to find that Old English also manifested "split genitives" (the term is Eilert Ekwall's (1943)). These were split in that a single genitive phrase occurred on both sides of the head noun. In (8.14) we see an example where the split element occurring to the right of the noun was a conjunct. Jespersen (1909, p. 300) notes that with conjuncts, splitting represents the usual word order in Old English.

(8.14) a. Inwæres   broþur   ond   Healfdenes
          Inwær's   brother   and   Healfden's
          Inwær's and Healfden's brother (*AS Chron.*, 878)
    b. Sodoma   lande   7   gomorra
         Sodom's   land   and   Gomorra
         The Sodomites' and the Gomorreans' land (*West Saxon Gospels* (Ms A), Matt 10.15)

In addition, appositional elements, where two DPs are in parallel, were usually split: the two elements occurred on either side of the head noun (8.15a–c), although (8.15d) was also possible, where *Ælfredes cyninges* is not split.

(8.15) a. Ælfredes godsune cyninges.
         King Alfred's godson. (*AS Chron.*, 890; Laud (Peterborough) [E] 1122))
    b. þæs cyninges dagum herodes.
         In the days of Herod the king. (*West Saxon Gospels* (Ms A), Matt 2.1)
    c. Iohannes dagum fulwihteres.
         From the days of John the Baptist. (*West Saxon Gospels* (Ms A), Matt 11.12)
    d. Ælfredes cyninges godsunu. (*AS Chron.*, 890 (Parker c. 900))
    e. *The book's cover about Rio (= The book about Rio's cover)
    f. *þæs cyninges   godsune   Frances
         the of king   godson   of France
         The king of France's godson

Splitting within DPs was restricted to conjuncts (8.14) and to appositional elements (8.15a–c). In particular, Old English did not show split constructions with a preposition phrase (PP), along the lines of (8.15e). So there was no general rule "extraposing" a PP. Nor does one find anything like (8.15f), where *Frances* has no thematic relation to *godsune*.

Split genitives in Old English had a structure along the lines of (8.16). *Ælfredes* was in the specifier of DP. *Godsune* assigned a thematic role and Case to the left and to the right.[5]

(8.16) $[_{DP\,Spec}$Ælfredes D $[_{NP}$ godsune [cyninges]]]

These grammars had an overt genitive case on the right or on the left of the head noun; and they had split genitives, where the head noun assigned the same

---

[5] Cynthia Allen (2002) argues that *cyninges* is an adjunct to *godsune* rather than a complement. This raises interesting questions which we shall not discuss here.

thematic role and Case in both directions. So much for splitting in Old English grammars.

Now for the mysterious changes. Middle and early Modern English also manifested split genitives but they included forms which are very different from the split genitives of Old English, as the examples of (8.17) show.

(8.17) a. The clerkes tale *of Oxenford*. (Chaucer, *Clerk's Tale*, Prologue)
b. The Wive's Tale *of Bath*. (Chaucer, *Wife of Bath's Tale*, Prologue)
c. Kyng Priamus sone *of Troy*. (Chaucer, *Troilus & Cressida*, I, 2)
d. This kynges sone of *Troie*. (Chaucer, *Troilus & Cressida*, III,1715)
e. The Archbishop's Grace *of York*. (Shakespeare, *1 Henry IV*, III.ii.119)

The meaning is "The clerk of Oxford's tale," "King Priam of Troy's son," etc, and the genitive is split in the same sense as in Old English grammars: the rightmost part of the genitive phrase (italicized) occurs to the right of the head noun which the genitive phrase modifies. Mustanoja (1960, p. 78) notes that "the split genitive is common all through ME [Middle English]" and is more common than the modern "group genitive," *The clerk of Oxford's tale*. Jespersen (1909, p. 293), exaggerating a little, calls this splitting "the universal practice up to the end of the fifteenth century." However, these Middle English split forms are different from those of Old English grammars, because the rightmost element is neither a conjunct nor appositional, and it has no thematic relation with the head noun, *tale*, *son*, *Grace*, but rather with the item to the left: *clerk*, *wife*, etc. How did these new split forms emerge and become so general?

We can understand the development of the new Middle English split genitives in light of the loss of the overt morphological case system and the theory of Case related to thematic role. Culicover (1997, pp. 37f.) discusses the "thematic case thesis," under which abstract Case realizes thematic-role assignment quite generally. This is where we seek to connect work on abstract Case with the morphological properties discussed by earlier grammarians.

Old English had four cases (nominative, accusative, genitive, and dative) and a vestigial instrumental, but they disappear in the period of the tenth to thirteenth century, the loss spreading through the population from the north to the south probably under the influence of the Scandinavian settlements (O'Neil 1978). In early Middle English, grammars emerged which lacked the morphological case properties of the earlier systems, in particular lacking a morphological genitive.

Put yourself now in the position of a child with this new, caseless grammar; your grammar has developed without morphological case. You are living in the thirteenth century; you would hear forms such as (8.15a) *Ælfredes godsune cyninges*, but the case endings do not register: that is what it means not to have morphological case in one's grammar. You are not an infant and you are old enough to have a partial analysis, which identifies three words. *Ælfredes* was construed as a "possessive" noun in the specifier of DP.

The modern "possessive" is not simply a reflex of the old genitive case. Morphological case generally is a property of nouns. On the other hand, "possessive" in modern English is a property of the DP and not of nouns: in (8.18a) *My uncle from Cornwall's cat* the possessor is the whole DP *My uncle from Cornwall*. Allen (1997) shows that the *'s* is a clitic attached to the preceding element and that the group genitive, where the clitic is attached to a full DP, is a late Middle English innovation.

(8.18) a. [DP [DP my uncle from Cornwall]'s cat]
        b. Poines his brother. (Shakespeare, *2 Henry IV*, 2.4.308)
        c. For Jesus Christ his sake. (1662 *Book of Common Prayer*)
        d. Mrs. Sands his maid. (*OED*, 1607)
        e. Job's patience, Moses his meekness, and Abraham's faith. (*OED*, 1568)

As the case system was lost, the genitive ending *es* was reanalyzed as something else, a Case-marking clitic. If *'s* comes to be a clitic in Middle English, which Case-marks DPs, this would explain why "group genitives" begin to appear only at that time, as Allen argued. Allen's analysis also predicts Jespersen's observation that splitting was the universal practice until the clitic became available.

It is likely that there was another parallel reanalysis of the genitive *es* ending, yielding the *his*-genitives which were current in the sixteenth and seventeenth centuries (8.18b,c) for "Poines' brother," "Christ's sake," etc. The genitive ending in *'s* was sometimes spelled *his*, and this form occurs even with females (8.18d), and occurs alongside possessive clitics (8.18e).

UG dictates that every phonetic DP has Case, as we sketched in chapter 3. The new caseless children reanalyzed the old morphological genitive suffix *es* as a clitic, which was recruited as a Case-marker. The clitic *'s* Case-marks the element in the specifier of the containing DP. So *Ælfred* has Case and the Case is realized through the *'s* marker (usually analyzed as the head D, as in the structure given for (8.19a); see also chapter 3). In short, the *Ælfredes* of the parents is reanalyzed as *Ælfred's*, although orthographic forms like *Ælfredes* occur in texts when mental grammars surely yielded *Ælfred's*. Orthographic *'s* is a recent innovation. So far, so good.

What about *cyninges* in (8.15a)? The evidence suggests that the phrase became (8.19a) *Ælfred's godsune king*. One finds phrases of just this form in (8.19b,c), where the post-nominal noun is not overtly Case-marked, and

Jespersen (1909, pp. 283f.) notes that these forms are common in Middle English.

(8.19) a. Ælfred's godsune king
[DP [DP Ælfred] D's [NP godsune [king]]]
b. The kynges metynge Pharao
Pharaoh the king's dream (Chaucer, *Book of the Duchess*, 282)
c. The Grekes hors Synoun
Sinon the Greek's horse (Chaucer, *Squire's Tale*, 209)

The forms of (8.19), where the rightmost element is appositional, are direct reflexes of OE split genitives like (8.15), corresponding exactly, except that the split element, *Pharao*, *Synoun*, has no overt Case. Despite the absence (for us new, caseless children – remember our thought experiment) of an overt, morphological genitive case, UG prescribes that the post-nominal DP must carry some abstract Case. After the loss of the morphological case system, it can no longer be realized as a genitive case ending. That means that there must be another way of marking/realizing the abstract Case in (8.19). Perhaps *Pharao* receives its Case by coindexing with the Case-marked *kynges*; the two forms are in apposition and therefore are coindexed and share the same thematic role. This is what one would expect if there is a one-to-one relationship between Case and thematic role, the key element of our theory of Case. In that event, no independent Case-marker is needed for *Pharao*.

There is another option for realizing Case on the rightmost element. The dummy preposition *of* could be used as a Case-marker, as it is in (8.17) (see chapter 3, note 11). This is not possible in *Ælfred's godsune king* or the phrases of (8.19), because if *of* were to Case-mark the DP, one would expect it also to assign a thematic role (given a one-to-one relation between Case and thematic role) and in that event the DP could not be interpreted as an appositional element. The sentences of (8.17), on the other hand, are not like those of (8.19) and have different meanings. In (8.17b), for example, *Wive* and *Bath* are not appositional, not coindexed, and therefore an independent Case-marker and thematic-role assigner is needed; this is the function of *of*. [6] Under this view, the emergence in Middle English of the new *N of DP* forms (8.17) is an automatic consequence of the loss of the morphological case system: *of* was introduced in order to Case-mark a DP which would not otherwise be Casemarked. In particular, the DP could not be Case-marked like the rightmost item in (8.19), which carries the same Case as *Ælfred's* because it has the same thematic role. *Of* assigns Case to a DP only if it has an independent thematic role.

---

[6] Nunnally (1985, p. 21) finds no genitival *of* phrases in his study of the OE translation of St. Matthew's Gospel (*of* was used frequently to show origin or agency, best translated by modern *from* or *by*).

With the introduction of the *of* Case-marker in these contexts, there is a further change and the split genitive construction is extended, as we have noted (8.17). In Old English, the post-nominal genitive always had a thematic relation with the head noun; one does not find expressions such as (8.15f) *þæs cyninges son Frances* "The king of France's son," where *Frances* is neither a conjunct nor appositional and is thematically related to "king" (Nunnally 1985, p. 148, Cynthia Allen, Willem Koopman, personal communication). In such a phrase, *Frances* could not be Case-marked by any adjacent element; in particular, it could not receive Case from *son* because it has no thematic relation with *son*. In Middle English, one does find post-nominal, split DPs even where there is no thematic relation with the head noun, and the post-nominal items are Case-marked by *of*. So, in (8.17a) *Oxenford* is construed with *clerkes* and not with *tale*, and it is Case-marked by *of*. It is crucial to note that the Middle English split expressions only involve *of* phrases: one does not find *The book's cover about Rio* for "the book about Rio's cover," mirroring the situation in Old English and showing that there is no general operation "extraposing" PPs in Middle English, any more than there was in Old English. Additionally, – and this is crucial – the post-nominal noun in (8.17) always has a thematic role of Locative/Source. We know of no claim to this effect in the literature but it has been pointed out to us by Cynthia Allen, Olga Fischer, and Willem Koopman in independent personal communications and it seems to be right. So, for example, one does not find forms like (8.20), where the post-nominal noun is a Theme (8.20a) or a Possessor (8.20b).

(8.20) a. *The portrait's painter of Saskia (= the portrait of Saskia's painter)
       b. *The wife's tale of Jim (= the wife of Jim's tale)

The fact that the *of* phrase is associated with a unique thematic role makes sense if UG prescribes a link between Case and thematic-role assignment. As we have noted, in Old English (8.15a) *Ælfredes godsune cyninges, godsune* assigns the same Case to the right and to the left, realized in both instances as an overt, morphological genitive case; it also assigns the same thematic role to the two DPs to which it assigns Case. That is what it means for the two DPs to be appositional (same Case, same thematic role), and all of this is easy to understand if Case and thematic-role assignment are linked at the level of UG. The same applies to conjuncts (8.14). Consequently, the extension of these split genitives in Middle English (to the new forms with *of*, (8.17)) is not surprising under a theory which allows nouns to assign Case and which links Case to thematic-role assignment.

This much we can understand under the theory of Case. The properties of the new grammar must have emerged in the way that they did, if children (a) heard expressions like *Ælfredes godsune cyninges* (8.15a), (b) did not have the morphological case system of their parents, and (c) were subject to a Case theory requiring all DPs to have Case (assigned and realized) and linking Case with the assignment of thematic roles. We have a tight explanation for the new properties of Middle English grammars. In particular, we explain the distinction between (8.17) and (8.19), with *of* occurring where there is no thematic relation with the head noun (8.17), but not where there is such a relation (8.19). We see that change is bumpy; if one element of a grammar changes, there may be many new phenomena (8.17). Children do not just match what they hear and they may produce innovative forms, as required by UG. UG defines the terrain, the hypothesis space, and a change in initial conditions (loss of morphological case) may have syntactic effects.[7]

This is an explanation for the form of the split genitives of (8.17) in Middle English. They were around for four centuries and then dropped out of the language. This was probably a function of the newly available clitic *'s* which made possible group genitives like *The clerk of Oxford's tale*; these became possible only when *'s* was construed as a clitic, which Case-marked DPs, and that in turn was a function of the loss of morphological cases, including the genitive in *es*.

Here we have taken a notion ("case") from traditional grammar, and construed Case as an element in cognitive grammars, in people's language organs. Phonetic DPs, DPs which are pronounced, have an abstract Case which must be realized somehow. This is required by UG, and abstract Cases are often realized as morphological cases. Children scan their linguistic environment for morphological cases and, if they find them, they serve to realize abstract Cases. If children do not find morphological cases, then different grammars emerge. In that event, a P or V (or other categories) may Case-mark a complement DP. We have examined here what happens when everything else remains constant. There came a point in the history of English when children ceased to find morphological cases. Those children were exposed to much the same linguistic experience as their parents, but the transparency of overt case endings had dropped below a threshold such that they were no longer attained. Given a highly restrictive theory of UG, particularly one linking Case-assignment by nouns to thematic-role assignment and requiring Cases to be realized on phonetic DPs, other things then had to change.

In this way our abstract theory of Case enables us to understand how some of the details of Middle English grammars were shaped, why things changed as they did and why Middle English grammars had their odd split genitives.

[7] Our account leaves open the question of *why* these extended split genitives (8.17) should have arisen. Lightfoot (1999) appeals to the reanalysis of one special type of Old English split genitive, those involving double names like *Thomasprest Doreward* (= priest of Thomas Doreward) and, crucially, those where the second part begins with *of*: *Rogereswarenner of Beauchamp* (= warrener of Roger of Beauchamp), which may have triggered the new split genitives.

8.5   Chaos

From the Greeks to Newton, people have believed in a predictable universe. Where unpredictable behavior was observed, for example in weather, the unpredictability was attributed to lack of knowledge: if we just knew more, we would have better weather forecasts. Pierre Simon Laplace said that he could specify all future states if he could know the position and motion of all particles in the cosmos at any moment. Recently, however, scientists in various fields have found that many systems are unpredictable despite the fact that they follow courses prescribed by deterministic principles. The key to understanding how systems may be both determinate and unpredictable – an oxymoron from the point of view of classical science – lies in the notion of sensitive dependence on initial conditions.

Predicting final outcomes – or indeed anything beyond the very short-term – becomes impossible for many types of system. Chaos incorporates elements of chance, but it is not random disorder. Rather, chaos theory tries to understand the behavior of systems that do not unfold over time in a linearly predictable manner. When viewed as a whole, these systems manifest definite patterns and structures. However, because the evolution of a chaotic system is so hugely complex and so prone to perturbation by contingent factors, it is impossible to discern its underlying pattern – its attractor – by looking at a single small event at a single point in time. At no single point can future directions be predicted from past history.

So it is with the emergence of a new species in evolutionary change, with changes in the political and social domain, and in grammar change. Change is not random, but we are dealing with contingent systems and we offer retrospective explanations, not predictions. Grammatical change is highly contingent, sensitive to initial conditions, chaotic in a technical sense. Linguists can offer satisfying explanations of change in some instances, but there is no reason to expect to find a predictive theory of change, offering long-term, linear predictions.

The emergence of a grammar in a child is sensitive to the initial conditions of the primary linguistic data. If those data shift a little, there may be significant consequences for the abstract system. A new system may be triggered, which generates a very different set of sentences and structures. There is nothing principled to be said about why the data should shift a little; those shifts often represent chance, contingent factors. Contingent changes in the distribution of the data (more accurately, changes in the "cues": Lightfoot 1999) may trigger a grammar which generates significantly different sentences and structures, and that may have some domino effects, as we have seen.

Changes in languages often take place in clusters: apparently unrelated superficial changes may occur simultaneously or in rapid sequence. Such clusters manifest a single theoretical choice which has been taken divergently. The singularity of the change can be explained by the appropriately defined theoretical choice. The principles of UG and the definition of the cues constitute the laws which guide change in grammars, defining the available terrain. Any given phenomenal change is explained if we show, first, that the linguistic environment has changed in such a way that some theoretical choice has been taken differently (say, a change in the inflectional properties of verbs), and, second, that the new phenomenon (*may*, *must*, etc. being categorized as I elements, for example) must be the way that it is because of some principle of the theory and the new inflectional system.

Sometimes we can explain domino effects of this type. Linguists have argued that a changing stress pattern may leave word-final inflection markings vulnerable to neutralization and loss. Loss of inflectional markings may have consequences for category membership and changes in category membership may have consequences for computational operations moving verbs to an I position. In that event, one establishes a link between a change in stress patterns and changes in the positions of finite verbs. Benjamin Franklin would understand: "For want of a nail, the shoe was lost; for want of a shoe the horse was lost; for want of a horse, the rider was lost." However, to say that there may be domino effects is not to say that there is a general directionality of the kind sought by nineteenth-century linguists and by modern typologists and grammaticalizationists.

What we cannot explain, in general, is why the linguistic environment should have changed in the first place (as emphasized by Lass 1997 and others). Environmental changes are often due to what we have called chance factors, effects of borrowing, changes in the frequency of forms, stylistic innovations, which spread through a community and, where we are lucky, can sometimes be documented by variation studies. Changes of this type need not reflect changes in grammars. But with a theory of language acquisition which defines the range of theoretical choices available to the child and specifies how the child may take those choices, one can predict that a child will converge on a certain grammar when exposed to certain environmental elements. This is where prediction is possible, in principle. We thus have a determinist theory of language acquisition, but not a determinist theory of history or of language change.

We have an interplay of chance and necessity, and appropriately so: changes are due to chance in the sense that contingent factors influence a child's PLD and make the triggering experience somewhat different from what the child's parent was exposed to. Necessity factors, the principles of UG and the cues, define the range of available options for the new grammar. We take a synchronic approach to history. Historical change is a kind of finite-state Markov process, where each state is influenced only by the immediately preceding state: changes have only local causes and, if there is no local cause, there is no change, regardless of the state of the grammar or the language at some previous time.

In that way, the emergence of a grammar in an individual child is sensitive to the initial conditions, to the details of the child's experience. So language change is chaotic, in a technical sense, in the same way that weather patterns are chaotic. The historian's explanations are based on available acquisition theories, and in some cases our explanations are quite tight and satisfying. Structural changes are interesting precisely because they have local causes. Identifying structural changes and the conditions under which they took place informs us about the conditions of language acquisition; we have indeed learned things about properties of UG and about the nature of acquisition by the careful examination of diachronic changes. Under this synchronic approach to change, there are no principles of history; history is an epiphenomenon and time is immaterial.

9   "Growing" a language

We have argued throughout this book that the cognitive system underlying a person's language capacity has intrinsic properties which are there by biological endowment. Those properties interact with contingencies resulting from exposure to a particular linguistic environment and the interaction yields a final state in which the person may communicate, perhaps some form of French. In that case, the person, Brigitte, will have incorporated from her environment the contingent lexical properties that *livre* is a word to refer to the novel she is reading and cooccurs with forms like *le* and *bon* (being "masculine"), *père* may refer to her father. She has also incorporated contingent structural properties: interrogative phrases like *quel livre* may be displaced to utterance-initial position, verbs raise to a higher functional position, and so on. We have described ways in which linguists have teased apart the intrinsic properties common to the species and the contingent properties resulting from individual experience. That work has been guided by the kind of poverty-of-stimulus arguments that we have discussed, by theoretical notions of economy and elegance, and by the specific phenomena manifested by the mature grammar under investigation.

Viewing a person's language capacity in this way and focusing on what we have called *I*-language leads one to ask novel questions about children and their linguistic development. The perspective we have sketched has already led to productive research and we have learned a great deal about the linguistic minds of young children. In many ways, results concerning the attainment of syntactic knowledge present the most dramatic examples of the bearing of this research on our overall thesis, and we focus on this area for much of the present chapter. Work in recent years has also shown remarkable things about the path by which children attain knowledge of the expression system of their language, however, and we turn briefly to those matters in section 9.5.

9.1   Principles of Universal Grammar: active early

If one postulates a principle of Universal Grammar (UG), one can ask whether it is available to children from birth or whether it is subject to a biological clock, becoming available only at a certain age, in the way that puberty or baldness or death are genetically determined and subject to timing constraints. In chapter 2 we discussed an experiment which showed that children manifest the hypothesized constraints about clitic nature of the reduced *'s* and that this is true at the earliest stage where they can be tested.

The same holds for another reduction process, whereby *want to* is often pronounced *wanna: I want to be happy* or *I wanna be happy*. Here, the *to* may be attached to the preceding *want* and then reduced to give the *wanna* form; but an intervening understood element blocks the reduction. For example, *Who do you want to see?* has the structure of (9.1a) (corresponding to the statement *You want to see Jill*) and it may be pronounced with the *wanna* form. *Who* is understood as the direct object (complement) of the verb *see*, indicated here by *x*.

(9.1) a. Who$_x$ do you want [$_{IP}$ $_1$to see x]?
       b. Who$_x$ do you want [$_{IP}$ x $_1$to go]?

However, when an understood element intervenes between *want* and *to*, *wanna* does not occur in the speech of most people. So an expression *Who do you want to go?* has the structure of (9.1b), where *who* is understood in the position *x* as the subject of the verb *go* (corresponding to the statement *I want Jill to go*). Structures like (9.1b) do not yield a pronunciation where *want to* is reduced to *wanna*.

The locality restriction discussed in chapter 3 also holds for the reduced *wanna* form: *to* attaches to *want* to yield the reduced form only if it is adjacent to and the top-most element in the complement of *want*. This is so in (9.1a) and therefore *want to* may be reduced. However, it is not true in the sentences of (9.2) and *want to* may not be reduced to *wanna*. We give some partial structure in (9.2aii,bii), enough to show that the *to* clause is not the complement of *want*. In (9.2aii) the IP *to win games* is not the complement of *want*; it acts as the subject of the next IP, which, in turn, is the complement of *want*. Similarly, *to vote for the incumbent is* not the complement of *want* in (9.2bii).

(9.2) a. i. They don't want to win games to be their only goal.
           ii. ... want [$_{IP}$ [$_{IP}$ $_1$to win games] $_1$to be their only goal]
       b. i. They expect people who continue to want to vote for the incumbent.
           ii. They expect [$_{IP}$ [$_{NP}$ people who continue to want] $_1$to vote for the incumbent]

A productive approach is to treat reduced *to* as a clitic, like the reduced *is* discussed in chapter 2, and it may attach to a higher *want*. Part of what a child growing a grammar needs to do is to determine the clitics in his or her linguistic environment, knowing in advance of any experience that these are small, un-stressed items left- or right-attached to an adjacent element in an appropriate structural relationship, with no other (phonetic or "understood") element intervening. This predetermined knowledge is contributed by the linguistic genotype and is what the child brings to language acquisition.

In this case too, experimenters have shown that the distinctions we have discussed do not result from learning and that the hypothesized genetic constraints are operative from the outset. They constructed situations in which children would be tempted to violate the relevant constraints. The fact that children conform to the hypothesized constraints, resisting the preferences for reduction in some contexts, shows that they have the constraints under investigation and they have them at the earliest stage where they might be manifested.

Stephen Crain and Rosalind Thornton developed an elicitation task that invited children to ask questions like (9.1b), *Who do you wanna go?*, if these were compatible with their grammars. They guessed that children would generally prefer the reduced *wanna* form whenever this was consistent with their grammars. This preference would be revealed in a frequency count of legitimate forms, like (9.1a) *Who do you wanna see?* Comparing the frequency of the reduced forms in these contexts with that of non-adult reduced forms would indicate whether or not children's grammars contained the hypothetical genetic constraint. If the genetic constraint is operative, there should be a significant difference in frequency; otherwise, not.

In the simplest case, an experimenter asked for a child's help in finding information about rats. Help was sought because the rat (a puppet) was too timid to talk to grown-ups. The experimenter said "The rat looks hungry. I bet he wants to eat something. Ask Ratty what he wants." And the children, who ranged in age from two years, ten months, to five years, five months, typically would ask "What do you wanna/want to eat?" In this example, the *wh*-word is understood as the complement of *eat* and the reduced form could occur freely, as in (9.1a). In fact, the reduced form occurred 59 percent of the time in these examples. So children do show a preference for the reduced form and that is the extent of it.

Something very different happened when the *wh*-word had to be understood in the subject position, as in (9.1b), *Who do you want to go?* The protocol for this experiment was that the experimenter would ask: "There are three guys in this story: Cookie Monster, a dog, and this baby. One of them gets to take a walk, one gets to take a nap, and one gets to eat a cookie. And the rat gets to choose who does each thing. So, **one** gets to take a walk, right? Ask Ratty who he wants." And the child would typically proceed: "Who do you want to take a walk?" Here *who* is understood as the subject of *take*, i.e. between *want* and *to*: who$_x$ you want [x to take a walk]? In these contexts the frequency of the reduced form was quite different: the reduced forms occurred 4 percent of the time. In fact, one child accounted for all three actual occurrences of the reduced form, which suggests that this particular child had some other analysis of *wanna* forms. So children prefer to use the reduced form in asking questions like (9.1a), but correctly resist this preference when it conflicts with UG principles. They use the reduced form in asking questions like (9.1a) but not in questions like (9.1b), so they manifest the hypothetical genetic constraint at a stage when their spontaneous production manifests very few instances of long-distance *wh*-movement. The ingenuity of the experiment shows that even at this stage the relevant principles are operating (Crain 1991).

The experiments we have described deal with elicited production, but comprehension studies also show that hypothetical genetic constraints are in effect in very young children, at the earliest stage where they can be tested. Thornton (1994) reported children's comprehension of yes/no questions containing negation, such as (9.3). The difference between the two forms lies in the structural position of the negative: in (9.3ai) the negative is inside the IP (partial structure given in (9.3aii)) but in (9.3bi) it has formed a word with *did* and moved out of the IP to C (9.3bii).

(9.3) a. i. Did any of the turtles not buy an apple?
       ii. [$_{CP}$ did [$_{IP}$ any of the turtles **not** buy an apple]]
   b. i. Didn't any of the turtles buy an apple?
       ii. [$_{CP}$ did**n't** [$_{IP}$ any of the turtles buy an apple]]

The position of the negative corresponds to two distinct interpretations. That correspondence between meaning and structural position follows from principles of UG, which we need not go into here; essentially, a negative has an effect on any element within its complement; logicians say that negatives have SCOPE over certain elements. The phenomenon is clear. Suppose that turtles A and B bought an apple but turtle C did not. Then if somebody asked question (9.3ai), an appropriate answer would be that turtle C did not. If somebody asked (9.3bi), then the appropriate answer would be very different: turtles A and B did. So children's responses to questions like (9.3ai,bi) reveal how they interpret negatives. In particular, responses to (9.3bi) show whether children interpret the negative in the higher structural position. This is worth testing because Thornton found that all her children **produced** non-adult negative questions. Most doubled the auxiliary verb (*What do you don't like?*) and one failed to move the auxiliary to the position of C: *What you don't like?*

In testing comprehension, Thornton found that the children had no difficulty interpreting negative questions in the adult fashion; significantly, all children were able to access interpretations like (9.3bi), where the negative needs to be interpreted in the position of C. She tested children between the ages of three and a half and four and a half. The comprehension test used a modified form of the Truth Value Judgement task (Crain 1991). A story was acted out by one experimenter and watched by the child and a second experimenter, who was playing the role of a puppet, in this case "Snail." At the end of each story, the experimenter asked Snail a targeted question. Snail had difficulty with the question ("That's a hard one . . ."), and requested help from the child. If the child was cooperative, she answered the question for Snail.[1] The scenarios used to test children's comprehension of questions like (9.3ai) and (9.3bi) were designed so that either (9.3ai) or (9.3bi) could be asked appropriately; children's answers, however, indicate their analysis of the structural position of the negative. Thornton found that, while these children made **production** errors with expressions like adult *What don't you like?*, their **comprehension** was adult-like and manifested the UG principles which determine the scope of negatives.

So there is a clear production/comprehension asymmetry, which, of course, is no surprise under the modular view of mind that we have articulated. Whatever it is that causes the delay in producing the adult forms, the fact that children interpret the negative questions in adult fashion shows that they have access to whatever principles of UG assign scope relations. The difficulty evidently lies with the behavior of the element *n't*: children produce non-adult questions which retain the *n't* in the IP until they figure out that *n't* may form part of a word with *did*[2] and move with it outside the IP to C.

Evidence suggests, then, that at least some principles of UG are available and operative at the earliest stage where they might be tested. The same might turn out to be true of all UG principles. But perhaps not. Some principles of UG may turn out to be subject to a puberty-like clock, emerging only at a certain age in a kind of "maturation." There is nothing implausible about that view and we know that it holds of some genetic properties in the physiological domain; so why not also in the cognitive domain?

In fact, the case that grammars mature in this fashion has been made. Some have argued that very young children have "semantically based" grammars and that they graduate to "syntactically based" grammars at a certain age just as tadpoles develop into frogs (Bowerman 1973; for discussion, see de Villiers and de Villiers 1985 and Gleitman and Wanner 1982). Others have argued that principles of the binding theory are not operative until they mature in the organism (Borer and Wexler 1987, Manzini and Wexler 1987). A little later we shall consider a claim that the principles of the binding theory are based on notions of linear precedence in very young children, later becoming structurally based. We do not find these maturation claims convincing and will not discuss them here, but there is nothing implausible in the general idea of maturation of genetic properties.

---

[1] The child was not asked the question directly, in order to alleviate any feeling she might have of being tested; in this setup, Snail is being quizzed, not the child. Here we are giving only the briefest description of the experiments, but the experimental techniques used for this kind of work require great ingenuity and are of enormous interest in themselves. For excellent discussion, see Crain and Thornton 1998.

[2] The most common account of this is to say that *n't* is a clitic, and attaches to *did* by cliticization. Zwicky and Pullum 1983, however, show that words like *didn't* actually represent inflected forms which exist only for a limited set of verbs, rather than cliticization. The difference between these two analyses does not bear on the point under consideration here, though.

9.2   New phenomena

The last experiment (dealing with the interpretation of (9.3)) illustrates the obvious fact that young children are not entirely similar to adults in their syntactic behavior, even if they seem to manifest at the earliest stage possible the hypothesized genetic constraints that we have discussed. In another study, Thornton analyzed an intriguing type of non-adult speech. She observed long-distance medial *wh*-questions like (9.4) in some three- and four-year-old children, where a copy of the *wh*-word shows up at the front of the clause where it is understood; such sentences do not occur in adult English, but analogues to them do occur in dialects of German and in other languages (Thornton 1995).

> (9.4) a. What do you think what pigs eat?
> b. Who do you think who eats trash?

Such phenomena had not been previously observed in the literature on child language acquisition but Thornton was struck by them in light of theoretical ideas about the displacement of *wh*-phrases. Recall that in chapter 3, where we discussed the derivation of sentences like *What city will the student visit?*, we noted that *wh*-phrases move to the front of an utterance. We noted (footnote 4 in chapter 3) that in a complex expression like *Who did Jay say that Fay saw?* (3.6b), movement is always local and the *wh*-phrase is copied first at the front of its own clause, then at the front of the next clause, and so on, as in (9.5).

> (9.5) Who$_i$ did Jay say [$_{CP}$ e$_i$ that Fay saw e$_i$]?

We know that movement is possible in an embedded clause (*I know who Fay saw*, which has the structure I know [$_{CP}$ who$_x$ Fay saw x]) and postulating that the movement is **always** local enables us to distinguish the well-formed *Who did you believe that Fay claimed that Ray saw?* from the ill-formed **What did you believe Fay's claim that Ray saw?*[3] Theorists postulated that movement is always local and successively cyclic, and Thornton observed children using overt *wh*-phrases in positions where they are always deleted in adult speech (9.4).

Not only did Thornton introduce expressions like (9.4) into the acquisition literature but she also noted further distinctions. After children stop using medial *wh*-words corresponding to a deleted complement (9.4a), they persist with them where they correspond to a deleted subject (9.4b). That developmental sequence illustrates principles of UG: the extra *wh*-word in subject extraction questions is

---

[3] The distinction is a function of a Subjacency condition which blocks movement across more than one bounding node (typically IP and DP in English grammars) and the claim that a *wh*-phrase moves to the specifier of CP (see chapter 3).

an overt manifestation of the special "agreement" properties needed to license an empty subject, as we discussed in chapter 3. Recall that a copied *wh*-phrase may not be deleted in the subject position of an embedded clause, unless it is licensed in some special, language-specific way (see the discussion following (3.18)); no such inhibitions constrain the deletion of a complement. That means that more has to be acquired from the environment in order for a person to delete a *wh*-phrase which is the subject of an embedded clause, and that explains why it takes a little longer.

There is a more primitive point to be made in this connection, primitive but of crucial importance: some children systematically produce things like (9.4), even though they never hear such sentences uttered by adult speakers of English. Children do not simply imitate models; they develop a system, a grammar, which at certain stages of development yields things which no child hears from English-speaking adults. When we study the development of these grammars (language organs), often we can understand the properties they have, even when they do not reflect what children have heard.

The sentences which children produce (e.g., (9.4)) make sense. They reflect properties of their language organs as we understand them, but they do not reflect what they hear from adults. In fact, the idea that children imitate adult speech would provide very little understanding of the stages that children go through and the kinds of things they say. And that idea cannot survive close observation of the things children actually **do** say, in comparison with the speech of the models available to them.

Another illustration of how grammatical theory has served as a diagnostic tool for acquisitionists, yielding discoveries about children's capacities, comes from the domain of so-called optional infinitives (Wexler 1994). We noted in chapter 8 that modal auxiliaries like *can*, *may*, etc. are generated as instances of Inflection (I) (9.6a) and may be displaced, moving to a higher functional position, as in (9.6b).

(9.6) a. Kim [$_I$ can] [$_{VP}$ understand the chapter].
b. [$_I$ Can] [$_{IP}$ Kim understand the chapter]?

In most European languages other than (modern) English, ordinary verbs may also move to the I position and then still further to a higher functional position. So a French sentence like *Elle lit les journaux* has the structure of (9.7a), where the verb *lit* has moved to the I position, as is clear in the corresponding negative (9.7b), where the finite *lit* has moved across the intervening *pas* (cf. *Ne pas lire les journaux . . .* , where the non-finite *lire* stays in its original position to the right of *pas*). *Lit-elle les journaux?* has the structure of (9.7c). Verb-second languages like Dutch and German are often analyzed with the same movement: *Met Hans bezoekt zij Amsterdam* "she is visiting Amsterdam with Hans" would have the structure of (9.8), where the finite verb *bezoekt* moves first to I and then to a higher position outside IP (Dutch has a head-final system, in which verbs and inflection elements occur at the right edge of their phrases).

(9.7) a. Elle [$_I$ lit$_i$] [$_{VP}$ e$_i$ les journaux].
      b. Elle ne [$_I$ lit$_i$] pas [$_{VP}$ e$_i$ les journaux].
      c. Lit$_i$ [$_{IP}$ elle e$_i$ [$_{VP}$ e$_i$ les journaux]].

(9.8) a. Met Hans bezoekt$_i$ [$_{IP}$ zij [$_{VP}$ Amsterdam e$_i$] e$_i$].

In general, as noted in chapter 3, movement takes place in order to check features. So *lit* and *bezoekt* have finite tense markers, which are checked in the I position. They may also have a feature which requires checking in a higher position, as in (9.7c) and (9.8).

David Poeppel and Ken Wexler (1993) noted that children acquiring grammars like these seem to go through an "optional infinitive stage": not only do they use adult-style finite verbs but they also use non-finite verbs in unembedded clauses, unlike adults. However, in a language like German or Dutch, the alternation is not random: the form of the verb correlates with its position in the clause. Finite verbs systematically appear in second position, as in (9.8), and non-finite verbs systematically occur clause-finally, in their original, base-generated position, showing up in infinitive forms (9.9).

(9.9) a. Thorsten   Caesar   haben.
        Thorsten   C (=doll   have
        Thorsten has (the doll) Caesar.
     b. Du   das   haben.
       you   that   have
       You have that.

Mieke Weverink (1989) supplied comparable examples from child Dutch (9.10), although no adult would produce such forms.

(9.10) a. Pappa   schoenen   wassen.
        Daddy   shoes   wash
        Daddy washes shoes.
      b. Pappa   nieuwe scooter   kopen.
        Daddy   new scooter   buy
        Daddy buys a new scooter.
      c. Ik   ook   lezen.
        I   also   read
        I'm reading too.
      d. Pappa   kranten   weg   doen
        Daddy   newspapers   away   do
        Daddy gets rid of the newspapers.

At this optional infinitive stage, children know that finite verbs may not occur (more technically, may not be "checked") in clause-final position in matrix
clauses, because they do not produce clause-final inflected verbs: *Pappa schoenen wast, *Pappa nieuwe scooter koopt. And they know that non-finite verbs
may not occur in an inflectional position and do not produce forms like *Pappa
wassen schoenen or *Ik lezen ook.

Comparable phenomena are found in young French children (Pierce 1992).
They alternate between the non-finite, non-adult forms of (9.11), where the verb
stays in its first, base-generated position inside the VP and to the right of the
negative marker pas, and the finite forms of (9.12), where the verb is finite and
therefore occurs in the I position where its finite features are checked, to the
left of pas.

(9.11) a. Pas [$_{VP}$ manger la poupée].
            Not eat the doll.
        b. Pas [$_{VP}$ tomber bébé].
            Not fall baby.
        c. Pas [$_{VP}$ attraper une fleur].
            Not catch a flower.

(9.12) a. Patsy est pas là-bas.
            Patsy is not down there.
        b. Marche pas.
            Walks not.
        c. Est pas mort.
            Is not dead.
        d. Trouve pas.
            Finds not.

There is now an extensive literature on optional infinitives, including in children with Specific Language Impairment (SLI) (Wexler, Rice, and Cleave 1995),
drawn from several languages. Much has been discovered about child language.
These discoveries show that while the children produce non-adult forms, which
they have not heard from their parents or older siblings, they nonetheless know
some very abstract principles of grammar, including head movement and the
properties of inflection which require head movement.

9.3   Experimental technique

Not only have we learned much about child language and found that children are subject to abstract principles of UG from the earliest testable stages,
but we have also discovered a lot about how to analyze children's capacities,
about experimental technique. In chapter 2, we noted that sometimes a pronoun

may precede its antecedent and sometimes not. This is the phenomenon of "backwards anaphora." So in (9.13a) (repeated from chapter 2), *he* may refer to Jay, but not in (9.13b). In both instances, *he* precedes *Jay*, but in (9.13b) *he* is also structurally higher than *Jay* in a sense that we shall not make precise here. It is Principle C of the binding theory which prevents *Jay* being coindexed with *he* in (9.13b), allowing it in (9.13a).[4]

> (9.13) a. When he entered the room, Jay was wearing a yellow shirt.
>   b. He was wearing a yellow shirt, when Jay entered the room.

Given what we said in the last section, we would expect children to conform to Principle C and to produce and understand sentences like (9.13) in the adult fashion. However, that is not what the early literature suggests. Larry Solan (1983) and Susan Tavakolian (1978) discussed experiments with children acting out sentences like (9.13), when provided with suitable toys.[5] The children were three- to eight-year-olds; not so young. For adults, (9.13a) may be interpreted as referring to two men, Jay and somebody unnamed; (9.13b) must be interpreted that way, involving two men. That interpretation is also open to children and the act-out studies found that children interpreted both types of sentences that way most commonly: two thirds of the time, in fact. This led to the conclusion that backwards anaphora does not exist in young children, that the conditions on coreference are purely linear and not structural in the early stages. Put differently, children do not permit the interpretation allowed by Principle C and are not subject to Principle C but rather only to a linear condition that a pronoun may never precede a noun to which it refers. However, the conclusion was premature.

First, one third of the responses, in fact, permitted backwards anaphora, with a pronoun referring to a noun to its right. Second, even if **all** responses disallowed backwards anaphora, that would not show that children were not subject to Principle C: perhaps they are only displaying a strong preference to have the pronoun refer to some second person unnamed in the sentence. To test adherence to Principle C one needs an experiment which shows that children sometimes allow backwards anaphora and that they reject it in the appropriate circumstances. Or not.

---

[4] The binding theory, one of the more resilient aspects of grammatical theory, divides nouns into three types: anaphors, pronouns, and everything else (sometimes called "names"). Anaphors are subject to Principle A and must be locally coindexed with a "higher" element (the technical notion is a "c-commanding" item). A pronoun must not be locally coindexed with a higher element, by Principle B. And Principle C requires that names not be coindexed with a higher element anywhere. See Chomsky 1981. In (9.13b) *he* is higher than *Jay* in the relevant sense, and therefore they may not be coindexed (Principle C); in (9.13a), on the other hand, *he* is contained in a subordinate clause and is not higher than *Jay* and therefore Principle C is irrelevant.

[5] The actual sentences used included *For him to kiss the lion would make the duck happy*, *That he kissed the lion made the duck happy*.

Crain and McKee (1986) constructed a Truth Value Judgement task, of the kind we saw earlier. Children were exposed to sentences like (9.14) (analogous to (9.13)), in situations where the pronoun was backwards anaphoric and in situations where the pronoun had another referent not mentioned in the sentence. They judged the truth value of the sentences.

(9.14) a. While he was dancing, the Ninja Turtle ate pizza.
       b. He was dancing while the Ninja Turtle ate pizza.

Sentence (9.14a) was presented twice, once where the Ninja Turtle was dancing and eating pizza and once where somebody else was dancing while the Ninja Turtle was eating pizza. Similar conditions attended the presentation of (9.14b), although no adult would use such a sentence in a situation in which the Ninja Turtle was dancing and eating pizza. For each scene, Kermit the Frog said what he thought happened in that trial, using sentences like (9.14a) or (9.14b). If Kermit said something appropriate, children could feed him something he liked; if Kermit said the wrong thing, children could get Kermit to eat something "yucky," like a rag or a cockroach, or to do push-ups. There is much to be said about the design of the experiment, but the results clearly showed that children correctly accepted the backwards anaphoric reading in sentences like (9.14a) about two thirds of the time. In addition, 90 percent of the time sentences like (9.14b) were correctly judged to be wrong in contexts displaying coreference. Thus even two- and three-year-olds allow backwards anaphora and reject it when structural conditions dictate that they should. Kermit ate some pretty unpleasant things as a consequence of the fact that these children behaved in accordance with Principle C.

The construction of a good experiment is far from trivial. We cannot simply observe children's spontaneous expressions, because it might be several years before a child is confronted with a situation which draws on her knowledge of Principle C in a way that can be measured. Crain and Thornton (1998, chs. 27–30) provide an excellent discussion of the design features of experiments relating to Principle C.

The literature is full of experiments showing that children do not know such-and-such at some early age, only coming to acquire some principle of UG at a later age. Since children's language differs from that of adults, one can easily allow extraneous factors to distort findings, as in the early experiments on Principle C. Confounding factors have led many researchers to conclude too hastily that children do not know certain principles of UG. In fact, we know of no good demonstration to this effect.

Consider another example. Hornstein and Lightfoot 1981 argued that children know in advance of any experience that phrase structure is hierarchical and not flat. So the structure of an expression *the second striped ball* would be that of

(9.15a) and the flat structure of (9.15b) would not be a candidate, precluded by UG.[6]

(9.15) a.

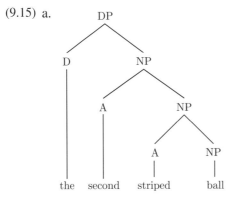

b.

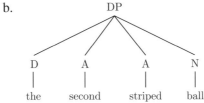

There were various reasons for this analysis and for the claim that flat structures are generally unavailable. In particular Hornstein and Lightfoot argued that if children allowed a flat structure they would never be exposed to positive data enabling them to acquire the correct hierarchical structure of adult language. Nonetheless, it was argued, for example by Matthei (1982), that children must operate with flat structures, because they have difficulty interpreting phrases like *the second striped ball*. Confronted with an array like that in figure 9.1 and asked to identify "the second striped ball," adults invariably identify the third ball but children often identify the second ball, which is also striped.

Figure 9.1   An array of objects

___

[6] Hornstein and Lightfoot stated their claims in terms of then-current notions of phrase structure, in which NP included determiners and intermediate N′ elements. Twenty years later, we translate their claims into present-day frameworks using DP, etc.

Hamburger and Crain 1984 then showed that the difficulty that children have in identifying "the second striped ball" in an array does not relate to their grammars; in fact, it cannot. They hypothesized that the difficulty might lie in the pragmatic complexity of identifying "the second striped ball" rather than in syntactic complexity. A dramatic improvement in children's responses was effected by two changes. First, children were given a pre-test session where they handled and counted sets of striped and unstriped balls. Second, if children were first asked to identify the first striped ball, forcing them to plan and execute part of what is involved in identifying the second striped ball, they then performed much better when asked to identify the second striped ball. As Crain put it, "these simplifying maneuvers made it possible for children to reveal mastery of the syntax and semantics of such expressions" (1991, p. 609).

Furthermore, Hornstein and Lightfoot had shown that the pronoun *one* refers to an NP and not a noun head (see note 6). Hamburger and Crain noted that if children employ such hierarchical structures, then, once they know the meaning of ordinals, they will behave in adult fashion when confronted with an array like that of figure 9.2 and asked "Point to the first striped ball; point to the second one," using the pronoun *one*. In fact, children pointed consistently to the fifth object in the array. Using *one* in this way indicates hierarchical structures like (9.15a) and is quite incompatible with the flat structure hypothesis ((9.15b)), if, as is generally assumed, pronouns corefer with syntactic constituents (because *second striped ball* is not a constituent in (9.15b); consequently children would be expected to identify the second ball, not the second striped ball).

Figure 9.2   Another array of objects

Here we have shown more instances where we can see that the language of young children manifests properties of UG at the earliest stages that we can test . . . **if** we do the experiments properly and are careful to tease out their syntactic capacities, designing the experiment to exclude extraneous confounding factors. As we learn more about experimental technique, so we shall learn more about children's linguistic capacities, and *vice versa*.

9.4   Nature of the trigger

In chapter 2, our analytical triplet had children endowed with UG, which develops into a mature grammar on exposure to primary linguistic data (9.16). Let us turn now to children's trigger experience and ask what it consists in, and we shall find that *I*-language notions are needed in order to define even children's initial experience, the primary linguistic data (PLD) that trigger the development of a mature grammar.

(9.16) primary linguistic data (Universal Grammar → grammar)

The **primary** linguistic data are positive and robust. That is, they consist of actual expressions which occur frequently enough for any child to hear them. As we observed in chapter 2, a rough-and-ready formulation would say that the PLD do not include negative data, information about what does not occur, nor exotic expressions, nor expressions used in exotic circumstances. Nor do they include paraphrase relations or indications of the scope of quantifiers. These are legitimate data, of course, part of what a grammar should characterize, part of the output of the emerging system, but plausibly not part of the input to language acquisition and so not "primary." These seem to be plausible assumptions about the input, but the proof will come if they support successful models of the form of (9.16), yielding optimal claims about UG and about mature grammars.

One might also argue that the PLD are structurally simple, that children do not need to hear complex expressions in order to develop a normal, mature grammar. Children do hear complex expressions, of course, and they may understand them, but they may not be a necessary part of experience. In that event, the question arises what one means by "simple."

Lightfoot (1991, 1994) has argued that children need exposure to simple, unembedded clauses and the front of an embedded clause, but not to anything more complex than that. This is degree-0 learnability, the idea that grammars are learnable by exposure only to unembedded structures. The relevant "unembedded" structures are defined in terms of the *I*-language, grammatical notion of a binding domain. So the PLD are drawn from unembedded binding domains.

Children need to learn, for example, which verbs are transitive and which are intransitive, and therefore need access to VPs which may or may not include a complement. Not everything, however, can be learned from simple, unembedded clauses. English speakers learn that the complementizer *that* may be omitted from the front of an embedded finite clause, unlike French *que* or Dutch *dat*, and that must require exposure to the front of an embedded clause, where sometimes *that* occurs and sometimes it does not. Similarly some verbs require that their complement clause be topped by a *wh*-item (*I wonder who she saw*) and others do not: *I believe that she saw Reuben.* This can only be learned, it would seem, by exposure to the front of an embedded clause. Furthermore, in English, some verbs allow a lexical subject in their infinitival complement, while their counterparts in other languages do not: *I expect/want her to see Reuben.* This fact about English verbs also can only be learned if children have access to embedded clauses.

Languages differ in the tenses of reported speech, the so-called sequence-of-tenses phenomenon. For example, if somebody says *Yesterday Fay said she was happy*, Fay's words might have been "I am happy" or "I was happy." In other languages the tense of the embedded clause manifests directly the tense of the direct speech. In these languages, if Fay said "I am happy," that would be reported as *Fay said that she is happy*. Again, it is hard to imagine how differences like this could be learned unless children have access to embedded clauses.

This suggests that children need access to simple, unembedded clauses and to the top of an embedded clause and to the highest inflectional position, but that may be enough. These are the positions for which the binding domain is not the immediate CP containing them, but the next CP up, which may be unembedded.[7] Lightfoot argued that children do not need access to structures more complex than this. Nothing about the mature grammar is to be learned from the fact that an embedded verb has a complement DP or that a relative clause has a certain tense.

Restricting the trigger in this way is a strong claim which runs against analyses in the literature. We will sketch three examples briefly. First, it was once argued that the verb *serve* selected a complement containing a transitive verb ((9.17a) vs. (9.17b)). If that were the right generalization, then children would need access to embedded verbs in order to learn it.

(9.17)   a. *The ice served to melt.
         b. The ice served to chill the beer.
         c. *Edison served to invent the light bulb.

However, that is not the right generalization, as can be seen by the ill-formedness of (9.17c), where the embedded verb is transitive. (9.17c) is ill-formed because it violates what is, in fact, the correct generalization, which is that the subject of *serve* must be an instrument, hence inanimate. Not only is the subject of *serve* an instrument, but it also acts as the understood subject of the embedded verb (*melt, chill, invent*). The correct generalization, that the subject of *serve* is an instrument, is learnable by exposure just to simple, unembedded clauses. All verbs with instrumental subjects are transitive (hence the ill-formedness of (9.17a)), but that is a deep fact which does not need to be learned, holding quite generally.

Second, several linguists (beginning with Rizzi 1982) had argued that the well-formedness of (9.18) in French and Italian indicates that IP is not a

---

[7] In note 4, we observed that an anaphor must be *locally* coindexed with a higher element. Comparably, pronouns are subject to the same local requirement. "Locally" means within its binding domain. An element's binding domain is usually the clause (CP) or DP which contains it. If the element is in a high structural position (namely in C, Spec of CP, or the subject of a non-finite IP), then its binding domain is the next CP up. See Chomsky 1981 for the details.

bounding node in those grammars (see note 3), unlike in the grammars of English speakers. Furthermore, this fact could be learned on exposure to complex sentences like those of (9.18), where there are two levels of embedding.

(9.18) a. Tuo fratello [CP a cui mi domando [CP che storie abbiano raccontato]] era molto preoccupato.
Your brother, to whom I wonder which stories they have told, is very troubled.

b. C'est à mon cousin [CP que je sais [CP lequel offrir]].
It is to my cousin that I know which to offer.

However, Lightfoot argued that the relevant conclusion (that IP is not a bounding node) could be drawn from simpler structures like those of (9.19). There *combien* (9.19a) and *ne* (9.19b) move across a DP and IP, as indicated (they are understood in the position marked e_i), and therefore (assuming that DP is always a bounding node) IP cannot be a bounding node in grammars allowing structures like these and the well-formedness of (9.18) follows.

(9.19) a. Combien$_i$ as [IP tu vu [DP e_i de personnes]]?
How many have you seen people?

b. Ne$_i$ ho visti [IP [DP molti e_i] corregli incontro].
Of-them I saw many run towards him.

Third, degree-0 learnability would preclude a generalization that a certain verb is deleted only in embedded clauses, as Andersson and Dahl 1974 argued for the Swedish auxiliary verb *ha*. *Ha* can be deleted in (9.20c) in an embedded clause, but it appears not to be deletable in a main clause (9.20a,b).

(9.20) a. Han hade sett henne.
He had seen her.

b. *Han *e* sett henne.

c. . . . att han (hade) sett henne.
. . . that he had seen her.

d. Allan kanske redan (har) skrivit sin bok.
Allan perhaps already has written his book.

Lightfoot showed that Andersson and Dahl's generalization was incorrect and that *ha* may be deleted in a matrix clause if the second position to which it would ordinarily move is already filled by an adverb like *kanske* "perhaps," as in (9.20d). This suggests that the correct generalization is that *ha* may be deleted quite generally, but in fact it fails to be deleted when moved to C (Swedish is a verb-second language, like Dutch and German, in which finite verbs typically move to C in matrix clauses). The restriction that it may not be deleted in C may then be understood in terms of the binding theory: if *ha* were deleted in that position, its deleted copy (trace) would not be bound – it would lack an antecedent. So *ha* may be deleted only in its original, base-generated position, where it is not needed as an antecedent for a deleted copy.

This would also explain the non-deletability of a moved *do* or modal auxiliary in English, as in (9.21); compare the non-moved *can* in (9.21c), which may be deleted. Under this analysis, the Swedish facts are not as peculiar as one might have thought and there are no special conditions to be learned, and nothing that requires children to learn anything from embedded binding domains.

(9.21) a. *Who did Jay greet and who Ray treat?
        b. *Who can Jay visit and who Ray eat with?
        c. Jay can visit Fay and Ray eat with Kay.

More productive syntax of this type followed, where better analyses were found by following through on the assumption that learning is based only on structures from unembedded binding domains. What is relevant here is that the notion of a binding domain is itself a grammatical, *I*-language notion, and that is what we need to define the limits to children's trigger experience. *I*-language notions are implicated in analyses of language acquisition from the outset.

In fact, there is a still more fundamental point: not only must the PLD be drawn from simple structures, but they are abstract structures themselves, not unanalyzed sentences. This is so-called cue-based acquisition, which we shall discuss below, but first let us consider other, more *E*-language-based approaches.

Chomsky's *Aspects of the theory of syntax* (1965), now a classic, viewed children as endowed with a metric evaluating the grammars which can generate the primary data to which they are exposed, along with appropriate structural descriptions for those data. The evaluation metric picks the grammar which conforms to the principles of UG and is most successful in generating those data and those structural descriptions. The child selects a grammar whose output matches her input as closely as possible.

The same point holds for more recent models. Gibson and Wexler (1994) posit a Triggering Learning Algorithm (TLA), under which the child–learner uses grammars to analyze incoming sentences and eventually converges on the correct grammar. If the child–learner cannot analyze a given sentence with the current grammar, then she follows a procedure to change one of the current parameter settings and then tries to reprocess the sentence using the new para-meter values. If analysis is now possible, then the new parameter value is adopted, at least for a while. So the TLA is error-driven and permits the child to reset a parameter when the current grammar does not give the right results. This model has the child seeking grammars which permit analysis of incoming data, where the data consist of more or less unanalyzed sentences.

Clark (1992) offers a similar kind of model, but one which differs from that of Gibson and Wexler in that the child does not revise particular parameter settings. Clark posits a Darwinian competition between grammars needed to parse sets of sentences. All grammars allowed by UG are available to each child, and some grammars are used more than others in parsing what the child hears. A "genetic algorithm" picks those grammars whose elements are activated most often. A Fitness Metric compares how well each grammar fares, and the fittest grammars go on to reproduce in the next generation, while the least fit die out. Eventually the candidate grammars are narrowed to the most fit, and the child converges on the correct grammar.

What these models have in common is that learners eventually match their input, in the sense that they select grammars which generate the sentences of the input. It is only accurate grammars of this type which are submitted to Chomsky's (1965) evaluation metric, and Gibson and Wexler's error-driven children react to inaccurate grammars by seeking new parameter settings until a sufficient degree of accuracy is achieved. The child converges on a grammar which analyzes the input successfully, where the input consists of sets of sentences.

There are problems with these input-matching, *E*-language-based approaches. First, the models will need great elaboration to deal with the fact, observed several times in this chapter, that children produce non-adult forms. That is, they operate with inaccurate grammars which do not match the input. The models will need to explain why certain inaccuracies are tolerated and others not.

Second, the models require extensive appeals to memory, because children resetting a parameter need to know the full set of sentences which required earlier resettings, lest they now be lost by picking the wrong parameter to reset.

Third, it is hard to see how these input-matching models can succeed when children are exposed to unusual amounts of artificial or degenerate data, which in fact are not matched. In particular, it is hard to see how they could account for the early development of creole languages, as described by Bickerton (1984, 1999) and others. In these descriptions, early creole speakers are not matching their input, which typically consists to a large degree of pidgin data. Pidgins are primitive communication systems, cobbled together from fragments of two or more languages. They are not themselves natural languages, and they tend not to last long, before giving way to a creole with all the hallmarks of a natural grammar. The first speakers of creoles go far beyond their input in some ways, and in other ways fail to reproduce what they heard from their models, arriving at grammars which generate sentences and structural descriptions quite different from those of their input.

Nowadays we can observe these effects in the development of deaf children acquiring various kinds of signing grammar. 90 percent of deaf children are born into hearing homes and are exposed initially to degenerate pidgin-like data, as their parents and older siblings learn an artificial gestural system in order to communicate in primitive fashion. Nonetheless, like early creole speakers, these deaf children go far beyond their models and develop natural systems.

Goldin-Meadow and Mylander (1990) show how deaf children go beyond their models in such circumstances and "naturalize" the system, altering the code and inventing new forms which are more consistent with what one finds in natural languages.[8]

Fourth, severe feasibility problems arise if acquisition proceeds by evaluating the capacity of grammars to generate sets of sentences. If UG provides binary parameters of variation, then 11 parameters permit 4,096 grammars, and 32 allow 8-9 billion grammars, and so on. The child eliminates grammars which fail to generate the sentences encountered. If we assume thirty to forty structural parameters and if children converge on a grammar by, say, age seven, then they eliminate grammars at a fantastic rate, several in each waking second on average. As if that problem is not enough, it is by no means clear that parameters can be kept down to between thirty and forty. If there are only thirty to forty structural parameters, then they must look very different from present proposals.

Cue-based acquisition offers a very different, more *I*-language-based approach. Under this view, advocated by Dresher 1999, Fodor 1998, Lightfoot 1999, and others, children do not evaluate grammars against sets of sentences. Rather, UG specifies a set of "cues" and children scan their linguistic environment for these cues and converge on a grammar accordingly. A cue is some kind of structure, an element of grammar, which is derived from the input. The cues are to be found in the mental representations which result from hearing, understanding, and "parsing" utterances ("parsing" means assigning structure and meaning to incoming speech signals). As a person understands an utterance, even partially, he or she has some kind of mental representation of the utterance. Similarly for children, but a child may only have a partial understanding of what is heard, hence a partial parse. The child scans those mental representations, derived from the input, and seeks the designated cues.

The child scans the linguistic environment for cues only in simple syntactic domains (this is the degree-0 learnability just discussed). Learners do not try to match the input; rather, they seek certain abstract structures derived from the input, and this shapes the emerging grammar without regard to the final result. That is, a child seeks cues and may or may not find them, regardless of the sentences that the emerging grammar can generate; the output of the grammar is entirely a by-product of the cues the child finds, and the success of the grammar is in no way evaluated on the basis of the set of sentences that it generates, unlike in the input-matching models.

So, for example, a child scans her environment for nouns and determiners. She would find the nouns *livre*, *idée*, and *vin* and the determiners *le*, *la*, and *mon*, if she lives in Paris; she finds *book*, *idea*, and *wine*, if she lives in Boston, and the determiners *the*, *that*, and *my*. Our Bostonian would also find a determiner *'s*,

---

[8] Newport (1999) extends these ideas and Kegl, Senghas, and Coppola (1999) report on the spectacular emergence of Nicaraguan Sign Language over the last twenty years.

which has no counterpart in French. She would find that this determiner also assigns Case to a preceding DP; she would discover this on exposure to an expression *the player's hat*, analyzed partially as [$_{DP}$ [$_{DP}$ the player] $_D$'s [$_{NP}$ hat]]. This partial analysis is possible, of course, only after the child has identified *player* and *hat* as separate words, both nouns projecting an NP, etc. In this way, the order in which cues are identified, the "learning path" (Lightfoot 1989), follows from dependencies among cues and follows from their internal architecture.

Our Parisian would also find the cue $_I$V, that is, instances of verbs occurring in an inflectional position (cf. chapter 8). She would find this on exposure to sentences like *Elle lit toujours les journaux* and understanding that *les journaux* is the complement of the finite verb *lit*. In that case, since verbs are first generated adjacent to their complement, there must be a partial analysis of (9.22a), which represents the movement of *lit* out of the verb phrase, across the adverb *toujours*, to the higher inflectional position. She would also find the cue when confronted with and partially understanding an expression *Lit-elle les journaux?*, which requires the partial analysis of (9.22b).

(9.22) a. Elle [$_I$ $_V$lit$_i$] [$_{VP}$ toujours $_V$e$_i$ les journaux].
   b. $_V$Lit$_i$ [$_{IP}$ elle $_I$e$_i$ [$_{VP}$ $_V$e$_i$ les journaux]]?

Our Bostonian, on the other hand, would not be confronted with any such expressions and would never be exposed to sentences which required postulating a verb raised to a higher inflectional position. Since she never finds the cue $_I$V, her grammar would never have such a verb-raising operation.

So children scan the environment for instances of $_I$V. This presupposes prior analysis: children may scan for this cue only after they have identified a class of verbs and when their grammars have a distinct inflectional position, I. The cue must be represented robustly in the PLD. The approach is entirely *I*-language based and children do not test or evaluate grammars against sets of sentences; in fact, the set of sentences generated by the emerging grammar is quite irrelevant – the chips fall where they fall.

Cue-based acquisition finesses the feasibility problems which arise for input-matching models. We are free to postulate 100 or 200 cues, if that is what analyses of different grammars require. That does not raise comparable feasibility problems for the child learner. Our child would not be evaluating quadrillions of grammars against sets of sentences, rejecting hundreds every waking second. Rather, the child would be scanning her environment for the 100 or 200 cues, much in the way that she scans her environment and identifies irregular past-tense verbs like *took, went, fit, spoke*, and so on. That task may raise difficulties that we do not now understand, but it does not raise the particular, devastating feasibility problems of input-matching parametric systems.

The cue-based approach has been productive for phonologists concerned with the parameters of stress systems (Dresher 1999) and it comports well with work on the visual system, which develops as organisms are exposed to very specific visual stimuli, such as horizontal lines (Hubel 1978, Hubel and Wiesel 1962, Sperry 1968). Current theories of the immune system are similar; specific antigens amplify preexisting antibodies. In fact, this kind of thing is typical of selective learning quite generally.

9.5   Acquiring sound patterns

Our discussion thus far in this chapter has been limited to the development of syntax, but of course the child also comes to control the sound pattern of the native language. Just as recent work on the acquisition of syntax makes it clear that, once we do the experiments correctly, children can be seen to have substantial elements of mature grammars earlier than had been thought, so current work makes it clear that the phonological system of the language organ arises rather earlier in the child's life than had long been thought, and in fact provides essential prerequisites for the development of syntactic knowledge. The sequence of events in the course of the acquisition of phonology is quite regular and shows every evidence of being driven by the organism's biological nature. This impression is confirmed by the parallels with another, quite undeniably biological developmental sequence: the emergence of song in oscine songbirds (one of the twenty-seven orders of living birds). While syntactic organization is apparently uniquely human, phonological form and its development show similarities – limited, but quite striking – to this aspect of the cognitive organization in very different species.

9.5.1   Children's early knowledge

The development of children's control of the speech patterns of the language they will speak is a subject that merits a book of its own – indeed, several books have been devoted to exactly this, as the experimental results of recent decades have shown how rich the child's early experience is in this area. Well before specific words or the principles of their combination are available, sophisticated knowledge of the patterns of their realization in sound (or gesture, in the case of deaf infants raised in the presence of adult signers) is already present. We summarize below what is generally accepted about a universal, culture-independent progression in the development of speech, following the very useful and accessible presentation by Bénédicte de Boysson-Bardies (1999).[9] We make no serious attempt to document these results independently or to give details of the experiments on which the conclusions are based, for which the reader is encouraged to consult the work just cited.

---

[9] See also Jusczyk 1997 and Kuhl 1999 for further amplification and references.

It has been known for many years that infants follow a regular progression in their sound productions during the first year or so of life. Between one and about five months, their vocalizations are often referred to as COOING: at this stage, they produce sounds resembling vowels and begin to control the process of phonation. Around seven months, they begin the stage known as BABBLING: early on, this consists of repetitive productions that rhythmically alternate consonants and vowels ("babababa," "mamamama," etc.). By around eight months, the vowels produced in babbling begin to approach those specific to the language spoken by their parents and others around them, and may alternate different syllables rather than repeating the same one. The intonation contours of babbling also begin to resemble those of their (soon to be) native language, and by the age of about ten months, it is possible to differentiate children on the basis of the linguistic environment in which they have developed.

This development is a crucial part of the infant's attaining control of language. We can see this in part from the behavior of congenitally deaf babies: up until the onset of babbling, their vocalizations are entirely comparable to those of hearing babies, but deaf babies do not babble. Around the age of seven months or so, their vocalizations diminish, and do not reemerge until later, at a point where they are dominated by syllables with labial consonants that the baby can **see** how to pronounce.

The absence of vocal babbling in deaf infants, however, does not mean that this stage of language development is absent. For deaf children raised among signing adults, there is indeed a linguistic environment: it is simply in another modality from that of hearing children. And it has been shown (Petitto and Marentette 1991) that these babies do indeed engage in manual "babbling" that evokes the constituent elements of signed language, a kind of manual activity that is qualitatively different from that of other children and that serves the same sort of function of attunement to a linguistic world as oral babbling does for the hearing child.

By around 10–15 months, children have arrived at a selection of vowel and consonant types appropriate to their native language. While babbling may persist, in the production of nonsense repetitions (generally with appropriate sentential intonation), the first stable words begin to appear by the end of the first year, and infants now come to use a consistent phonetic form to refer to an object. Around 20–24 months, when most (though by no means all) children have a vocabulary of roughly 250 to 300 words, they begin to combine words in meaningful ways and produce their first sentences.

A child's early productions are of course available for observation, and the path of development sketched above has been documented for some time. It is naturally rather harder to study the sequence of events in the development of perception, since we cannot directly observe what is going on in the mind of the prelinguistic child. Recent years have seen the emergence and refinement of a number of ingenious experimental techniques for drawing conclusions about a child's perceptual abilities, however, and we do know quite a bit about the sequence in which linguistic perceptual ability arises.

Even before birth, it has been demonstrated that the fetus responds to auditory input, recognizing changes in sounds and reacting preferentially to the sound of the mother's voice. At birth (or as soon thereafter as it is practical to do experiments), infants can discriminate sounds along all of the dimensions used by the world's languages. They also can detect changes in intonation patterns, while recognizing the sameness of a speech sound under variations in intonation.

At (or shortly after) birth, infants show a preference for the prevailing intonation patterns of their "mother tongue." Up to the age of 2 months, infants show no right-ear advantage for speech (though they do show a left-ear advantage for musical contrasts). By 3 or 4 months, though, a right-ear advantage for speech is present. The importance of this lies in the fact that (as we will note in chapter 10) the primary language areas in the brains of most humans are in the left hemisphere, to which the right ear provides the most direct access.

By the age of 5 months, infants can make some connections between visual and auditory information. Around 6 months, infants show a preference for speech containing the vowel sounds of the language spoken around them. At about the same time, they are able to detect the prosodic cues for the boundaries of clauses in different languages, despite the fact that it will be some time before they actually produce utterances that could be said to be structured into "clauses." Around 8–10 months, their sensitivity to prosodic organization increases still further, and they can be shown to be sensitive to phrase boundaries within clauses – obviously an important ability if they are to be in a position to impose a syntactic organization on their linguistic input, as we have assumed at a number of points in this book. Although they do not yet produce stable words at this point, they can still be shown to prefer word forms that respect the stress patterns of their native language, and the constraints on sequences of sounds that are characteristic of it.

Already, around the age of 10 months, infants' ability to discriminate sound contrasts that are not used in the language spoken around them is greatly reduced. This degradation of the phonetic perceptual virtuosity they are born with will continue as they acquire their native language, and adults have considerable difficulty hearing sound contrasts not present in their native language (Japanese speakers distinguishing [r] from [l], English speakers hearing French or Spanish [p] vs. [b], etc.), contrasts which they could discriminate as babies. When the same physical acoustic dimensions are presented in a non-speech signal, however, adults perceive them with roughly the same accuracy regardless of native language, showing that it is specifically linguistic perception that becomes preferentially tuned to the dimensions of contrast utilized in a particular language.

These observations suggest something like the following course of development. At birth, the child's perceptual system is capable of making a range of auditory discriminations. Both speech and general auditory processing have roughly the same capacities. During the first months of life, the quality of the speech around the child results in a "tuning" of the speech perception system that begins to focus on the kinds of sound found in the surrounding language. At around six months, the child begins to experiment with his own vocal apparatus, discovering the connections between articulation and sound. As the perceptual system becomes tuned to a specific language, and integrated with the motor system, it comes to disregard distinctions that do not occur in this language. This has no effect on non-speech perception, however.

This process of progressive refinement seems to proceed as a product of the availability of evidence. Notice that the child in the womb has access to some limited information about speech: the rhythm and intonation pattern of the mother's speech, but little or nothing else. And, in fact, we can demonstrate some specialization for those patterns right after birth.

It has long been considered that this sort of development takes place during a specific stage in life: the "critical" or "sensitive" period. For some aspects of language learning, we have actual evidence that if the right kind of stimulus is not present during the right age (roughly, up to puberty), learning does not take place.[10] In the domain of speech, there is little relevant information: the few known studies of children deprived of linguistic input during their early years did not apparently include the kind of perceptual tests that would tell us how normal their speech perception systems were.

We can show, however, that in "late" bilinguals (people who learn a second language well, but after childhood), as opposed to "early" bilinguals, there are processing differences: imaging studies seem to show that the latter use overlapping brain regions to process the two languages, while the former use distinct regions. This suggests that whatever we learn after the period of normal first-language acquisition, we learn in a different way.

Why should this be true? One possibility is that it is just a part of development: certain mechanisms cut in at a particular point, and cut out at a particular point. A slightly less metaphysical point of view, however is the following. In the early years of life, the brain develops vast numbers of new synapses, peaking at about 2 years of age. Over the next several years, neurons die and synapses wither, resulting in a specifically limited organization. Neuron death levels out at around age 7, while overall synaptic organization is determined by around the age of puberty. If we assume that the role of experience is to shape and mold this specific organization, then whatever is in place by puberty is what we are "stuck with."

---

[10] For a survey of the classic cases relevant to this issue, and their interpretation, see Curtiss 1988.

9.5.2   Birds' development of song

Somewhat surprisingly, perhaps, much the same story seems to be characteristic of song learning in oscine birds (suborder *Passeres*) – but not of the communication systems of other animals, or even other communication systems in the same animals.[11] In some birds, song is learned, in the sense that some interaction with the environment is required for normal development. In other birds, however, the song is completely innate: a young phoebe, for instance, will sing nearly correctly at the age of about 2 weeks, and the course of the bird's improvement depends solely on improved control of the vocal apparatus with physical maturation. Crucially, these birds will sing correctly if (a) raised in isolation from other phoebes; or (b) deafened shortly after hatching. This is not true for birds that learn: these birds need experience and models, or else their vocalizations will resemble pathetic squawks rather than real species-typical song.

It is conventional to distinguish true song from other avian vocalizations, referred to as "calls." Bird song is opposed to bird calls in its complexity, in its ontogeny, and also in the underlying neural structures. To cite Marler (1999, pp. 295f.):

Most calls seem to be innate . . . In most birds the song is also innate. In only three of the 27 orders of birds is there unequivocal evidence of vocal learning. These are the parrots, the hummingbirds, and above all . . . the oscine songbirds . . . Oscines [have] uniquely complex vocal apparatus, and [a] specialized network of brain nuclei that constitutes the "song system," lacking from the brains of suboscines, and as far as we know, from the brains of all birds with *innate* songs.

On the other hand, "parrots seem to have achieved a similar end by their own neuroanatomically distinct neural system, apparently independently evolved" (Marler 1999, p. 296). The neural organization in hummingbirds shows some initial similarities to that of oscines, but little evidence has been collected on these species.

Song may range from a simple series of a few more or less identical notes through long arias that may last 10 seconds or more. The difference between songs and calls is only in part a categorial one. Marler (1999, pp. 295f.) describes songs (as opposed to calls) as

especially loud, longer in duration than calls, often highly patterned, with a variety of acoustically distinct notes . . . often a male prerogative, with many functions, the most obvious of which are signaling occupation of a territory and maintenance of sexual bonds. Songs are sometimes seasonal and sometimes given year round . . . Some learned

---

[11] There is a vast literature on song and other acoustic communication in birds, including the development of this ability as a function of differences among species. Our presentation here relies especially on work by Peter Marler (1970, 1991, 1999, and elsewhere), along with other research represented by chapters in Kroodsma and Miller 1996. Marler has explored the parallels (and differences) between the development of song in birds and of language in human infants in great detail, and his work has given rise to a great deal of further exploration of these issues.

birdsongs are relatively simple, on a par with those that are *innate*. Other *learned* songs are extraordinarily complex, with individual repertoires numbering in the tens, hundreds, and in a few cases, even in the thousands.

Songs are quite distinctive from one species to another, of course. The song itself is made up of a number of separate notes, of different types. These occur in a particular sequence, and the sequence is essentially the same across repetitions. These matters are important: female song sparrows, for instance, respond preferentially to songs that are (a) composed of "song sparrow" notes, and (b) follow "song sparrow" patterns. Experiments show that female receptiveness is sensitive to both of these dimensions.

In fact, as Marler observes, the same bird will typically have a repertoire of several different songs (two to ten, or even many more in other species), generally similar but distinct. All of these songs serve the same purpose, however: to claim territory. Different songs do not convey different messages. Females appreciate the variety, though: diversity of the male's repertoire helps attract mates, even though it cannot be shown to be linked to any other objectively valuable genetic characteristic.

Songs often – maybe usually – display differences of dialect. That is, there may be local variations that characterize the song. These are not genetic: if you move a baby bird into a different area, he will learn the local dialect. Females may even prefer locally appropriate variation, providing evidence that although in most species they do not sing, females do some song learning too.

The role of learning is quite diverse across species. In some species (e.g. cuckoo), even a rather complicated song is clearly innate, since it is sung without learning. This is adaptive for this bird, since cuckoos typically lay their eggs in other birds' nests, with the result that the babies would not have other cuckoos around to serve as models for song learning. In other species, though, learning is definitely involved. This may consist in identifying some particular conspecific individual's song and copying it, perhaps picking up the right pattern from within a range of possible choices (chaffinch), perhaps relatively free learning (bullfinch).

The course of learning seems to involve four periods.[12] First is the acquisition of a song model from experience during days 15–35 after birth. The bird does not sing yet, but it is during this time that he is listening – and song models heard at this time are internalized and saved. This is followed by a period in which the bird produces SUBSONG, from roughly 25–40 days, consisting of relative soft, broad band, unstructured sounds. This stage is thought to be the process by which a young bird calibrates his vocal instrument, akin to babbling in human infants. At about 35 to 80 days, the bird begins to produce PLASTIC SONG, and

---

[12] The timings cited here for these periods are for white crowned sparrows, the bird Marler studied first in detail. Other species will vary somewhat from these precise ages, while following the same overall sequence of development.

this period is marked by the gradual approximation of the young male's song output to the stored model(s). Finally, at about 90 days, the adult song is fixed (or "crystallized") in its permanent form. In some species, several different songs are sung during plastic song and all but one are dropped at the stage of crystallization.

Much of this is actually highly parallel to human language acquisition, given the fact that the bird only has to learn to speak, as it were, and not to say anything: he has to develop a command of phonology, but not syntax. The stages of song learning, and the role of a critical (or "sensitive") period (during which input has to be available, or else song will not develop normally) are just like what we find in human infants. Quite clearly, a given bird has a specific range of systems that it is capable of learning, providing an obvious parallel with the role of UG in determining the range of human languages that are accessible to the child. The bird does not have to learn how song works: it only has to learn which song to sing, within a narrowly constrained range.

Similarly, we can note that at least some birds, during the "plastic song" phase, produce song elements that are not the same as any they have actually heard, but which still fall within the range of possible song for that species. This is comparable to the fact that children's "errors" during language learning correspond to different possible grammatical systems, at a stage where they are still working out just what system the language they are learning instantiates. In birds, these "errors" may well persist in adult song as creative innovations (a form of "sound change"?).

This sequence shows us how a particular kind of learning takes place. It seems quite incontrovertible that this learning sequence is determined by the bird's biology: vary the species, and the range of systems that can be acquired changes, regardless of the nature of input. Song sparrows cannot learn to be bluebirds, although they **can** learn to sing somewhat like swamp sparrows (a closely related species with a rather different song) if that is the only model available.

While the localization of human language functions in the brain is known only sketchily, as we will see in chapter 10, the corresponding issues in the neuroanatomy of birds are understood in much greater detail. The control of song is centered in connections among several specific, neuroanatomically distinct areas (especially those known as HVc, MAN, and RA). In song birds, there are basically four functions that are subserved by this specialized apparatus:

(9.23)   a. Initiating non-song calls
         b. Initiating and controlling song
         c. Perceiving song
         d. Learning song

One of the major findings in human neurophysiology is HEMISPHERIC ASYMMETRY: the fact that although the two sides of the brain are roughly similar anatomically, they are specialized in somewhat different ways for particular functions. For instance, as we will discuss in chapter 10, most structural language functions are concentrated (in most adult right-handed males) in the left hemisphere, while non-structural, emotional, paralinguistic function is mostly in the right. Since birds have two hemispheres too, we might ask whether their brains are lateralized as well.

The answer seems to be: yes and no. Lesioning different sides of the bird's brain has slightly different results on the song. Actually, that is somewhat puzzling, since birds do not have a *corpus callosum* connecting the two hemispheres, which are largely independent of one another (though there are a few connections). Each hemisphere controls motor activity on the corresponding side of the animal. A bird's syrinx has two independently controllable parts, and it might be thought that the right syrinx would be a right brain function and the left syrinx a matter for the left brain.[13] But in fact physical coupling makes it more complex than this: what the bird does with the muscles on one side also affects the configuration of the other. It seems that different, but interrelated, parts of the song can be controlled separately by the two hemispheres. This is not the same kind of lateralization we find in humans, as far as we can tell.

It is particularly interesting to note that the motor control areas that are involved in song production are also involved in song perception. Williams and Nottebohm (1985) have shown that zebra finch motor areas, right down to the nucleus innervating the syrinx, respond when the bird is hearing roughly conspecific song, but much less when the bird hears stimuli with auditory properties that could not be song; not even when it hears its own song backwards. This is obvious support for the motor theory of speech perception (mentioned above in chapter 6), at least for birds, since the system whose basic function is to control production also plays a role in perception. This does not mean that the bird is literally singing along (though birds probably come closer to this than people): it just means that the production system is involved, and hence that its dimensions of control can be expected to play a part in perception.

Other interesting results from neurological investigations concern the mechanisms involved in learning. For one thing, a comparison of species in which song is learned (e.g., zebra finches) and those in which it is unlearned (e.g., phoebes) shows that brain areas that are essential to song production and learning in the former (e.g., HVc) are simply absent in the latter. Birds that learn have not one but two pathways that are involved in song production, one of which seems to be specially involved in learning, because it becomes redundant

---

[13] Birds do not have the kind of contralateral organization that connects the right side of the human body to the left hemisphere, and *vice versa*.

once song is crystallized. This shows that specialized brain physiology is intimately connected with the learning process, which is of course related to the notion that song learning (though not the specific song) is innate.

While human infants display a relatively uniform pattern of linguistic development, different species of birds behave somewhat differently with respect to learning. In most species (e.g., zebra finch), song is learned once, in the first year, and stays constant through the rest of life. In other species, though, new songs are learned each year: this is the case with the canary. It turns out that when we look at the birth and death of neurons in the song-relevant parts of the bird brain, cell birth and death are associated with song learning and song forgetting, respectively. Interestingly, when we compare canaries with zebra finches, we find that neurogenesis occurs in close-ended learners (that is, those who learn their song(s) once and for all), but in contrast to open-ended learners, this process is generally arrested after the first year of life. These observations provide a neurological basis for the observation that learning is associated with critical or sensitive periods, and that the timing of these is a consequence of physical changes that play themselves out in the stages of a bird's maturation.

No one would seriously doubt that the control of birdsong is largely organized as a function of the bird's neuroanatomy, and thus of its biology. In some birds, the whole development is innate, since the bird can come to sing its song with little or no environmental input. In the birds we have been discussing, though, the song control system develops on the basis of an interaction with data provided by the environment. The productivity of this interaction is rather precisely dependent on physical changes in the bird's neuroanatomy, changes that are clearly controlled by its specific genetic program.

All of this is strongly consistent with the picture of human language learning as similarly driven by human biology: normal language acquisition in humans, also, takes place preferentially during a specific stage of maturation. But just as what a bird is capable of learning is a function of its species-specific biology, so also what we are capable of learning as a first language is undoubtedly determined by our genetic program. Our language organ is distinctly biological in nature.

9.6   Conclusion

There is, of course, much more to be said about grammars and their acquisition, as well as the development of phonology (including more detailed aspects than we have attended to above); and there is an enormous technical literature. Here we have tried to show how the biological view of grammars, focusing on the internal representations occurring in individual brains, influences the way one studies the acquisition of linguistic knowledge in young children. In this connection, we have outlined a rigorously *I*-language-based approach.

Meanwhile, we have an approach to the riot of differences that we find in the languages of the world and even within languages: there is a universal language faculty and it is this UG which makes us accessible to one another, defining the ways in which we analyze our linguistic experience. As children, our linguistic experience varies tremendously; no two children experience the same set of sounds and sentences. Nonetheless, the approach we have sketched enables us to understand the universality of our development, why we categorize the linguistic world so similarly and can talk to each other despite the enormous variation in our childhood experience.

10   The organic basis of language

Our ability to speak and understand a natural language results from – and is made possible by – a richly structured and biologically determined capacity specific both to our species and to this domain. In this chapter we review arguments that show that the language faculty is a part of human biology, tied up with the architecture of the human brain, and distinct at least in significant part from other cognitive faculties. We also discuss some of the work that has tried to link the language organ with specific brain tissue and its activity.

Previous chapters have explored the structure of various components of our language organ, and some aspects of the course by which that structure arises. Some component of the mind must be devoted to language, and in its original state (determined by Universal Grammar (UG)), prior to any actual linguistic experience, it seems predisposed to infer certain quite specific sorts of system on the basis of limited and somewhat degenerate data. This is what we mean when we say that our language organ can be described by a grammar, and the shape of particular grammars is determined by the system of UG as this interprets the primary linguistic data available during the period of growth of the language organ.

Thus far, our description is largely an abstract or **functional** one: that is, it does not depend on the specific properties of the physical system that realizes it. For a parallel, consider the nature of multiplication. We can characterize the function of multiplication over the natural numbers in terms of some general properties (commutativity, associativity, etc.), together with some specific results. Any computation that produces those results, consistent with the general properties of multiplication, counts as multiplication: repeated addition, binary shift-and-add strategies, the kind of logarithmic addition that used to be implemented on slide rules, etc. Multiplication remains the same function, regardless of the algorithm by which we compute it.[1]

Suppose we take a specific algorithm, for concreteness' sake – perhaps the standard one we learn in grade school, by which we carry out multi-digit

---

[1] The discussion here is based on the kind of analysis of cognitive functions proposed by David Marr (1982).

multiplications one place at a time, with carrying, etc. That algorithm seems quite clearly specified, but in fact it can be implemented in various ways: with the paper and pencil technique we learned in school (at least prior to the ubiquity of calculators), on mechanical adding machines, old-fashioned moving-wheel adding machines, an abacus, digital computers, etc. The inner workings of all of these devices differ in various ways – even specifying the algorithm does not tell us exactly how the system does it, at the level of implementation.

Much of what we have seen in previous chapters concerning language remains at the functional level. We can determine properties of languages, often very abstract and surprising ones; and we can establish the properties which UG must have in order to allow the learner to establish a particular instance of the "language function" on the basis of the kind of data available, but there are myriad ways in which this function could be "computed" and (at least as far as we know) few limits in principle on the kind of mechanism with which that computation could be carried out.[2] Silicon-based forms of artificial life (such as contemporary digital computers) cannot at present fully replicate human knowledge of language, let alone the acquisition of that knowledge, but we have no particular reason to believe that the existing limitations reflect some special property of the stuff of which we (as opposed to our workstations) are made.

Nonetheless, when we ask how our knowledge of language is implemented, there is some fact of the matter: that is, there is some physical aspect of human beings that realizes the knowledge in question, and something that renders this knowledge accessible in the observed way in the cases of real, physical human beings. We maintain that there is no serious alternative to the notion of a language organ: that is, a highly specialized aspect of our cognitive organization which is common to all of us, particular to humans, specialized for the tasks it performs (i.e., specific to the domain of language), and determined by human biology – specifically including (though not limited to) the organic structure of the human brain.

A commonly posed alternative to this position is the notion that language is a product not of human biology but of human culture. On that view, language might be seen as something that develops within every human society, for reasons having to do with the imperatives of social interaction, but without further determination beyond the constraints imposed on effective communication in naturally occurring human societies. Every known human society has

---

[2] In the terms above, the study of the "algorithms" by which humans carry this out is referred to as the study of language or speech PROCESSING, and forms a part of the discipline of psycholinguistics. We have said virtually nothing about processing in this book, which is not at all meant to deny its significance. There are many different views of language processing that could all correspond to the same picture of the properties of the language organ in the sense we have been pursuing; and furthermore, for any particular theory of processing, there are in principle many ways in which it could be carried out by actual physical systems.

conventions of dress, of table manners, etc., but there is no particular reason to believe that this is due to a faculty for fashion, etiquette, etc., which is embodied somehow in the human genome. If language were nothing but another form of social convention, there would be no reason for it to be treated differently.

But the proposition that language is only one more socially determined arti-fact, with the differences among the world's languages mere cultural accidents, is belied by the deep and detailed similarities that evidently exist among them, as the research of the last forty years or so has made clear.[3] A particularly striking instance of the commonality of the human language faculty is supplied by the manual languages which develop in Deaf communities independently of one another or of the language of the surrounding hearing community, and which share fully in the fundamental properties we have explored in the case of spoken languages. We must conclude that the profound structural similarities between signed and spoken languages,[4] including not only the basic princi-ples of their organization but the specific path of their development, the brain regions associated with their control, and many other features, can be neither the result of simple shared history nor necessary consequences of the articula-tory/acoustic/auditory modality of spoken language. They must, rather, derive from shared biology.

The notion that human language acquisition is primarily a matter of cul-tural transmission, rather than biologically driven maturation in the presence of relevant experience, is also undermined by instances of the development of structurally deficient pidgins into the essentially normal linguistic systems found in creoles. The deep reorganization of pidgins into creoles which takes place as an essentially automatic result of transmission through the natural language learning process in new generations of children, provides additional support for the richness of the genotypic system involved in linguistic devel-opment (Lefebvre 1998, Bickerton 1999). This kind of reorganization can be observed on a daily basis in the emergence of the gestural languages of the Deaf. Ninety percent of Deaf children are born into hearing homes, and often such children are exposed initially to a kind of pidgin, as their parents struggle to learn some kind of manual system of communication. Nonetheless the children reorganize their experience and attain more or less natural, creole-like systems (Lightfoot 1999, pp. 170–173).

The language faculty has properties typical of a bodily organ, a specialized structure which carries out a particular function. Some organs, like the blood and the skin, interact with the rest of the body across a widespread, complex interface, and all organs are integrated into a complex whole. Often the limits to an organ are unclear, and anatomists do not worry about whether the hand is

---

[3] It is increasingly clear that the superficial diversity of the world's languages conceals striking commonalities among them. For an introduction to the evidence for this, see Baker 2001, who considers a stunningly wide range of languages in a highly accessible way.

[4] See Newport 1999, Supalla 1990, Anderson 1993 among other sources for some discussion.

an organ or whether this designation should be reserved for one of its fingers. If we think of an organ as a distinguishable aspect of an organism's structure, intrinsic to and determined by its biological nature and implementing a particular function, then the human capacity for language can be viewed in those terms.

10.1   Only humans have language organs

It appears that the capacity for language in the sense we have been developing is specific to humans, and lacks significant parallels even in those species closest to us, including the higher apes. This conclusion follows from the failures of a half century of intensive efforts to teach human languages to individuals of other species, especially chimpanzees and other primates.

The failure of attempts to teach spoken languages to non-human primates was initially attributed to deficiencies in these animals' vocal apparatus. To overcome this, attention shifted in the 1960s to studies based on manual languages such as American Sign Language (ASL; Gardner and Gardner 1969). Research has demonstrated that ASL and other natural signed languages have the structural properties of spoken languages,[5] but obviously without requiring a human-like vocal tract. While some relatively minor differences in the structure and control of the hands exist between humans and other primates, it is reasonably clear that the basic articulatory demands of, e.g., ASL are well within the limits of dexterity of chimpanzees and other primates.

Despite this, however, the animals in these experiments have never been shown to acquire even the rudiments of the syntactic, lexical, or phonological systems of natural languages.[6] This has been repeatedly challenged by members of the ape language research community, especially in connection with more recent experiments involving bonobos ("pygmy chimpanzees" – *pan paniscus*) (Savage-Rumbaugh et al. 1993, 1998), but the fact remains that nothing resembling the natural human capacity for free, recursive syntactic combination, the systematicities of relations among lexical items, or the organization of sound (or sign) structure based on systematic, patterned combinations of a limited number of basic components has been shown in any serious scientific work to date.

---

[5] See Klima and Bellugi 1979, Perlmutter 1991 and a rich technical literature. Note that there is considerable controversy about the extent to which the input to which the apes in these experiments were exposed actually constituted a natural language like ASL, as opposed to a system that lacked essential properties of ASL.

[6] For discussion of this work during the period when it was particularly prominent, see Petitto and Seidenberg 1979, Terrace et al. 1979, Wallman 1992. Unfortunately, the negative conclusions that arose from careful examination of these experiments held little appeal for the general public, and the impression has gradually grown that some higher apes have been successfully taught to use a human natural language. Despite the fascinating abilities that these apes have in fact displayed, such a conclusion is simply not correct. See Anderson (forthcoming) for review of these and other issues from the more general perspective of animal communication systems.

In contrast to the failure of these attempts to instill in primates a syntactic, lexical, or phonological ability comparable to that which appears naturally and spontaneously in every normal human child, a capacity for arbitrary symbolic reference **has** been elicited in some higher apes (Premack 1978, 1980, 1990, Savage-Rumbaugh 1986, Savage-Rumbaugh et al. 1986, Savage-Rumbaugh 1987, Seidenberg and Petitto 1987, Savage-Rumbaugh, Shanker, and Taylor 1998) and perhaps even in other animals, such as parrots (Pepperberg 2000). This is extremely interesting, since such use of arbitrary symbols had not seemed to occur in nature in non-human species. The demonstration that in some cases it is nonetheless within their cognitive capacities is quite surprising and important. It does not, however, compromise the conclusion that the systematic syntactic, morphological, and phonological properties of human language are provided by our language organ as a consequence of our specific genotype, and as such are outside the capacity of non-humans.

This should hardly come as a great surprise, since every species has some unique systems and capacities (and lacks others) as determined by its specific genotype – inaccessible in the absence of the appropriate biology. It is not far-fetched to compare the situation regarding language in other animals with the fact that humans, even with intensive training, are incapable of free flight. So birds fly, and humans talk.

The functional properties of our language organ develop along a regular maturational path, such that it seems appropriate to see our linguistic knowledge as "growing" rather than being "learned." As with the visual system, much of the detailed structure we find is "wired in," though triggering experience is necessary to set the system in operation and to determine some of its specific properties.

In this respect, human language shows fascinating and detailed analogies (as well, of course, as significant dis-analogies) with the development of song in birds (Marler 1970, 1991), a system we explored in section 9.5.2 and which is quite uncontroversially to be attributed to properties of the animal's specific biology rather than to some system of generalized learning or the like.

We marvel at the exotic structure and precise elaboration of systems such as the bat's echo-location facility, or the entirely different sonar systems of dolphins, the electric field sensitivity (and communication based on it) of certain fish, etc. (Hughes 1999). No serious scientist would question that these are faculties quite specific in their structure and development to the individual species concerned, and that no amount of structured training will enable even the brightest or most sensitive human child to find insects by emitting short pulses of high frequency sound and listening for their reflection. Why, then, should we doubt that the intricacies of the human language faculty would be similarly unique to our own species, especially given the repeated failure of attempts to prove otherwise?

One might, of course, reject the validity of this analogy, and say that humans lack certain skills of bats or electric fish because they lack the appropriate sensory organs. But what, after all, is an "appropriate sensory organ"? Precisely some bit of tissue which is specialized, as a result of the animal's biological organization, to be sensitive to certain environmental events. But that is exactly what we claim for the language organ: it is a biologically determined aspect of certain tissue (primarily in the brain), rendering it uniquely sensitive to linguistic events in the environment, and allowing the development of a highly specialized capacity as a consequence of that environmental interaction.

The importance of quite species-specific determination in these matters cannot be underestimated: we must not imagine that an animal's capacities develop simply through the application of very generally defined cognitive systems to the problems posed by its *Lebenswelt*. Many animals have noses, and olfactory cortex, but no matter how much a man may desire truffles, he cannot find them by their scent without the aid of his dog or pig. Similarly, non-human primates certainly have ears to hear with and (with more qualification) a vocal tract capable of producing sound; or hands and eyes capable of producing and identifying signs; but this does not appear to endow even the cleverest of them with the capacity for human language.

Of course, if one defines "language" generally enough, perhaps simply as "structured communication" or the like, there is every reason to think that a vast range of organisms display something of the sort, but we have seen in earlier chapters that the human language organ has a much more specific and substantive content than that – a content which in the final analysis has no significant parallels in any other species.

10.2   Language is a function of the brain

What can we say about the physical implementation of language – about the "hardware" that the language program runs on? The nature and capacity of the system seem clearly to be specified (at least in part) as an aspect of the biological structure of the organism. We can show that from the fact that disruptions in the system seem to be heritable, as we will note in the following section. It is also clear that language ability is not simply another aspect of general intelligence or overall cognitive capacity. It looks as if there must be some specific part of the organism where a distinctive language organ resides.

So where should we expect to find it, in anatomical terms? That may seem obvious: in the brain. Interestingly enough, however, the relation of the brain to capacities such as language has not always appeared self-evident. Historically, we find mention in Babylonian and Assyrian cuneiform tablets from *c.* 2000 BC of a connection between disorders of intelligence and brain disease. In an Egyptian record from *c.* 1700 BC, we find mention of a connection between a brain injury and the fact that the affected individual suffered a loss of speech. In later theorizing, though, the relation of the brain to cognition (including language) became somewhat more obscure: Aristotle, for instance, taught that the brain was really a large sponge, whose function was to serve as a radiator to cool the blood.

Only fairly recently (in historical terms), with the development of good microscopes – and then later, with the development of more elaborate imaging facilities – did it become possible to see enough of the structure of the brain as an organ to develop any kind of coherent picture of its organization and functions. The notion that the brain, and the nervous system more generally, is a collection of cells that communicate with one another at specific connection points (the neuron doctrine) dates only from the nineteenth century.

On a larger scale, there have been two distinct views of the brain that have been in contention for much of recent history. One of these has its modern origins in the theories of Franz Gall. Gall believed that the brain is composed of a large number of very specific faculties, each specialized for a very limited sort of function. He offered specific charts of this kind of organization (see figure 10.1).

Gall also held the view that exercising a particular mental faculty caused the corresponding part of the brain to enlarge, pressing against the skull and producing corresponding bulges (or, in the case of underutilized faculties, depressions). The result was supposed to be palpable irregularities in the surface of the skull, which an appropriately trained interpreter could use as indices of personality traits. That gave rise to the pseudo-science of phrenology, which tended to give "faculty psychology" a bad name from which it has still not completely recovered. There is no logical necessity, however, to the connection between this sort of thing and the notion that the mind (as represented in the brain) has a number of distinct components, modules, or faculties . . . among them, the language organ.

At the beginning of the nineteenth century, the neurologist Marie-Jean-Pierre Flourens (1824) performed experiments on animals in which he excised parts of their brains and then looked to see what specific abilities were affected. By and large, what he found was that all of his experimental subjects were affected globally: that is, rather than losing just one particular function, Flourens' experimental subjects were all turned into vegetables. From this he concluded (Flourens 1846), in explicit reaction against Gall's views, that cognitive capacities are not localized in the brain, but rather distributed globally, so that injury to any part results in a general degradation. This view that the brain represents a single very general faculty, rather than a lot of individual and specific ones, is sometimes called the "aggregate field" view of the brain: the view caricatured by Pinker (1994) as that of the "brain as meatloaf."

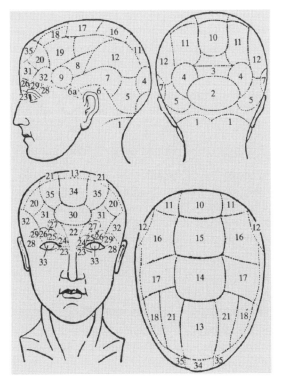

1. Amativeness	2. Philoprogenitiveness	3. Concentrativeness
4. Adhesiveness	5.Combativeness	6. Destructiveness
6a. Alimentiveness	7. Secretiveness	8. Acquisitiveness
9. Constructiveness	10. Self-esteem	11. Love of approbation
12. Cautiousness	13. Benevolence	14. Veneration
15. Conscientiousness	16. Firmness	17. Hope
18. Wonder	19. Ideality	20. Wit
21. Imitation	22. Individuality	23. Form
24. Size	25. Weight	26. Colour
27. Locality	28. Number	29. Order
30. Eventuality	31. Time	32. Tune
33. Language	34. Comparison	35. Causality

Figure 10.1 The personality organs of the human brain, according to Gall and his followers Johann Spurzheim and George Combe

While the aggregate field view seems somewhat implausible in many ways, it is quite attractive on one particular notion of the nature of human beings. If we view most higher mental faculties as actually properties of an incorporeal soul, or something of the sort, it seems natural to say that the brain is just a large, functionally amorphous structure that serves as the locus for the effects of the soul on the body (and perhaps *vice versa*), but nothing more precise than that. If, on the other hand, we hold that specific faculties are anatomically localized, this increases the extent to which we see those faculties as grounded in the properties of specific material (brain tissue) in the physical world; and as a result, the materialist view of the basis of the mind becomes much more congenial. Indeed, in 1802, Gall was forced by conservative Catholic authorities and the Austro-Hungarian emperor to stop lecturing in Vienna (and soon after, to leave Austria) precisely because he was seen to be "championing materialism, atheism, and fatalism bordering on heresy" (Finger 2000, p. 124).

In the late nineteenth and early twentieth century, however, an accumulation of results suggested that the localist view is correct, at least in part. As people looked into the question in more detail, it became clear that very specific injuries can result in rather specific functional impairments, rather than general degradation (as in the case of Flourens' animal subjects). And in this connection, the study of language has played a central role.

10.2.1   Language localization in the brain

Nowadays, it is a generally accepted research assumption that brain functions are localized. For instance, evidence from a number of sources makes it clear that core aspects of language function are located predominantly in the left hemisphere in normal, right-handed, adult males.[7] This evidence includes (a) brain damage: left but usually not right hemisphere stroke often produces disorder or breakdown in language functions; (b) the Wada test: sodium amytal is injected in the major artery supplying one or the other hemisphere, which allows us to effectively suppress its activity. When this happens, we find that language function is affected when the left hemisphere is anesthetized in this way; (c) commissurotomy: severing the connections between the hemispheres allows us to explore their functions separately; (d) imaging studies, which show clearly that particular left hemisphere areas are metabolically and electro-chemically active during language-related tasks; and (e) stimulation studies, such as those made possible in presurgical examination of epileptic patients through the implantation of subdural grids.

We should note that when we investigate these questions of localization, we find that the organization of language in the brain is entirely comparable regardless of the modality of the language: that is, signers seem to use the

---

[7] Some (but not all) left-handed individuals have an opposite lateralization of language functions. Lateralization is less prominent in young children, and develops in part as an aspect of maturation. And some recent studies (e.g., Shaywitz et al. 1995) suggest that the asymmetries of language function between hemispheres are less pronounced in women than in men, a result which is consistent with the evidence that anatomical asymmetries between Broca's area and the analogous brain region in the right hemisphere are less pronounced in women than in men (Uylings et al. 1999).

same parts of their brains for language as speakers. Sign aphasias are entirely comparable to conditions affecting spoken language, and we can find evidence that the linguistic use of visual information is the responsibility of different parts of the brain from its non-linguistic use (Poizner, Klima, and Bellugi 1987). ASL is produced and perceived in the visual spatial modality, as opposed to spoken languages, and right hemisphere lesions often produce marked visuospatial deficits. Nonetheless, signers (like speakers) with left hemisphere strokes often display significant problems with language, while those with right hemisphere strokes display essentially normal (signed or spoken) language in the presence of such spatial deficits as left hemi-neglect (essentially ignoring the existence of the left half of their visual field). We can thus see that it is **language** and not (just) **speech** which is primarily based in the left cerebral hemisphere.

However, this overall localization of language function in the left hemisphere has been seen in recent years to be a significant oversimplification (Kosslyn et al. 1999). Rather more language function can be identified in the right hemisphere (by the kinds of arguments suggested above) than was once thought, and there is considerable individual variation in these matters.

10.2.2   Studying the functional anatomy of language

Of course, it would be nice to be able to say something much more specific than just that language functions are (generally) located in the left hemisphere. Actually, though, there is little reason to expect detailed maps of language areas in the brain to emerge soon. In an exploration of the specifics of localization, George Ojemann and his colleagues (1989) studied over a hundred preoperative epilepsy patients, using direct cortical stimulation. They discovered that stimulation in precise locations could interrupt naming ability – but apart from the fact that by and large, the relevant sites were in the perisylvian region, the exact locations varied tremendously from one individual to the next.[8] Still, we would like to have as much precise information as possible. What techniques are there for exploring these matters, and what does the evidence suggest?[9]

For most areas of cognition (other than language) that have been explored in detail, researchers have an enormous advantage that is not available to those studying language: animal models. The human visual and auditory systems, as well as systems underlying other sensory modalities, motor control, and much else, have close analogs in other animals, and we permit ourselves to study these in ways that are completely excluded in the case of other humans. Much has been

[8] These differences are important in determining appropriate sites for surgery to ameliorate epileptic conditions.

[9] We certainly cannot cover all of this emerging field here, nor is it necessary to do so to make our overall point about the biological nature of the language organ. The papers in Brown and Hagoort 1999 provide a summary of recent views and results, in much greater depth.

learned about, say, the visual system by studying cats and monkeys: removing selective bits of brain tissue and observing the resultant deficits, implanting electrodes directly into individual neurons in the intact brain and measuring its activity, disturbing neural development in various ways and observing the results, etc. We have learned much about these systems in animals evolutionarily close to us, and our understanding of the role of various cortical areas in visual processing is relatively precise. These animal models, in turn, have generally turned out to be valid in their essentials for the human visual system as well. The corresponding studies have not been carried out directly on humans, for obvious moral and ethical reasons, but it appears we can largely dispense with them, given what we know about other animals.

When we come to language, however, this path to knowledge is closed to us, for the precise reason that no other animal besides *homo sapiens* possesses a language organ, so far as we know. To understand the precise role of the brain in language, we must start from the very beginning – and our options are relatively limited, for the same reasons we cannot study the human visual system in the kind of detail the monkey visual system has been explored. With few exceptions, we are limited to the evidence provided by non-intrusive experimental methods, or to interpreting what we might call the "experiments of nature": the consequences of localized brain damage, as caused by stroke, trauma, or other accidents.

Evidence from language deficits   The primary source of evidence to date concerning the precise localization of language functions has come from the study of language deficits, or aphasia. The logic of this is to attempt to infer the distinctness of the mechanisms underlying particular functions from the evidence of patients who have suffered brain damage, and in whom these functions are differentially affected. When we find a patient who can write to dictation, but cannot repeat what we say, we presume something like the following: auditory processing is intact, as is the patient's access to the lexicon, but there is a problem going from the lexicon to a spoken output. This implies the potential distinctness of brain regions serving this last function. We then look to the location of the lesions in our patient, and infer that the function(s) impaired must have been located in (or at least essentially dependent on) the area(s) destroyed.

The original, basic step in this study was made by Paul Broca, who in 1861 described a patient with good comprehension of language but severely impaired production. At the time, the only way to find out where the brain was in fact damaged in such cases was to wait for a post-mortem autopsy; and Broca's patient had a lesion specifically in the left posterior frontal lobe. Broca studied eight patients with similar language deficits, and found that in each case subsequent autopsies revealed lesions in the left hemisphere (generally in the same overall area, though it appears the actual lesions were rather diverse). This led Broca to announce that "Nous parlons avec l'hémisphère gauche!" More specifically, a particular kind of language deficit could now be associated with damage to a relatively specific part of the brain, now referred to as "Broca's area" (though see Uylings et al. 1999 for some of the difficulties in defining that notion more precisely in anatomical terms).

This result provided important impetus for the development of brain science, and in the 1870s others discovered that electrical stimulation of the brain could result in movements of very specific parts of an animal's anatomy. In fact, it was possible to correlate particular locations in the cortex with particular motor activities, resulting in a topographic map of the primary motor strip that shows an obvious resemblance to the body – with interesting differences, largely related to the fact that some small body parts (the vocal organs, e.g.) require disproportionately large amounts of controlling tissue, while other body parts (the trunk and abdomen, e.g.) require less than their relative size would suggest.

A familiar and amusing exercise is to relate the brain tissue subserving primary motor control with the parts of the body, resulting in a sort of "homunculus" analogy (cf. figure 10.2).

More recent research suggests there are actually several of these "body maps" in the brain, rather more diffused, and with some variation in structure in different instances. Similar maps link areas of brain tissue bit by bit with the visual field, with the frequency response range of the cochlea, etc. Neuroscientific research is usually based on the view that activities are rather precisely localized. And of course, once the plausibility of this position was well established, many other researchers got busy looking for the specific localization of a variety of functions – such as language.

In the late 1870s, Carl Wernicke proposed another rather specific relation between brain lesion and functional deficit. This involved a class of patients whose production is relatively fluent but who have a deficit in comprehension. This pattern was associated with left posterior temporal lobe lesions, affecting the area now known as Wernicke's area. Wernicke noted that Broca's area is quite near the motor areas responsible for control of speech articulators, and "Broca's aphasics" have trouble producing fluent speech. "Wernicke's area," on the the other hand, is close to areas of the brain responsible for auditory comprehension, and "Wernicke's aphasics" have comprehension diffculties. Wernicke therefore suggested that language production is controlled by Broca's area, and comprehension by Wernicke's area.

But Wernicke's main contribution was the suggestion that only some of the brain basis of cognitive structures such as language is to be found in the localization of specific functions. Much of the way cognitive systems work, according to him, involves interconnections among these specific functions. Thus, on this view both the localists and the aggregate field people were partly

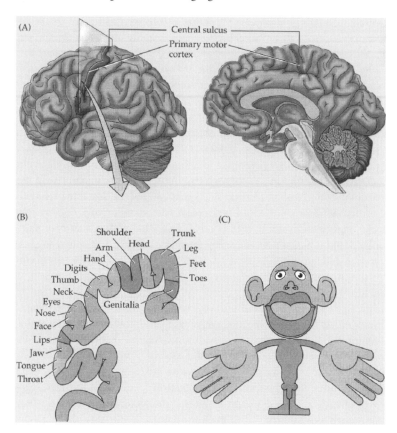

Figure 10.2   Topographic map of the body musculature in the primary motor
cortex (from Purves et al. 1997, p. 316)

right: some functions are local, but mental functioning involves making overall
patterns of connections among these functions.

On this basis, Wernicke predicted another kind of aphasia, one that would
be based not on a lesion in Broca's area or Wernicke's area, but rather on
impaired connections between the two. Such a patient ought to have relatively
spared production and comprehension, but to be very bad at tasks that involved
connecting the two, such as repetition. Patients displaying just this sort of
deficit ("Conduction aphasia") were later actually found, providing one of those
wonderful instances that are all too rare in science of the confirmation of an
empirical prediction made on theoretical grounds.

How much can we refine and extend the information provided by cases
of language pathology in order to derive a more precise picture? As one

might expect, clinicians have gone far beyond the classification of "Broca's," "Wernicke's," "Conduction" aphasics, etc. There are many clinical "syndromes" that have been identified, and one might expect it to be possible to look for the locus of brain damage in each case to get a sense of what goes on where.

Unfortunately, as more and more patients are documented, it becomes clearer that each is an individual, and the deficits patients show are subtly specific. In part, the interpretive difficulties arise from the fact that lesions are rarely precise, and a variety of functions are inevitably implicated when a large area of brain tissue is affected. But some neuropsychologists argue that so much individual variation exists among brain-damaged individuals that the only way to learn about cognition is to study each one as an individual, *sui generis*. Lumping patients with similar but distinct lesions together and averaging over them – e.g., treating a population of "Broca's aphasics" as being comparable – necessarily loses important detail on this view. Categories like "Broca's" or "agrammatic" aphasia may conceal as much as they reveal, by averaging out the differences among distinct patients.

Indeed, aphasic symptoms can be exquisitely detailed. This is particularly obvious in the anomias: patients can lose the ability to name quite precise categories, such as animate objects, abstract objects, plants . . . one of us recalls once hearing the neuropsychologist Frieda Newcombe describe a patient who had lost the ability to name green vegetables, but nothing else.

Given the diffuse and contradictory evidence from attempting to correlate anomias with lesion sites, it is vanishingly unlikely that this will ever lead to the discovery of "the green vegetable center" in the brain; but even so, we learn something more general from the cumulative effect of such cases. They suggest that our knowledge of words is organized in such a way that semantically similar items share some brain mechanisms.

Another bit of evidence in the same direction is provided by Tourette's Syndrome patients. These people have a variety of involuntary seizures, including occasional episodes in which they suddenly start to shout out strings of blasphemies and obscenities. Now since there seems to be no reason to assume that these have any specific semantic content, it would appear that somehow the patient's brain has obscenities organized together as well as items similar in substance, at least if we take Tourette's Syndrome to be a localized brain disorder of some sort.

A major problem in studying the brain through the deficits of aphasic patients is that the ability to localize is rather poor, since most aphasias result from rather comprehensive lesions. Also, the system as we study it in an aphasic is an abnormal one: **perhaps** just the normal with something missing (as the logic of most research seems to assume), but more likely with something missing and something else added in the mind/brain's attempt to make up for the deficits. It would clearly be much better if we could study people without brain damage, and in ways that let us see finer spatial detail.

In summary, evidence from brain lesions suggests that a number of important language functions are largely based in certain areas in the left hemisphere, especially around the perisylvian fissure. There is good reason to believe that subcortical structures have considerable importance as well, but these have been much less accessible to study and so are much less well understood. There seems little hope that we can go much further than this toward localizing components of the language organ on the basis of deficit studies, however.

Evidence from non-invasive imaging   So how can we go about examining what goes on in the rather well protected tissue of the brain so as to explore the neurological underpinnings of cognitive phenomena (including language)? X-ray is one way to study the inside of a normal head, but even forgetting about radiation, this is not useful for our purposes, because it does not show soft tissue. Rather better is Magnetic Resonance Imaging (MRI), a technique that shows the soft tissue in considerable detail. From a series of MRI scans at regular spatial intervals, it is possible to reconstruct the three dimensional structure of the brain tissue with some precision. But of course a picture of the tissue itself, no matter how detailed, fails to reveal what the brain is **doing**. For this, we need an indication of the activity taking place in the brain's individual neurons and groups of neurons.

Even at the level of the individual neuron, this activity is incredibly complicated. It involves large numbers of tiny channels through which chemical ions of various sorts can (or cannot) pass, resulting in changes in the electrical charge at various points in the neuron. When certain such electro-chemical events occur, they result in the release of a variety of other substances (neurotransmitters) that effect the state of other neurons with which a given neuron is in contact. A full picture of what is going on in even the simplest process with cognitive content is surely bewilderingly complex – and, of course, we have to arrive at our picture without actually penetrating the skull or introducing observing instruments into the brain itself.

Two general approaches to the problem of imaging the brain's activity have evolved in recent years. One of these is based on the fact that neural activity requires energy, and when a region of the brain becomes more active, it requires an increase in local blood flow. If we can identify such regions of greater blood flow, we can infer from their associated metabolic activity that something interesting might be going on there. The other approach relies on the fact that neural activity implies the flow of electrical current. While incredibly slight, this current flow can under some circumstances be detected externally. In addition, when current flows it produces a magnetic field, and this also can be detected under some conditions. We discuss the potential results of these two sorts of study in turn.[10]

Hemodynamic methods. One way of imaging metabolic activity (blood flow) in the brain from outside is the technique of Positron Emission Tomography (PET), which has in fact produced the great majority of the technicolor pictures of working brains that appear in the popular literature. This technique involves injecting subjects with radioactively "tagged" water, whose presence in particular areas of brain tissue reflects blood flow (and thus, by inference, metabolic levels). The location from which radiation is emitted can be detected with considerable accuracy from outside the head, and areas where more of this radioactivity can be measured can be assumed to be more active than others.

Despite the immediate appeal of the pictures that derive from PET experiments, the technique is quite limited in its application to the study of cognitive phenomena that take place rapidly, as most language processing surely does. It tells us where activity is taking place, but temporal resolution is quite poor: on the order of 30 seconds for a single picture. A longer period is required between images, to allow for the decay of the radioactive isotope in the tagged water from the earlier dose; and the radioactivity involved means that only a dozen or so images can be collected from a given subject. These physical limitations mean that any experiment inevitably involves a number of subjects whose images under parallel conditions must be averaged to obtain significance. Also, since it is relative increase in activity that is of interest, not just absolute levels of blood flow, these experiments generally involve "subtractive" designs, in which two conditions (in one of which the function of interest is involved, but not the other) are compared. One image is then "subtracted" from the other to obtain a picture of the brain regions whose activity is presumably correlated with the function under study.

These experimental details are by no means insignificant, because they make the results extremely difficult to interpret in terms of cognitive functioning. For one thing, pairs of conditions that have an appropriately "subtractive" character have proven difficult if not impossible to construct. Although good spatial resolution is possible with this technique, that advantage is partially lost as a result of the need to average across the different brains of several subjects. There is also the fact that increased blood flow to a region implies that overall, it has greater metabolic needs; but if some of a group of neurons increase their activity while others decrease, no such net increase in flow will be observed.

Despite these difficulties, PET has been used to explore some more interesting issues about how language is represented in the brain. Differences in processing between words and other stimuli can be detected, but only in an

---

[10] See Rugg 1999 for a good survey of these methods, their possibilities and their limitations.

overall fashion that averages over long periods of time and many events. Jaeger and her colleagues (1996) studied the processing of regular *vs.* irregular verbs in English using PET, and concluded that these are stored in the brain in ways that imply different cognitive mechanisms. Such studies are still a matter of static pictures, though: the experiment involves having several subjects each do the same thing over and over, which yields a single picture that represents the whole period. The possible inferences to the functions of the language organ are limited, at best. Poeppel (1996) discusses a series of PET experiments that purport to identify brain regions active in phonological processing, and concludes that a combination of weak experimental designs and intrinsic limitations of the method result in essentially no significant result.

Another way of imaging blood flow is by the use of f(unctional)MRI: the same method noted above, but with much more powerful magnets than those normally used for static imaging of tissue. Somewhat paradoxically, the blood draining from very active tissue is richer in oxygen than that draining from less active tissue. The extent to which hemoglobin is affected by a strong external magnetic field depends on its oxygen content, so these differences in metabolic activity can result in an effect that can be measured from outside the head in the presence of a powerful magnet.

The images that are possible with fMRI have even better spatial resolution than PET images, and since they can be acquired within about 100 milliseconds for a single "slice," their temporal resolution is better as well. In addition, since they involve no radiation exposure, there is no resulting limit in the number of images that can be collected from a single subject, thus avoiding the problems of intersubject normalization and averaging.

Despite these advantages, fMRI is still some distance from providing a satisfactory approach to cognitive events, because its temporal resolution is still somewhat too coarse to allow us to capture the dynamics of what brain tissue is doing at an appropriate level. It also presents some problems of its own (extreme sensitivity to slight movements, non-uniform imaging of tissue in different regions, high noise level of the apparatus) which limit its usefulness. Nonetheless, as experimental designs are developed which allow the study of more sophisticated cognitive functions ("event-related fMRI"), its virtues, especially in terms of spatial resolution, will make contributions to studies of the localization of language functioning in the brain.

One important problem with the majority of studies conducted using these hemodynamic techniques is that they are designed by researchers who have little or no familiarity with the concepts, methods, results, and research issues of those working on language from a linguistic point of view. Most are based on studies of individual words, rather than active use of language; they typically involve visual presentation of written material, rather than the linguistically more natural mode of aural presentation; and in general they make almost no contact with the literature on grammars. Linguists certainly cannot expect to be able to pose their questions directly and find answers in brain images; but if those designing the experiments have no real sense of what is known about the structure of the language organ, it is unlikely that they will find interesting answers, either. One of our hopes in writing this book is to improve on this situation. In any event, linguists and neuroscientists are increasingly cooperating in this work, especially as the greater benefits of fMRI are realized by both communities.

Electro-chemical methods. As mentioned above, as an alternative to the imaging of blood flow as a clue to neural activity, we can attempt to measure the consequences of electrical current flow in the neuron. This can be done either on the basis of scalp measurements of current flow (electroencephalogram, or EEG) or by using special sensors to record the patterns of magnetic field variation that result from that flow. Each of these has its strengths and its disadvantages, as summarized well by Kutas, Federmeier, and Sereno 1999. The overwhelming advantage of both methods over hemodynamic imaging is its vastly improved temporal resolution: changes on the order of a millisecond can be recorded, making it possible to study language processing on the temporal scale on which it occurs.

The primary technique presently in use to study dynamics of processing is the measurement of Event Related Potentials (ERP) – low level changes in the scalp EEG signal that can be coordinated with linguistically interesting events. This has been widely employed in studying syntactic processing (Hagoort, Brown, and Osterhaut 1999), and a number of characteristics of the ERP signal have been identified that appear to correlate well with language functions. ERP imaging has been applied in a large number of studies of the dynamics of linguistic processing. Interestingly, and unlike the experimental literature based on hemodynamic methods, much more of the ERP literature on language has been driven by questions asked by linguists (rather than neuroscientists). An important reason for this is the fact that the equipment involved is vastly less expensive: even some departments of linguistics can afford to develop an ERP facility, while PET and fMRI remain more or less the exclusive province of medical schools and their immediate affiliates.

The basis of ERP studies is the measurement of electrical potentials that can be detected on the scalp – but that has some serious disadvantages. One of these is the fact that although it is possible to record the signal with millisecond accuracy, the related issue of connecting the signal to a particular area of brain tissue has been shown to be unsolvable in principle: it is effectively impossible to reconstruct the three-dimensional location of the subdural brain activity that gave rise to the measured signal without additional information. A second issue is the fact that only when a substantial number of neurons are active in a simultaneous, synchronized fashion will there be a detectable signal. Much brain activity fails to meet this threshold, and accordingly cannot be recorded this way.

A different technique called Magneto-EncephaloGraphy (MEG) shows great promise of being able to image actual electro-chemical events of very short duration (like ERP), while retaining high spatial accuracy (like fMRI). This is based on the detection of the magnetic fields associated with neural activity: like the hemodynamic methods, this requires elaborate and expensive apparatus, but its development has been driven more by questions of the study of cognitive activity than by medical diagnostic considerations, and as a result, linguists have been active participants in organizing the research agendas that have been explored (see the papers in Marantz, Miyashita, and O'Neil 2000 for some examples).

This technique too has technical problems which limit the extent to which it can be considered the holy grail in the study of cognitive processes (Kutas, Federmeier, and Sereno 1999). Like ERP, it is only sensitive to the activity of substantial numbers of neurons acting together: indeed, these neurons must all be aligned in the same way, and this must be on a tangent to the surface of the skull in the relevant region. Some neural events related to language meet these criteria: as a result, MEG has made progress in identifying interesting aspects of neural functioning (see, e.g., Poeppel and Marantz 2000), but it is obviously far from providing a way of looking at language-related brain activity in general.

Can we image the language organ? The hemodynamic methods of investigating brain function thus provide us with observational techniques that have quite good spatial resolution, but very poor temporal resolution; while electrophysiological studies give excellent temporal resolution but (at least in the case of ERP) very little (or quite ambiguous) spatial information. Is it possible to improve on these approaches? Current research pursues this goal from several perspectives. For example, fMRI studies conducted in concert with ERP recordings can provide the additional spatial information needed to improve the interpretation of the ERP signal. This kind of work is difficult to organize, and still in its infancy, but it shows some promise of reducing the limitations of each technique.

Does this mean that we can realistically expect to be able to present a fully objective physical picture of the activity of the language organ, once the experimental techniques available are suitably refined? We can certainly anticipate an increase in our understanding of the physical underpinnings of that activity. For example, in a series of papers (Poeppel 1996, Hickok and Poeppel 2000, Poeppel and Marantz 2000), David Poeppel and his colleagues have examined the neurological basis of speech perception, whereby physical signals in the auditory system are transformed into symbolic mental representations that enter into further computation. One might imagine that it would be fairly straightforward to identify the functional neuroanatomy of speech perception: it is tightly linked to a single sensory modality,[11] unlike higher-level lexical or syntactic processes. However, it has proved surprisingly difficult to characterize. Poeppel argues that the difficulty stems in part from the fact that the neural systems supporting "speech processing" vary as a function of the task: the neural systems involved in discriminating syllables under laboratory conditions overlap only partially with those involved in natural, on-line comprehension of spoken language. Progress can be made in disentangling these results on the basis of a variety of imaging techniques, but only in the presence of well-worked-out theories of the cognitive functions involved. The images do not, as it were, bear their interpretations on their sleeves. Similarly, Phillips (2001) discusses the complexity of relating acoustic signals to higher-level lexical representations, using electro-physiological results to refine theories of the abstract, functional representations.

On a more cautionary note, let us not forget that none of these techniques give us a way to examine what the neuron is actually doing: although we talk about neurons "firing," current flow is not the same thing as the complex electro-chemistry of real neurons, where a variety of neurotransmitters having diverse effects are in play. There is accordingly no reason to believe that, if the functioning of the language organ is somehow reducible to (or representable in terms of) the activity of neurons, blood or current flow is the right level of analysis. And, so far, we have no way of getting information from outside the head about these more detailed matters.

A more fundamental point here is that the representations provided by non-invasive imaging techniques are not simply the unvarnished reality of brain activity, but a significant abstraction from it: they represent some features of these events (metabolic or electromagnetic correlates of the coordinated activity of a large number of spatially associated neurons), but omit much else. There is no reason *a priori* to believe that the specific abstractions provided by these technologies will correspond in a particularly close way to the kinds of abstraction we need to understand our functional descriptions of the language organ. We have already seen in chapter 6, for example, that the dimensions of a linguistically relevant (phonetic) representation of speech correspond only in a rather indirect way to what is measurable in the acoustic signal. There is no particular reason to expect that the fit between brain imaging data and other

---

[11] This is true to the extent we disregard work suggesting that non-auditory evidence for the activity of the speech apparatus – visual observation of the talker's face, for instance, as in the classical "McGurk effect" (McGurk and MacDonald 1976) – can also enter into our perception of speech. And of course the kind of "analysis-by-synthesis" view of perception discussed in chapter 4 further complicates the extent to which we can expect speech perception to be simply a matter of transforming the information provided by the peripheral auditory system alone.

aspects of language function need be any closer than this. We may, of course, be able to make inferences about functional organization from evidence of this sort – at least, if we have sufficiently articulated theories in both domains to make it possible to confront each with the other. Even adopting a thoroughly materialist view of the language organ as a cognitive function arising from the activity of the brain and nervous tissue, though, we are hardly committed to the proposition that the kinds of physical phenomena we can measure are exactly and exhaustively coextensive with that function.

The conclusion to be drawn from the remarks above is that while we can be quite sure that the language organ is a biologically determined aspect of human physiology, and that it arises primarily as an aspect of the electro-chemical activity of the brain (more specifically, in most individuals, of the left cerebral hemisphere), we do not yet have techniques that would allow us to relate specific cognitive events to specific neurophysiological (electro-chemical) events in particular assemblages of neurons with any certainty. What evidence we have suggests that the relevant events are rather complex and implicate substantial regions of cortical and subcortical tissue, at least some of which subserves other functions as well as language. And in any event, the cognitive interpretation of that activity can only be offered in the presence of a fully articulated picture of its functional nature: of the language organ, as we have interpreted that notion in this book.

10.3   Language is a particular faculty

The language organ is thus not comparable to, say, the kidney, in having a clear and specifiable anatomical localization (at least in the present state of our knowledge). Our understanding of the localization of cognitive function in brain tissue is currently too fragmentary and rudimentary to allow for clear claims of this sort. Certain areas of the brain (both cortical and subcortical) can be shown to subserve functions essential to language, in the sense that lesions in these areas disrupt language functioning, sometimes in remarkably specific ways (Mayeux and Kandel 1991), but inferences from this evidence to claims that, for example, "language is located in Broca's (and/or Wernicke's) area" are quite unwarranted. Indeed, even the overall localization of language function in the left cortical hemisphere has been seen in recent years to be a significant oversimplification, as we noted above.

But in fact, even if it were to become clear that there is no real segregation between language-related and non-language-related brain tissue, it would still be useful and important to treat the language capacity as a discrete and speci-fiable human biological system in functional if not anatomical terms, on the basis of arguments of the sort we have adduced.

The domain-specificity of the language faculty is supported by the extensive literature documenting dissociations between control of language structure and of other aspects of cognition. Where a system operates and is subject to discrete impairment independently of other systems, it is a candidate for modular status. Thus in the domain of the senses, one can be deaf without being blind, and *vice versa*, which supports (though it does not by itself require) the claim that hearing and sight are the products of distinct systems. Neil Smith (in press) provides an excellent discussion of this point. He discusses the case of a linguistic "savant" Christopher, whose hand–eye coordination is severely impaired and whose psychological profile shows "moderate to severe disability in performance tasks, but results close to normal in verbal tasks." Despite low general intelligence, not only is his language essentially unimpaired, but in fact he has an astonishing capacity to pick up languages; see Smith and Tsimpli 1995 for more extensive documentation and analysis.

In contrast, the phenomenon known as Specific Language Impairment (SLI; for an overview, see Joanisse and Seidenberg 1998) represents an apparently genetically determined condition in which language ability is impaired in fairly precise ways in the presence of otherwise normal abilities in other domains: most SLI children are cognitively normal but fail to develop age-appropriate linguistic capacities (Bishop 1997). The homogeneity of the cases which have been grouped together under this diagnosis is quite controversial, but in support of the biological nature of the faculty in question, the distribution of SLI in some well-studied populations has been shown in both epidemiological and genetic studies (Tomblin 1997) to be that of a relatively simple Mendelian trait (Gopnik 1990, Gopnik and Crago 1991), perhaps even with a specific, identifiable chromosomal location. Researchers have postulated a range of grammatical deficits associated with this genetic abnormality (Clahsen, Bartke, and Gollner 1997, Gopnik 1997, van der Lely 1996); see Levy and Kavé 1999 for a useful overview.

Smith (in press) points to other dissociations:

Just as intelligence and language are dissociable, so also is it possible to separate linguistic ability and Theory of Mind, with autistic subjects lacking in the latter but (potentially, especially in the case of Asperger's Syndrome – see Frith 1991) language being retained within normal limits. Some Down's Syndrome children provide a contrary scenario, with their Theory of Mind being intact, but their linguistic ability moderately to severely degraded.

Similarly we find "submodular" dissociations within the language organ, suggesting that grammars have their own internal modules. Smith points to dissociations between the lexicon and the computational system. Christopher's talent for learning second languages "is restricted largely to mastery of the morphology and the lexicon, whilst his syntactic ability rapidly peaks and then stagnates ... [A] reverse dissociation [is] found in the case of children with Spinal Muscular Atrophy, who seem to develop a proficient syntactic rule system but have correspondingly greater difficulty with lexical development" (see

Sieratzki and Woll in press). Edwards and Bastiaanse (1998) address this issue for some aphasic speakers, seeking to distinguish deficits in the computational system from deficits in the mental lexicon.

We also know that focal brain lesions can result in quite specific language impairments in the presence of normal cognitive abilities, and *vice versa* (Caplan 1987). Friedmann and Grodzinsky (1997) argue that agrammatic aphasics may be unable to compute certain abstract structural elements ("functional categories"), while Grodzinsky (2000) identifies much of agrammatism with a disorder specifically impairing the computation of movement relations, localized in the classical "Broca's area." Ingham (1998) describes a young child in similar terms, arguing that she lacked one particular functional category.

This modular view runs contrary to a long tradition, often associated with Jean Piaget, which claims that language is dependent on prior general cognitive capacities and is not autonomous and modular (Piaget and Inhelder 1968, Piattelli-Palmarini 1980). Such a claim is undermined by the kinds of dissociations that have been observed, however. Bellugi et al. (1993) have shown, for example, that Williams Syndrome children consistently fail to pass seriation and conservation tests but nonetheless use syntactic constructions whose acquisition is supposedly dependent on those cognitive capacities. Clahsen and Almazan (1998) demonstrate that Williams Syndrome children have good control of the rule-governed aspects of syntax and word formation, but are severely impaired in certain irregular, memory-based functions, while SLI children display an essentially symmetrical pattern of affected and spared abilities. More generally, language and other cognitive abilities dissociate in development just as they do in acquired pathology (Curtiss 1988).

10.4   Conclusions

The psychologist Eleanor Rosch once said that she wanted her new field to be empirical but not barbarically so. The key to successful scientific work is to find a level of abstraction at which one can state interesting generalizations. The point of our book has been to demonstrate that generative grammarians have found an appropriate level of abstraction in the notion of *I*-language, which has enabled them to understand the language faculty better. The details of that abstraction make up the focus of empirical work of the kind that we have described.

Does the appropriate level of abstraction incorporate the deletion operations that we discussed in chapter 3? Perhaps yes, if what we sketched endures, as ideas about constituent structure and the binding theory have endured now for long periods. Or perhaps not. In fact, most likely not. As work progresses, our ideas about deletion will probably come to be seen in a different light, related to other ideas, whose connections we do not now see, and the technology will change. That is what it means to work at a certain level of abstraction, constantly refining and revising hypotheses. It is striking that generative theories of grammar have been reformulated fairly radically a number of times over the last several decades in all the domains that we have sketched in this book. Each of those reformulations has involved rethinking analyses across the board, but grammarians have always dealt with primitives which are abstract and formal, involving categories like N, V, [Coronal], structure-building and lexical operations, deletion, indices, and the like. These are elements of the *I*-language abstraction and they are enduring elements.

Rosch's "barbarism" comes if one tries to work at inappropriate levels of abstraction. At several points earlier in the book we have contrasted the work we have described with so-called *E*-language approaches, where the primitives are drawn from the external world of sounds, words, and sentences: low-level abstractions. We have shown that a person's language capacity can hardly begin to be described at that level. The kinds of distinctions between well-formed and ill-formed sentences discussed in chapter 3 require a higher level of abstraction and cannot be captured in the *E*-language approaches which dominated earlier periods of the field and continue to be pursued in certain quarters.

One cannot understand major facts about the bumpy way in which languages change from generation to generation, if one limits oneself to describing languages in terms of low-level units like sounds, morphemes, words, and sentences. Those *E*-language approaches lead to Rosch's "barbarism," we would say. When confronted with the kinds of distinctions we have indicated, they invoke vague analogical notions, or Cyclopean ideas that certain kinds of languages tend to change to other kinds of languages, sliding down some mystical, diachronic slope (cf. chapter 8), or global pronouncements that children slowly learn to match their input (cf. chapter 9). The knives just are not sharp enough to make the right distinctions, to capture the details, and these approaches are not adequate to analyze language as a cognitive phenomenon. They might perhaps be adequate to analyze languages from other points of view, in their social dimensions or as literary tools, though we doubt that, as well.

At the other end of the spectrum, someone might argue that the language faculty is brain based, and that therefore one should work at still higher levels of abstraction and describe it in terms of brain operations, analyzing cortical matter and synapses. We have indicated in this chapter that interesting work is emerging which seeks to correlate what we know about language with what we know about the brain. At this stage of our knowledge, however, observations of the brain are unlikely to reveal the kinds of distinctions discussed in earlier chapters, and there is no reason to stipulate that work on the brain should be privileged. If syntacticians, working with their formal abstractions, can discover the distinctions among the sentences of English discussed in chapter 3 and then tease apart information which is plausibly native, intrinsic to the species, distinguishing it from crucial information which English speakers derive from their external experience, and if that enables them to understand aspects of linguistic diversity, distinctions between Italian, Swedish, and Banni-Hassan, then they have a productive research program. That program will, surely, enable us to understand better the kinds of distinctions which occur in brain-damaged, aphasic patients or how Williams Syndrome children differ from others in their language acquisition. It will also help those conducting brain imaging studies to ask more substantive questions about the functions that neural activity might correspond to. If the program doesn't help brain scientists, then something is wrong and ideas need to be adjusted, either those of the grammarian or those of the brain scientist, or more likely, both. If the program does help, then the productivity of the program is increased. That is why it is important that generative grammarians attend to the literature on language acquisition, aphasia, and brain processes, and why acquisitionists, aphasiologists, and neurophysiologists should attend to the grammatical literature. It is the importance of that interaction that drove us to write this book.

Humanists often complain about scientific work becoming narrower and narrower, but Sir Peter Medawar (1967, p. 115) argued that the opposite is actually the case in the sciences:

One of the distinguishing marks of modern science is the disappearance of sectarian loyalties. Newly graduated biologists have wider sympathies today than they had in my day, just as ours were wider than our predecessors'. At the turn of the century an embryologist could still peer down a microscope into a little world of his own. Today he cannot hope to make head or tail of development unless he draws evidence from bacteriology, protozoology, and microbiology generally; he must know the gist of modern theories of protein synthesis and be pretty well up in genetics.

This kind of breadth is what we aspire to in the cognitive sciences, particularly in work on language organs.

To study brain processes with only minimal knowledge of work on grammars is to restrict oneself to another kind of barbarism in understanding language. One may claim that "human linguistic and cognitive ability can be traced back to learned motor responses" (Lieberman 2000, p. 2), but one restricts oneself to barbarism by failing to connect that idea to the details of what we know about human linguistic and cognitive function. We are beginning to discover interesting things about brain operations, and of course we want to connect them to what we know about language. That means that people who work on imaging the electro-chemical activity of the brain or on aphasia should know about grammatical analyses conducted at the functional level we have described, and that grammarians should know something of what we are beginning to learn about brain processes. In this way, each group benefits in refining its approach to learning more about people's language organs.

In fact, people work at levels where they believe that they can make significant progress. Strikingly, over the last forty years work on syntax and phonology has blossomed and led to countless discoveries. A good case can be made that studies of children's language have blossomed more recently, say over the last ten years, and that we are learning a great deal along the lines of what we described in chapter 9. On the other hand, it is less clear that comparable productivity has been achieved in studies of aphasia over recent years. All this can change and aphasiologists might discover some productive tools which will enable them, over the next decade, perhaps, to make discoveries in a way comparable to what has happened in syntax and language acquisition. We would bet that aphasiologists might discover useful tools in the grammatical and acquisitional literature – or elsewhere, of course. Hunches about future progress and the discovery of useful tools guide people in figuring out what they want to study in graduate school, as they prepare to undertake careers in the cognitive sciences.

So there are different levels at which one might work. *E*-language levels do not look at all promising for work on the language faculty as an element of human cognition. *I*-language approaches of the kind we have described have been very productive, we contend. Brain-based approaches so far have not led to much understanding about the language faculty, but there has been some and, now that we have better tools, it is likely that we shall learn much more in this domain in the near future, hoping for some correspondence between what we find about brain processes and the nature of *I*-language structures and their acquisition.

What we seek quite broadly is a theory of the mind, seen as an element of nature. Chomsky (2000, ch. 4) has construed the kind of work we have described as a development of the rational psychology of the seventeenth century: there are "principles or notions implanted in the mind [that] we bring to objects from ourselves [as] a direct gift of Nature, a precept of natural instinct . . . common notions [and] intellectual truths [that are] imprinted on the soul by the dictates of Nature itself, [which, though] stimulated by objects [are not] conveyed" by them (Herbert of Cherbury 1624/1937, p. 133). We try to discover the "principles or notions implanted in the mind" that are a "direct gift" of nature. We begin with common-sense formulations. If we observe that Juan knows Spanish, we focus on a state of the world, including a state of Juan's brain. He knows how to interpret certain linguistic signals, certain expressions. We might try to characterize that knowledge and to ask how his brain reached this state, how his language organ developed in the interplay of nature and nurture. Inquiry leads to empirical hypotheses about biological endowment, information derived from the environment, the nature of the state attained, how it interacts with other systems of the mind, and so on.

One conducts that inquiry as best one can, typically invoking deeper and deeper abstractions as one moves beyond common-sense formulations. There is no *a priori* reason why analyses must be stated at one particular level of abstraction. One uses those levels that lead to productive insights. In particular, there is no reason why everything must be stated in terms of brain physiology. If somebody claimed that there were such reasons, we would want to know whether they should be stated in terms of what we know of the chemistry of the brain or at a still higher level of abstraction, in terms of some kind of particle physics. Nor is there any reason to require that grammatical analyses be reducible in some transparent way to what is now known about brain physiology. We have very little idea how the nervous system computes simple, arithmetical operations, but that does not mean that algorithmic accounts of arithmetic should be discarded as an account of human computational capacity because they have no demonstrable basis in what we now understand of brain processes.

Working at different levels of abstraction is normal practice. One wants to unify various theories about the world by discovering correspondences between them, but that does not necessarily entail the kind of REDUCTION which took place in the mid-twentieth century, when much of biology was reduced to biochemistry. That was a rare event in the history of science. More usually, one or other of the sciences has to be reformulated, sometimes radically, before unification can proceed. Chomsky gives the example of nineteenth-century chemistry: its accounts of molecules, interactions, properties of elements, etc. was in no way continuous with or harmonious with physics, as then understood. "By the 1930s, physics had radically changed, and the accounts (themselves modified) were 'continuous' and 'harmonious' with the new quantum physics" (Chomsky 2000, p. 82).

One picks research strategies which are opportune at any given time. We have tried to show here that an approach to the language faculty which sees it as part of our cognitive make-up can be fruitful, if one proceeds at the levels of abstraction that we have illustrated, teasing apart intrinsic and extrinsic properties and postulating abstract grammars. We believe that these abstract grammars are represented in the brain somehow and we are beginning to learn something of how that might be, hoping to learn more along those lines over the near, foreseeable future.

It is no news that things mental, of the mind, are emergent properties of the brain. We are not much better at saying **how** they emerge than our predecessors were when such ideas were expressed in the seventeenth century, but perhaps we do have better ideas about the nature of things mental, most strikingly in the domains of language and vision. Those ideas should be pursued, while neuroscientists, informed by grammatical work, discover how grammatical operations are implemented at the cellular level; and grammarians should attend to work in neuroscience, which may suggest that they have cut the empirical cake wrongly. We already have some convergences, for example in work on aphasia showing that inflectional morphology is quite distinct from other linguistic processes (see remarks by Alfonso Caramazza in Gazzaniga 1996, pp. 131–151). That is how we shall elaborate a cognitive physiology.

Perhaps one day progress in these domains will lead to some understanding of consciousness, but that seems more remote, harder to foresee. It is more useful, we think, to pursue for now the kinds of abstractions and idealizations where we have some understanding, notably regarding vision and language organs, in the hope and expectation that they will provide better tools for tackling more remote problems, working towards an understanding of consciousness, rationality, morality, emotions, and other attributes of the natural world, the world of human beings and their cognitive capacities.

References

Allen, C. 1997. Investigating the origins of the "group genitive" in English. *Transactions of the Philological Society* **95**. 111–131.

2002. Case and Middle English genitive noun phrases. In Lightfoot 2002. 57–80.

Anderson, S. R. 1974. *The organization of phonology*. New York: Academic Press.

1976. On the description of consonant gradation in Fula. *Studies in African Linguistics* **7**. 93–136.

1978. Syllables, segments and the northwest Caucasian languages. In *Syllables and segments*, ed. by A. Bell and J. B. Hooper. 47–58. Amsterdam: North-Holland.

1981. Why phonology isn't "natural." *Linguistic Inquiry* **12**. 493–539.

1985. *Phonology in the twentieth century*. Chicago: University of Chicago Press.

1988. Objects (direct and not so direct) in English and other languages. In *On language: a Festschrift for Robert Stockwell*, ed. by C. Duncan-Rose, T. Vennemann and J. Fisiak. 279–306. Beckenham, Kent: Croom-Helm.

1990. The grammar of Icelandic verbs in *-st*. In *Icelandic syntax*, ed. by J. Maling and A. Zaenen. Syntax & Semantics 24. 235–273. New York: Academic Press.

1992. *A-morphous morphology*. Cambridge: Cambridge University Press.

1993. Linguistic expression and its relation to modality. In *Current issues in ASL phonology*, ed. by G. R. Coulter. Phonetics and Phonology 3. San Diego: Academic Press.

2000. Reflections on "on the phonetic rules of Russian." *Folia Linguistica* **34**. 1–17.

forthcoming. *Doctor Dolittle's delusion: animal communication and the nature of human language*.

Anderson, S. R. and D. W. Lightfoot. 1999. The human language faculty as an organ. *Annual Review of Physiology* **62**. 697–722.

Andersson, A-B. and O. Dahl. 1974. Against the penthouse principle. *Linguistic Inquiry* **5**. 451–454.

Aronoff, M. 1976. *Word formation in generative grammar*. Cambridge, MA: MIT Press.

1988. Two senses of *lexical*. *Proceedings of the Eastern States Conference on Linguistics* **5**. 13–23.

Baker, M. 2001. *The atoms of language*. New York: Basic Books.

Barbosa, P., D. Fox, P. Hagstrom, M. McGinnis and D. Pesetsky, eds. 1998. *Is the best good enough?* Cambridge, MA: MIT Press.

Barbour, J. 2000. *The end of time*. Oxford: Oxford University Press.

Bates, E. A. and J. L. Elman. 1996. Learning rediscovered. *Science* **274**. 1849–1850.

Bauer, L. 1995. *The emergence and development of SVO patterning in Latin and French*. Oxford: Oxford University Press.

Bazell, C. E. 1952. The correspondence fallacy in structural linguistics. *Studies by Members of the English Department, Istanbul University* **3**. 1–41.

Beard, R. 1995. *Lexeme-morpheme base morphology: a general theory of inflection and word formation*. Albany: SUNY Press.

Beckman, M., J. Edwards and J. Fletcher. 1992. Prosodic structure and tempo in a sonority model of articulatory dynamics. In Docherty and Ladd 1992. 68–86.

Bellugi, U., S. Marks, A. Bihrle and H. Sabo. 1993. Dissociation between language and cognitive functions in Williams Syndrome. In *Language development in exceptional circumstances*, ed. by D. Bishop and K. Mogford. Hillsdale, NJ: Lawrence Erlbaum.

Berthier, M. L., A. Rutz, M. I. Massone, S. E. Starkstein and R. C. Leiguarda. 1991. Foreign accent syndrome: behavioral and anatomical findings in recovered and non-recovered patients. *Aphasiology* **5**. 129–147.

Bickerton, D. 1984. The language bioprogram hypothesis. *Behavioral and Brain Sciences* **7**. 173–221.

  1999. How to acquire language without positive evidence: what acquisitionists can learn from creoles. In DeGraff 1999. 49–74.

Bishop, D. V. M. 1997. *Uncommon understanding: development and disorders of language comprehension in children*. London: Psychology.

Bittner, M. 1987. On the semantics of the Greenlandic antipassive and related constructions. *International Journal of American Linguistics* **53**. 194–231.

Blake, B. 1994. *Case*. Cambridge: Cambridge University Press.

Bloch, B. 1941. Phonemic overlapping. *American Speech* **16**. 278–284.

Bloomfield, L. 1933. *Language*. New York: Holt.

  1939. Menomini morphophonemics. *Travaux du cercle linguistique de Prague* **8**. 105–115.

  1962. *The Menomini language*. New Haven: Yale University Press. [Charles F. Hockett, ed.].

Blumstein, S. E., M. P. Alexander, J. H. Ryalls, W. Katz and B. Dworetzky. 1987. On the nature of the foreign accent syndrome: a case study. *Brain and Language* **31**. 215–244.

Boas, F., ed. 1911. *Handbook of American Indian languages*. Bulletin 40, part I. Bureau of American Ethnology.

Boatman, D., B. Gordon, M. Stone and S. Anderson. 1994. Studies of articulatory timing in normal and foreign accent syndrome speech. *Brain and Language* **47**. 549–552.

Borer, H. and K. Wexler. 1987. The maturation of syntax. In *Parameter setting*, ed. by T. Roeper and E. Williams. 123–172. Dordrecht: Reidel.

Bowerman, M. F. 1973. Structural relationships in children's utterances: syntactic or semantic? In *Cognitive development and the acquisition of language*, ed. by T. E. Moore. New York: Academic Press.

Boyce, S. E., R. A. Krakow and F. Bell-Berti. 1991. Phonological underspecification and speech motor organization. *Phonology* **8**. 219–236.

Brentari, D. 1995. Sign language phonology: ASL. In *The handbook of phonological theory*, ed. by J. A. Goldsmith. 615–639. Cambridge, MA: Blackwell.

Briscoe, E. 2000. Grammatical acquisition: innovative bias and coevolution of language and the language acquisition device. *Language* **76**. 245–296.

Broe, M. B. and J. B. Pierrehumbert. 2000. *Papers in laboratory phonology* vol. V: *Acquisition and the lexicon*. Cambridge: Cambridge University Press.

Browman, C. and L. Goldstein. 1990a. Gestural specification using dynamically-defined articulatory structures. *Journal of Phonetics* **18**. 299–320.

1990b. Tiers in articulatory phonology, with some implications for casual speech. In Kingston and Beckman 1990. 341–346.

1992a. Articulatory phonology: an overview. *Phonetica* **49**. 155–180.

1992b. Targeted and targetless schwas. Paper presented at International Phonologie-tagung, Krems, Austria.

1992c. "Targetless" schwa: an articulatory analysis. In Docherty and Ladd 1992. 26–56.

1998. Competing constraints on intergestural coordination and self-organization of phonological structures. Read at Current Trends in Phonology, II, Royaumont, France.

Browman, C. P., L. M. Goldstein, D. N. Honoroff, A. Jebbour and E. Selkirk. 1998. Gestural organizations underlying syllable structure in Tashlhiyt Berber. Read at Current Trends in Phonology, II, Royaumont, France.

Brown, C. M. and P. Hagoort, eds. 1999. *The neurocognition of language*. Oxford: Oxford University Press.

Byrd, D., A. Kaun, S. Narayanan and E. Saltzman. 2000. Phrasal signatures in articulation. In Broe and Pierrehumbert. 70–87.

Byrd, D. and E. Saltzman. 1998. Intragestural dynamics of multiple prosodic boundaries. *Journal of Phonetics* **26**. 173–199.

Caplan, D. 1987. *Neurolinguistics and linguistic aphasiology*. Cambridge: Cambridge University Press.

Carbary, T. J., J. P. Patterson and P. J. Snyder. 2000. Foreign accent syndrome following a catastrophic second injury: MRI correlates, linguistic and voice pattern analyses. *Brain and Cognition* **43**. 78–85.

Choi, J. D. 1992. *Phonetic underspecification and target interpolation: an acoustic study of Marshallese vowel allophony*. Working Papers in Phonetics 82. Los Angeles: Phonetics Laboratory, UCLA.

Chomsky, N. 1959. Review of B. F. Skinner, *Verbal Behavior*. *Language* **35**. 547–578.

1964. The logical basis of linguistic theory. *Proceedings of the ninth international congress of linguists*, Cambridge, MA, August 27–31, 1962, ed. by H. G. Lunt. 914–978. The Hague: Mouton.

1965. *Aspects of the theory of syntax*. Cambridge, MA: MIT Press.

1975. *Reflections on language*. New York: Pantheon.

1981. *Lectures on government and binding*. Dordrecht: Foris.

1986. *Knowledge of language*. New York: Praeger.

1995. *The minimalist program*. Cambridge, MA: MIT Press.

2000. *New horizons in the study of language and mind*. Cambridge: Cambridge University Press.

Chomsky, N. and M. Halle. 1968. *The sound pattern of English*. New York: Harper & Row.

Clahsen, H. and M. Almazan. 1998. Syntax and morphology in Williams Syndrome. *Cognition* **68**. 167–198.

Clahsen, H., S. Bartke and S. Gollner. 1997. Formal features in impaired grammars: a comparison of English and German SLI children. *Essex Research Reports in Linguistics* **14**. 42–75.

Clark, R. 1992. The selection of syntactic knowledge. *Language Acquisition* **2**. 83–149.

Coulter, G. R. ed. 1993. *Current issues in ASL Phonology*. Phonetics and Phonology 3. San Diego, CA: Academic Press.

Crain, S. 1991. Language acquisition in the absence of experience. *Behavioral and Brain Sciences* **14**. 597–650.

Crain, S. and C. McKee. 1986. The acquisition of structural restrictions on anaphora. In *Proceedings of North Eastern Linguistics Society 16*, ed. by I. S. Berman, J. Choe and J. McDonough. 94–110. Amherst, MA: University of Massachusetts, GLSA.

Crain, S. and R. Thornton. 1998. *Investigations in Universal Grammar: a guide to experiments on the acquisition of syntax and semantics*. Cambridge, MA: MIT Press.

Culicover, P. 1997. *Principles and parameters: an introduction to syntactic theory*. Oxford: Oxford University Press.

Curtiss, S. 1988. Abnormal language acquisition and the modularity of language. In *Linguistics: the Cambridge survey*, ed. by F. J. Newmeyer. Vol. II. 96–116. Cambridge: Cambridge University Press.

Darnell, R. 1990. *Edward Sapir*. Berkeley: University of California Press.

Darwin, C. 1874. *The descent of man*. New York: Appleton. [Second edition, 1889.]

Dawkins, R. 1976. *The selfish gene*. Oxford: Oxford University Press.

de Boysson-Bardies, B. 1999. *How language comes to children*. Cambridge, MA: MIT Press.

de Saussure, F. 1879. *Mémoire sur le système primitif des voyelles dans les langues indo-européennes*. Leipzig: Tübner.

1974. *Cours de linguistique générale*. critical edn. Paris: Payot. [Prepared by Tullio de Mauro.]

DeGraff, M., ed. 1999. *Language creation and change: creolization, diachrony and development*. Cambridge, MA: MIT Press.

Dekkers, J., F. van der Leeuw and J. van deWeijer, eds. 2000. *Optimality theory: phonology, syntax and acquisition*. Oxford: Oxford University Press.

deVilliers, J. and P. deVilliers. 1985. The acquisition of English. In *The crosslinguistic study of language acquisition*, ed. by D. Slobin. 27–139. Hillside, NJ: Lawrence Erlbaum.

Di Sciullo, A-M. and E. Williams. 1987. *On the definition of word*. Cambridge, MA: MIT Press.

Dobzhansky, T. 1970. *Genetics of the evolutionary process*. New York: Columbia University Press.

Docherty, G. J. and D. R. Ladd, eds. 1992. *Papers in laboratory phonology*, Vol. II: *Gesture, segment, prosody*. Cambridge: Cambridge University Press.

Dresher, B. E. 1999. Charting the learning path: cues to parameter setting. *Linguistic Inquiry* **30**. 27–67.

Dresher, B. E. and W. Idsardi. 1999. Prerequisites for a theory of diachronic adaptation. *Zeitschrift für Sprachwissenschaft* **18**. 212–215.

Dumézil, G. 1975. *Le verbe oubykh: études descriptives et comparatives*. Mémoires de l'Académie des Inscriptions et Belles-lettres 1. Paris: Imprimerie Nationale.

Edwards, S. and R. Bastiaanse. 1998. Diversity in the lexical and syntactic abilities of fluent aphasic speakers. *Aphasiology* **12**(2). 99–117.

Ekwall, E. 1943. *Studies on the genitive of groups in English*. Lund: Gleerup.

Engdahl, E. 1985. Parasitic gaps, resumptive pronouns, and subject extractions. *Linguistics* **23**. 3–44.

Finger, S. 2000. *Minds behind the brain*. Oxford: Oxford University Press.

Flourens, M.-J.-P. 1824. *Récherche expérimentale sur les propriétés et les fonctions du système nerveux dans les animaux vertébrés*. Paris: Ballières.

1846. *Phrenology examined*. Philadelphia: Hogan & Thompson. Translated from the 2nd French edition (1842) by C. de L. Meigs.

Fodor, J. D. 1998. Unambiguous triggers. *Linguistic Inquiry* **29**. 1–36.

Fowler, C. A. 1990. Some regularities of speech are not consequences of formal rules: Comments on Keating's paper. In Kingston and Beckman 1990. 476–489.

Friedmann, N. and Y. Grodzinsky. 1997. Tense and agreement in agrammatic production: pruning the syntactic tree. *Brain and Language* **56**. 397–425.

Frith, U. 1991. *Autism and Asperger Syndrome*. Cambridge: Cambridge University Press.

Fujimura, O. 1994. C/D model: a computational model of phonetic implementation. In *Language computations*, ed. by E. S. Ristad. 1–20. American Mathematical Society.

Gardner, R. A. and B. T. Gardner. 1969. Teaching sign language to a chimpanzee. *Science* **165**. 664–672.

Gazzaniga, M. S. 1996. *Conversations in the cognitive neurosciences*. Cambridge, MA: MIT Press.

Gibson, E. and K. Wexler. 1994. Triggers. *Linguistic Inquiry* **25**. 407–454.

Gleitman, L. and E. Wanner. 1982. Introduction. In *Language acquisition: the state of the art*, ed. by E. Wanner and L. Gleitman. 3–48. Cambridge: Cambridge University Press.

Goldin-Meadow, S. and C. Mylander. 1990. Beyond the input given: the child's role in the acquisition of language. *Language* **66**. 323–355.

Gopnik, M. 1990. Feature blindness: a case study. *Language Acquisition* **1**(2). 139–164.

1997. Language deficits and genetic factors. *Trends in Cognitive Sciences* **1**. 5–9.

Gopnik, M. and M. Crago. 1991. Familial aggregation of a developmental language disorder. *Cognition* **39**. 1–50.

Graff-Radford, N. R., W. E. Cooper, P. L. Colsher and A. R. Damasio. 1986. An unlearned foreign "accent" in a patient with aphasia. *Brain and Language* **28**. 86–94.

Greenberg, J. H. 1963. Some universals of grammar with particular reference to the order of meaningful elements. In *Universals of language*, ed. by J. H. Greenberg. 73–112. Cambridge, MA: MIT Press.

Grimm, J. 1848. *Geschichte der deutschen Sprache*. Vol. I. Leipzig: Weidmannsche Buchhandlung.

Grimshaw, J. 1990. *Argument structure*. Cambridge, MA: MIT Press.

Grodzinsky, Y. 2000. The neurology of syntax: language use without Broca's area. *Behavioral and Brain Sciences* **23**. 1–21.

Guy, G. R. 1991a. Contextual conditioning in variable lexical phonology. *Language Variation and Change* **3**. 223–239.

1991b. Explanation in variable phonology: an exponential model of morphological constraints. *Language Variation and Change* **3**. 1–22.

Hagoort, P., C. M. Brown and L. Osterhaut. 1999. The neurocognition of syntactic processing. In Brown and Hagoort 1999. 273–316.

Hale, K. 1976. The adjoined relative clause in Australia. In *Grammatical categories in Australian languages*, ed. by R. M. W. Dixon. 78–105. Canberra: Australian Institute of Aboriginal Studies.

Halle, M. 1957. On the phonetic rules of Russian. Unpublished paper read to the Annual Meeting of the Linguistic Society of America, Chicago.

1959. *The sound pattern of Russian*. The Hague: Mouton.

Hamburger, H. and S. Crain. 1984. Acquisition of cognitive compiling. *Cognition* **17**. 85–136.

Harris, Z. 1951. *Methods in structural linguistics*. Chicago: University of Chicago Press.

Haspelmath, M. 1999a. Are there principles of grammatical change? *Journal of Linguistics* **35**. 579–596.

1999b. Optimality and diachronic adaptation. *Zeitschrift für Sprachwissenschaft* **18**. 180–205.

1999c. Why is grammaticalization irreversible? *Linguistics* **37**. 1043–1068.

Hauser, M. D. and M. Konishi, eds. 1999. *The design of animal communication*. Cambridge, MA: MIT Press.

Herbert of Cherbury. 1624/1937. *De veritate*. University of Bristol Studies Number 6. Translated by M. H. Carré.

Hickok, G. and D. Poeppel. 2000. Towards a functional neuroanatomy of speech perception. *Trends in Cognitive Sciences* **4**. 131–138.

Hockett, C. F. 1947. Problems of morphemic analysis. *Language* **23**. 321–43.

Hoenigswald, H. 1963. On the history of the comparative method. *Anthropological Linguistics* **5**. 1–11.

Hombert, J.-M. 1976. Consonant types, vowel height and tone in Yoruba. *UCLA Working Papers in Phonetics* **33**. 40–54.

Hopper, P. J. and E. Traugott. 1993. *Grammaticalization*. Cambridge: Cambridge University Press.

Hornstein, N. and D. Lightfoot. 1981. Introduction. In *Explanation in linguistics: the logical problem of language acquisition*, ed. by N. Hornstein and D. Lightfoot. 9–31. London: Longman.

Householder, F. W. 1965. On some recent claims in phonological theory. *Journal of Linguistics* **1**. 13–34.

Hovav, M. R. and B. Levin. 1992. -*er* nominals: implications for the theory of argument structure. In *Syntax and the lexicon*, ed. by T. Stowell and E. Wehrli. Syntax & Semantics 26. 127–153. San Diego: Academic Press.

Hubel, D. 1978. Vision and the brain. *Bulletin of the American Academy of Arts and Sciences* **31**(7). 28.

Hubel, D. and T. Wiesel. 1962. Receptive fields, binocular interaction and functional architecture in the cat's visual cortex. *Journal of Physiology* **160**. 106–154.

Hughes, H. C. 1999. *Sensory exotica*. Cambridge, MA: MIT Press.

Ingham, R. 1998. Tense without agreement in early clause structure. *Language Acquisition* **7**. 51–81.

Jackendoff, R. S. 1975. Morphological and semantic regularities in the lexicon. *Language* **51**. 639–71.

1983. *Semantics and cognition*. Cambridge, MA: MIT Press.

1990. *Semantic structures*. Cambridge, MA: MIT Press.

1994. *Patterns in the mind*. New York: Basic Books.

Jaeger, J. J., A. H. Lockwood, D. L. Kemmerer, R. D. Van Valin, B. W. Murphy and H. G. Khalak. 1996. A positron emission tomography study of regular and irregular verb morphology in English. *Language* **72**. 451–497.

Janda, R. D. 2001. Beyond "pathways" and "unidirectionality": On the discontinuity of language transmission and the counterability of grammaticalization. *Language Sciences* **23**. 265–340.

Jespersen, O. 1909. *Progress in language*. London: Swan Sonnenschein. [Second edition.]

Joanisse, M. and M. Seidenberg. 1998. Specific language impairment: a deficit in grammar or processing? *Trends in Cognitive Sciences* **2**. 240–247.

Johnson, K., E. Flemming and R. Wright. 1993. The hyperspace effect: phonetic targets are hyperarticulated. *Language* **69**. 505–528.

Joseph, B. 2001. Is there such a thing as grammaticalization? *Language Sciences* **23**. 163–186.

Jusczyk, P. 1997. *The discovery of spoken language*. Cambridge: MIT Press.

Kagaya, R. 1971. Laryngeal gestures in Korean stop consonants. *Annual Bulletin, Research Institute of Logopedics and Phoniatrics, University of Tokyo* **5**. 15–23.

Keating, P. 1988. Underspecification in phonetics. *Phonology* **5**. 275–292.

Kegl, J. A., A. Senghas and M. Coppola. 1999. Creation through contact: sign language emergence and sign language change in Nicaragua. In DeGraff 1999. 179–237.

Keller, E. 1987. The cortical representation of motor processes of speech. In *Motor and sensory processes of language*, ed. by E. Keller and M. Gopnik. 125–162. Hillsdale, NJ: Lawrence Erlbaum.

Kenstowicz, M. 1994. *Phonology in generative grammar*. Cambridge: Blackwell.

Kingston, J. and M. Beckman, eds. 1990. *Papers in laboratory phonology*, Vol. I: *Between the grammar and the physics of speech*. Cambridge: Cambridge University Press.

Kingston, J. and R. L. Diehl. 1994. Phonetic knowledge. *Language* **70**. 419–454.

Kiparsky, P. 1982. Word formation and the lexicon. In *Proceedings of the 1982 Mid-America linguistics conference*, ed. by F. Ingemann. 3–29. Lawrence: University of Kansas.

1984. On the lexical phonology of Icelandic. In *Nordic prosody*, Vol. III, ed. by C.-C. Elert, I. Johansson and E. Strangert. 135–164. Stockholm: University of Umeå (Almqvist and Wiksell).

1993. Variable rules. Unpublished paper read at Rutgers Optimality Workshop.

1996. The shift to head-initial VP in Germanic. In *Studies in comparative Germanic syntax*, ed. by H. Thráinsson, S. J. Epstein and S. Peters. 140–179. Dordrecht: Kluwer.

Kisseberth, C. 1970a. On the functional unity of phonological rules. *Linguistic Inquiry* **1**. 291–306.

1970b. Vowel elision in Tonkawa and derivational constraints. In *Studies presented to Robert B. Lees by his students*, ed. by J. Sadock and A. Vanek. 109–138. Edmonton: Linguistic Research.

Klima, E. and U. Bellugi. 1979. *The signs of language*. Cambridge, MA: Harvard University Press.

Kosslyn, S. M., M. S. Gazzaniga, A. M. Galaburda and C. Rabin. 1999. Hemispheric specialization. In *Fundamental neuroscience*, ed. by M. J. Zigmond, F. E. Bloom, S. C. Landis, J. L. Roberts and L. R. Squire. 1521–1542. San Diego: Academic Press.

Kroch, A. 1989. Reflexes of grammar in patterns of language change. *Language Variation and Change* **1**. 199–244.

Kroodsma, D. E. and E. H. Miller, eds. 1996. *Ecology and evolution of acoustic communication in birds*. Ithaca, NY: Cornell University Press.

Kuhl, P. K. 1999. Speech, language and the brain: innate preparation for learning. In Hauser and Konishi 1999. 419–450.

Kuipers, A. H. 1960. *Phoneme and morpheme in Kabardian*. The Hague: Mouton.

Kurowski, K. M., S. E. Blumstein and M. Alexander. 1996. The foreign accent syndrome: a reconsideration. *Brain and Language* **54**. 1–25.

Kutas, M., K. D. Federmeier and M. I. Sereno. 1999. Current approaches to mapping language in electromagnetic space. In Brown and Hagoort 1999. 359–392.

Lakoff, R. T. 1972. Another look at drift. In *Linguistic change and generative theory*, ed. by R. P. Stockwell and R. Macauley. 172–198. Bloomington: Indiana University Press.

Langacker, R. W. 1969. Pronominalization and the chain of command. In *Modern studies in English*, ed. by D. Reibel and S. Schane. 160–186. Englewood Cliffs, NJ: Prentice-Hall.

Lasnik, H. 1999. *Minimalist analysis*. Oxford: Blackwell.

Lass, R. 1980. *On explaining linguistic change*. Cambridge: Cambridge University Press.

1997. *Historical linguistics and language change*. Cambridge: Cambridge University Press.

Laughren, M. 1988. Toward a lexical representation of Warlpiri verbs. In *Thematic relations*, ed. by W. Wilkins. Syntax and Semantics 21. 215–242. San Diego: Academic Press.

Lefebvre, C. 1998. *Creole genesis and the acquisition of grammar*. Cambridge: Cambridge University Press.

Lehiste, I. 1970. *Suprasegmentals*. Cambridge, MA: MIT Press.

Levy, Y. and G. Kavé. 1999. Language breakdown and linguistic theory: a tutorial overview. *Lingua* **107**. 95–113.

Liberman, A. M. and I. G. Mattingly. 1985. The motor theory of speech perception revised. *Cognition* **21**. 1–36.

Lieberman, P. 2000. *Human language and our reptilian brain: the subcortical bases of speech, syntax and thought*. Cambridge, MA: Harvard University Press.

Lightfoot, D. W. 1989. The child's trigger experience: Degree-0 learnability. *Behavioral and Brain Sciences* **12**. 321–334.

1991. *How to set parameters: arguments from language change*. Cambridge, MA: MIT Press.

1994. Degree-0 learnability. In *Syntactic theory and first language acquisition: crosslinguistic perspectives*, ed. by B. Lust, G. Hermon and J. Kornfilt. Vol. II. 453–171. Hillsdale, NJ: Lawrence Erlbaum.

1999. *The development of language: acquisition, change and evolution*. Oxford: Blackwell.

ed. 2002. *Syntactic effects of morphological change*. Oxford: Oxford University Press.

Lindblom, B. 1990. Explaining phonetic variation: a sketch of the H and H theory. In *Speech production and speech modelling*, ed. by W. J. Hardcastle and A. Marchal. 403–439. Dordrecht: Kluwer Academic.

Locke, J. 1993. *The child's path to spoken language*. Cambridge, MA: Harvard University Press.

MacDonnell, A. 1916. *A Vedic grammar for students*. Oxford: Oxford University Press.

Manzini, R. and K. Wexler. 1987. Parameters, binding theory, and learnability. *Linguistic Inquiry* **18**. 413–444.

Marantz, A., Y. Miyashita and W. O'Neil, eds. 2000. *Image, language, brain*. Cambridge, MA: MIT Press.

Marchand, H. 1969. *The categories and types of present-day English word formation*. München: Beck. [Second edition.]

Marler, P. 1970. Birdsong and human speech: could there be parallels? *American Scientist* **58**. 669–674.

   1991. Song-learning behavior: the interface with neuroethology. *Trends in Neurosciences* **14**. 199–206.

   1999. On innateness: are sparrow songs "learned" or "innate"? In Hauser and Konishi 1999. 293–318.

Marr, D. 1982. *Vision*. San Francisco: Freeman.

Matthei, E. 1982. The acquisition of prenominal modifier sequences. *Cognition* **11**. 201–332.

Matthews, G. H. 1955. A phonemic analysis of a Dakota dialect. *International Journal of American Linguistics* **21**. 56–59.

Mattingly, I. G. and M. Studdert-Kennedy, eds. 1991. *Modularity and the motor theory of speech perception*. Hillsdale, NJ: Lawrence Earlbaum.

Mayeux, R. and E. R. Kandel. 1991. Disorders of language: the aphasias. In *Principles of neural science*, ed. by E. Kandel, J. H. Schwartz and T. M. Jessel. 839–851. New York: Elsevier.

McCarthy, J. J. 1981. A prosodic theory of non-concatenative morphology. *Linguistic Inquiry* **12**. 373–418.

McCawley, J. D. 1999. Why surface syntactic structure reflects logical structure as much as it does, but only that much. *Language* **75**. 34–62.

McGurk, H. and J. MacDonald. 1976. Hearing lips and seeing voices. *Nature* **264**. 746–748.

Medawar, P. 1967. *The art of the soluble*. London: Methuen.

Monrad-Kröhn, G. H. 1947. Dysprosody or altered "melody of language". *Brain* **70**. 405–415.

Morris Jones, J. 1913. *A Welsh grammar*. Oxford: Clarendon.

Mustanoja, T. 1960. *A Middle English syntax*. Helsinki: Société Néophilologique.

Nash, D. 1986. *Topics in Warlpiri grammar*. New York: Garland.

Nespor, M. and I. Vogel. 1986. *Prosodic phonology*. Dordrecht: Foris.

Newmeyer, F. J. 1998. *Language form and language function*. Cambridge, MA: MIT Press.

Newport, E. L. 1999. Reduced input in the acquisition of signed languages: contributions to the study of creolization. In DeGraff 1999. 161–178.

Niyogi, P. 2002. The computational study of diachronic linguistics. In Lightfoot 2002. 351–65.

Niyogi, P. and R. Berwick. 1997. A dynamical systems model for language change. *Complex Systems* **11**. 161–204.

Nunes, J. 1995. Linearization of chains and sideward movement. PhD thesis. University of Maryland. College Park, MD.

Nunnally, T. 1985. The syntax of the genitive in Old, Middle, and Early Modern English. PhD thesis. University of Georgia.

Ojemann, G., J. Ojemann, E. Lettich and M. Berger. 1989. Cortical language organization in left, dominant hemisphere. *Journal of Neurosurgery* **71**. 316–326.

O'Neil, W. 1978. The evolution of the Germanic inflectional systems: a study in the causes of language change. *Orbis* **27**. 248–285.

Orešnik, J. and M. Pétursson. 1977. Quantity in modern Icelandic. *Arkiv för Nordisk Filologi* **92**. 155–171.

Paradis, C. and D. LaCharité. 1997. Preservation and minimality in loanword adaptation. *Journal of Linguistics* **33**. 379–430.

Paul, H. 1880. *Prinzipien der Sprachgeschichte*. Tübingen: Niemeyer.

Payne, D. L. 1998. Maasai gender in typological and applied perspective. Read at 29th Annual Conference on African Linguistics, Yale University.

Pepperberg, I. M. 2000. *The Alex studies: cognitive and communicative abilities of grey parrots*. Cambridge, MA: Harvard University Press.

Perlmutter, D. M. 1991. The language of the Deaf. *New York Review of Books* **38**(6). 65–72. [Review of Sacks 1989.]

Petitto, L. A. and P. F. Marentette. 1991. Babbling in the manual mode: evidence for the ontogeny of language. *Science*. 251. 1493–1496.

Petitto, L. and M. Seidenberg. 1979. On the evidence for linguistic abilities in signing apes. *Brain and Language* **8**. 162–183.

Phillips, C. 2001. Levels of representation in the electrophysiology of speech perception. *Cognitive Science* **25**. 711–731.

Piaget, J. and B. Inhelder. 1968. *The psychology of the child*. London: Routledge.

Piattelli-Palmarini, M., ed. 1980. *Language and learning: the debate between Jean Piaget and Noam Chomsky*. London: Routledge and Kegan Paul.

1986. The rise of selective theories: a case study and some lessons from immunology. In *Language learning and concept acquisition: foundational issues*, ed. by W. Demopoulos and A. Marras. 117–130. Norwood, NJ: Ablex.

1989. Evolution, selection, and cognition: from "learning" to parameter setting in biology and the study of language. *Cognition* **31**. 1–44.

Pierce, A. 1992. *Language acquisition and syntactic theory: a comparative analysis of French and English child grammars*. Dordrecht: Kluwer.

Pierrehumbert, J. 1990. Phonological and phonetic representation. *Journal of Phonetics* **18**. 375–394.

Pierrehumbert, J. and D. Talkin. 1992. Lenition of /h/ and glottal stop. In Docherty and Ladd 1992. 90–117.

Pinker, S. 1994. *The language instinct*. New York: William Morrow.

Poeppel, D. 1996. A critical review of PET studies of phonological processing. *Brain and Language* **55**. 317–351.

Poeppel, D. and A. Marantz. 2000. Cognitive neuroscience of speech processing. In Marantz et al. 2000. 29–50.

Poeppel, D. and K. Wexler. 1993. The full competence hypothesis of clause structure in early German. *Language* **69**. 1–33.

Poizner, H., E. S. Klima and U. Bellugi. 1987. *What the hands reveal about the brain*. Cambridge, MA: MIT Press.

Premack, D. 1978. Chimpanzee problem-solving: a test for comprehension. *Science* **202**. 532–535.

1980. Representational capacity and accessibility of knowledge: the case of chimpanzees. In Piattelli-Palmarini 1980. 205–221.

1990. Words: What are they, and do animals have them? *Cognition* **37**. 197–212.

Prince, A. and P. Smolensky. 1993. Optimality theory: constraint interaction in generative grammar. Manuscript, Rutgers University and University of Colorado.

Purves, D., G. J. Augustine, D. Fitzpatrick, L. C. Katz, A.-S. LaMantia and J. O. McNamara, eds. 1997. *Neuroscience*. Sunderland, MA: Sinauer.

Rask, R. K. 1818. *Undersøgelse om det gamle Nordisk eller Islandske sprogs oprindelse.* Copenhagen: Gyldendals.

Reinhart, T. 1976. The syntactic domain of anaphora. PhD thesis. Massachusetts Institute of Technology.

Rizzi, L. 1982. Violations of the *wh*-island constraint and the subjacency condition. In *Issues in Italian syntax*, ed. by L. Rizzi. 49–76. Dordrecht: Foris.

1990. *Relativized minimality*. Cambridge, MA: MIT Press.

Roberts, I. 1993. A formal account of grammaticalization in the history of Romance futures. *Folia Linguistica Historica* **13**. 219–258.

Ross, J. R. 1967. On the cyclic nature of English pronominalization. *To honor Roman Jakobson*. The Hague: Mouton.

1969. Auxiliaries as main verbs. In *Studies in philosophical linguistics*, ed. by W. Todd. Vol. I. Evanston: Great Expectations.

Rugg, M. D. 1999. Functional neuroimaging in cognitive neuroscience. In Brown and Hagoort 1999. 15–36.

Sacks, O. 1989. *Seeing voices*. Berkeley: University of California Press.

Sapir, Edward. 1921. *Language*. New York: Harcourt, Brace & World.

1925. Sound patterns in language. *Language* **1**. 37–51.

1929. The status of linguistics as a science. *Language* **5**. 207–214.

1938. Why cultural anthropology needs the psychiatrist. *Psychiatry* **1**. 7–12.

1994. *The psychology of culture*. Berlin: Mouton de Gruyter. Reconstructed and edited by Judith T. Irvine.

Savage-Rumbaugh, E. S. 1986. *Ape language: from conditioned response to symbol.* New York: Columbia University Press.

1987. Communication, symbolic communication, and language: reply to Seidenberg & Petitto. *Journal of Experimental Psychology: General* **116**. 288–292.

Savage-Rumbaugh, E. S., K. McDonald, R. A. Sevcick, W. D. Hopkins and E. Rupert. 1986. Spontaneous symbol acquisition and and communicative use by pygmy chimpanzees (*Pan Paniscus*). *Journal of Experimental Psychology: General* **115**. 211–235.

1993. Language comprehension in ape and child. *Monographs of the Society for Research in Child Development* **58**. 1–221.

Savage-Rumbaugh, E. S., S. G. Shanker and T. J. Taylor. 1998. *Apes, language, and the human mind*. New York: Oxford University Press.

Schleicher, A. 1848. *Über die Bedeutung der Sprache für die Naturgeschichte des Menschen*. Weimar: Hermann-Böhlau.

1861–62. *Compendium der vergleichenden Grammatik der indogermanischen Sprachen*. Weimar: Hermann-Böhlau.

1863. *Die Darwinische Theorie und die Sprachwissenschaft*. Weimar: Hermann-Böhlau.

Seidenberg, M. and L. Petitto. 1987. Communication, symbolic communication, and language: comment on Savage-Rumbaugh *et al. Journal of Experimental Psychology: General* **116**. 279–287.

Shaywitz, B., S. Shaywitz, K. Pugh, T. Constable, P. Skudlasrski, R. Fulbright, R. Bronen, J. Fletcher, D. Shankweiler, L. Katz and J. Gore. 1995. Sex differences in the functional organization for language. *Nature* **373**. 607–609.

Shlonsky, U. 1988. Complementizer cliticization in Hebrew and the ECP. *Natural Language and Linguistic Theory* **6**. 191–206.

Sieratzki, J. and B. Woll. in press. Toddling into language: precocious language development in motor-impaired children with spinal muscular atrophy. *Lingua*.

Sievers, E. 1881. *Grundzüge der Phonetik*. Leipzig: Breitkopf & Hartel.

Smith, N. V. in press. Dissociation and modularity. In *Mind, brain and language: multidisciplinary perspectives*, ed. by M. T. Banich and M. Mack. Hillsdale, NJ: Lawrence Erlbaum.

Smith, N. V. and I. M. Tsimpli. 1995. *The mind of a savant: language-learning and modularity*. Oxford: Blackwell.

Solan, L. 1983. *Pronominal reference: child language and the theory of grammar*. Dordrecht: Reidel.

Sperry, R. 1968. Plasticity of neural maturation. *Developmental Biology Supplement* **2**. 306–27.

Stevens, K. and M. Halle. 1967. Remarks on analysis by synthesis and distinctive features. In *Models for the perception of speech and visual form*, ed. by W. Whaten-Dunn. 88–102. Cambridge, MA: MIT Press.

Supalla, S. 1990. Segmentation of manually coded English: problems in the mapping of English in the visual/gestural mode. PhD thesis. University of Illinois.

Tavakolian, S. 1978. Children's comprehension of pronominal subjects and missing subjects in complicated sentences. *University of Massachusetts occasional papers 4: Papers in the structure and development of child language*, ed. by H.Goodluck and L. Solan. 37–83. Amherst, MA: University of Massachusetts Graduate Student Linguistic Association.

Terrace, H. S., L. A. Pettito, R. J. Sanders and T. G. Bever. 1979. Can an ape create a sentence? *Science* **206**. 891–902.

Thornton, R. 1994. Children's negative questions: a production/comprehension asymmetry. In *Proceedings of Eastern States Conference on Linguistics 1994*, ed. by J. Fuller, H. Han and D. Parkinson. 306–317. Ithaca: Cornell University Department of Linguistics.

   1995. Referentiality and *wh*-movement in child English: juvenile dlinkuency. *Language Acquisition* **4**. 139–175.

Tomblin, J. B. 1997. Epidemiology of specific language impairment. In *The inheritance and innateness of grammars*, ed. by M. Gopnik. 91–110. New York: Oxford University Press.

Trubetzkoy, N. S. 1939. *Grundzüge der Phonologie*. Travaux du cercle linguistique de Prague.

Uylings, H. B. M., L. I. Malofeeva, I. N. Bogolepova, K. Amunts and K. Zilles. 1999. Broca's language area from a neuroanatomical and developmental perspective. In Brown & Hagoort 1999. 319–336.

van der Lely, H. K. J. 1996. Specifically language impaired and normally developing children: verbal passive *vs.* adjectival passive sentence interpretation. *Lingua* **98**. 243–272.

van Gelderen, E. 1997. *Verbal agreement and the grammar behind its "breakdown": minimalist feature checking*. Tübingen: Max Niemeyer.

Vennemann, T. 1975. An explanation of drift. In *Word order and word order change*, ed. by C. N. Li. 269–302. Austin: University of Texas Press.

Wallman, J. 1992. *Aping language*. Cambridge: Cambridge University Press.

Warner, A. R. 1995. Predicting the progressive passive: parametric change within a lexicalist framework. *Language* **71**. 533–557.

1997. The structure of parametric change and V movement in the history of English. In *Parameters of morphosyntactic change*, ed. by A. van Kemenade and N. Vincent. 380–393. Cambridge: Cambridge University Press.

Watkins, C. 1976. Toward Proto-Indo-European syntax: problems and pseudo-problems. In *Diachronic syntax*, ed. by S. Steever, C. Walker and S. Mufwene. 305–326. Chicago: Chicago Linguistic Society.

Weverink, M. 1989. The subject in relation to inflection in child language. Master's thesis. Utrecht University.

Wexler, K. 1994. Optional infinitives, head movement, and the economy of derivations. In *Verb movement*, ed. by D. W. Lightfoot and N. Hornstein. 305–350. Cambridge: Cambridge University Press.

Wexler, K., M. Rice and P. Cleave. 1995. Specific language impairment as a period of extended optional infinitives. *Journal of Speech and Hearing Research* **38**. 850–863.

Williams, H. and F. Nottebohm. 1985. Auditory responses in avian vocal motor neurons: a motor theory for song perception in birds. *Science* **229**. 279–282.

Wright, J. 1910. *Grammar of the Gothic language*. Oxford: Clarendon.

Yang, C. D. 2002. Grammar competition and language change. In Lightfoot 2002. 367–380.

Zwicky, A. M. and G. K. Pullum. 1983. Cliticization vs. inflection: English *n't*. *Language* **59**. 502–13.

Index

a- adjectives 154
Acquired Foreign Accent Disorder 128–9, 128 n5
agent nouns 149, 153
Allen, C. 177 n5, 179, 181
Almazan, M. 238
anaphora 195–6, 195 n4
Anderson, S. R. 76, 88, 112, 118, 121, 218 n4, 219 n6
Andersson, A.-B. 201
apes 219–20, 219 n5–6
aphasia *see* language deficits
apophony 138
Arabic 138, 148, 148 n10, 149
    Banni-Hassan 60
    Saudi 118
Aronoff, M. 132, 133, 134, 154
Articulatory Phonology 124–5
Asperger's Syndrome 237
autism 237
auxiliary verbs *see* modal auxiliaries

babbling 207
Baker, M. 218
Banni-Hassan Arabic 60
Barbour, J. 162
Bastiaanse, R. 238
Bates, E. A. 34, 35
Bauer, L. 159–60
Bazell, C. E. 148 n9, 155
be 168–71, 172, 173
    see also is/'s
Beard, R. 148, 155
Beckman, M. 126
behaviorism 13–14, 15, 16
Bell-Berti, F. 120
Bellugi, U. 219 n5, 225, 238
Berthier, M. L. et al. 128 n5
Bickerton, D. 203
bilingualism 209
binding theory 33 n6, 33 n7, 190, 195–6, 195 n4, 200–2, 200 n7

birdsong 210–14, 220
Bishop, D. V. M. 237
Bittner, M. 145–7
biuniqueness condition 77–8, 80–1, 83
Blake, B. 62
Bloch, B. 86, 148 n9
Bloomfield, L. 12, 13–14, 85–6, 112, 132
Boas, F. 4, 12, 148, 155
Boatman, D. et al. 129 n6
Borer, H. 190
borrowing 93–6, 109
Bowerman, M. F. 190
Boyce, S. E. 120
brain
    aggregate field view 222, 223–4
    birds 212, 213–14, 213 n13
    body maps 227, 228*f*
    Broca's area 227, 238
    and cognition 221–2
    electroencephalograms (EEG) 233
    Event Related Potentials (ERP) 233–4
    functional anatomy 225–36, ix–x
    functional MRI (fMRI) 232–3, 234
    language localization 208, 213, 224–5, 224 n7, 236
    Magnetic Resonance Imaging (MRI) 230
    Magneto-EncelphaloGraphy (MEG) 234
    materialist view 222, 223*f*, 224
    neural activity 230–1, 235, 240–1
    non-invasive imaging 230–6
    Positron Emission Tomography (PET) 231–2, 233
    Wernicke's area 227
    see also language deficits
Bresnan, J. 53
Broca, P. 226–7
Broca's area 227, 238
Browman, C. 121, 123, 124–5, 127
Brown, C. M. 225 n9, 233
Byrd, D. 126 n4

Caplan, D. 238
Caramazza, A. 243
case
    of 180–1, 180 n6, 182
    Case theory 63–5
    ergative languages 143, 143 n6
    Middle English 175, 178, 179, 180, 181–2
    morphological/abstract links 65–6
    morphological case 61–3
    Old English 62, 176–8, 180 n6, 181,
        182 n7
    possessive 179
    scope generalization 147
    syntactic effects of loss 175–82
    thematic roles 175–6, 178, 180, 181
    see also genitives
Choi, J. D. 121
Chomsky, N. 15–16, 34, 42, 89, 102, 115,
        202, 203, 241, 242, vi, xii, xv
Circassian languages 120, 150, 150 n11
cladograms 7–8
Clahsen, H. 238
Clark, R. 202–3
Cleave, P. 194
clitics 27–8, 30–1, 187–8
cognition 37–8, 221–2, xiii–xiv
cognitive science 16–17, 241–3
Combe, G. 223*f*
consonant clusters 97–9, 101, 106–9
constraints 101
    Eval 104, 105
    faithfulness 102–4
    Fixed Subject 53
    Gen 104, 105
    harmony principles 104–5
    markedness 101, 102–4
    richness of the base 105
Coppola, M. 204 n8
copy theory of movement 43–5
Correspondence Fallacy 148 n9
Crago, M. 237
Crain, S. 38–9, 188–9, 196, 198
creole languages 203, 218
Culicover, P. 178
Curtiss, S. 209 n10, 238

Dahl, O. 201
Dakota 84–5
Darwin, C. 11
de Boysson-Bardies, B. 206
de Saussure, F. 12, 13, 74, 76, 135
deafness *see* signing and signers
degree-0 learnability 199–202, 204
deletion
    deleting copies 47–52
    diversity 55–61

and *I*-language 238–9
    incorporation 52–5
    merger 43–5
    that deletion 45–7
derived nominals 142–3, 148, 149
determiner phrases (DPs) 43 n1, 63–5,
        175–6, 177
deVilliers, J. and P. 190
devoicing 98–9
Di Sciullo, A.-M. 132
Diehl, R. L. 113 n1
displacement 44
Down's Syndrome 237
DPs *see* determiner phrases
Dresher, B. E. 204, 205
drift 158–9
Dumézil, G. 150
Dutch 192–4

E-language 12–15, 239, 241, xv
Edwards, J. 126
Edwards, S. 238
Ekwall, E. 176
electroencephalograms (EEG) 233
Elman, J. L. 34, 35
epenthesis 98–9
-er nominals 142–3, 148, 149, 153
ergative languages 143, 143 n6
"Eskimo" 135 n1
    see also West Greenlandic
Event Related Potentials (ERP) 233–4

faithfulness 102–4
Federmeier, K. D. 233, 234
Finger, S. 224
Finnish 62, 147
Fischer, O. 181
Fixed Subject Constraint 53
Flemish, West 57–8
Flemming, E. 123
Fletcher, J. 126
Flourens, M.-J.-P. 222
fMRI (functional Magnetic Resonance
        Imaging) 232–3, 234
Fodor, J. D. 204
Fowler, C. A. 118, 119, 120
French
    binding theory 200–1
    borrowing into Fula 93–7, 93 n1
    branching system 159–60
    deletion 56 n9, 57
    negative markers 160
    pouvoir 163–4
    verb movement 192, 194, 205
Friedmann, N. 238
Frith, U. 237

Fujimura, O. 125
Fula 93–7, 93 n1

Gall, F. 222, 223*f*, 224
Gazzaniga, M. S. 243
gender 150–1
genitives
   endings 160–1
     group genitive 179, 182
     split 175, 176–8, 181, 182, 182 n7
German 78, 136, 193
Gibson, E. 202, 203
Gleitman, L. 190
Goldin-Meadow, S. 204
Goldstein, L. 121, 123, 124–5, 127
Gopnik, M. 237
grammars
   change 161–2
   generative theories 238–9, 240
   historical view 8–9
   as language organ 35–7, 40
   maturation 190
   nature of 23–5
   real-time acquisition 38–40
   rules 84, 89, 90
   see also Universal Grammar (UG)
grammaticalization 160–1
   English auxiliary verbs 162–75
Great Vowel Shift 9–10
Greenberg, J. H. 42, 158
Greenlandic, West 136, 145–6, 147
Grimm, J. 11
Grimm's Law 9–10, 11
Grimshaw, J. 142
Grodzinsky, Y. 23, 238
Guy, G. R. 123 n3

Hackel, E. 8, 129 n6
Hagoort, P. 225 n9, 233
Hale, K. 44 n2
Halle, M. 79 n4, 83–5, 87–8, 89, 90,
     102, xvii
Hamburger, H. 198
Harris, Z. 86
Haspelmath, M. 160 n1, 161 n2
have 173
Hebrew 58–9, 138, 148
Herbert of Cherbury 241
historical linguistics 5–12
Hockett, C. F. 85, 137
Hombert, J.-M. 117, 117*f*
Hornstein, N. 196–7, 197 n6, 198
Householder, F. W. 86, 89
Hovav, M. R. 142
Hubel, D. 37, 38
Hughes, H. C. 220

I-language 15–17, 75, 83–91, 238–9, 241,
     xii, xv
Icelandic 138, 139–41
inflection 174
Ingham, R. 238
Inhelder, B. 238
International Phonetic Alphabet (IPA) 124, 130
is/'s 18–19, 25–32, 38–9
Italian 59–60, 200–1

Jackendoff, R. S. 70, 136 n2, 137 n3, 155
Jaeger, J. J. et al. 232
Janda, R. D. 161, 161 n2
Jespersen, O. 11–12, 176, 178, 180
Joanisse, M. 237
Johnson, K. 123
Jones, M. 41
Joseph, B. 161

Kabardian 120
Kagaya, R. 119
Kavé, G. 237
Keating, P. 119
Kegl, J. A. 204 n8
Keller, E. 129
Kingston, J. 113 n1
Kiparsky, P. 123 n3, 161
Klima, E. 219 n5
Klima, E. S. 225
Koopman, W. 181
Korean 80–2, 119–20
Krakow, R. A. 120
Kroch, A. 166
Kroodsma, D. E. 210 n11
Kuipers, A. H. 120
Kutas, M. 233, 234
Kwakw'ala (Kwakiutl) 102–3

labialized velars 102–3
Lakoff, R. T. 158, 159
language
   as brain function 221–36, 239–40
   and culture 217–18
   diversity 55–61, 55 n8
   functional anatomy 225–36
   identity 14–15
   as knowledge 16, 92, 111
   localization in the brain 208, 213,
     224–5, 224 n7, 236
   organic basis 216–19, 221
   and other species 219–21, 219 n5–6
   as particular faculty 236–8
   processing 216–17, 217 n2
language acquisition 1–3
   analytical triplet 36–8
   binding theory 195–6, 200–2

language acquisition (*cont.*)
  cue-based acquisition 204–6
  degree-0 learnability 199–202, 204
  evaluation metric 202, 203
  experimental technique 194–8
  Fitness Metric 203
  learning path 205, 207
  linguistic genotype 15–16, 22–3, 31, 33–4, 36–7
  optional infinitives 192–4
  phrase structure 196–8
  poverty of the stimulus 18–21, 25–33, 34–6
  primary linguistic data (PLD) 162, 167, 168, 199
  real-time acquisition of grammars 38–40
  sequence-of-tenses phenomenon 200
  sound patterns 206–9
  speech perception 207–9
  syntax 186–206
  trigger 2, 36–7, 198–206
  Triggering Learning Algorithm (TLA) 202, 203
  Truth Value Judgement tasks 189, 196
  UG principles 186–90
  wh-phrases 45, 191–2
language change
  analogical change 9
  case loss 175–82
  chaos 183–5
  drift 158–9
  English auxiliary verbs 162–75
  evolutionary explanation 159–60
  grammar change 161–2
  grammaticalization 160–1
  long-term directionality 157–61
  sound change 6, 7, 9–11
  spread through populations 166
  time 162
  word order typologies 158–9
language deficits 2, 3, 128–9, 222, 224–5, 226–30, 237–8, 241
  see also Specific Language Impairment (SLI)
language organ 3, 16, 221, ix
langue 12, 13
Laplace, P. S. 183
Lasnik, H. 173
Lass, R. 159, 184
Latin 159–60
Laughren, M. 143, 145
Lehiste, I. 116 n2
Levin, B. 142
Levy, Y. 237
lexical items 135

lexicon 105, 132–5
  derivational relations 153–4, 155–6
  mental lexicon 171, 172–3, 174
  optimization 105–6
  organization 155–6
  productivity 152–4
  word classes 153
  words and "morphemes" 134–52
LF (logical form) 115
Liberman, A. M. 113
Liebermann, P. 240
Lightfoot, D. W. 161 n3, 167, 168, 175 n4, 182 n7, 196–7, 197 n6, 198, 199, 201–2, 204, 205, 218
Lindblom, B. 123
linguistic genotype *see* Universal Grammar (UG)
linguistic knowledge 16, 92, 111
  see also phonological knowledge
linguistic relativity 4
linguistic savants 237–8
linguistics
  as discipline x–xi, xiv
  historical development xi–xiii
  as history 5–12
  and mind/brain 3–5
  as study of *E*-language 12–15
  as study of *I*-language 15–17
Locke, J. 127
logical form (LF) 115

Maasai 150–1
MacDonald, J. 235 n11
MacDonnell, A. 41
Magnetic Resonance Imaging (MRI) 230
  functional (fMRI) 232–3, 234
Magneto-EncephaloGraphy (MEG) 234
Manzini, R. 190
Marantz, A. 234
Marchand, H. 154
Marentette, P. F. 207
markedness 101, 102–4
Marler, P. 210–11, 210 n11, 211 n12, 220
Marr, D. 216 n1
Marshallese 121
Matthei, E. 197
Matthews, G. H. 84
Mattingley, I. G. 113
McGurk, H. 235 n11
McKee, C. 196
meaning 136, 136 n2, 137
Medawar, P. 240
MEG (Magneto-EncephaloGraphy) 234
Meillet, A. 160
Menomini 85–6

mental lexicon 171, 172–3, 174
metathesis 145, 145 n8
Middle English 164, 175, 178, 179, 180,
    181–2
Miller, E. H. 210 n11
Miyashita, Y. 234
modal auxiliaries 162–75
    be 168–71, 172, 173
    category membership 164, 166, 167–8, 171,
        173
    distribution 162–4
    morphological distinction 166
    nature of change 164–6
    past tense forms 167
    and *thou* 171–2
    V-to-I operation 168, 171
mondegreens 70
Monrad-Kröhn, G. H. 128
More, Sir Thomas 165
morphemes 132, 135–52
    content 138–47
        derivation and change 143–7
        subtractive morphosyntax 141–3
        subtractive semantics 139–41
    directionality in word formation 150–2
    form 137–8
    solidarity of form and content 147–50
morphological relatedness 136
morphology
    case 61–3
    and category membership 173–4
    productivity 152–4
    see also morphemes
morphophonemics
    and *I*-language 83–91
    representations 80–3
MRI *see* Magnetic Resonance Imaging
Mustanoja, T. 178
mutation 138
Mylander, C. 204

Nash, D. 143
negation 160, 189–90, 190 n2
Newcombe, F. 229
Newmeyer, F. J. 161, 161 n2
Newport, E. L. 204 n8, 218 n4
Norwegian 58
Nottebohm, F. 213
nouns
    agent nouns 149, 153
    binding theory 195 n4
    derived nominals 142–3, 148, 149
    -er nominals 142–3, 148, 149, 153
Nunes, J. 65 n12
Nunnally, T. 180 n6, 181

of 180–1, 180 n6, 182
Ojemann, G. et al. 89 225
Old English 62, 164, 176–8, 180 n6, 181,
    182 n7
O'Neil, W. 178, 234
Optimality Theory 99–106, 110
optional infinitives 192–4
oronyms 70
Osterhaut, L. 233

Paradis, C. 93 n1
parole 12, 13
Paul, H. 6
Payne, D. L. 150
Pepperberg, I. M. 220
perception
    analysis by synthesis 79
    in birdsong 213
    in child development 207–9
    motor theory 113–14, 213
    neurological basis 234–5
Perlmutter, D. M. 219 n5
PET *see* Positron Emission Tomography
Petitto, L. 219 n6, 220
Petitto, L. A. 207
PF *see* phonological form
Phillips, C. 235
philology 5–6
phonemes 75
phonemics *see* phonology
phonetic representation 68, 69–70, 76 n2
    biuniqueness condition 77–8, 80–1, 83
    discreteness of phonetic dimensions 124–5
    distinctive features 70, 72
    hidden intended effects 123–4
    linguistic basis for 112–13, 114–27
    measurable "unintended" effects 115–22
        laryngeal specifications in Korean
            119–20
        pitch microcontours 116–18, 117*f*
        schwa 121–2
        vowel length effects 118–19
        vowel quality differences 120–1
    and phonological form 77–80, 115,
        129–30
    segmental independence 70, 71
    segmentation 70–1
    timing effects 126–7
phonetics 10–11, 67–8
    faithfulness 102–4
    International Phonetic Alphabet 124, 130
    markedness 101, 102–4
    theory 68–73
    see also phonetic representation
phonological form (PF) 77–80, 115, 130

phonological knowledge
  borrowing 93–6, 109
  constraints *vs.* rules 99–110
  rules 96–9
phonological representations 68, 74–7,
    76 n2
  biuniqueness condition 77–8, 80–1, 83
  fully specified basic variant 76
  fully specified surface variant 76
  incompletely specified 75–6
  morphophonemic representations 80–3
  nature of 111–12
  and phonetic form 77–80, 115, 130
  underspecification 119–20
phonology 67, 68, 73
  articulatory 124–5
  auto-segmental representations 90–1
  generative 83, 84, 89, 100
  history 83–91
  morphophonemic representations 80–3
  sound change 6, 7, 9–11
  sound pattern acquisition 206–14
  theory 73, 87
  see also phonological form; phonological
    knowledge; phonological
    representations
phrase structure 28–31, 196–8
physiology ix–x
Piaget, J. 238
Piattelli-Palmarini, Massimo 238
pidgins 203, 218
Pierce, A. 194
Pierrehumbert, J. 112, 124, 125
Pinker, S. 222, xvi
pitch microcontours 116–18, 117*f*
PLD *see* primary linguistic data
Poeppel, D. 193, 232, 234–5
Poizner, H. 225
Polish 62, 63
Positron Emission Tomography (PET)
    231–2, 233
poverty-of-stimulus problem 18–21, 25–33,
    34–6
Premack, D. 220
preterite-presents 166–7
primary linguistic data (PLD) 162, 167,
    168, 199
Prince, A. 99, 100
pronouns 19, 32–3, 61–2, 195 n4, 200 n7
prosodic hierarchy 28
psychiatry 4–5
Pullum, G. K. 190 n2

Rask, R. K. 11
recursive devices 43–4
Rice, M. 194
rider/writer 86–7

Rizzi, L. 56, 57, 200
Roberts, I. 161 n3
Rosch, E. 238, 239
Ross, J. R. 164
Rugg, M. D. 231 n10
rules 84, 88–9, 90, 92, 96–9, 100–1, 152
Russian 83–4

Saltzman, E. 126 n4
Sapir, Edward 4–5, 12, 17, 76, 158, 159
Sapir-Whorf Hypothesis 4
Saudi Arabic 118
Savage-Rumbaugh, E. S. et al. 219, 220
Schleicher, A. 7–8, 11
schwa 121–2
segmental independence 70, 71
segmentation 70–1
Seidenberg, M. 219 n6, 220, 237
Senghas, A. 204 n8
Separation Hypothesis 155
Sereno, M. I. 233, 234
serve 200
Shanker, S. G. 220
Siberian Yupik 136
Sieratzki, J. 238
Sievers, E. 11
signing and signers
  apes 219–20, 219 n5–6
  aphasia 225
  brain function 224–5
  language acquisition 203–4, 204 n8,
    206, 207
  language faculty 2, 67, 218
signs 13, 135, 153
SLI *see* Specific Language Impairment
Smith, N. V. 237
Smolensky, P. 99, 100
sociolinguistics 3–4, xi
Solan, L. 195
sound change 6, 7, 9–11
sound patterns
  babbling 207
  birdsong development 210–14
  children's acquisition 206–9
  cooing 207
  perception 207–9
  see also phonetics; phonology
Specific Language Impairment (SLI) 194,
    237, 238
speech
  microprosody 126, 127–9
  perception 79, 113–14, 207–9, 234–5
  physical properties 113
split genitives 175, 176–8, 181, 182, 182 n7
Spurzheim, J. 223*f*
Stevens, K. 79 n4
structural linguistics 13

Studdert-Kennedy, M. 113
Supalla, S. 218 n4
Swedish 59, 109, 201–2
syllables 28
syntax
    children's acquisition 186–206
    emergence within linguistics 41–2
    generative 110
    merger and deletion 43–5
        deleting copies 47–52
        diversity 55–61
        incorporation 52–5
        that deletion 45–7
    see also case

Talkin, D. 125
Tavakolian, S. 195
Taylor, T. J. 220
tense 200
Terrace, H. S. et al. 219 n6
that deletion 45–7
thematic roles 175–6, 178, 180, 181
Thornton, R. 38–9, 188–90, 191–2, 196
thou 171–2
TLA *see* Triggering Learning Algorithm
Tomblin, J. B. 237
tone languages 117–18
Tourette's Syndrome 229
trace 26 n4
tree diagrams 7–8
trigger 2, 36–7, 173, 198–206
Triggering Learning Algorithm (TLA) 202,
    203
Trubetzkoy, N. S. 87, 112
Tsimpli, I. M. 237

underspecification 119–20
Universal Grammar (UG) 15–16, 22, 36–7
    Case 176, 179, 180, 182
    constraints 101, 103, 109
    deletion principle 47, 61, 65
    grammatical categories 167
    principles 31, 33–4, 186–90
    production/comprehension asymmetry
        189–90
utterances 28
Uylings, H. B. et al. 224 n7, 227

van Gelderen, E. 161
Vata 59
verbs
    affixal 172–3
    be 168–71, 172, 173
    featural 173
    have 173
    is/*'s* 18–19, 25–32, 38–9

movement 192–3, 205
preterite-presents 166–7
serve 200
subjunctive forms 167
want to/*wanna* 187–9
West Circassian 150
see also modal auxiliaries
visual system 37, 206, 226
voice assimilation 106–9
vowels
    Great Vowel Shift 9–10
    length effects 118–19
    quality differences 120–1
    schwa 121–2

Wallman, J. 219 n6
Wanner, E. 190
want to/*wanna* 187–9
Warlpiri 143–5, 147
Warner, A. R. 168–71
Watkins, C. 175
Wells, R. 148 n9
Wernicke, C. 227, 228
Wernicke's area 227
West Circassian 150, 150 n11
West Flemish 57–8
West Greenlandic 136, 145–6, 147
Weverink, M. 193–4
Wexler, K. 190, 192, 193, 194, 202, 203
wh-phrases 45, 191–2
who/*whom* 159
Wiesel, T. 37
Williams, E. 132
Williams, H. 213
Williams Syndrome 238
Woll, B. 238
words 28, 131–2
    classes 153
    derivational relations 153–4, 155–6
    directionality in formation 150–2
    lexical items 135
    lexical organization 155–6
    lexicon 132–5
    monotonicity in formation 137–47
    and "morphemes" 135–52
    productivity 152–4
    solidarity of form and content 147–50
Wright, J. 41
Wright, R. 123
writer/*rider* 86–7

Yale morpheme 148 n9, 155
Yoruba 117–18, 117*f*
Yupik 136

Zwicky, A. M. 148, 190 n2